Beginning Database Design

Gavin Powell

WILEY

Wiley Publishing, Inc.

Beginning Database Design

Published by
Wiley Publishing, Inc.
10475 Crosspoint Boulevard
Indianapolis, IN 46256
www.wiley.com

Copyright © 2006 by Wiley Publishing, Inc., Indianapolis, Indiana

Published by Wiley Publishing, Inc., Indianapolis, Indiana

Published simultaneously in Canada

ISBN-13: 978-0-7645-7490-0
ISBN-10: 0-7645-7490-6

Manufactured in the United States of America

10 9 8 7 6 5 4 3 2 1

1B/RV/RR/QV/IN

Library of Congress Control Number is available from the publisher.

For general information on our other products and services or to obtain technical support, please contact our Customer Care Department within the U.S. at (800) 762-2974, outside the U.S. at (317) 572-3993 or fax (317) 572-4002.

Wiley also publishes its books in a variety of electronic formats. Some content that appears in print may not be available in electronic books.

Beginning Database Design

Books are to be returned on or before
the last date below.

This book is dedicated to Jacqueline — my fondest pride and joy.

About the Author

Gavin Powell has a Bachelor of Science degree in Computer Science, with numerous professional accreditations and skills (including Microsoft Word, PowerPoint, Excel, Windows 2000, ERWin, and Paintshop, as well as Microsoft Access, Ingres, and Oracle relational databases, plus a multitude of application development languages). He has almost 20 years of contracting, consulting, and hands-on educating experience in both software development and database administration roles. He has worked with all sorts of tools and languages, on various platforms over the years. He has lived, studied, and worked on three different continents, and is now scratching out a living as a writer, musician, and family man. He can be contacted at oracledbaexpert@earthlink.net or info@oracledbaexpert.com. His Web site at http://www.oracledbaexpert.com offers information on database modeling, database software, and many development languages. Other titles by this author include *Oracle Data Warehouse Tuning for 10g* (Burlington, MA: Digital Press, 2005), *Oracle 9i: SQL Exam Cram 2 (1Z0-007)* (Indianapolis: Que, 2004), *Oracle SQL: Jumpstart with Examples* (Burlington, MA: Digital Press, 2004), *Oracle Performance Tuning for 9i and 10g* (Burlington, MA: Digital Press, 2003), *ASP Scripting* (Stephens City, VA: Virtual Training Company, 2005), *Oracle Performance Tuning* (Stephens City, VA: Virtual Training Company, 2004), *Oracle Database Administration Fundamentals II* (Stephens City, VA: Virtual Training Company, 2004), *Oracle Database Administration Fundamentals I* (Stephens City, VA: Virtual Training Company, 2003), and *Introduction to Oracle 9i and Beyond: SQL & PL/SQL* (Stephens City, VA: Virtual Training Company, 2003).

Credits

Senior Acquisitions Editor
Jim Minatel

Development Editor
Kevin Shafer

Technical Editor
David Mercer

Production Editor
Pamela Hanley

Copy Editor
Susan Hobbs

Editorial Manager
Mary Beth Wakefield

Production Manager
Tim Tate

Vice President & Executive Group Publisher
Richard Swadley

Vice President and Publisher
Joseph B. Wikert

Project Coordinator
Michael Kruzil

Graphics and Production Specialists
Jonelle Burns
Carrie A. Foster
Denny Hager
Joyce Haughey
Jennifer Heleine
Alicia B. South

Quality Control Technicians
Laura Albert
Leeann Harney
Joe Niesen

Proofreading and Indexing
TECHBOOKS Production Services

Contents

Contents

Part II: Designing Relational Database Models 71

Contents

Contents

Contents

Contents

Introduction

This book focuses on the relational database model from a beginning perspective. The title is, therefore, *Beginning Database Design*. A *database* is a repository for data. In other words, you can store lots of information in a database. A *relational database* is a special type of database using structures called tables. Tables are linked together using what are called *relationships*. You can build tables with relationships between those tables, not only to organize your data, but also to allow later retrieval of information from the database.

The process of relational database model design is the method used to create a relational database model. This process is mathematical in nature, but very simple, and is called *normalization*. With the process of normalization are a number of distinct steps called Normal Forms. Normal Forms are: 1st Normal Form (1NF), 2nd Normal Form (2NF), 3rd Normal Form (3NF), Boyce-Codd Normal Form (BCNF), 4th Normal Form (4NF), 5th Normal Form (5NF), and Domain Key Normal Form (DKNF). That is quite a list. This book presents the technical details of normalization and Normal Forms, in addition to presenting a layman's version of normalization. Purists would argue that this approach is sacrilegious. The problem with normalization is that it is so precise by attempting to cater to every possible scenario. The result is that normalization is often misunderstood and quite frequently ignored. The result is poorly designed relational database models. A simplified version tends to help bridge a communication gap, and perhaps prepare the way for learning the precise definition of normalization, hopefully lowering the incline of the learning curve.

Traditionally, relational database model design (and particularly the topic of normalization), has been much too precise for commercial environments. There is an easy way to interpret normalization, and this book contains original ideas in that respect.

You should read this book because these ideas on relational database model design and normalization techniques will help you in your quest for perhaps even just a little more of an understanding as to how your database works. The objective here is to teach you to make much better use of that wonderful resource you have at your fingertips — your personal or company database.

Who This Book Is For

People who would benefit from reading this book would be anyone involved with database technology, from the novice all the way through to the expert. This includes database administrators, developers, data modelers, systems or network administrators, technical managers, marketers, advertisers, forecasters, planners — anyone. This book is intended to explain to the people who actually make use of database data (such as in a data warehouse) to make forecasting predictions for market research and otherwise. This book is intended for everyone. If you wanted some kind of clarity as to the funny diagrams you find in your Microsoft Access database (perhaps built for you by a programmer), this book will do it for you. If you want to know what on earth is all that stuff in the company SQL-Server or Oracle database, this book is a terrific place to start — giving just enough understanding without completely blowing your mind with too much techno-geek-speak.

To find further information, the easiest place to search is the Internet. Search for a term such as "first normal form," or "1st normal form," or "1NF," in search engines such as http://www.yahoo.com. Be aware that not all information will be current and might be incorrect. Verify by crosschecking between multiple references. If no results are found using Yahoo, try the full detailed listings on http://www.google.com. Try http://www.amazon.com and http://www.barnesandnoble.com where other relational database modeling titles can be found.

What This Book Covers

The objective of this book is to provide an easy to understand, step-by-step, simple explanation of designing and building relational database models. Plenty of examples are offered, and even a multiple chapter case study scenario is included, really digging into and analyzing all the details. All the scary, deep-level technical details are also here—hopefully with enough examples and simplistic explanatory detail to keep you hooked and absorbed, from cover to cover.

As with all of the previous books by this author, this book presents something that appears to be immensely complex in a simplistic and easy to understand manner. The profligate use of examples and step-by-step explanations builds the material into the text.

Note that the content of this book is made available "as is." The author assumes no responsibility or liability for any mishaps as a result of using this information, in any form or environment.

How This Book Is Structured

This book is divided into four parts. Each part contains chapters with related material. The book begins by describing the basics behind relational database modeling. It then progresses onto the theory with which relational database models are built. The third part performs a case study across four entire chapters, introducing some new concepts, as the case study progresses. In Part IV, new concepts described in the case study chapters are not directly related to relational database modeling theory. The last part describes some advanced topics.

It is critical to read the parts in the order in which they appear in the book. Part I examines historical aspects, describing why the relational database model became necessary. Part II goes through all the theory grounding relational database modeling. You need to know why the relational database model was devised (from Part I), to fully understand theory covered in Part II. After all the history and theories are understood, you can begin with the case study in Part III. The case study applies all that you have learned from Part I and Part II, particularly Part II. Part IV contains detail some unusual information, related to previous chapters by expanding into rarely used database structures and hardware resource usage.

This book contains a glossary, allowing for the rapid look up of terms without having to page through the index and the book to seek explicit definitions.

❑   *Part I: Approaching Relational Database Modeling* — Part I examines the history of relational database modeling. It describes the practical needs the relational database model fulfilled. Also included are details about dealing with people, extracting information from people and existing systems, problematic scenarios, and business rules.

 ❑   *Chapter 1: Database Modeling Past and Present* — This chapter introduces basic concepts behind database modeling, including the evolution of database modeling, different types of databases, and the very beginnings of how to go about building a database model.

 ❑   *Chapter 2: Database Modeling in the Workplace* — This chapter describes how to approach the designing and building of a database model. The emphasis is on business rules and objectives, people and how to get information from them, plus handling of awkward and difficult existing database scenarios.

 ❑   *Chapter 3: Database Modeling Building Blocks* — This chapter introduces the building blocks of the relational database model by discussing and explaining all the various parts and pieces making up a relational database model. This includes tables, relationships between tables, and fields in tables, among other topics.

❑   *Part II: Designing Relational Database Models* — Part II discusses relational database modeling theory formally, and in detail. Topics covered are normalization, Normal Forms and their application, denormalization, data warehouse database modeling, and database model performance.

 ❑   *Chapter 4: Understanding Normalization* — This chapter examines the details of the normalization process. Normalization is the sequence of steps (normal forms) by which a relational database model is both created and improved upon.

 ❑   *Chapter 5: Reading and Writing Data with SQL* — This chapter shows how the relational database model is used from an application perspective. A relational database model contains tables. Records in tables are accessed using Structured Query Language (SQL).

 ❑   *Chapter 6: Advanced Relational Database Modeling* — This chapter introduces denormalization, the object database model, and data warehousing.

 ❑   *Chapter 7: Understanding Data Warehouse Database Modeling* — This chapter discusses data warehouse database modeling in detail.

 ❑   *Chapter 8: Building Fast-Performing Database Models* — This chapter describes various factors affecting database performance tuning, as applied to different database model types. If performance is not acceptable, your database model does not service the end-users in an acceptable manner.

❑   *Part III: A Case Study in Relational Database Modeling* — The case study applies all the formal theory learned in Part I and Part II—particularly Part II. The case study is demonstrated across four entire chapters, introducing some new concepts as the case study progresses. The case study is a steady, step-by-step learning process, using a consistent example relational database model for an online auction house company. The case study introduces new concepts, such as analysis and design of database models. Analysis and design are non-formal, loosely defined processes, and are not part of relational database modeling theory.

❑ *Chapter 9: Planning and Preparation Through Analysis* — This chapter analyzes a relational database model for the case study (the online auction house company) from a company operational capacity (what a company does for a living). Analysis is the process of describing what is required of a relational database model — discovering what is the information needed in a database (what all the basic tables are).

❑ *Chapter 10: Creating and Refining Tables During the Design Phase* — This chapter describes the design of a relational database model for the case study. Where analysis describes what is needed, design describes how it will be done. Where analysis described basic tables in terms of company operations, design defines relationships between tables, by the application of normalization and Normal Form, to analyzed information.

❑ *Chapter 11: Filling in the Details with a Detailed Design* — This chapter continues the design process for the online auction house company case study — refining fields in tables. Field design refinement includes field content, field formatting, and indexing on fields.

❑ *Chapter 12: Business Rules and Field Settings* — This chapter is the final of four chapters covering the case study design of the relational database model for the online auction house company. Business rules application to design encompasses stored procedures, as well as specialized and very detailed field formatting and restrictions.

❑ *Part IV: Advanced Topics* —Part IV contains a single chapter that covers details on advanced database structures (such as materialized views), followed by brief information on hardware resource usage (such as RAID arrays).

❑ *Appendices* — Appendix A contains exercise answers for all exercises found at the end of many chapters ion this book. Appendix B contains a single Entity Relationship Diagram (ERD) for many of the relational database models included in this book.

What You Need to Use This Book

This book does not require the use on any particular software tool — either database vendor-specific or front-end application tools. The topic of this book is relational database modeling, meaning the content of the book is not database vendor-specific. It is the intention of this book to provide non-database vendor specific subject matter. So if you use a Microsoft Access database, dBase database, Oracle Database, MySQL, Ingres, or any relational database — it doesn't matter. All of the coding in this book is written intentionally to be non-database specific, vendor independent, and as pseudo code, most likely matching American National Standards Institute (ASNI) SQL coding standards.

You can attempt to create structures in a database if you want, but the scripts may not necessarily work in any particular database. For example, with Microsoft Access, you don't need to create scripts to create tables. Microsoft Access uses a Graphical User Interface (GUI), allowing you to click, drag, drop, and type in table and field details. Other databases may force use of scripting to create tables.

The primary intention of this book is to teach relational database modeling in a step-by-step process. It is not about giving you example scripts that will work in any relational database. There is no such thing as universally applicable scripting — even with the existence of ANSI SQL standards because none of the relational database vendors stick to ANSI standards.

This book is all about showing you how to build the database model — in pictures of Entity Relationship Diagrams (ERDs). All you need to read and use this book are your eyes, concentration, and fingers to turn the pages.

Any relational database can be used to create the relational database models in this book. Some adaptation of scripts is required if your chosen database engine does not have a GUI table creation tool.

Conventions

To help you get the most from the text and keep track of what's happening, a number of conventions are used throughout the book.

Examples that you can download and try out for yourself generally appear in a box like this:

```
Example title
```

This section gives a brief overview of the example.

Source

This section includes the source code.

```
Source code
Source code
Source code
```

Output

This section lists the output:

```
Example output
Example output
Example output
```

Try It Out

Try It Out is an exercise you should work through, following the text in the book.

1. They usually consist of a set of steps.
2. Each step has a number.
3. Follow the steps through one by one.

How It Works

After each *Try It Out*, the code you've typed is explained in detail.

> **Boxes like this one hold important, not-to-be forgotten information that is directly relevant to the surrounding text.**

Tips, hints, tricks, and asides to the current discussion are offset and placed in italics like this.

As for styles in the text:

❑ New terms and important words are *italicized* when introduced.

❑ Keyboard strokes are shown like this: Ctrl+A.

❑ File names, URLs, and code within the text are shown like so: `persistence.properties`.

❑ Code is presented in two different ways:

```
In code examples we highlight new and important code with a gray background.
```

```
The gray highlighting is not used for code that's less important in the present
context, or has been shown before.
```

Syntax Conventions

Syntax diagrams in this book use Backus-Naur Form syntax notation conventions. Backus-Naur Form has become the de facto standard for most computer texts.

❑ *Angle Brackets: < ... >* — Angle brackets are used to represent names of categories, also known as substitution variable representation. In this example <table> is replaced with a table name:

```
SELECT * FROM <table>;
```

Becomes:

```
SELECT * FROM AUTHOR;
```

❑ *OR: |* — A pipe or | character represents an OR conjunction meaning either can be selected. In this case all or some fields can be retrieved, some meaning one or more:

```
SELECT { * | { <field>, ... } } FROM <table>;
```

❑ *Optional: [...]* — In a SELECT statement a WHERE clause is syntactically optional:

```
SELECT * FROM <table> [ WHERE <field> = ... ];
```

❑ *At least One Of: { ... | ... | ... }* — For example, the SELECT statement must include one of *, or a list of one or more fields:

```
SELECT { * | { <field>, ... } } FROM <table>;
```

This is a not precise interpretation of Backus-Naur Form, where curly braces usually represent zero or more. In this book curly braces represent one or more iterations, never zero.

Errata

Every effort has been made to ensure that there are no errors in the text or in the code; however, no one is perfect, and mistakes do occur. If you find an error in one of our books, such as a spelling mistake or faulty piece of code, your feedback would be greatly appreciated. By sending in errata you may save another reader hours of frustration and at the same time you will be helping us provide even higher quality information.

To find the errata page for this book, go to `http://www.wrox.com` and locate the title using the Search box or one of the title lists. On the book details page, click the Book Errata link. On this page you can view all errata that has been submitted for this book and posted by Wrox editors. A complete book list including links to each book's errata is also available at `www.wrox.com/misc-pages/booklist.shtml`.

If you don't spot "your" error on the Book Errata page, go to `www.wrox.com/contact/techsupport.shtml` and complete the form there to send the error you have found. The information will be checked and, if appropriate, a message will be posted to the book's errata page and the problem will be fixed in subsequent editions of the book.

p2p.wrox.com

For author and peer discussion, join the P2P forums at p2p.wrox.com. The forums are a Web-based system for you to post messages relating to Wrox books and related technologies and interact with other readers and technology users. The forums offer a subscription feature to e-mail you topics of interest of your choosing when new posts are made to the forums. Wrox authors, editors, other industry experts, and your fellow readers are present on these forums.

At `http://p2p.wrox.com` you will find a number of different forums that will help you not only as you read this book, but also as you develop your own applications. To join the forums, follow these steps:

1. Go to `p2p.wrox.com` and click the Register link.
2. Read the terms of use and click Agree.
3. Complete the required information to join as well as any optional information you want to provide and click Submit.

You will receive an e-mail with information describing how to verify your account and complete the joining process.

> *You can read messages in the forums without joining P2P, but you must join to post your own messages.*

After you join, you can post new messages and respond to messages other users post. You can read messages at any time on the Web. If you would like to have new messages from a particular forum e-mailed to you, click the Subscribe to this Forum icon by the forum name in the forum listing.

For more information about how to use the Wrox P2P, be sure to read the P2P FAQs for answers to questions about how the forum software works as well as many common questions specific to P2P and Wrox books. To read the FAQs, click the FAQ link on any P2P page.

Beginning Database Design

Part I
Approaching Relational Database Modeling

In this Part:

Database Modeling
Past and Present

"...a page of history is worth a volume of logic." (Oliver Wendell Holmes)

Why a theory was devised and how it is now applied, can be more significant than the theory itself.

This chapter gives you a basic grounding in database model design. To begin with, you need to understand simple concepts, such as the difference between a database model and a database. A *database model* is a blueprint for how data is stored in a database and is similar to an architectural approach for how data is stored — a pretty picture commonly known as an *entity relationship diagram* (a database on paper). A *database*, on the other hand, is the implementation or creation of a physical database on a computer. A database model is used to create a database.

In this chapter, you also examine the evolution of database modeling. As a natural progression of improvements in database modeling design, the relational database model has evolved into what it is today. Each step in the evolutionary development of database modeling has solved one or more problems.

The final step of database modeling evolution is applications and how they affect a database model design. An *application* is a computer program with a user-friendly interface. End-users use interfaces (or screens) to access data in a database. Different types of applications use a database in different ways — this can affect how a database model should be designed. Before you set off to figure out a design strategy, you must have a general idea of the kind of applications your database will serve. Different types of database models underpin different types of applications. You must understand where different types of database models apply.

It is essential to understand that a well-organized design process is paramount to success. Also, a goal to drive the design process is equally as important as the design itself. There is no sense designing or even building something unless the target goal is established first, and kept foremost in mind.

This chapter, being the first in this book, lays the groundwork by examining the most basic concepts of database modeling.

By the end of this chapter, you should understand why the relational database model evolved. You will come to accept that the relational database model has some shortcomings, but after many years it is still the most effective of available database modeling design techniques, for most application types. You will also discover that variations of the relational database model depend on the application type, such as an Internet interface, or a data warehouse reporting system.

In this chapter, you learn about the following:

- ❑ The definition of a database
- ❑ The definition of a database model
- ❑ The evolution of database modeling
- ❑ The hierarchical and network database models
- ❑ The relational database model
- ❑ The object and object-relational database models
- ❑ Database model types
- ❑ Database design objectives
- ❑ Database design methods

Grasping the Concept of a Database

A *database* is a collection of information—preferably related information and preferably organized. A database consists of the physical files you set up on a computer when installing the database software. On the other hand, a database model is more of a concept than a physical object and is used to create the tables in your database. This section examines the database, not the database model.

By definition, a database is a structured object. It can be a pile of papers, but most likely in the modern world it exists on a computer system. That structured object consists of *data* and *metadata*, with metadata being the structured part. Data in a database is the actual stored descriptive information, such as all the names and addresses of your customers. Metadata describes the structure applied by the database to the customer data. In other words, the metadata is the customer table definition. The customer table definition contains the fields for the names and addresses, the lengths of each of those fields, and datatypes. (A *datatype* restricts values in fields, such as allowing only a date, or a number). Metadata applies structure and organization to raw data.

Figure 1-1 shows a general overview of a database. A database is often represented graphically by a cylindrical disk, as shown on the left of the diagram. The database contains both metadata and raw data. The database itself is stored and executed on a database server computer.

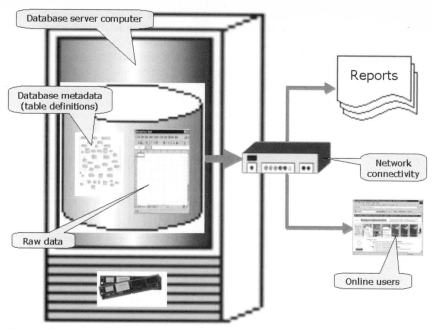

Figure 1-1: General overview of a database.

In Figure 1-1, the database server computer is connected across a network to end-users running reports, and online browser users browsing your Web site (among many other application types).

Understanding a Database Model

There are numerous, precise explanations as to what exactly a *database model* or *data model* is. A database model can be loosely used to describe an organized and ordered set of information stored on a computer. This ordered set of data is often structured using a data modeling solution in such a way as to make the retrieval of and changes to that data more efficient. Depending on the type of applications using the database, the database structure can be modified to allow for efficient changes to that data. It is appropriate to discover how different database modeling techniques have developed over the past 50 years to accommodate efficiency, in terms of both data retrieval and data changes. Before examining database modeling and its evolution, a brief look at applications is important.

What Is an Application?

In computer jargon, an *application* is a piece of software that runs on a computer and performs a task. That task can be interactive and use a graphical user interface (GUI), and can execute reports requiring the click of a button and subsequent retrieval from a printer. Or it can be completely transparent to end-users. *Transparency* in computer jargon means that end-users see just the pretty boxes on their screens and not the inner workings of the database, such as the tables. From the perspective of database modeling, different application types can somewhat (if not completely) determine the requirements for the design of a database model.

An *online transaction processing* (OLTP) database is usually a specialized, highly *concurrent* (shareable) architecture requiring rapid access to very small amounts of data. OLTP applications are often well served by rigidly structured OLTP transactional database models. A *transactional database model* is designed to process lots of small pieces of information for lots of different people, all at the same time.

On the other side of the coin, a *data warehouse* application that requires frequent updates and extensive reporting must have large amounts of properly sorted data, low concurrency, and relatively low response times. A data warehouse database modeling solution is often best served by implementing a denormalized duplication of an OLTP source database.

Figure 1-2 shows the same image as in Figure 1-1, except that in Figure 1-2, the reporting and online browser applications are made more prominent. The most important point to remember is that database modeling requirements are generally determined by application needs. It's all about the applications. End-users use your applications. If you have no end-users, you have no business.

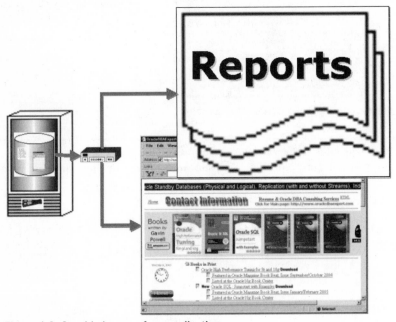

Figure 1-2: Graphic image of an application.

The Evolution of Database Modeling

The various data models that came before the relational database model (such as the hierarchical database model and the network database model) were partial solutions to the never-ending problem of how to store data and how to do it efficiently. The relational database model is currently the best solution for both storage and retrieval of data. Examining the relational database model from its roots can help you understand critical problems the relational database model is used to solve; therefore, it is essential that you understand how the different data models evolved into the relational database model as it is today.

The evolution of database modeling occurred when each database model improved upon the previous one. The initial solution was no virtually database model at all: the *file system* (also known as *flat files*). The file system is the operating system. You can examine files in the file system of the operating system by running a `dir` command in DOS, an `ls` command in UNIX, or searching through the Windows Explorer in Microsoft Windows. The problem that using a file system presents is no database structure at all.

Figure 1-3 shows that evolutionary process over time from around the late 1940s through and beyond the turn of the millennium, 50 years later. It is very unlikely that network and hierarchical databases are still in use.

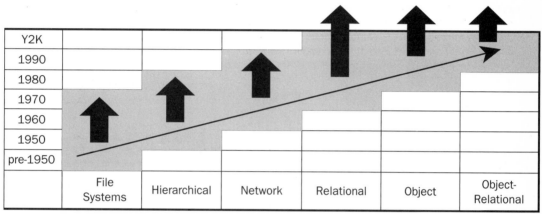

	File Systems	Hierarchical	Network	Relational	Object	Object-Relational
Y2K						
1990						
1980						
1970						
1960						
1950						
pre-1950						

Figure 1-3: The evolution of database modeling techniques.

File Systems

Using a file system database model implies that no modeling techniques are applied and that the database is stored in *flat files* in a file system, utilizing the structure of the operating system alone. The term "flat file" is a way of describing a simple text file, containing no structure whatsoever — data is simply dumped in a file.

> *By definition, a comma-delimited file (CSV file) contains structure because it contains commas. By definition, a comma-delimited file is a flat file. However, flat file databases in the past tended to use huge strings, with no commas and no new lines. Data items were found based on a position in the file. In this respect, a comma-delimited CSV file used with Excel is not a flat file.*

Any searching through flat files for data has to be explicitly programmed. The advantage of the various database models is that they provide some of this programming for you. For a file system database, data can be stored in individual files or multiple files. Similar to searching through flat files, any relationships and validation between different flat files would have to be programmed and likely be of limited capability.

Hierarchical Database Model

The hierarchical database model is an inverted tree-like structure. The tables of this model take on a child-parent relationship. Each *child table* has a single *parent table*, and each parent table can have multiple child tables. Child tables are completely dependent on parent tables; therefore, a child table can exist only if its parent table does. It follows that any entries in child tables can only exist where corresponding parent entries exist in parent tables. The result of this structure is that the hierarchical database model supports *one-to-many* relationships.

Figure 1-4 shows an example hierarchical database model. Every task is part of a project, which is part of a manager, which is part of a division, which is part of a company. So, for example, there is a one-to-many relationship between companies and departments because there are many departments in every company. The disadvantages of the hierarchical database model are that any access must originate at the root node, in the case of Figure 1-4, the Company. You cannot search for an employee without first finding the company, the department, the employee's manager, and finally the employee.

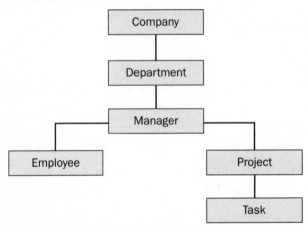

Figure 1-4: The hierarchical database model.

Network Database Model

The network database model is essentially a refinement of the hierarchical database model. The network model allows child tables to have more than one parent, thus creating a networked-like table structure. Multiple parent tables for each child allows for *many-to-many* relationships, in addition to one-to-many relationships. In an example network database model shown in Figure 1-5, there is a many-to-many relationship between employees and tasks. In other words, an employee can be assigned many tasks, and a task can be assigned to many different employees. Thus, many employees have many tasks, and visa versa.

Figure 1-5 shows how the managers can be part of both departments and companies. In other words, the network model in Figure 1-5 is taking into account that not only does each department within a company have a manager, but also that each company has an overall manager (in real life, a Chief Executive Officer, or CEO). Figure 1-5 also shows the addition of table types where employees can be defined as being of different types (such as full-time, part-time, or contract employees). Most importantly to note from Figure 1-5 is the new Assignment table allowing for the assignment of tasks to employees. The creation of the

Assignment table is a direct result of the addition of the multiple-parent capability between the hierarchical and network models. As already stated, the relationship between the employee and task tables is a many-to-many relationship, where each employee can be assigned multiple tasks and each task can be assigned to multiple employees. The Assignment table resolves the dilemma of the many-to-many relationship by allowing a unique definition for the combination of employee and task. Without that unique definition, finding a single assignment would be impossible.

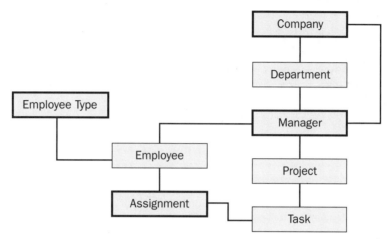

Figure 1-5: The network database model.

Relational Database Model

The relational database model improves on the restriction of a hierarchical structure, not completely abandoning the hierarchy of data, as shown in Figure 1-6. Any table can be accessed directly without having to access all parent objects. The trick is to know what to look for — if you want to find the address of a specific employee, you have to know which employee to look for, or you can simply examine all employees. You don't have to search the entire hierarchy, from the company downward, to find a single employee.

Another benefit of the relational database model is that any tables can be linked together, regardless of their hierarchical position. Obviously, there should be a sensible link between the two tables, but you are not restricted by a strict hierarchical structure; therefore, a table can be linked to both any number of parent tables and any number of child tables.

Figure 1-7 shows a small example section of the relational database model shown in Figure 1-6. The tables shown are the Project and Task tables. The PROJECT_ID field on the Project table uniquely identifies each project in the Project table. The relationship between the Project and Task tables is a one-to-many relationship using the PROJECT_ID field, duplicated from the Project table to the Task table. As can be seen in Figure 1-7, the first three entries in the Task table are all part of the *Software sales data mart* project.

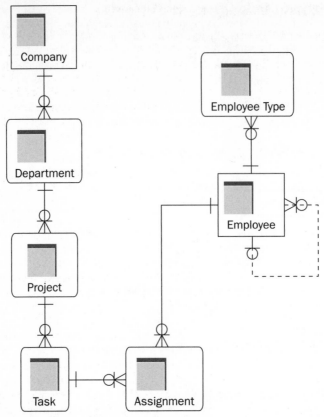

Figure 1-6: The relational database model.

PROJECT_ID	DEPARTMENT_ID	PROJECT *Project*	COMPLETION	BUDGET
1	1	Software sales data mart	4-Apr-05	35,000
2	1	Software development costing application	24-Apr-05	50,000
3	2	Easy Street construction project	15-Dec-08	25,000,000
4	1	Company data warehouse	31-Dec-06	250,000

TASK_ID	PROJECT_ID	TASK *Task*
1	1	Acquire data from outside vendors
2	1	Build transformation code
3	1	Test all ETL process
4	2	Assess vendor costing applications
5	3	Hire an architect
6	3	Hire an engineer
7	3	Buy lots of bricks
8	3	Buy lots of concrete
9	3	Find someone to do this because we don't know how

Figure 1-7: The relational database model — a picture of the data.

Relational Database Management System

A *relational database management system* (RDBMS) is a term used to describe an entire suite of programs for both managing a relational database and communicating with that relational database engine. Sometimes Software Development Kit (SDK) front-end tools and complete management kits are included with relational database packages. Microsoft Access is an example of this. Both the relational database and front-end development tools, for building input screens, are all packaged within the same piece of software. In other words, an RDBMS is both the database engine and any other tools that come with it. RDBMS is just another name for a relational database product. It's no big deal.

The History of the Relational Database Model

The relational database was invented by an IBM researcher named Dr. E. F. Codd, who published a number of papers over a period of time. Other people have enhanced Dr. Codd's original research, bringing the relational database model to where it is today.

Essentially, the relational database model began as a way of getting groups of data from a larger data set. This could be done by removing duplication from the data using a process called *normalization*. Normalization is composed of a number of steps called *normal forms*. The result was a general data access language ultimately called the Structured Query Language (SQL) that allowed for queries against organized data structures. All the new terms listed in this paragraph (including normalization, normal forms, and SQL) are explained in later chapters.

Much of what happened after Dr Codd's initial theoretical papers was vendor development and involved a number of major players. Figure 1-8 shows a number of distinct branches of development. These branches were DB2 from IBM, Oracle Database from Oracle Corporation, and a multitude of relational databases stemming from Ingres (which was initially conceived by two scientists at Berkeley). The more minor relational database engines such as dBase, MS-Access, and Paradox tended to cater to single-user, small-scale environments, and often included free front-end application development kits.

The development path of the different relational database vendors proceeded as follows. Development from one database to another usually resided in different companies, and was characterized by movement of personnel rather than of database source code. In other words, the people invented the different databases (not the companies), and people moved between different companies. Additionally, numerous object databases have been developed. Object databases generally have very distinct applications. Some object databases have their roots in relational technology, once again in terms of the movement of personnel skills.

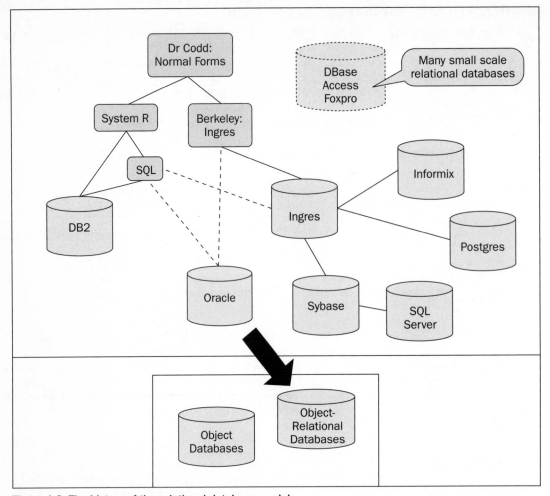

Figure 1-8: The history of the relational database model.

Object Database Model

An object database model provides a three-dimensional structure to data where any item in a database can be retrieved from any point very rapidly. Whereas the relational database model lends itself to retrieval of groups of records in two dimensions, the object database model is efficient for finding unique items. Consequently, the object database model performs poorly when retrieving more than a single item, at which the relational database model is proficient.

The object database model does resolve some of the more obscure complexities of the relational database model, such as removal of the need for types and many-to-many relationship replacement tables. Figure 1-9 shows an example object database model structure equivalent of the relational database model structure shown in Figure 1-6. The assignment of tasks to employees is catered for using a collection inclusion in the manager, employee, and employee specialization classes. Also note that the different types of employees are catered for by using specializations of the employee class.

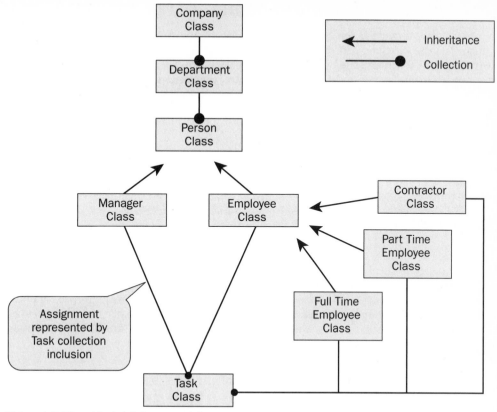

Figure 1-9: The object database model.

Another benefit of the object database model is its inherent ability to manage and cater for extremely complex applications and database models. This is because of a basic tenet of object methodology whereby highly complex elements can be broken down into their most basic parts, allowing explicit access to, as well as execution against and within those basic parts. In other words, if you can figure out how all the little pieces work individually, it makes the big picture (complex by itself) a combination of a number of smaller, much simpler constituent pieces.

A discussion of the object database model in a book covering the relational database model is important because many modern applications are written using object methodology based SDKs such as Java. One of the biggest sticking points between object programmed applications and relational databases is the performance of the mapping process between the two structural types: object and relational. Object and relational structure is completely different. It is, therefore, essential to have some understanding of object database modeling techniques to allow development of efficient use of relational databases by object-built applications.

Object-Relational Database Model

The object database model is somewhat spherical in nature, allowing access to unique elements anywhere within a database structure, with extremely high performance. The object database model performs extremely poorly when retrieving more than a single data item. The relational database model, on the other hand, contains records of data in tables across two dimensions. The relational database model is best suited for retrieval of groups of data, but can also be used to access unique data items fairly efficiently. The object-relational database model was created in answer to conflicting capabilities of relational and object database models.

Essentially, object database modeling capabilities are included in relational databases, but not the other way around. Many relational databases now allow binary object storage and limited object method coding capabilities, with varying degrees of success. The biggest issue with storage of binary objects in a relational database is that potentially large objects are stored in what is actually a small-scale structural element as a single field-record entry in a table. This is not always strictly the case because some relational databases allow storage of binary objects in separate disk files outside the table's two-dimensional record structures.

The evolution of database modeling began with what was effectively no database model whatsoever with file system databases, evolving on to hierarchies to structure, networks to allow for special relationships, onto the relational database model allowing for unique individual element access anywhere in the database. The object database model has a specific niche function at handling high-speed application of small data items within large highly complex data sets. The object-relational model attempts to include the most readily accountable aspects of the object database model into the structure of the relational database model, with varying (and sometimes dubious) degrees of success.

Examining the Types of Databases

At this stage, we need to branch into both the database and application arenas because the choice of database modeling strategy is affected by application requirements. After all, the reason a database you build a database is to service some need. That need is influenced by one or more applications. Applications should present user-friendly interfaces to end-users. End-users should not be expected to know anything at all about database modeling. The objective is to provide something useful to a banker, an insurance sales executive, or anyone else most likely not in the computer industry, and probably not even in a technical field. You need to take into account the function of what a database achieves, rather than the complicated logic that goes into designing the specific database.

Databases functionally fall into three general categories:

❑ Transactional

❑ Decision support system (DSS)

❑ Hybrid

Transactional Databases

A *transactional database* is a database based on small changes to the database (that is, small transactions). The database is transaction-driven. In other words, the primary function of the database is to add new data, change existing data, delete existing data, all done in usually very small chunks, such as individual records.

The following are some examples of transactional databases:

❑ *Client-Server database* — A client-server environment was common in the pre-Internet days where a transactional database serviced users within a single company. The number of users could range from as little as one to thousands, depending on the size of the company. The critical factor was actually a mixture of both individual record change activity and modestly sized reports. Client-server database models typically catered for low concurrency and low throughput at the same time because the number of users was always manageable.

❑ *OLTP database* — OLTP databases cause problems with concurrency. The number of users that can be reached over the Internet is an unimaginable order of magnitude larger than that of any in-house company client-server database. Thus, the concurrency requirements for OLTP database models explode well beyond the scope of previous experience with client-server databases. The difference in scale can only be described as follows:

> ❑ *Client-server database* — A client-server database inside a company services, for example, 1,000 users. A company of 1,000 people is unlikely to be corporate and global, so all users are in the same country, and even likely to be in the same city, perhaps even in and around the same office. Therefore, the client-server database services 1,000 people, 8 hours per day, 5 days a week, perhaps 52 weeks a year. The standard U.S. work year is estimated at a maximum of about 2,000 hours per year. That's a maximum of 2,000 hours per year, per person. Also, consider how many users will access the database at exactly the same millisecond. The answer is probably 1! You get the picture.

> ❑ *OLTP database* — An OLTP database, on the other hand, can have millions of potential users, 24 hours per day, 365 days per year. An OLTP database must be permanently online and concurrently available to even in excess of 1,000 users every millisecond. Imagine if half a million people are watching a home shopping network on television and a Web site appears offering something for free that everyone wants. How many people hit the Web site at once and make demands on the OLTP database behind that Web site? The quantities of users are potentially staggering. This is what an OLTP database has to cater to — enormously high levels of concurrent database access.

Decision Support Databases

Decision support systems are commonly known as DSS databases, and they do just that — they support decisions, generally more management-level and even executive-level decision-type of objectives. Following are some DSS examples:

❑ *Data warehouse database* — A *data warehouse* database can use the same data modeling approach as a transactional database model. However, data warehouses often contain many years of historical data to provide effective forecasting capabilities. The result is that data warehouses can become excessively large, perhaps even millions of times larger than their counterpart OLTP source databases. The OLTP database is the source database because the OLTP database is the database where all the transactional information in the data warehouse originates. In other words, as data becomes not current in an OLTP database, it is moved to a data warehouse database. Note the use of the word "moved," implying that the data is copied to the data warehouse and deleted from the OLTP database. Data warehouses need specialized relational database modeling techniques.

❑ *Data mart* — A *data mart* is essentially a small subset of a larger data warehouse. Data marts are typically extracted as small sections of data warehouses, or created as small section data chunks during the process of creating a much larger data warehouse database. There is no reason why a data mart should use a different database modeling technique than that of its parent data warehouse.

❑ *Reporting database* — A *reporting database* is often a data warehouse type database, but containing only active (and not historical or archived) data. A simple reporting database is of small size compared to a data warehouse database, and likely to be much more manageable and flexible.

Data warehouse databases are typically inflexible because they can get so incredibly large.

Hybrid Databases

A *hybrid database* is simply a mixture containing both OLTP type concurrency requirements and data warehouse type throughput requirements. In less-demanding environments (or in companies running smaller operations), a smaller hybrid database is often a more cost-effective option, simply because there is one rather than two databases — fewer machines, fewer software licenses, fewer people, the list goes on.

This section has described what a database does. The function of the database can determine the way in which the database model is built. The following section goes back to the database model design process, but approaching it from a conceptual perspective.

Understanding Database Model Design

Do you really need to design stuff? When designing a computer system or a database model, you might wonder why you need to design it. And exactly what is *design*? Design is to writing software like what architecture is to civil engineering. Architects learn all the arty stuff such as where the bathrooms go and how many bathrooms there are, and whether or not there are bathrooms. If the architecture were left to the civil engineers, they might forget the bathrooms or leave the occupants of the completed structure with Portaloos or outhouses.

Civil engineers ensure that it all stands up without falling down on our heads. Architects make it habitable. So, where does that lead us with software, database modeling, and having to design the database model? Essentially, the design process involves putting your ideas on paper before actually constructing your object, and perhaps experimenting with moving parts and pieces around a bit just to see what they look like. Civil engineers are not in the habit of erecting millions of tons of precast concrete slabs into the forms of bridges and skyscrapers and then moving bits around (such as whole corners and sections of structures) just to see what the changes look like. You see my point. You must design it and build it on paper first. You could use something like a computer-aided design (CAD) package to sort out the *seeing what it looks like* stage. In terms of the database model, you must design it before you build it and then start filling it with data and hooking it up to applications.

Database design is so important because all applications written against that database model design are completely dependent on the structure of that underlying database. If the database model must be altered at a later stage, everything constructed based on the database model probably must be changed and perhaps even completely rewritten. That's all the applications — and I mean all of them! That can get very expensive and time consuming. Design the database model in the same way that you would design an application — using tools, flowcharts, pretty pictures, Entity Relationship Diagrams (ERDs), and anything else that might help to ensure that what you intend to build is not only what you need, but also will actually work, and preferably work without ever breaking.

Of course, liability issues place far more stringent requirements on the process of design for architects and civil engineers when building concrete structures than that compared with computer systems. Just imagine how much it costs to build a skyscraper! Skyscrapers can take 10 years to build. The cost in wages alone is probably in the hundreds of millions. A computer system, however, and database model that ultimately turns into a complete dud as a result of poor planning and design can cost a company more money than it is prepared to spend and perhaps more than a company is even able to lose.

Design is the process of ensuring that it all works without actually building it. Design is a little like testing something on paper before spending thousands of hours building it in possibly the wrong way.

Design is needed to ensure that it works before spending humungous amounts of money finding out that it doesn't. The idea is to fix as many teething problems and errors in the design. Fixing the design is much easier than fixing a finished product. A design on paper costs a fraction of what building and implementing the real thing would cost. Waste a small amount of money in planning, rather than lose more than can be afforded when it's too late to fix it.

Defining the Objectives

Defining objectives is probably the single most important task done in planning any project, be it a skyscraper or a database model. You could, of course, just start anywhere and dive right into the project with your eyes shut. But that is not planning. The more you plan what you are going to do, the more likely the final result will fit your requirements.

Aside from planning, you must know what to plan in the first place. *Defining the objectives* is the basic step of defining how you are going to get from A to B.

So, now that you know you have to plan your steps, you also have to know what the steps are that you are planning for (be those steps the final result or smaller steps in between). There are, of course, a number of points to guide the establishment of design objectives for a proper relational database model design:

❑   *Aim for a well-structured database model* — A well-structured database model is simple, easy to read, and easy to comprehend. If your company has a database model made up of 50 pieces of A4-sized paper taped to an entire wall, and links between tables taking 20 minutes to trace, you have a problem. That problem is poor structure. If you are interviewed as a contractor to sort out a problem like this, you might be faced with a Herculean task.

❑   *Data integrity* — Integrity is a set of rules in a database model, ensuring that data is not lost within the database, and that data is only destroyed when it should be.

❑ *Support both planned queries and ad-hoc or unplanned queries* — The fewer ad-hoc queries, the better, of course, and in some circumstances (such as very high-concurrency OLTP databases), ad-hoc queries might have to be banned altogether, or perhaps shifted to a more appropriate data warehouse platform.

An ad-hoc query is a query that is submitted to the database by a non-programmer such as a sales executive. People who are not programmers are not expected to know how to build the most elegant solution to a query and will often write queries quite to the contrary.

❑ Ad-hoc queries can cause serious performance issues. Customer-facing applications that require millisecond response times (which depend solely on a high-performance OLTP database) do not get along well with ad-hoc queries. Don't risk losing your customers and wind up with no business to speak of. Do not allow anyone to do anything ad-hoc in an application-controlled OLTP database.

❑ *Support the objectives of the business* — Highly normalized table structures do not necessarily represent business structures directly. Denormalized, data warehouse, fact-dimensional structures tend to look a lot more like a business operationally. The latter is acceptable because a data warehouse is much more likely to be subjected to ad-hoc queries by management, business planning, and executive staff. Subjecting a customer-facing OLTP database to ad-hoc activity could be disastrous for operational effectiveness of the business. In other words, don't normalize a database model simply because the rules of normalization state this is the accepted practice. Different types of databases, and even different types of application, are often better served with less application of normalization.

❑ *Provide adequate performance for any required change activity* — Be it single record changes in an OLTP database or high-speed batch operations in a data warehouse (or both), this is important.

❑ *Each table in a database model should preferably represent a single subject or topic* — Don't over-design a database model. Don't create too many tables. OLTP databases can thrive on more detail and more tables, but not always. Data warehouses can fall apart when data is divided up into too many tables.

❑ *Future growth must always be a serious consideration* — Some databases can grow at astronomical rates. Where data warehouse growth is potentially predictable from one load to the next, sometimes OLTP database growth can surprise you with sudden interest in an Internet site because of advertising, or just blind luck. When a sudden jump in online user interest increases load on an OLTP database astronomically, however, a database model that is not designed for potential astronomical growth could lose all newly acquired customers just as quickly as their interest was gained — overnight!

The computer jargon term commonly used to assess the potential future growth of a computer system is scalability. Is it scalable?

❑ *Future changes can be accommodated for, but potential structural changes can be difficult to allow for* — Parts of the various different types of database models naturally allow extension and enhancement. Some parts do not allow future changes easily. Some arguments for future growth state that more granularity and normalization are essential to allow for future growth, whereas other opinions can state exactly the opposite. This objective can often depend on company requirements. The problem with allowing for future growth in a database model is that it is much easier to allow for database size growth by adding new data. Adding new metadata structures is also not necessarily a problem. On the contrary, changing existing structures can cause serious problems, particularly where relationships between tables change, and even sometimes simply adding new fields to tables. Any table changes can affect applications. The best way to deal with this issue is to code applications generically, but generic coding can affect overall performance. Other ways are to black box SQL database access code either in applications or the database.

The term "black box" implies chunks of code that can function independently, where changes made to one part of a piece of software will not affect others.

❑ Minimize dependence between applications and database model structures if you expect change. This makes it easier to change and enhance both database model and application code in the future.

Changes to underlying database model structure can cause huge maintenance costs. Minimizing dependence between application database access code and database model structures might help this process, but this can result in inefficient generic coding. No matter what, database model changes nearly always result in unpleasant application code changes. The important point is to build the application properly as well as the database model. Changes are unavoidable in applications when a database model is altered, but they can be adequately planned for.

Catering to all these objectives could cause you a real headache in designing your database model. They are only guidelines with possibilities both good and bad, and then all only potentially arising at one point or another. However, the positive results from using good database model design objectives are as follows:

❑ From an operational perspective, the most important objective is fulfilling the needs of applications. OLTP applications require rapid response times on small transactions and high concurrency levels—in other words, lots and lots of users, all doing the same stuff and at exactly the same time. A data warehouse has different requirements, of course, and a hybrid type of database a mixture of both.

❑ Queries should be relatively easy to code without producing errors because of lack of data integrity or poor table design. Table and relationship structures must be correct.

❑ The easier applications can be built, the better. In general, the less co-dependence between database model and application, the better. In tightly controlled OLTP application environments where no ad-hoc activity is permitted, this is easy. Where end-users are allowed to interact more directly with the database such as in a data warehouse, this becomes more difficult.

❑ Changing data and metadata is always an issue, and from an operational perspective, data changes are more important. Changing table structures would be nice if it were always easy, but metadata changes tend to affect applications adversely no matter how unglued applications and database structures are.

Strive for the best you can in the given circumstances, budget, and requirements.

That's ideally where you want to be when your database model design is built, implemented, and applications using your database are running and performing their tasks up to the operational expectations of the business. In other words, you are in business and business has improved substantially both in turnover and efficiency after your company has invested large sums of money in computerization.

Looking at Methods of Database Design

So far, you have looked at why a design process is required and why you need to define objectives to give the design process a goal at which to aim. So, the question you might be asking is how do you go about designing a database model?

There are various methodologies available for designing database models. Each of these different approaches consists of a number of steps. The following sequence of steps to database model design seems the most sensible for a book such as this.

❑ *Requirements analysis* — Collect information about the nature of the data, features required, and any specialized needs such as expected output responses. This step covers what is needed, so simply analyze it and write it down. Talk to the customer and company employees to get a better idea of exactly what they need.

❑ *Conceptual design* — This is where you get to use the fancy graphical tools and draw the pretty pictures — Entity Relationship Diagrams (ERDs). This step includes creation of tables, fields within those tables, and relationships between the tables. This step also includes normalization. Later chapters describe all aspects of conceptual design. Figure 1-10 shows a simple ERD for an online store selling books.

❑ *Logical design* — Create database language commands to generate table definitions. Some tools used for creating ERDs allow generation of data definition language (DDL) scripting; however, they are likely to generate generic scripts. Be sure that you check anything generated before executing in any specific database engine.

   Data definition language (DDL) is made of the commands used to change metadata in a database, such as creating tables, changing tables, and dropping tables.

❑ *Physical design* — Adjust database language commands to alter the database model for the underlying physical attributes of tables. For example, you might want to store large binary objects in separate, underlying files to that of standard relational record-field data.

❑ *Tuning phase* — This step includes items such as appropriate indexing, further normalization, or even denormalization, security features, and anything else not covered by the previous steps.

These separate steps are interchangeable, repeatable, iterative, and really *anything-able*, according to various different approaches used for different database engines and different database designer personal preferences. Some designers may even put some of these steps into single steps and divide others up into more detailed sets of subset steps. In other words, this is all open to interpretation. The only thing I do insist that should be universal is that you draw the ERDs and build tables well before you build metadata table creation code, placing visual design prior to physical implementation.

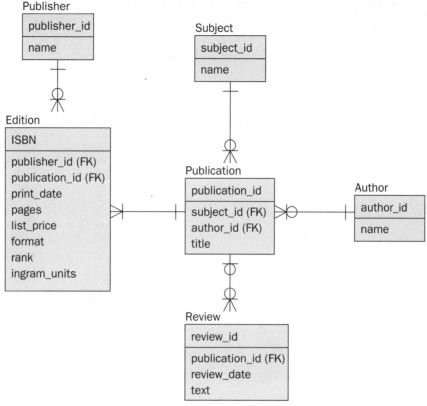

Figure 1-10: A simple online bookstore database model ERD

Summary

In this chapter, you learned about:

❑ The differences between a database, a database model, and an application

❑ The hierarchical and network database models

❑ The relational database model

❑ The object and object-relational database models

❑ Why different database models evolved

❑ The relational database model is the best all round option available

❑ Database design depends on applications

❑ Database types

❑ Database design objectives and methods

The next chapter discusses database modeling in the workplace, examining topics such as business rules, people, and unfavorable scenarios.

Database Modeling in the Workplace

"A common mistake that people make when trying to design something completely foolproof is to underestimate the ingenuity of complete fools." (Douglas Adams)

The only fool is the data model designer who assumes to know all.

Chapter 1 described database model design history, the different types of applications, and how those applications affect the basic structure of a database model. This chapter expands on that overall perspective by describing how to approach database modeling.

Data modeling in the workplace includes the modeling (or design) of a company's operations. Business rules are sometimes by definition a gray area, but they attempt to define how a business operates — that is, what a company does to earn its keep. There can be a distinct difference between end-user interpretation of operations and the interpretation of a database modeler. Both interpretations are usually correct, but simply formulated from a different perspective.

People are so important to a database model designer. Those people are nearly always end-users. It is important for a database modeler to find out what people need. People skills are required. The end-users have all the facts, especially if a database does not yet exist. If a database already exists, that existing database might be useful, might even be a hindrance, or both. There can be different approaches when dealing with people (both technical people and non-technical people) when trying to create a database design, either in a consulting or more permanent role. Getting correct information from the right people is critical to the pre-design process. A database is built for a company that will use it. Build for the people who will use it.

You might need to build for developers or end-users, or even both. It depends on who gets access to that database. A database modeler must know who to get information from, and what types of employee roles give what types of information. Whereas an employee may be microcosmic, a manager could be macrocosmic. That's a little akin to the difference between a weather report for your local town and the entire country. For example, manager and employee perspectives can be very different. A database designer must understand that management level has a birds-eye view and employees have a more localized perspective to fill in the details for you.

After you read this chapter, you should have an understanding that people are a very important factor in database model design, whether a database already exists or not. This chapter describes how to prepare a database design, and, in particular, some various difficult-to-manage scenarios that you could encounter in database model design. By the end of this chapter you should understand how to approach building a database model.

In this chapter, you learn about the following:

- ❑ Business rules
- ❑ Database structure of business rules
- ❑ How to deal with people
- ❑ Listen as much as talk when analyzing a design
- ❑ Getting information from end-users
- ❑ End-users specifications versus database model design
- ❑ The importance of an in-house technical perspective
- ❑ The bird's eye view from management
- ❑ Some unfavorable scenarios

Understanding Business Rules and Objectives

You can create a beautifully appropriate database model with clearly defined objects, using a set of clearly defined database design methodological steps. Elegant solutions, however, must be practical and useful. You must understand that you are designing for practical application, not elegance, and the most elegant solution is not always the most practical. The importance of understanding the nature of the business is paramount to understanding how best to model that business in a database.

Some of the operational aspects of a business will be built into a database model design, even into the bare structure itself in the form of the tables and the relationships between those tables. For example, in Figure 2-1, you can see that books are defined by a number of factors because of the relationships between the PUBLICATION table that contains books and all other tables directly related to those books. The PUBLICATION table defines a book as having a subject (classification or genre), being written by an author, possibly having reviews, and possibly being available in multiple editions. All editions are usually printed by the same publisher but not always.

The representation of the business in the database model ERD shown in Figure 2-1 is that there are relationships between the different tables. What these relationships do is logically enforce relationships between different data items in that database model structure. Understanding the nature of the business or the structure of data and the daily flow of information is key (if not *the* key) to understanding how to build a database model for that business.

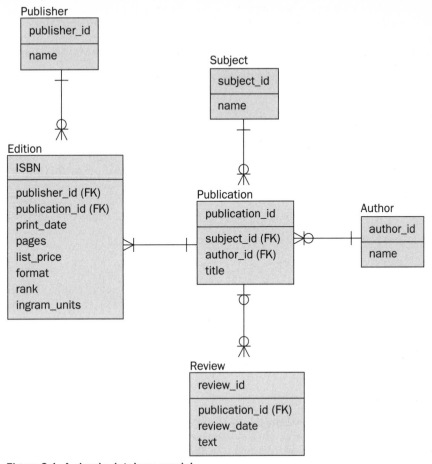

Figure 2-1: A simple database model.

This discussion leads to the sometimes sorely misunderstood topic called *business rules*. The term "business rules" is often open to interpretation as to exactly what it means. A relational database model allows the implementation of the most significant business rules into its basic structure. That basic structure is the relationships between tables. Business rules are applied by enforcing the validity of those relationships.

What Are Business Rules?

Business rules for an organization are essentially the processes and flows of whatever is involved in the daily workings of that organization — in other words, the operation of that business and the decisions made to execute the operational processes of that organization. What does the organization do to operate? What is its task? What is the meaning and purpose of its existence? How does it make its money? Hopefully, it does turn a profit.

Business rules essentially have great scope for definition and redefinition, even in a single organization. Essentially, business rules cover the following aspects of an organization:

❑ Any types of organizational policies of any form and at all levels of the organization

❑ Any types of calculations or formulas (such as loan amortization calculations for a mortgage lending company)

❑ Any types of regulations (such as rules applied because of legal requirements, self-imposed restrictions, or industry-standard requirements)

Simple business rules can be implemented in a database model by creating relationships between tables. For example, in Figure 2-1, a book (PUBLICATION) requires at least one author. This relationship is enforced in the diagram as being one and only one author who can have zero, one, or many publications.

In Figure 2-1, the relationship between the PUBLICATION and AUTHOR tables determines that an author can exist, but the author does not have to have any books published. On the contrary, a publication cannot exist unless it has an author. This relationship is somewhat sensible because if an author never wrote a book, the book never existed.

It could, of course, be argued that an unpublished author is not an author by trade; however, that is a minor detail. The point is that the relationship forces the database model to accept only books that have actually been written by someone, on the basis that a book written by no one has never been written because no one wrote it. The enforcement of entry of author prior to the name of the book helps to ensure that the book does actually exist in the real world. This is how a database model can help to implement simple business rules. The business rule is that a non-existent book cannot be entered into the database.

Other business rules can be implemented and enforced using coding and other specialized constraint types. *Coding* implies programming code, in whatever language is appropriate. *Constraints* are things that place restrictions on values stored in a database. For example, field values in table records can be validated for each entry. Only allowing a field to take on the value M or F to represent Male or Female is another example of business rule application because there is no such gender that is not male or female.

The Importance of Business Rules

I have had conversations with managers along the lines of, *"no business rules in the database please,"* or, *"as many business rules in the database as possible please."* Both of these statements are nonsensical because both do not apply to a certain extent. A relational database model cannot avoid defining some business rules simply because of the existence of relationships between tables and enforcement of referential integrity.

And then there is individual field validation, such as allowing or prohibiting NULL values on individual fields. On the other hand, any type of complex validation processing may require the use of database-stored procedures or method coding (in an object database) to provide comprehensive business rule validation in the database.

> *A stored procedure (also sometimes called a "database procedure") is a chunk of code stored within and executed from within a database, typically on data stored in a database, but not always.*

Implementing business rules using stored procedures can be used to provide comprehensive accommodation of business rules; however, it is not a recommended path to good database performance for a relational database. On the contrary, storing chunks of code as methods is the best route for an object database because of the black box effect of the object data model.

> The term "black box" implies chunks of code that can function independently, where changes made to one part of a piece of software, will not affect others.

Because this book is essentially about designing good relational database models, the object aspect is somewhat irrelevant. Perhaps it merely reinforces that complex business logic should be left to the application if developers must resort to database procedural code to enforce it. Most especially, avoid triggers and database events for enforcing relationships between tables.

A *trigger* can also be called a *database event trigger* or a *database rule*. A trigger is a chunk of code that executes when a specified event occurs. For example, adding a new record to a table can be used to trigger an event. Referring to Figure 2-1 again, adding a new author could fire a trigger making a log entry into a logging or auditing table. Unless you are building an expert system, do not to use this type of database-automated response coding for the application of database model level complex business rules. You will likely get serious performance deficiencies if you do not heed this particular warning.

Incorporating the Human Factor

What is meant by the *human factor*? You cannot create a database model without the involvement of the people who will ultimately use that database model. It is of no consequence if they are technical people such as computer programmers, or end-users such as executives wanting forecast plans from a data warehouse. There is only one important thing to remember about company employees: as a whole, they know their business, how it operates, and how it works.

Many database model designers with vast experience can often go into a new company and draw on past experiences that they gained in similar organizations. This is nearly always the case for experienced designers, but there are often exceptional situations in any company that even experience can't prepare for.

You can find out exactly what is needed by talking to the people who will use the database model you are about to design for them. Talk to their developers and their end-users. Your first task is to talk with and listen to company personnel. By talking and listening, you can discover how to design a better database model for them

People as a Resource

The people the database model is being built for can often tell you the most about what should be in the model, and sometimes even how pieces within that model should relate to each other. Remember, however, that those people are usually non-technical and know nothing about database model design. The database designer applies technical skills to the thoughts and statements of the users (be that verbal or written down). Both users and designers have equal weight to add to this process.

In fact, even though I keep stressing the point of listening (always assuming the customer is right), essentially the users are people who you (the designer) gathers information from as to how the model should be designed and what should be in it — even down to the size and datatypes of fields in tables.

Ultimately, you (the designer) are 95 percent responsible for figuring out the design and building the database model. The end-users can give you many small pointers. From their perspective, it all makes sense. From your perspective, information from end-users can often feel like a stream of jumbled-up facts. It is your job to un-jumble everything and to make complete sense of it. Take time to think. Remember, design is largely a planning process, and thinking about various options is a big part of that planning process.

All you really need to do is to organize everything into sequences of logical, mathematical steps. Those logical bits and pieces get placed into a logically structured database model. It is the database designer's responsibility to figure out all this logical organization. It is not that the end-users do not know their business, but they are likely to think of it in terms of priorities and how they react to different situations — plus how important each task on their desk is related to the importance of the running of their business.

There also may be indirect effects in play as well where a specific employee thinks something is important because he or she has been managed and motivated in a specific direction. Of course, it is likely that the manager or even the manager's manager is aware of the importance of a specific task, but a lower-level employee may not be aware of why something is significant or not. Everything is subjective at this stage. The database designer must be objective, clinical, analytical, and (above all) precise.

So, now you have an impression of perhaps what people (being end-users, employees within a company) can tell you about the database model you are about to design. Perhaps you have also been made aware that some things company employees tell you can be misleading. If people are misleading you, it is more than likely that they are explaining something to you in a specific case type of scenario. That specific case scenario is the way they see it as specific to their particular business, company, the city they work and live in, or any number of other reasons.

Designing a database model is an abstraction of specifics. *Abstraction* is a logical or mathematical process, designed to make handling of specific situations much easier. Abstraction attempts to compartmentalize different activities, ultimately processing at the compartment level, and not the activity level. What in a business environment could be two distinctly different things could be identical when properly abstracted.

So, what does all that jargon mean? For example, a car salesman may picture selling a Ford and selling a Chevy as two distinctly different processes. Fords and Chevys could be in different lots. They could have different service agreements. There could be many other differences as well. From the perspective of the database modeler, however, both Ford and Chevy are automobiles, they are both either automatic transmissions or stick-shift, and they are both sold.

Whereas end-users see specifics, database model designers should look for common elements for abstraction.

Once again, you as the data modeler are ultimately responsible for designing their database. The database model designer has the final say on what a database model should do and what it should look like. This is important to remember. Even though managers and employees alike understand their specific roles, not only could their perspective on tasks and procedures be microcosmic in nature, but also they could misunderstand the concept that some abstraction is required to create an effective and efficient database model. A database model must take all special circumstances into account, but it must remain abstract. To reiterate an important point, what could seem like a special circumstance or situation for an end-user could very well be easily catered for by a future database model — essentially an abstraction of special circumstances.

Take into account everything people tell you, but don't get sidetracked, misled, or confused because the database model designer's perspective is much more abstract than that of an end-user. End-user perspectives are either at ground level or operationally based. A database model is a logical (and even mathematical) abstraction that tries to accommodate for all possible circumstances, within reason, of course. Otherwise, the database model will be more complex than sometimes it is possible for applications to find useful. Have you ever encountered a database model design in a company, covering an entire wall? This harbors potential for a scary situation.

Talking to the Right People

There are different types of people. Some people are more technically aware than others; however, this does not imply that those who are technically aware are your best source of information. In my experience, the people with the most knowledge of a business are usually the managers, usually executive level in small companies, and somewhere in the middle in larger companies. In a small company, executive-level people are easy to access. In a larger company, getting executive time is difficult (if not impossible) and probably not effective for your purposes. For large companies, the best option is the high-level managers with a good overall picture of the business. These people can allocate the database designer more time than people further down on the scale who know the business well, perhaps someone who has both technical and business operational skills.

As a database model designer, your entry point is the person who you bill and who signs your check. You may see this person only once. Even if your recruiter is in the Human Resources (HR) department, be sure that you get the recruiter's help right off the bat in getting introductions to who might be able to help you best in your quest to create the most appropriate database model design possible.

A database designer must talk to different types of people on multiple levels and in multiple skills arenas, in the same company. It is beneficial to get a balance of levels and skills to help get a better overall picture of requirements. There can be quite a distinct contrast between the perspective of management and that of the nitty-gritty details of employees on the floor getting their hands dirty in specific job functions. Obviously, how much detail is required is largely dependent on how complex the business is and also on how much of that complexity is to be computerized.

For example, a simple invoicing system requiring only that bills be sent out excluding details of what is being sent out makes a simple book retailer require the same data modeling complexity as that of an auto parts manufacturer. Of course, if the evolving application is to include part numbers, colors, materials of which items are made, correct parts for different types of cars, how things are made, precise measurements, the list goes on — there is a complexity issue. How complicated can selling books get? Quite typically, retail is simplistic when it comes to computerization. Manufacturing can be extremely complex, especially when parts and pieces manufactured are custom-made as well as off-the-shelf.

The more complexity a database model requires, the more questions you must ask. The more questions there are to ask, the larger the amount of detail and potential layering within the structure of a design solution. In conclusion, the more questions you have, the more people you might want to talk to, and, thus, the more people in different roles you will probably need to talk to as well. Take a breath!

Perhaps the central theme of database modeling (especially for relational database modeling in OLTP databases) is that abstraction is the order of the day. Greater levels of abstraction are more often needed when special-case scenarios crop up frequently. The more special-case scenarios you get, the more likely you will begin to observe similarities between those supposedly opposing special-case scenarios. Your objective is to create a single set of tables and relationships to cover as much of the operational functioning of a company as possible. If a separate set of tables is created for every special-case scenario, you will have too many tables and, therefore, no reduction in complexity (probably what the company was aiming at by computerizing). An extremely complex database model is not the objective. Application developers and end-users need simplicity. Without adequate simplicity, your database model design might be impossible to use, particularly in the case of end-users and a data warehouse.

The job of a database modeler is simplicity through abstraction. *Abstraction* is this sense of the word is the amalgamation of different aspects of company operations into a succinct set of tables and relationships joining those tables together. One simple rule is the more people you talk to about how to build their database model, the more likely you get a general overall picture (also the more likely you can get completely confused). The higher up the management scale you get, the more of a global picture you get. The problem with the management level is that they can leave out crucial details. Therefore, you must talk to the regular employees in specific job functions as well. Some managers might be able to point you at the right employees with whom you should talk.

Overall, the number of people you must talk to depends on how complex the required database model should be. With simple database models, you can sometimes get away with using the elements of a paper-based system alone to build a database model.

In more technical companies that include computer personnel skills (such as programmers, systems and database administrators, and so on), these people can possibly provide you with the most valuable of input; however, technical people can also be obstructive. Technical people, even in-house technical people, often do not have a clear perspective in terms of what end-users might need. In fact, more often than not, in-house technical people are less aware of end-user needs within a company than consulting people. Outside consulting help can often give a fresh perspective.

Getting the Right Information

When it comes to getting the right information, the question that should perhaps first be asked is, "What is the right information?" Do you know the correct information? As an outsider, the answer is "probably not." As an insider, the answer is "perhaps." There is a distinct advantage in using outside people to do essentially a task that not only treads on people's toes, but also has the threat of introducing change. No one likes change. An in-house employee cannot reach across departments, asking 101 people 101 questions, from all over the company, without having to negotiate large tangled knots of political red tape.

Politics within companies is not always the case; however, environments that are difficult to deal with are common. Sometimes a consultant can either drive the process, or help get around the obstacles. Another (perhaps more quirky) fact is that the more a consultant costs, the more significant the consultant is to the company in terms of the relative cost perspective. Obviously, the higher the cost, the higher the approval-rated signature is for the consultant's bill (thus, the higher the level of management the consultant deals with and, therefore, the more likely that consultant will be effective). Obviously, all of this depends on company size, composition, political issues...the list is endless. On the contrary, in many situations, in-house people are the best option.

> Don't get a completely negative opinion of company politics. Political maneuvering has its purpose. The larger companies get, the more complex people issues and the human factor can become. Simple chain of command can often be misconstrued as politicking. In other words, politics is not always as unproductive as you might think. Every facet of a situation has its purpose. If a situation is wholly negative, perhaps you should attempt to use it to your own advantage in getting the job done.

Getting the right information is really an extension of talking to the right people, in that the correct detail comes from the mouths of the people who know how a company functions operationally. This is not a derogatory statement. The database designer must figure out what should and should not be listened to, and taken into account. Some company employees have a birds-eye view; others have a detailed picture of specific aspects of how a company makes its living on a daily basis.

Another way to look at it is this. The more people you talk to in a greater number of sections and levels of a company, the more likely you (as a database model designer) will get a better perspective, perhaps even to the point of being able to dissimilate between correct and incorrect information and advise. The danger of talking to far too many people, taking account of some and not implementing suggestions and or requests of others, could certainly ruffle some feathers (not to mention completely confusing the database model designer). The situation might even be a delicate balance between producing a good structure and not upsetting anyone. Strike a balance. The database model must be correct, but it also has to be acceptable to the users. If there really are special scenarios, maintain them as special cases and not abstractions. Abstraction will save a database model from complexity, but could also make it unusable.

Finally, if you are an outside consultant, bear in mind that what you think is correct and what you think is incorrect may not be the reality of the situation. You could be completely wrong. Try not to ruffle any feathers while analyzing for and building your database model design because you want people to use your database. There is no point in building a database design if it is not accepted because people simply don't like you. Strive to be liked, as well as achieving technical aims, and your efforts are unlikely to be wasted. Many technical people think that being liked is unimportant. They are wrong!

It's not what you know, it's who you know. It's also not what you say, but how you say it!

Never assume that you know more than in-house employees, but also realize that you do have some experience; otherwise, you would not be there. A combination of your skills and the knowledge of others can help you build a good database model design. Balance all perspectives and opinions to find the best solution. That solution should also be agreeable to as many of the participants as possible (including yourself). You as the database designer are important as well because ultimately you designed it and you are responsible for it. When you know you are correct, insist gently (but firmly), but also acquiesce when someone else might be correct. Consider all possibilities and don't let your own ego get in the way of your own success. Ensuring that a database model design comes into enthusiastic use is just as important as making sure the design is correct.

Above all, listen! Listen, learn, and examine every piece of information you are given. If a piece of information is not given, ask for it. If a snippet of information is essential and one person does not or cannot provide it, ask another. Achieve your objectives, but be careful not to tread on people's toes. The material discussed here can be found in a sales handbook. It is all basic common sense, and, yes, it is largely selling—selling yourself, your skills, your experience, and your ideas. When building a database model for a company, be it a brand new concept or a rebuild of something that is already there, you are potentially introducing change. Some people inside the company may react badly to potential change. Be aware of that, work around it, and work with it.

Dealing with Unfavorable Scenarios

Quite often, the best environment for which to design is a completely non-computerized environment. Common in many database model design projects are what can only be called "unfavorable" and sometimes even "ugly" scenarios. Sometimes those ugly scenarios have to do with people. Those are best avoided; however, there are some commonly encountered situations where the people involved are only too willing to assist you in helping themselves out of a difficult database model problem.

> *With any existing database model and any type of conversion, be it from a legacy database on a mainframe, a paper-based system, or even a spreadsheet program, get as much information as possible on what the new database model is supposed to achieve. Work backward from that point.*

Computerizing a Pile of Papers

This can, in some ways, be the easiest problem to solve, and also, in some ways, the most difficult. The fact is nothing exists in the way of a computerized database and quite often the paper pile and its attached trail can show you (in great detail) exactly how the database model should look. Paper-based systems are sometimes very accurate and very detailed. They must also take all possibilities into account, and have been designed for all possible eventualities over many years.

A problematic situation with a paper-based system is that it has often not been meticulously designed, and has more or less grown into what it is because of necessity. The obvious result is a complete nightmare of different types of paper with a lot of duplicated information, conflicting information, and a whole plethora of potential problems. In this extreme situation, you can use the basic format of paper documents to build basic table structures and possibly establish the operational aspects of the business.

Sometimes it is possible to find one person in an organization who knows how it all works. Sometimes it's up to you to figure it out. In an extreme situation of total confusion, it is best to approach a database model design cautiously and get some kind of verification from people who understand operational functioning of the business. These people likely enjoy applying their knowledge to the creation of a database model. And better still, they also understand your database model design much better when it comes to final handover to the client. Further still, they might even point out other factors such as field additions and special cases that as an outsider you would never be able to see.

The easiest way through a paper system is to collect as much printed material as you can and then start categorizing it. This task might be easier if you can find someone in the organization who can help you through this categorization process. Just be sure that the person actually does know about both the paper system and the operational function of the business. Someone who doesn't know zip could well confuse the heck out of you. Also, exchanging them later on for someone who is in the know could ruffle feathers. Choose wisely if you have a choice. Ask the manager or executive who hired you to pick the person. Ensure that it is the executive who wanted you in the company. You don't want to get involved in any petty politicking.

Computerizing a pile of papers always looks like a daunting task. It isn't! In fact, it is very possible that by the time a company decides to computerize a paper system, the company will be more than willing to assist you in this most daunting of tasks because they might very well be trying to get rid of all those pesky pieces of paper they are constantly having to fill in and correct.

Converting Legacy Databases

Converting legacy databases can often be the most difficult of tasks. Sometimes the databases are partially inaccessible or difficult to access at best. Sometimes the databases may even be in existence using network or even hierarchical database modeling techniques. These database model structures can be extremely large and complex and, therefore, very difficult to decipher.

As with a paper system, find someone who knows all about the database to help you; otherwise, dig into the database yourself, allow plenty of time for analysis, and verify structure. In the worst case, analyze applications as well as the database model to confirm the operational functionality of the database and that it actually does what it should do. It could very well be the case that a new database model is required because the legacy database and software was incorrectly built in the first place, or that requirements have drastically changed since its inception. If things have changed, you should find someone or something that makes these differences very obvious, either inside or outside of the database and applications, or both. It's better to find an expert in the company first. Once again, you will get much farther, much faster, and with much more ease, by talking to people and asking questions.

Homogenous Integration of Heterogeneous Databases

In scientific terms, a *heterogeneous system* is a system consisting of dissimilar parts. And, obviously, a *homogenous system* is the complete opposite consisting of similar parts, or parts being of a uniform structure throughout. In terms of database models, some of the much more sophisticated (largely very expensive) database engines allow for the creation of homogenous integration of heterogeneous databases. In other words, it is possible to transparently link multiple types of databases, using different database engines, perhaps even including legacy databases, and really any type of database that can be catered for with whichever database is being used to perform the integration. The idea is to retrieve data from the *controlling database*, the one establishing the homogeneous, seamless, transparent interface, and manage data in any number of underlying databases.

These maps or overlying homogeneous structures usually require what are called *gateways*, which are essentially database links from one database to another. The link is passed through a specialized driver, which allows the controlling database to talk to another database. Typically, these gateways are restricted to access only the commonly used databases. Any connections or gateways to older network or hierarchical databases could be implemented by manual coding. That is complicated and probably not worth the development effort.

The fact is this—all computer software, including databases and their incorporated database models, have a fixed *life cycle*. That life cycle is the cycle of usefulness within acceptable limits of cost effectiveness. There comes a point where older legacy software is either too expensive to maintain or can be easily replaced. At that point, there is simply no reason to retain and not rewrite older software. Other than that, older legacy software and databases (depending on how old they are) can present enormous problems for management in finding people to maintain those older systems.

Converting from Spreadsheets

Spreadsheets are always fun at first because they look like flat files. When looking into spreadsheet files, however, you can find all sorts of complexities with formulas on multiple levels and even multiple related sheets. Paper-based and legacy-system spreadsheets require analysis, requirements specifications of what should exist, and preferably the person who built the spreadsheet.

The benefit of converting something like a spreadsheet into a database model is that the spreadsheet is likely to be a lot less complex than a mainframe-based legacy network database or a paper-based system. The reason why is likely to be because the company keeps losing copies of the spreadsheet or spreadsheets. Loss can occur from bad hardware, but most likely they occur because of human error caused by accidental deletions or copying. People lose things all the time. Spreadsheet or any single-user based system, unless its something built in a legacy piece of software like dBase, is unlikely to present too much history; however, complexity is certainly a possibility.

Sorting Out a Messed-up Database

Sorting out a messed-up database implies that there is a relational database in existence, but that the database model is a complete mess. Expect to find invalid data, orphaned records, and other such wonderful problems. Once again, establish what is needed first before starting to go through it willy-nilly. After you establish what the records are supposed to look like, you might even find that there are only a few minor structural errors or relationship errors that can be easily repaired.

Even though a task like this can seem daunting, it really only has two very distinct steps. First, establish and build the correct structure. If the company has decided that the existing structure is problematic, the company probably has plenty of ideas on how to fix it. The company probably also knows who can give you all the correct information. Second, copy data across to new tables, if necessary.

Summary

In this chapter, you learned about:

- ❑ Business rules are partially built into a relational database model design
- ❑ Talk to users to get the information you need
- ❑ Abstraction requires management perspective
- ❑ Assess the culture of in-house technical people to understand their perspective
- ❑ Higher-level personnel in small companies are more accessible than those in large companies
- ❑ Different types of people in different roles can give differing perspectives
- ❑ Talk to the right people to get the right information in a specific topic area
- ❑ Unfavorable scenarios are difficult conversion situations, but not necessarily as daunting as they seem

The next chapter begins the discussion of the technical details of the relational database model itself by introducing all the various terms and concepts, the building blocks of the relational database model.

Database Modeling
Building Blocks

"Well begun is half done." (Aristotle)

Begin at the beginning by starting with the simple pieces.

This chapter introduces the building blocks of the relational database model by discussing and explaining all the various parts and pieces making up a relational database model. For example, a table is probably the most important piece in the puzzle of the relational database model, where fields or fields in tables are perhaps of less significance but still essential to the semantics of the model as a whole.

So far, this book has covered the historical evolution of database models, how different applications and end-user needs affect database type, the basics of the art of database design, plus various human factors influencing design. Before describing how a data model is built, you must know what all the pieces are. You need a basic knowledge of all the parts and pieces constituting the relational database model. This chapter describes all those parts and pieces needed for future chapters, which will cover the process of creating and refining relational database models.

In a book such as this, the objective is to teach an understanding of the relational database model by whatever means necessary. Previous chapters have used approaches such as a history of database models to describe the benefits and reasons for the evolution of the relational database model, as it exists today. Various aspects of this book have already gone into some detail to describe some basic and fundamental concepts, with deliberate succinctness.

At this point, this book could jump straight into the workings of the normalization process using normal forms. Normalization is used to *granularize* and organize data for use in a database. It is also assumed, having purchased this book, that the concept of a table in a relational database model is completely unfamiliar to you. So, I shall have to err on the side of caution and proceed to devote this entire chapter to describing all the various parts and pieces of what makes up a relational database model. You have to begin with the elements that make up the relational database model before proceeding to learn how to create relational database models.

If you have all the details in this chapter committed to memory and well understood, you can skip it if you are really strapped for time. However, I do recommend you read this chapter in its entirety. There are concepts, ideas, and object aspects of data modeling described in this chapter that you will not find in most books of this nature. I have taken the liberty of expanding on the basic structure of the relational database model and adding little bits and pieces here and there such as materialized views and auto counter sequences. For example, even though materialized views are not a part of the normalization process used to create a relational database model, materialized views can have a most profound effect on the behavior of data warehouses, particularly in the area of performance.

> *The process of normalization and the application of normal forms are covered in detail in Chapter 4. All you have to know at this stage is that normalization is the method or formula used to divide data up into separate tables — according to a bunch of rules. So, when the term normalization is mentioned, simply assume it implies that new tables are being created or more streamlined versions of existing tables are being devised.*

Views are included in this chapter. A view is not the same thing as a materialized view, which are relegated to a final section covering specialized objects. Materialized views and auto counters are included. As a performance tuner, I don't believe in using views for anything other than security purposes, and I still wouldn't recommend even that practice. Views are often used by developers to prototype or speed up development. The result is usually drastically poor performance in production. I prefer not to promote the use of views in general. In addition, views can be used to get around or skirt poor database model design. Like I said, I prefer not to suggest use of views too strongly, by reason of past experience.

This chapter describes all the pieces that compose the relational database model. All of the constituents of the relational database model help to create an organized logical structure for managing data in a database. The organized logical structure is a relational database model.

In this chapter, you learn about the following:

- ❑ Information, data, and data integrity
- ❑ Tables
- ❑ Fields, columns, and attributes
- ❑ Rows, records, and tuples
- ❑ Datatypes
- ❑ Validation and NULL values
- ❑ Relations, relationships, and some normalization
- ❑ Entity Relationship Diagrams (ERDs)
- ❑ Primary and foreign keys
- ❑ Referential integrity
- ❑ Indexes
- ❑ Specialized objects (views and materialized views)

So, arm in arm and onward we shall go! Let's begin with a conceptual perspective.

Information, Data and Data Integrity

Information refers to knowledge or the way in which knowledge is communicated. Values in a database are made up of data, which is essentially information. Validity is determined by the integrity of data. The integrity of data is the correct form of data. The following list leads off the definitions of basic terms and concepts:

❑ *The concept of information* — Information is knowledge or the communication of knowledge. Knowledge is accumulated and derived by processes including those of experience, events, or static information (such as a set of statistical values). In computer jargon, information is data that is stored in a database, processed by programs, or even transmitted over a network such as the Internet (between multiple users).

❑ *The concept of data* — Data is composed of unique, specifically formatted items of information. Unique data item values are stored in slots in a database, processed as individual values by coded programs, and transmitted across networks of wires, or even communicated with electromagnetic signals to and from satellites (all over the world, and beyond).

❑ *The concept of a computer program* — Programs are sets of precise instructions, used to manipulate and process changes to a database.

❑ *The concept of a datatype* — Datatypes comprise the forms data can take, such as numbers, dates, strings, and others.

❑ *The concept of data integrity* — The integrity of data is the validity of data. Possible compromises to data integrity include human error at data entry, network transmission errors, software bugs and virus infections, hardware malfunction, disk errors, and natural disasters. Countering compromises to data integrity is mostly a pre-emptive process, rather than a re-active process. In other words, the best solution is to attempt to prevent data integrity loss. The most significant prevention mechanisms are database backups (regularly), computer security (in all forms), and properly designed interfaces restricting how data is entered by data entry users. Solving the problem after the fact often utilizes something called a *parity check* (such as when transmitting over a network), which is simply a check of something, of itself.

Understanding the Basics of Tables

In data model theory, a *table* is a bucket into which data is poured. The idea of the relational database model and normalization is that data in a specific table is directly associated with all other items in that same table — that would be each field as exaggerated in Figure 3-1, pictured as the horizontal dimension.

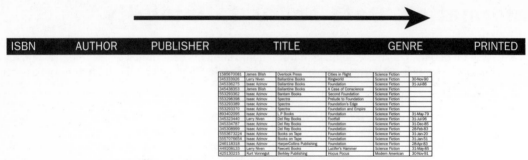

Figure 3-1: Table fields express the metadata (horizontal) dimension.

Records are repeated over and over again in the vertical dimension, duplicating field structures from the horizontal dimension, as exaggerated in Figure 3-2.

ISBN	AUTHOR	PUBLISHER	TITLE	GENRE	PRINTED
1585670081	James Blish	Overlook Press	Cities in Flight	Science Fiction	
345333926	Larry Niven	Ballantine Books	Ringworld	Science Fiction	30-Nov-90
345336275	Isaac Azimov	Ballantine Books	Foundation	Science Fiction	31-Jul-86
345438353	James Blish	Ballantine Books	A Case of Conscience	Science Fiction	
553293362	Isaac Azimov	Bantam Books	Second Foundation	Science Fiction	
553298398	Isaac Azimov	Spectra	Prelude to Foundation	Science Fiction	
553293389	Isaac Azimov	Spectra	Foundation's Edge	Science Fiction	
553293370	Isaac Azimov	Spectra	Foundation and Empire	Science Fiction	
893402095	Isaac Azimov	L P Books	Foundation	Science Fiction	31-May-79
345323440	Larry Niven	Del Rey Books	Footfall	Science Fiction	31-Jul-96
345334787	Isaac Azimov	Del Rey Books	Foundation	Science Fiction	31-Dec-85
345308999	Isaac Azimov	Del Rey Books	Foundation	Science Fiction	28-Feb-83
5553673224	Isaac Azimov	Books on Tape	Foundation	Science Fiction	31-Jan-20
5557076654	Isaac Azimov	Books on Tape	Foundation	Science Fiction	31-Jan-51
246118318	Isaac Azimov	HarperCollins Publis	Foundation	Science Fiction	28-Apr-83
449208133	Larry Niven	Fawcett Books	Lucifer's Hammer	Science Fiction	31-May-85
425130215	Kurt Vonnegut	Berkley Publishing	Hocus Pocus	Modern American	30-Nov-91

Figure 3-2: Table records duplicate the set of fields into the tuples or data (vertical) dimension.

A table is effectively a structure containing fields across it in one dimension defining the structure of records repeatedly added to that table. In other words, all records in the same tables have the same field structure applied to them. Figure 3-3 shows a picture demonstrating a pile of books on the left, passed through a table structure represented by the miniature ERD in the center, resulting in the structured data set on the right, duplicated as the table records from Figure 3-2.

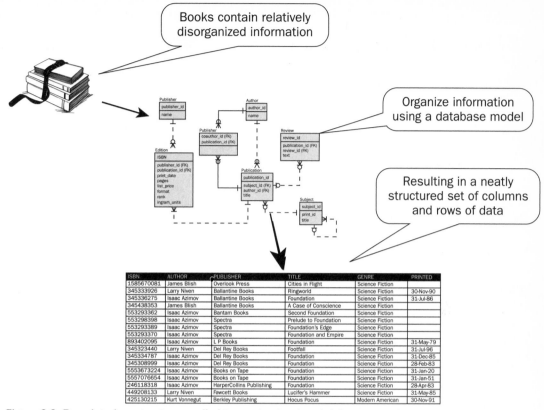

Books contain relatively disorganized information

Organize information using a database model

Resulting in a neatly structured set of columns and rows of data

ISBN	AUTHOR	PUBLISHER	TITLE	GENRE	PRINTED
1585670081	James Blish	Overlook Press	Cities in Flight	Science Fiction	
345333926	Larry Niven	Ballantine Books	Ringworld	Science Fiction	30-Nov-90
345336275	Isaac Azimov	Ballantine Books	Foundation	Science Fiction	31-Jul-86
345438353	James Blish	Ballantine Books	A Case of Conscience	Science Fiction	
553293362	Isaac Azimov	Bantam Books	Second Foundation	Science Fiction	
553298398	Isaac Azimov	Spectra	Prelude to Foundation	Science Fiction	
553293389	Isaac Azimov	Spectra	Foundation's Edge	Science Fiction	
553293370	Isaac Azimov	Spectra	Foundation and Empire	Science Fiction	
893402095	Isaac Azimov	L P Books	Foundation	Science Fiction	31-May-79
345323440	Larry Niven	Del Rey Books	Footfall	Science Fiction	31-Jul-96
345334787	Isaac Azimov	Del Rey Books	Foundation	Science Fiction	31-Dec-85
345308999	Isaac Azimov	Del Rey Books	Foundation	Science Fiction	28-Feb-83
5553673224	Isaac Azimov	Books on Tape	Foundation	Science Fiction	31-Jan-20
5557076654	Isaac Azimov	Books on Tape	Foundation	Science Fiction	31-Jan-51
246118318	Isaac Azimov	HarperCollins Publishing	Foundation	Science Fiction	28-Apr-83
449208133	Larry Niven	Fawcett Books	Lucifer's Hammer	Science Fiction	31-May-85
425130215	Kurt Vonnegut	Berkley Publishing	Hocus Pocus	Modern American	30-Nov-91

Figure 3-3: Raw data has structure applied to create structured data.

Tables contain fields and records. Fields apply structure to records, whereas records duplicate field structure an indefinite number of times.

Records, Rows, and Tuples

The terms record, row, and tuple all mean the same thing. They are terms used to describe a record in a table. Figure 3-4 shows the structure of fields applied to each record entry in a table. There is really nothing to understand other than that a table can have multiple fields, whereas that set of fields can have many records created in that table, and data can subsequently be accessed according to the field structure of the table, record by record.

ISBN	AUTHOR	PUBLISHER	TITLE	GENRE	PRINTED
1585670081	James Blish	Overlook Press	Cities in Flight	Science Fiction	
345333926	Larry Niven	Ballantine Books	Ringworld	Science Fiction	30-Nov-90
345336275	Isaac Azimov	Ballantine Books	Foundation	Science Fiction	31-Jul-86
345438353	James Blish	Ballantine Books	A Case of Conscience	Science Fiction	
553293362	Isaac Azimov	Bantam Books	Second Foundation	Science Fiction	
553298398	Isaac Azimov	Spectra	Prelude to Foundation	Science Fiction	
553293389	Isaac Azimov	Spectra	Foundation's Edge	Science Fiction	
553293370	Isaac Azimov	Spectra	Foundation and Empire	Science Fiction	
893402095	Isaac Azimov	L P Books	Foundation	Science Fiction	31-May-79
345323440	Larry Niven	Del Rey Books	Footfall	Science Fiction	31-Jul-96
345334787	Isaac Azimov	Del Rey Books	Foundation	Science Fiction	31-Dec-85
345308999	Isaac Azimov	Del Rey Books	Foundation	Science Fiction	28-Feb-83
5553673224	Isaac Azimov	Books on Tape	Foundation	Science Fiction	31-Jan-20
5557076654	Isaac Azimov	Books on Tape	Foundation	Science Fiction	31-Jan-51
246118318	Isaac Azimov	HarperCollins Publishing	Foundation	Science Fiction	28-Apr-83
449208133	Larry Niven	Fawcett Books	Lucifer's Hammer	Science Fiction	31-May-85
425130215	Kurt Vonnegut	Berkley Publishing	Hocus Pocus	Modern American	30-Nov-91

Rows repeat the column structure of the table

Figure 3 -4: Records repeat table field structure.

So far, this chapter has examined tables, plus the fields and records within those tables. The next step is to examine relationships between tables.

Fields, Columns and Attributes

The terms field, column, and attribute all mean the same thing. They are all terms used to describe a field in a table. A *field* applies structure and definition to a chunk of data within each repeated record. Data is not actually repeated on every record, but the structure of fields is applied to each record. So, data on each record can be different, both for the record as a whole, and for each field value. Note the use of the term "can be" rather than "is," implying that there can be duplication across both fields and records, depending on requirements and constraints. A constraint constrains (restricts) a value. For example, in Figure 3-5 the second box showing NOT NULL for the first three fields specifies that the ISBN, PUBLISHER_ID, and PUBLICATION_ID fields can never contain NULL values in any record.

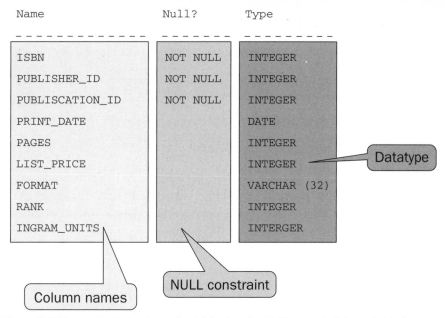

Figure 3-5: The vertical structure of a table showing fields, constraints and datatypes.

Examine Figure 3-5 again. The left column shows the name of fields in the table. This particular table is used to contain separate editions of the same book. Separate editions of a single book can each be published by different publishers. Thus, the PUBLISHER_ID field is included in the EDITION table. Note various other fields such as the PUBLICATION_ID field - uniquely identifying a unique book name, which is stored in the PUBLICATION table. The PUBLICATION table represents each book uniquely regardless of the existence of multiple editions of the same title or not. The International Standard Book Number (ISBN) uniquely identifies a book on an international basis, and is distinct for each edition of a book.

Also note the datatypes shown in Figure 3-5. Datatypes are shown as INTEGER, DATE, or VARCHAR(32). These three field types restrict values to be of certain content and format. INTEGER only allows whole numbers, all characters consisting of digits between 0 and 9, with no decimal point character. DATE only allows date entries where specific formatting may apply. Most databases will have a default format for date values. If the default format is set to *dd/mm/yyyy*, an attempt to set a date value to 12/31/2004 will cause an error because the day and month values are reversed. Effectively, datatypes can constrain values in fields in a similar way to that of the previously specified NOT NULL constraint does. Similar to constraints, datatypes can restrict values, so datatypes are also a form of field value constraining functionality.

Whereas fields apply structure to records, datatypes apply structure and restrictions to fields and values in those fields.

Datatypes

There are many different types of *datatypes*, which vary often more in name than anything else with respect to different database engines. This section describes all different variations of datatypes, but without targeting any specific vendor database engine.

Datatypes can be divided into three separate sections:

❑ *Simple datatypes* — These are datatypes applying a pattern or value limitation on a single value such as a number.

❑ *Complex datatypes* — These include any datatypes bridging the gap between object and relational databases, including items such as binary objects and collection arrays. Specifics on complex datatypes are not strictly necessary for this book as they are more object-oriented than relational in nature.

❑ *Specialized datatypes* — These are present in more advanced relational databases catering to inherently structured data such as XML documents, spatial data, multimedia objects and even dynamically definable datatypes.

Simple Datatypes

Simple datatypes include basic validation and formatting requirements placed on to individual values. This includes the following:

❑ *Strings* — A string is a sequence of one or more characters. Strings can be fixed-length strings or variable-length strings:

  ❑ *Fixed-length strings* — A fixed-length string will always store the specified length declared for the datatype. The value is padded with spaces even when the actual string value is less than the length of the datatype length. For example, the value NY in a CHAR(3) variable would be stored as NY plus a space character. Fixed-length strings are generally only used for short length strings because a variable-length string (discussed next) requires storage of both value and length. Fixed-length strings are also more efficient for ensuring fixed record lengths of key values. Figure 3-6 shows an FXCODE field representing a foreign exchange currency code, always returning three characters even when the currency code is less than three characters in length. A case in point is the defunct currency code DM (Deutsche Marks, German currency), returning DM plus a space character, yielding a total of three characters.

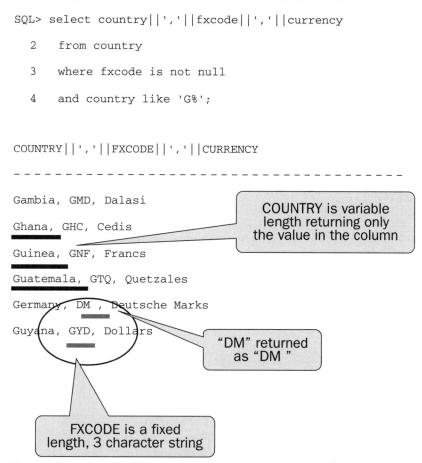

```
SQL> select country||','||fxcode||','||currency

  2     from country

  3     where fxcode is not null

  4     and country like 'G%';


COUNTRY||','||FXCODE||','||CURRENCY

- - - - - - - - - - - - - - - - - - - - - - - - - - - - - - - - - - - - -

Gambia, GMD, Dalasi

Ghana, GHC, Cedis

Guinea, GNF, Francs

Guatemala, GTQ, Quetzales

Germany, DM , Deutsche Marks

Guyana, GYD, Dollars
```

COUNTRY is variable length returning only the value in the column

"DM" returned as "DM "

FXCODE is a fixed length, 3 character string

Figure 3-6: Fixed-length strings and variable-length strings.

❑   *Variable-length strings* — A variable-length string allows storage into a datatype as the actual length of the string, as long as a maximum limit is not exceeded. The length of the string is variable because when storing a string of length less than the width specified by the datatype, the string is not padded (as is the case for fixed-length strings). Only the actual string value is stored. Storing the string XXX into a variable length string datatype of ten characters in length stores the three characters only, and not three characters padded by seven spaces. Different databases use different naming conventions for variable-length string datatypes. VARCHAR(n) or TEXT(n) are common naming formats for variable-length strings. Figure 3-6 shows variable-length strings on country names (COUNTRY), returning only the names of the countries and no padding out to maximum length as for fixed-length strings.

❑ *Numbers* — Numeric datatypes are often the most numerous field datatypes in many database tables. The following different numeric datatype formats are common:

    ❑ *Integers* — An integer is a whole number such that no decimal digits are included. Some databases allow more detailed specification using small integers and long integers, as well and standard-sized integer datatypes. Figure 3-7 shows three whole number integer datatypes in the fields SINT, INT, and LONGINT. SINT represents a small integer, INT an integer, and LONGINT a long integer datatype.

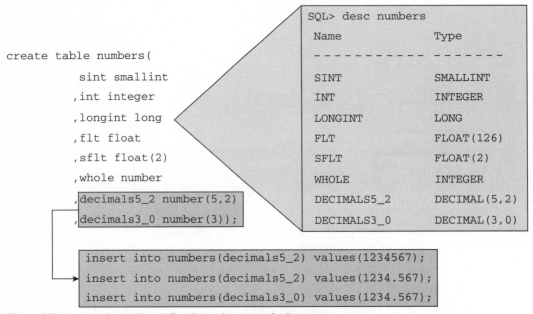

Figure 3-7: Integer, decimal, and floating-point numeric datatypes.

    ❑ *Fixed-length decimals* — A fixed-length decimal is a number, including a decimal point, where the digits on the right side of the decimal are restricted to a specified number of digits. For example, a DECIMAL(5,2) datatype will allow the values 4.1 and 4.12, but not 4.123. However, the value 4.123 might be automatically truncated or rounded to 4.12, depending on the database engine. More specifically, depending on the database engine the value to the left of the decimal, the number 5 in DECIMAL(5,2), can be interpreted in different ways. In some databases the value 5 limits the number of digits to the left of the decimal point; in other databases, 5 limits the total length of the number, and that total length may include or exclude the decimal point. Thus, in some databases, DECIMAL(5,2) would allow 12345.67 and some databases 12345.67 would not be allowed because the entire number contains too many digits. So, the value 5 can specify the length of the entire number, or only the digits to the left of the decimal point. In Figure 3-7 assume that DECIMAL(5,2) implies 2 decimals with total digits of 5 at most, excluding the decimal point. So in Figure 3-7 the fields DECIMALS5_2 and DECIMALS3_0 allow fixed length decimal values. All INSERT commands adding values to the two DECIMALS5_2 and DECIMALS3_0 fields will fail because decimal length, or overall field length specifications for the datatypes have not been adhered to.

❑ *Floating points* — A floating-point number is just as the name implies, where the decimal point "floats freely" anywhere within the number. In other words, the decimal point can appear anywhere in the number. Floating-point values can have any number of digits both before and after the decimal point, even none on either side. Values such as 1000, 1000.12345, and 0.8843343223 are valid floating-point numbers. Floating point values are likely to be less efficient in storage and retrieval than fixed-length decimals and integers because they are less predictable in terms of record length and otherwise. Figure 3-7 shows a 32-byte length floating-point datatype and a relatively unlimited length floating point datatype.

For most databases, any INSERT commands into the float fields exceeding length requirements (such as 32 bytes for SFLT) will not produce errors because values added will likely be truncated and converted to exponential (scientific) notation when too large or too small, as shown in Figure 3-8.

```
insert into numbers(sflt) values(5.2234);

insert into numbers(sflt) values(55444);

insert into numbers(sflt) values(449998234590782340895);

insert into numbers(sflt) values(0.00000499998234590782340895);
```

```
SQL> select sflt from numbers;


        SFLT

    - - - - - -

            5

        60000

    4.0000E+20

        .000005
```

Figure 3-8: Adding values to floating-point datatype fields.

❑ *Dates and times* — Dates can be stored as simple dates or dates including timestamp information. In actuality, simple dates are often stored as a Julian date or some other similar numbering system. A *Julian date* is a time in seconds from a specified start date (such as January 1, 1960). When simple date values are set or retrieved in the database, they are subjected to a default formatting process spitting out to, for example, a *dd/mm/yyyy* format excluding seconds (depending on default database formatting settings, of course). A timestamp datatype displays both date and time information regardless of any default date formatting executing in the database (sometimes stored as a special timestamp datatype). Figure 3-9 shows the difference between dates with timestamps and dates without timestamps.

```
SQL> select isbn, print_date AS Printed,
  2     to_char(print_date, 'DD/MM/YYYY HH24:MI:SS') AS TimeStamp
  3     from edition where print_date is not null;


       ISBN   PRINTED      TIMESTAMP
   --------   -------      ----------------

    893402095 | 31-MAY-79 | 31/05/1979 00:12:01

    345308999 | 28-FEB-83 | 28/02/1983 04:55:03

    345336275 | 31-JUL-86 | 31/07/1986 03:44:33

   5557076654 | 31-JAN-51 | 31/01/1951 09:41:00

   5553673224 | 31-JAN-20 | 31/01/2020 22:15:20

    246118318 | 28-APR-83 | 28/04/1983 10:17:10

    345334787 | 31-DEC-85 | 31/12/1985 08:13:45

    449208133 | 31-MAY-85 | 31/05/1985 00:01:12

    345323440 | 31-JUL-96 | 31/07/1996 03:00:30

    345333926 | 30-NOV-90 | 30/11/1990 21:04:40

    425130215 | 30-NOV-91 | 30/11/1991 16:43:53
```

Database specific format

Timestamp format

Figure 3-9: Dates with timestamps and dates without timestamps.

Complex Datatypes

Complex datatypes encompass object datatypes. Available object datatypes vary for different relational databases. Some relational databases provide more object-relational attributes and functionality than others. Complex datatypes include any datatypes breaching the object-relational database divide including items such as binary objects, reference pointers, collection arrays and even the capacity to create user defined types. Following are some complex datatypes:

❑ *Binary objects*—Purely binary objects were created in relational databases to help separate binary type data from regular relational database table record structures. A large object such as a graphic is so very much larger than the length of an average table record containing all strings and numbers. Storage issues can become problematic. Relational databases use many different types of underlying disk storage techniques to make the management of records in tables more efficient. A typical record in a table may occupy at most 2 KB (sometimes known as a *page* or *block*), and often much less. Even the smallest of graphic objects used in Web site applications easily exceeds the size of a record—and each record in a table could have a unique graphic object. Therefore, storing a graphic object with each record in the underlying operating system block structure completely ruins any kind of specialized storage structure performance tuned for simple table record strings and numbers storage. Binary objects were created to physically separate binary values from traditional table record values. The obvious extension to this concept was creation of binary objects to store anything in binary format, reducing storage, even items such as large strings, sound files, video, XML documents . . . the list goes on.

❑   *Reference pointers*—In the C programming language, a *reference pointer* is a variable containing an address on disk or in memory of whatever the programmer wants to point at. A pointer provides the advantage of not having to specify too much in advance with respect to how many bytes the pointer value occupies. Some relational databases allow the use of pointers where a pointer points to an object or file stored externally to the database, pointing from a field within a table, to the object stored outside the database. Only the address of the externally stored object is stored in the table field. This minimizes structural storage effects on relational tables as often is the result of storing binary objects in table records. Pointers are generally used for pointing to static binary objects. A static object does not change very often.

❑   *Collection arrays*—Some relational databases allow creation of what an object database would call a collection. A *collection* is a set of values repeated structurally (values are not necessarily the same) where the array is contained within another object, and can only be referenced from that object. In the case of a relational database, the containment factor is the collection being a field in the table. Collection arrays can have storage structures defined in alternative locations to table fields as for binary objects, but do not have to be as such. Collection arrays, much like program arrays, can be either fixed length or dynamic. A *dynamic array* is a variable-length array, and is actually a pointer. When using a *fixed-length array*, the programmer must specify the length of the array before using it.

❑   *User-defined types*—Some relational databases allow programmable or even on-the-fly creation of user-defined types. A user-defined type allows the creation of new types. Creation of a new type means that user-defined datatypes can be created by programmers, even using other user-defined types. It follows that fields can be created in tables where those fields have user-defined datatypes.

Specialized Datatypes

Specialized datatypes take into account datatypes that are intended for contained complex data objects. These specialized datatypes allow types with contained inherent structure (such as XML documents, spatial data, and multimedia objects).

Constraints and Validation

Relational databases allow *constraints*, which restrict values that are allowed to be stored in table fields. Some relational databases allow the minimum of constraints necessary to define a database as being a relational database. Some relational databases allow other constraints in addition to the basics. In general, constraints are used to restrict values in tables, make validation checks on one or more fields in a table, or even check values between fields in different tables. Following are some examples of constraints:

❑   NOT NULL — This is the simplest of field level constraints, making sure that a value must always be entered into a field when a record is added or changed.

❑   *Validation check* — Similar to a NOT NULL constraint, a validation checking type of constraint restricts values in fields when a record is added or changed in a table. A check validation constraint can be as simple as making sure a field allowing only M for Male or F for Female, will only ever contain those two possible values. Otherwise, check validation constraints can become fairly complex in some relational databases, perhaps allowing inclusion of user written functions running SQL scripting.

❑   *Keys* — Key constraints include primary keys, foreign keys, and unique keys. All these key types are discussed briefly later on in this chapter and further in later chapters in this book. Key constraints allow the checking and validation of values between fields in different tables. Primary and foreign keys are essentially the implementation of relationships between parent and child tables. Those relationships or relations are the source of the term *relational database*.

Some relational databases allow constraints to be specified at both the field level or for an entire table as a whole, depending on the type of constraint.

Understanding Relations for Normalization

By dictionary definition, the term *normalization* means to make normal in terms of causing something to conform to a standard, or to introduce consistency with respect to style and content. In terms of relational database modeling, that consistency becomes a process of removing duplication in data, among other factors. Removal of duplication tends to minimize redundancy. Minimization of redundancy implies getting rid of unneeded data present in particular places, or tables.

In reality, normalization usually manages to divide information into smaller, more manageable parts, preferably not too small. The most obvious redundancies can usually be removed without getting too deeply mathematical about everything. Commercially speaking, primary objectives are usually to save space and organize data for usability and manageability, without sacrificing performance. All this is often a juggling act and commonly partially ironed out by trial and error. Additionally the demands of intensely busy applications and end-user needs can tend to necessitate breaking the rules of normalization in many ways to meet performance requirements. Rules are usually broken simply by not applying every possible layer of normalization. Normal Forms beyond 3rd Normal Form are often ignored and sometimes even 3rd Normal Form itself is discounted.

Normalization can be described as being one of introduction of granularity, removal of duplication, or minimizing of redundancy, or simply the introduction of tables, all of which place data into a better organized state.

Normalization is an incremental process. In other words, each Normal Form layer adds to whatever Normal Forms have already been applied. For example, 2nd Normal Form can only be applied to tables in 1st Normal Form, and 3rd Normal Form only applied to tables in 2nd Normal Form, and so on. Each Normal Form is a refinement of the previous Normal Form. Similarly 3rd Normal cannot be applied to tables in 4th Normal Form because by definition tables in 4th Normal Form are cumulatively already in 3rd Normal Form.

Benefits of Normalization

Effectively minimizing redundancy is another way of describing removal of duplication. removing duplication is as follows:

❑   Physical space needed to store data is reduced.

❑   Data becomes better organized.

❑   Normalization allows changes to small amounts of data (namely single records) to be made to one table at once. In other words, a single table record is updated when a specific item is added, changed, or removed from the database. You don't have to search through an entire database to change a single field value in a single record, just the table.

Potential Normalization Hazards

There are potential problems in taking this redundancy minimization process too far. Some detailed aspects of the positive effects of normalization mentioned previously can have negative side effects, and sometimes even backfire, depending on the application focus of the database. Performance is always a problem with too much granularity caused by over-application of normalization. Very demanding concurrency OLTP databases can be very adversely affected by too much granularity. Data warehouses often require non-technical end-user access and over-granularity tends to make table structure more technically oriented to the point of being impossible to interpret by end-users. Keep the following in mind:

❑   Physical space is not nearly as big a concern as it used to be, because disk space is one of the cheapest cost factors to consider (unless, of course, when dealing with a truly huge data warehouse).

❑   Too much minimization of redundancy implies too much granularity and too many tables. Too many tables can lead to extremely huge SQL join queries. The more tables in a SQL join query, the slower queries execute. Performance can be so drastically affected as to make applications completely useless.

❑   Better organization of data with extreme amounts of redundancy minimization can actually result in more complexity, particularly if end-users are exposed to database model structure. The deeper the level of normalization, the more mathematical the model becomes, making the model "techie-friendly" and thus very "user-unfriendly." Who is accessing the database, end-users or OLTP applications?

Tables are connected to each other with relationships. Examine what a relationship is and how it can be represented.

Representing Relationships in an ERD

Tables can have various types of relationships between them. The different types of inter-table relationships that can be formed between different tables can be best described as displayed in Entity Relationship Diagrams (ERDs).

onships between those tables. Figure 3-10 shows an example ERD for
lished books. Figure 3-10 shows what an ERD is and what it looks like.
complicated or inscrutable about ERDs.

entity in an ERD.

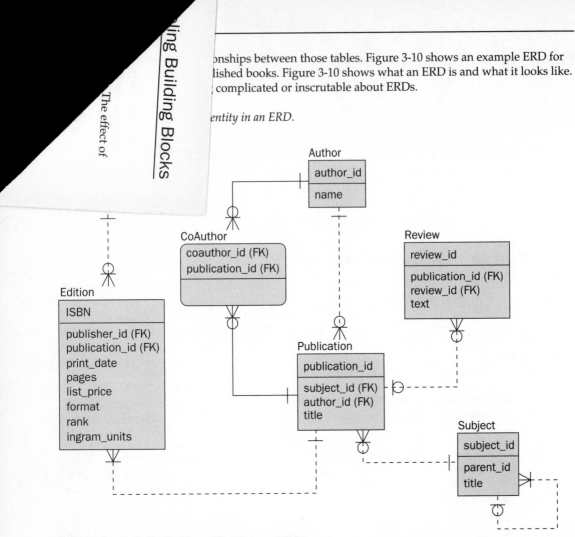

Figure 3-10: An Entity Relationship Diagram (ERD).

At this point, you don't need to understand how relationships are created between the tables shown in Figure 3-10. Creating the relations is a little too advanced for this chapter and will be covered in later chapters, mostly in Chapter 4.

Crows Foot

A *crow's foot* is used to describe the "many" side of a one-to-many or many-to-many relationship, as highlighted in Figure 3-11. A crow's foot looks quite literally like the imprint of a crow's foot in some mud, with three splayed "toes." (How many toes a crow has exactly I am not sure.) By now, you should get the idea that many toes implies more than one and thus many, regardless of how many toes a crow actually has. Figure 3-11 shows a crow's foot between the AUTHOR and PUBLICATION tables, indicating a one-to-many relationship between AUTHOR and PUBLICATION tables.

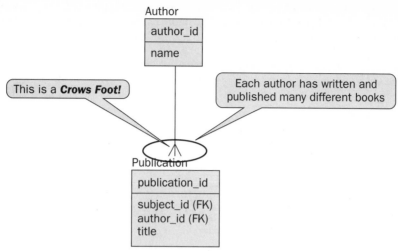

Figure 3-11: A crow's foot represents the many sides of a one-to-many relationship.

One-to-One

One-to-one relationships are often created to remove frequently NULL valued fields from a table. They are hopefully rare in relational database models, unless in exceptional circumstances because the price of storage space is cheap. One-to-one relationships are typical of 4th Normal Form transformations (see Chapter 4) where potentially NULL valued fields are removed from the parent table, possibly saving storage space. Not only is storage space cheap in modern times, but variable-length records in most relational databases tend to make this type of normalization bad for performance. SQL code joins get bigger as more tables are created. SQL code with more tables in joins can cause serious performance issues. Bad database performance means slow applications and unhappy users looking to pay your competitors what they pay you.

Figure 3-12 shows a one-to-one relationship between the EDITION and RANK tables such that for every EDITION entry, there is exactly one RANK entry, and visa versa.

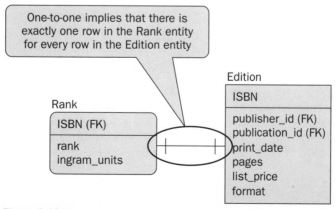

Figure 3-12: A one-to-one relationship implies exactly one entry in both tables.

Figure 3-13 shows the equivalent of the one-to-one table structure representation using real data. ISBN numbers 198711905 and 345308999 both have RANK and INGRAM_UNITS value entries, and thus appear in the RANK table as unique records.

In Figure 3-13, there is exactly one record in the EDITION table for every record in the RANK table, and visa versa.

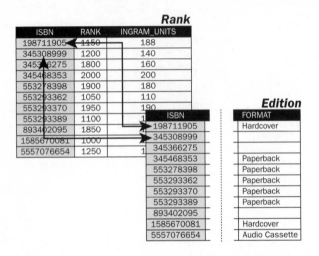

Figure 3-13: A one-to-one relationship implies exactly one entry in both tables.

One-to-Many

One-to-many relationships are extremely common in the relational database model between tables. Figure 3-14 shows that an AUTHOR table record can have many publications because an author can publish many books (PUBLICATION record entries).

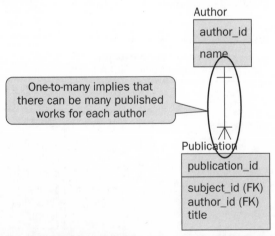

Figure 3-14: One-to-many implies one entry to many entries between two tables.

Figure 3-15 shows a data diagram with authors on the right of the diagram and their respective publications on the left, in a one-to-many relationship. One author has two titles, another five titles, another three titles, two authors have one each, and two other authors have nothing published at all — at least not in this database.

PUBLICATION_ID	SUBJECT_ID	AUTHOR_ID	TITLE
1	7	2	Cities in Flight
2	7	2	A Case of Conscience
3	7	3	Foundation
4	7	3	Second Foundation
5	7	3	Foundation and Em
6	7	3	Foundation's Edge
7	7	3	Prelude to Foundat
9	7	4	Lucifer's Hammer
10	7	4	Footfall
11	7	4	Ringworld
8	15	6	The Complete Works of Shakespeare
12	16	7	Hocus Pocus

AUTHOR_ID	NAME
1	Orson Scott Card
2	James Blish
3	Isaac Azimov
4	Larry Niven
5	Jerry Pournelle
6	William Shakespeare
7	Kurt Vonnegut

Figure 3-15: One-to-many implies one entry to many entries between two tables.

Many-to-Many

A *many-to-many relationship* means that for every one record in one table there are many possible records in another related table, and visa versa (for both tables). The classic example of a many-to-many relationship is many students enrolled in many courses at a university. The implication is that every student is registered for many courses and every course has many students registered. The result is a many-to-many relationship between students and courses. This is not a problem as it stands; however, if an application or end-user must find an individual course taken by an individual student, a uniquely identifying table is required. Note that this new table is required only if unique items are needed by end-users or an application.

In Figure 3-16, from left to right, the many-to-many relationship between PUBLISHER and PUBLICATION tables is resolved into the EDITION table. A publisher can publish many publications and a single publication can be published by many publishers. Not only can a single publication be reprinted, but other types of media (such as an audio tape version) can also be produced. Additionally those different versions can be produced by different publishers. It is unlikely that a publisher who commissions and prints a book will also produce an audio tape version of the same title. The purpose of the EDITION table is to provide a way for each individual reprint and audio tape copy to be uniquely accessible in the database.

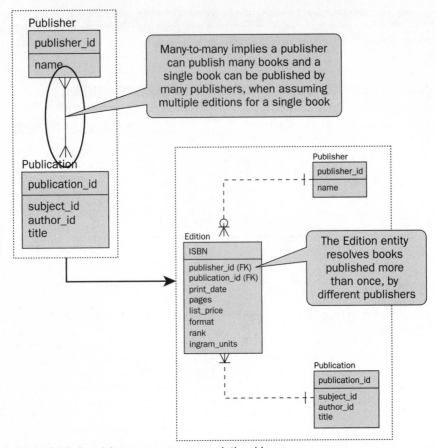

Figure 3-16: Resolving a many-to-many relationship.

In Figure 3-17 there are seven different editions of the publication *Foundation*. How is this so? Isaac Azimov is an extremely popular author who wrote books for decades. This particular title was written many years ago and has been in print ever since. Searching for this particular publication without the unique ISBN number unique to each edition would always find seven editions in this database. If only one of the *Books On Tape* editions was required for a query, returning seven records rather than only one could cause some serious problems. In this case, a many-to-many join resolution table in the form of the EDITION table is very much needed.

TITLE	PUBLISHER	ISBN	PRINTED
Cities in Flight	Overlook Press	1585670081	
A Case of Conscience	Ballantine Books	345438353	
Foundation	**HarperCollins Publishing**	**246118318**	28-A...
Foundation	**Books on Tape**	**5553673224**	...1-Jan-2...
Foundation	**Books on Tape**	**5557076654**	31-Jan-51
Foundation	**Del Rey Books**	**345334787**	31-Dec-85
Foundation	**Del Rey Books**	**345308999**	28-Feb-83
Foundation	**L P Books**	**893402095**	31-May-79
Foundation	**Ballantine Books**	**345336275**	31-Jul-86
Second Foundation	Bantam Books	553293362	
Foundation and Empire	Spectra	553293370	
Foundation's Edge	Spectra	553293389	
Prelude to Foundation	Spectra	553298398	
Lucifer's Hammer	Fawcett Books	449208133	31-May-85
Footfall	Del Rey Books	345323440	31-Jul-96
Ringworld	Ballantine Books	345333926	30-Nov-90

> Each edition is uniquely identified by ISBN – unique to each new edition of the same title

Figure 3-17: Resolving a many-to-many relationship.

Zero, One, or Many

Relationships between tables can be zero, one, or many. *Zero* implies that the record does not have to exist in the target table; *one with zero* implies that it can exist; *one without zero* implies that it must exist; and *many* simply implies many. The left side of Figure 3-18 shows a one-to-zero (or exactly one) relationship between the RANK and EDITION tables. What this implies is that an EDITION record does not have to have a related RANK record entry. Because the zero is pointing at the RANK table, however, the same is not the case in reverse. In other words, for every RANK entry, there must be exactly one record in the EDITION table; therefore, individual editions of books do not have to be ranked, but a ranking requires a book edition to rank. There is no point having a ranking without having a book to rank — in fact, it is impossible to rank something that does not exist.

Similarly, on the right side of Figure 3-18, a publisher can be a publisher, if only in name, even if that publisher currently has no books published. When you think about that, in reality it sounds quite silly to call a company a publisher if it has no publications currently produced. It's possible, but unlikely. However, this situation does exist in this database as a possibility. For example, a publisher could be bankrupt where no new editions of its books are available, but used editions of its books are still available. This does happen. It has happened.

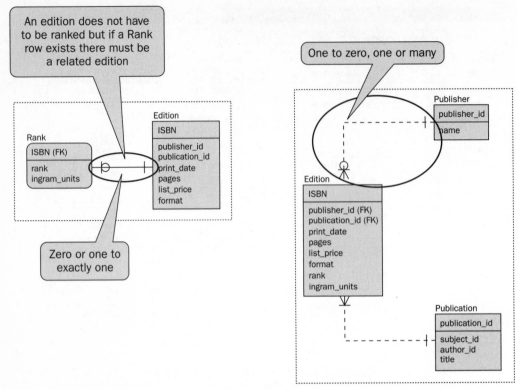

Figure 3-18: One implies a record must be present and zero the record can be present.

Figure 3-19 shows the equivalent of the one-to-one table structure representation using similar but a little more data than the data in Figure 3-13. ISBNs 198711905 and 345308999 both have RANK and INGRAM_UNITS value entries and thus appear in the RANK table as unique records. On the contrary, the edition with ISBN 246118318 does not have any information with respect to rank and Ingram unit values, and thus RANK and INGRAM_UNITS field values would be NULL valued for this edition of this book. Since values are NULL valued, there is no record in the RANK table for the book with ISBN 246118318.

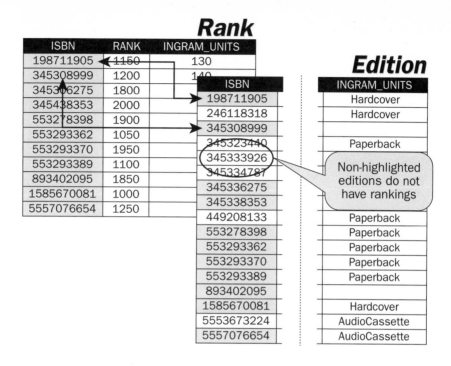

Figure 3-19: One implies a record must be present and zero the record can be present.

Identifying and Non-Identifying Relationships

Figure 3-20 shows identifying relationships, non-identifying relationships, and dependent tables. These factors are described as follows:

- ❑ *Identifying relationship* — The child table is partially identified by the parent table, and partially dependent on the parent table. The parent table primary key is included in the primary key of the child table. In Figure 3-20, the COAUTHOR table includes both the AUTHOR and PUBLICATION primary keys in the COAUTHOR primary key as a composite of the two parent table fields.

- ❑ *Non-identifying relationship* — The child table is not dependent on the parent table such that the child table includes the parent table primary key as a foreign key, but not as part of the child table's primary key. Figure 3-20 shows a non-identifying relationship between the AUTHOR and PUBLICATION tables where the PUBLICATION table contains the AUTHOR_ID primary key field from the AUTHOR table. However, the AUTHOR_ID field is not part of the primary key in the PUBLICATION table.

- ❑ *Dependent entity or table* — The COAUTHOR table is dependent on the AUTHOR and PUBLICATION tables. A dependent table exists for a table with an identifying relationship to a parent table.

- ❑ *Non-dependent entity or table* — This is the opposite of a dependent table.

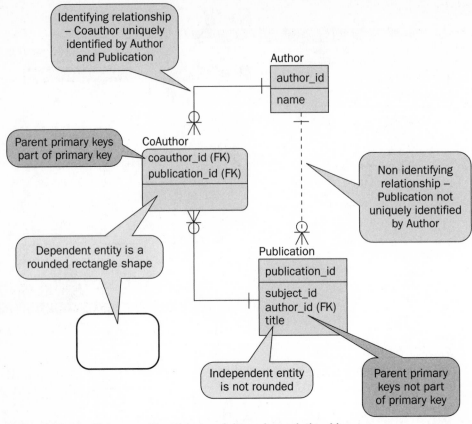

Figure 3-20: Identifying, non-identifying, and dependent relationships

Keys are used to identify and ultimately retrieve records from a database at a later date.

Understanding Keys

Relational databases use the terms *index* and *key* to indicate similar concepts. An *index* is like an index in a book — used to find specific topics, on specific pages, in a book, very quickly (without having to read the entire book). Similarly, an *index* in a relational database is a copy of a part of a table, perhaps structured in a specific format such as a BTree index. An index can be created on any field in a table. A *key*, on the other hand, is more of a concept than a physical thing because a key is also an index. In a relational database, however, a key is a term used to describe the fields in tables linking tables together to form relationships (such as a one-to-many relationship between two tables).

A key is both a key and an index. A key is an index because it copies fields in a table into a more efficient searching structure. A key is also a key, its namesake, because it creates a special tag for a field, allowing that field to be used as a table relationship field, linking tables together into relations. There are three types of keys: a primary key, a unique key, and a foreign key.

Primary Keys

A *primary key* is used to uniquely identify a record in a table. Unique identification for each record is required because there is no other way to find a record without the possibility of finding more than one record, if the unique identifier is not used. Figure 3-21 shows primary key fields of AUTHOR_ID for the AUTHOR table and PUBLICATION_ID for the PUBLICATION table, each being primary key fields for the two tables.

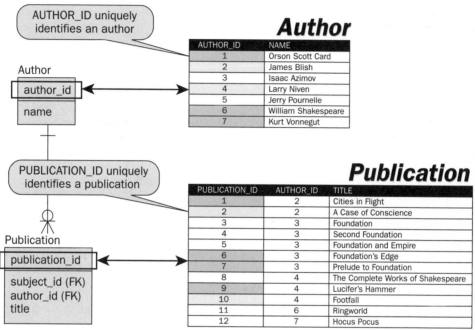

Figure 3-21: A primary key uniquely identifies a record in a table.

Unique Keys

Like a primary key, a *unique key* is created on a field containing only unique values throughout an entire table. In Figure 3-21, and throughout the rest of this chapter, you may be wondering why integers are used as primary keys rather than the name of an author or a publication, and otherwise. The reason why will be explained later in this book but in general integer value primary keys are known as *surrogate keys* because they substitute as primary keys for names.

For example, the AUTHOR_ID field in the AUTHOR table is a surrogate primary key as a replacement or surrogate for creating the primary on the AUTHOR table NAME field, the full name of the author. It is very unlikely that there will be two authors with the same name. Surrogate keys are used to improve performance.

So, why create unique keys that are not primary keys? If surrogate keys are used and the author name is required to be unique, it is common to see unique keys created on name fields such as the AUTHOR table NAME and the PUBLICATION table TITLE fields. A unique key ensures uniqueness across a table. A primary key is always unique, or at least a unique key; however, a primary key is also used to define relationships between tables. Unique keys are not used to define relationships between tables.

The `AUTHOR` table could be created with a simple script such as the following:

```
CREATE TABLE Author
(
        author_id INTEGER NOT NULL,
        name VARCHAR(32) NULL,
        CONSTRAINT XPK_Author PRIMARY KEY (author_id),
        CONSTRAINT XUK_A_Name UNIQUE (name)
);
```

In this script, the primary key is set to the `AUTHOR_ID` field and the name of the author is set to be unique to ensure that the same author is not added twice, or that two authors do not use the same pseudonym.

Foreign Keys

Foreign keys are the copies of primary keys created into child tables to form the opposite side of the link in an inter-table relationship—establishing a relational database relation. A foreign key defines the reference for each record in the child table, referencing back to the primary key in the parent table.

Figure 3-22 shows that the `PUBLICATION` table has a foreign key called `AUTHOR_ID` (`FK`). This means that each record in the `PUBLICATION` table has a copy of the parent table's `AUTHOR_ID` field value, the `AUTHOR` table primary key value, in the `AUTHOR_ID` foreign key field on the `PUBLICATION` table. In other words, an author can have many books published and available for sale at once. Similarly, in Figure 3-22, the `COAUTHOR` table has a primary key made up of two fields, which also happens to comprise the combination or composite of a two foreign key relationship back to both the `AUTHOR` table and the `PUBLICATION` table.

The `PUBLICATION` table could be created with a simple script such as the following:

```
CREATE TABLE Publication
(
        publication_id INTEGER NOT NULL,
        subject_id INTEGER NOT NULL,
        author_id INTEGER NOT NULL,
        title VARCHAR(64) NULL,
        CONSTRAINT XPK_Publication PRIMARY KEY (publication_id),
        CONSTRAINT FK_P_Subject FOREIGN KEY (subject_id) REFERENCES Subject,
        CONSTRAINT FK_P_Author FOREIGN KEY (author_id) REFERENCES Author,
        CONSTRAINT XUK_P_Title UNIQUE (title)
);
```

In this script, the primary key is set to the `PUBLICATION_ID` field. The fields `SUBJECT_ID` and `AUTHOR_ID` are set as two foreign key reference fields to the `SUBJECT` and `AUTHOR` tables, respectively. A unique key constraint is applied to the title of the publication, ensuring copyright compliance.

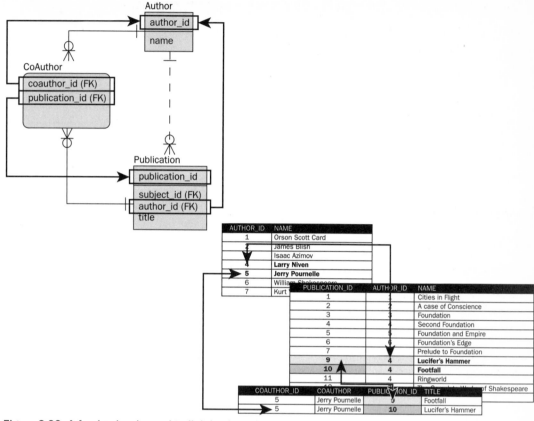

Figure 3-22: A foreign key is used to link back to the primary key of a parent table.

There will be more explanation of the how and why of primary and foreign keys Chapter 4. At this point, simply remember that a primary key uniquely identifies each record in a table. A foreign key is a copy of the primary key copied from a parent table, establishing a relationship between parent and child tables. A unique key simply ensures the uniqueness of a value within a table.

Try It Out   **Creating Some Simple Tables**

Figure 3-23 shows some data. Do the following exercise:

1. Create two related tables linked by a one-to-many relationship.

2. Assign a primary key field in each table.

3. Assign a foreign key field in one table.

BAND NAME	TRACK	DESCRIPTION
Nirvana	Come As You Are	Bass reverb
Greetings From Limbo	The Right Line	Country groove
Pearl Jam	Fatal	Deadly
Foo Fighters		
Greetings From Limbo	Ashes	Heavy
Red Hot Chili Peppers	My Friends	Hmmm
Red Hot Chili Peppers	Otherside	Hmmm again
Red Hot Chili Peppers	Californication	Hot and dry
Pearl Jam	Immortality	Just imagine
Nirvana	About A Girl	Lots of lovely bass
Red Hot Chili Peppers	Suck My Kiss	No thanks
Pearl Jam	Around The Bend	Nuts!
Red Hot Chili Peppers	University Speaking	OK
Nirvana	The Man Who Sold The World	Sell out!
Stone Temple Pilots		
Greetings From Limbo	Greetings From Limbo	The Wizard of Oz
Red Hot Chili Peppers	Under The Bridge	Where's that confounded bridge?
Soundgarden		
Nirvana	Polly	Who's that?

Figure 3-23: Band names, tracks, and silly descriptions.

How It Works

You are asked for two tables from three fields. One table has one field and the other table has two fields. The three fields are conveniently arranged. Look for a one-to-many relationship by finding duplicated values. The data is inconveniently and deliberately unsorted.

1. The first column contains the names of numerous different bands (musical groups) and the second column a track or song name. Typically, different bands or musical groups create many tracks. A one-to-many relationship exists between the band names and track names.

2. Band names in the first column are duplicated. Track names and descriptions are not. This supports the solution already derived in step 1.

3. Band names are the only duplicated values, so they make up the table on the parent side of the one-to-many relationship. The other two columns make up the table on the child side of the relationship.

4. The track name must identify the track uniquely. The description is just silly.

Figure 3-24 shows three viable solutions with Option 3 being the better of all of the three options because surrogate keys are used for the primary and foreign keys. Option 2 is better than Option 1 because in Option 2 the one-to-many relationship is a non-identifying relationship, where the primary key on the TRACK table is not composite key.

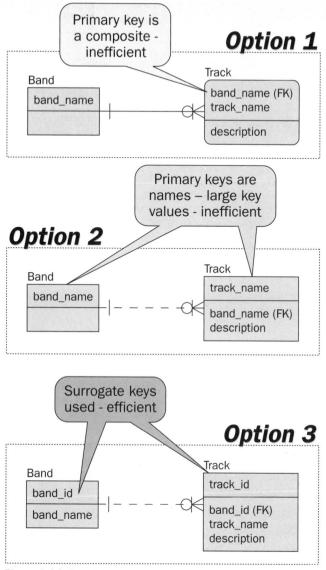

Figure 3-24: Band names, tracks, and silly descriptions represented as an ERD.

Understanding Referential Integrity

Referential Integrity functions just as its name states: It ensures the integrity of referential relationships between tables as defined by primary and foreign keys. In a relation between two tables, one table has a primary key and the other a foreign key. The primary key uniquely identifies each record in the first table. In other words, there can be only one record in the first table with the same primary key value. The foreign key is placed into the second table in the relationship such that the foreign key contains a copy of the primary key value from the record in the related table.

So, what is Referential Integrity? Referential Integrity ensures the integrity of relationships between primary and foreign key values in related tables. Most relational database engines use what are often called *constraints*. Primary and foreign keys are both constraints. Remember, a constraint is a piece of metadata defined for a table defining restrictions on values. A primary key constraint forces the primary key field to be unique. A primary key constraint is also forced to make checks against any foreign key constraints referenced back to that primary key constraint. Referencing (or referential) foreign key constraints can be in any table, including the same table as the primary key constrained field referenced by the foreign key (a self join). A foreign key constraint uses its reference to refer back to a referenced table, containing the primary key constraint, to ensure that the two values in the primary key field and foreign key field match.

Simply put, primary and foreign keys automatically verify against each other. Primary and foreign key references are the connections establishing and enforcing Referential Integrity between tables. There are some specific circumstances to consider in terms of how Referential Integrity is generally enforced:

A primary key table is assumed to be a parent table and a foreign key table a child table.

❑   When adding a new record to a child table, if a foreign key value is entered, it must exist in the related primary key field of the parent table.

Foreign key fields can contain NULL values. Primary key field values can never contain NULL values as they are required to be unique.

❑   When changing a record in a parent table if the primary key is changed, the change must be cascaded to all foreign key valued records in any related child tables. Otherwise, the change to the parent table must be prohibited.

The term "cascade" implies that changes to data in parent tables are propagated to all child tables containing foreign key field copies of a primary key from a parent table.

❑   When changing a record in a child table, a change to a foreign key requires that a related primary key must be checked for existence, or changed first. If a foreign key is changed to NULL, no primary key is required. If the foreign key is changed to a non-NULL value, the foreign key value must exist as a primary key value in the related parent table.

❑   When deleting a parent table record then related foreign key records in child tables must either be cascade deleted or deleted from child tables first.

Understanding Indexes

Indexes are not really part and parcel of the relational database model itself; however, indexes are so important to performance and overall database usability that they simply have to be introduced without going into the nitty-gritty of how each different type of index functions internally. It is important to understand the fundamentals of indexes and their different types and attributes to get a basic understanding as to why exactly indexing is so important for relational databases in general.

What Is an Index?

An index is usually and preferably a copy of a very small section of table, such as a single field, and preferably a short length field. The act of creating an index physically copies one or more fields to be indexed into a separate area of disk other than that of the table. In some databases, indexes can be stored in a file completely separated from that of the table. Different databases are structured differently on a physical level. The important factor is the underlying physical separation. When a table is accessed, a process usually called an *Optimizer* decides whether to access the table alone, scanning all the records in the table, or if it is faster to read the much smaller index in conjunction with a very small section of the table.

> *All relational databases have some type of SQL execution optimization process. It is usually called the Optimizer.*

An index essentially behaves like an index in the back of a book or the table of contents at the front of a book. When searching for details on a specific topic, it is much easier to find the term in the index or table of contents first, and then use a page reference number to find the information within the pages of the text. Reading the entire book every time you want to find a definition for a single term would be far too time-consuming to be useful, probably making the book completely useless as a reference. Most technical books are used as reference guides in one form or another.

Following are some things to be avoided when indexing:

❑ *Creating too many indexes* — Too many indexes on a table can result in very slow database change responses. This is because every change to a table updates every index attached to it, as well as the table. The more indexes created for a table, the more physical changes are required.

❑ *Indexing too many fields* — Indexing too many fields not only makes the use of the indexes by queries more complex, but also makes the indexes too large physically. An index must be relatively much smaller than a table, and should be created on as few fields from that table as is possible.

Alternate Indexing

Alternate indexing really comes from the terms "alternate index," "secondary index," "tertiary index," or just plain "indexing." Specific use of terminology depends on the database in use. These terms all mean the same thing. Alternate indexes are an alternate to the primary relational structure organized by primary and foreign key indexes. Alternate indexes are alternate because they are in addition to primary and foreign key indexes and exist as alternate sorting methods to those provided by primary and foreign keys. By definition, the unique key indexes described in a previous section of this chapter are essentially alternate indexes, as well as being unique constraints.

Foreign Key Indexing

Relationships between tables such as that between the AUTHOR and PUBLICATION tables shown in Figure 3-21 can allow the foreign key in the child table not only to be duplicated (one-to-many) but also to be NULL valued in the child table (one-to-zero, one or many). In other words, in Figure 3-21, each author can have multiple publications or an author does not have to have any publications at all. Because foreign keys are allowed to be NULL valued and do not have to be unique, indexes must be created on those foreign key fields manually.

Because primary keys must be unique, a relational database should automatically create internal unique indexes on primary keys.

Commands similar to the following commands could be used to create indexes on foreign key fields, for the CREATE TABLE command on the PUBLICATION table shown previously in this chapter:

```
CREATE INDEX XFK_P_Author ON Publication(author_id);
CREATE INDEX XFK_P_Publisher ON Publication(subject_id);
```

Types of Indexes

It is important to have a brief understanding of different types of indexing available in relational databases. Some of the smaller-scale database engines (such as dBase, Paradox, and MS Access) might offer little or no variation on index types allowed, generally using BTree type indexing. Types of indexes in various relational database engines are as follows:

❑   *BTree index* — BTree means "binary tree" and, if drawn out on a piece of paper, a BTree index looks like an upside down tree. The tree is called "binary" because binary implies two options under each branch node: branch left and branch right. The binary counting system of numbers contains two digits, namely 0 and 1. The result is that a binary tree only ever has two options as leafs within each branch — at least that is the theory, not being precisely the case in all databases. BTree indexes are sometimes improperly named as they are not actually binary meaning two — branches can have more than two leafs contained within them. Naming conventions are largely immaterial in this situation. Essentially, a BTree consists of a root node, branch nodes, and ultimately leaf nodes containing the indexed field values in the ending (or leaf) nodes of the tree. Some BTree construction and searching methods in some databases are highly efficient for both reading and changing of data, automatically changing the structure of the BTree index without any overflow.

Overflow is bad for indexing because changes are placed outside of the optimized index structure. Enough changes and overflow can destroy the efficiency of an index, eventually rendering it useless and drastically deteriorating rather than generally improving table access performance.

Figure 3-25 shows an example of what a typical relational database BTree index might look like.

❑   *Bitmap index* — A Bitmap index contains binary representations for each record using 0's and 1's. Bitmap indexes are often misused and are extremely vulnerable to overflow over long periods of time. Values cannot be slotted into the existing Bitmap index structure as readily as can be done when updating a BTree index. Figure 3-26 shows a graphical type structure of the internal machinations of a Bitmap index where two bitmaps are created for two values of M for male and F for female. When M is encountered, the M bitmap is set to 1 and the F bitmap is set to 0. In general, Bitmap indexes can be disappointing, even in environments where they are supposedly highly beneficial.

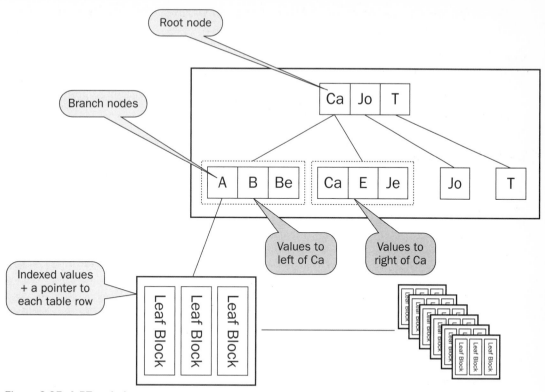

Figure 3-25: A BTree index.

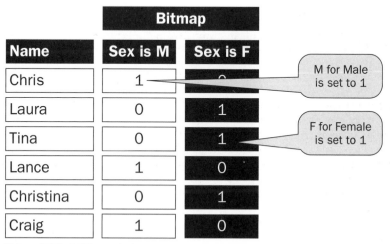

Figure 3-26: A Bitmap index.

❑ *ISAM index* — Indexed Sequential Access Method (ISAM) uses a simple structure with a list of record numbers. ISAM indexes are used in various database engines. ISAM indexes are best used for static data as their internal list structure prohibits easy changes, making them extremely vulnerable to index overflow.

❑ *Hash table* — A hash table is a copy of data but rearranged into a different and more efficiently accessed order depending on a hashing algorithm. For example, a hashing algorithm takes a string and creates a number from that string. The number created by a specific string is always the same and is thus placed in a position in an index, sorted based on the hash-calculated value. Hash indexes can be highly efficient for read access, but are best avoided when subjected to any kind of data changes. Hash tables are likely to overflow worse than Bitmap indexes because there is absolutely no scope whatsoever for changes. The only way to push record changes from table to index is by regenerating the entire hash table index.

❑ *Index Organized Table* — An Index Organized Table (IOT) builds a table in the sorted order of an index, typically using a BTree index. IOTs can actually work fairly well in many types of databases, but you must remember that index record length is much longer than normal because index leaf blocks contain all fields in the entire record length of a table. Also, if the IOT is not read in indexed order, obviously all records in the table are read, and thus the index is ignored. Because the table is built in the structure of an index, however, not reading the table in IOT indexed order could be seriously problematic for performance.

Different Ways to Build Indexes

Indexes can usually be built in various different ways to accommodate however they might be used. Once again, some relational databases allow all of these options, some allow some, and some allow none.

❑ *Ascending or descending index* — An index can be built sorted in a normally ascending order (such as A, B, C) or in descending order (such as C, B, A).

❑ *Unique index* — Indexes values must be unique (can't contain duplicate values).

❑ *Non-unique index* — Non-unique indexes contain duplicated or repeated values in the index.

It is normal to create both unique indexes and non-unique indexes.

❑ *Composite index* — Indexes can be built on more than a single field and are known as composite field indexes, multiple field indexes, or just plain old composite indexes. The most efficient type of index is a single field index containing an integer.

❑ *Compressed indexes* — Some databases allow compression of composite indexes where repeated prefix values are effectively indexed within the index, removing duplications within prefixed indexed fields. In other words, a composite index containing three fields can be accessed using a single value of the first field.

❑ *Reverse key indexes* — This is a really weird and unusual one. Only a very select few databases allow building of indexes such that indexed field values are stored as reverse strings. When adding gazillions of records at once to the same index in a very busy database, adding sequential index values (not reversed) adds many records all at once to the same physical space in the index. The result is what some relational databases call *locking* and other relational databases call *hot blocking*. The result is the same — gridlock! Reverse keys make the index values not sequential in terms of where they are physically written to disk. The result is no locking, no hot blocking, no gridlock, and, thus, much better performance.

Other than tables, keys, and indexes, there are other types of objects. These other object types are more easily defined as data management objects and only loosely definable as data modeling objects. Management of data is the administration process occurring on a production system, long after completion of the data modeling process.

Introducing Views and Other Specialized Objects

So far in this chapter, topics covered have included tables, relationships between tables, and indexes attached to tables. You should understand the basic structure of a table, and that the relationships between tables are determined by primary keys in parent tables linked to foreign keys in child tables. Foreign keys are copies of primary key field values from parent tables. Indexing is important to understand not directly from a modeling perspective, but that indexes are used to superimpose a different order on top of the order created by the very structure of the relationships between tables, imposed by primary and foreign keys.

Other than all these wonderful indexing things, there are further possibilities within relational databases that some database engines allow and some do not. It is important to know that specialized objects exist as options for expansion to a relational database model, as extensions to both the underlying physical structure of a database and the overlying logical structure (the tables and indexes). Following are a few examples:

❑   *Views* — A view is essentially a query definition and does not contain any data. A view is not a physical copy of data and does not contain any data itself. A view is merely a logical overlay of existing tables. Every execution against a view executes the query contained within the view against all underlying tables. The danger with using views is filtering a query against a view, expecting to read a very small portion of a very large table. Any filtering should be done within the view because any filtering against the view itself is applied after the query in the view has completed execution. Views are typically useful for speeding up the development process but in the long run can completely kill database performance.

❑   *Materialized views* — Materialized views are available in some very large capacity type relational databases. A materialized view materializes underlying physical data by making a physical copy of data from tables. So, unlike a view as described previously, when a query is executed against a materialized view, the materialized view is physically accessed rather than the underlying tables. The objective is to free the underlying tables for other uses, effectively creating two separate physical copies. Materialized views are often used to aggregate large data sets down to smaller sized data sets, in data warehouses and data marts. The biggest potential problem with materialized views is how often they are refreshed and brought up to date with any changes to their underlying tables. Another attribute of materialized views is the ability of some database engines to allow a query directed at an underlying table to be automatically redirected to a physically much smaller materialized view, sometimes called *automated query rewrite*. Queries can be automatically rewritten by the query Optimizer if the query rewrite can help to increase query performance.

❑ *Clusters*—Clusters are used in very few databases and have been somewhat superceded by materialized views. In the past, clusters were used to pre-create physical copies of entire field level sections of heavily accessed tables, especially in SQL joins. Unlike materialized views, clusters do not allow for automatic refresh and are normally manually maintained.

❑ *Sequences and auto counters*—An auto counter field is a special datatype, sometimes called a *non-static internal function*, allowing automated generation of sequential number values (thus the term "sequence"). Typically, auto counters are used for primary key surrogate key generation on insertion of new records into a table.

❑ *Partitioning and parallel processing*—Some databases allow physical splitting of tables into separate partitions, including parallel processing on multiple partitions and individual operations on individual partitions. One particularly efficient aspect of partitioning is the capability when querying a table to read fewer than all the partitions making up a table, perhaps even a single partition.

Summary

In this chapter, you learned about:

❑ Building tables containing fields, datatypes, and simple validation

❑ The different types of relationships between tables

❑ Representing relations in ERDs

❑ Defining referential integrity relationships between tables using primary and foreign keys

❑ The types and uses of indexes

❑ The types and uses of specialized objects such as views, materialized views, and auto counters

The next chapter discusses the very heart of the relational database model by examining the process of normalization through the application of normal forms.

Exercises

1. Write two CREATE TABLE commands for the tables in Option 3 of Figure 3-24. Make sure that all primary key, foreign key, and any potentially necessary unique keys are included.

2. Write CREATE INDEX commands to create all indexes on any foreign keys indicated in the CREATE TABLE command written for the previous question.

Part II

Designing Relational Database Models

In this Part:

Understanding Normalization

"There are two rules in life: Rule #1: Don't sweat the small stuff. Rule #2: Everything is small stuff." (Finn Taylor)

Life is as complicated as we make it — normalization can be simplified.

This chapter examines the detail of the normalization process. Normalization is the sequence of steps by which a relational database model is both created and improved upon. The sequence of steps involved in the normalization process is called *Normal Forms*. Essentially, Normal Forms applied during a process of normalization allow creation of a relational database model as a step-by-step progression.

Previous chapters have examined history and applications, plus various other factors involved in database model design. Chapter 3 introduced all the parts and pieces involved in a relational database model. This chapter now uses the terminology covered in Chapter 3 and explains how to build a relational database model. Subsequent chapters examine more advanced details of relational database modeling such as denormalization and SQL, both of which depend on a good understanding of normalization.

This chapter describes the precise steps involved in creation of relational database models. These steps are the 1st, 2nd, and 3rd Normal Forms, plus the rarely commercially implemented Boyce-Codd, 4th, 5th, and Domain Key Normal Forms. The Normal Forms steps are the progressive steps in the normalization process.

In this chapter, you learn about the following:

- ❑   Anomalies
- ❑   Dependency and determinants
- ❑   Normalization
- ❑   A layman's method of understanding normalization

❑   A purist, academic definition of normalization

❑   1st, 2nd, 3rd, Boyce-Codd, 4th, 5th, and Domain Key Normal Forms

❑   Normalization and referential integrity as expressed by primary and foreign keys

What Is Normalization?

The academic definition of normalization is the accepted format of Normal Forms definition. I like to label normalization as academic because the precise definitions of Normal Forms are often misunderstood in a commercial environment. In fact, the truth is that language use in the exact definitions for Normal Forms is so very precise and carefully worded that problems are caused. Many database designers do not understand all facets of normalization—in other words, how it all really works. A lot of this is a result of such precise use of language. After all, we are now in a global economy. There are a multitude of database architects who do not speak English, have a limited command of the English language, and should not be expected to be well-versed in either respect.

In general, normalization removes duplication and minimizes redundant chunks of data. The result is better organization and more effective use of physical space, among other factors.

Normalization is not always the best solution. For example, in data warehouses, there is a completely different approach. In short, normalization is not the be-all and end-all of relational database model design. This chapter also describes a brief user-friendly interpretation of Normal Forms. It is just as important to understand Normal Forms from a more academic, more precise but possibly less commercially viable perspective. The problem with the academic approach to normalization is that it seems to insist on always expecting a designer to apply every Normal Form layer in every situation. In my experience, in a commercial environment this is nearly always a mistake. The trouble with the deeper and more precisely refined aspects of normalization is that normalization tends to over-define itself for the sake of simply defining itself further.

Before going into the details of normalization, some specifics should be covered briefly, including the concept of anomalies and some rather technical mathematical jargon.

The Concept of Anomalies

The intention of relational database theory is to eliminate anomalies from occurring in a database. Anomalies can potentially occur during changes to a database. An anomaly is a bad thing because data can become logically corrupted. An *anomaly* with respect to relational database design is essentially an erroneous change to data, more specifically to a single record. To put this into perspective, data warehouses can add and change millions of records in single transactions, making accounting for anomalies over zealous. In the interests of mathematical precision, explicit definition is required. Why? Mathematics is very precise and anomalies always should be accounted for. That is just the way it is.

Consider the following:

❑   *Insert anomaly*—Caused when a record is added to a detail table, with no related record existing in a master table. In other words, adding a new book in Figure 4-1 requires that the author be added first, assuming, of course, that the author does not already exist.

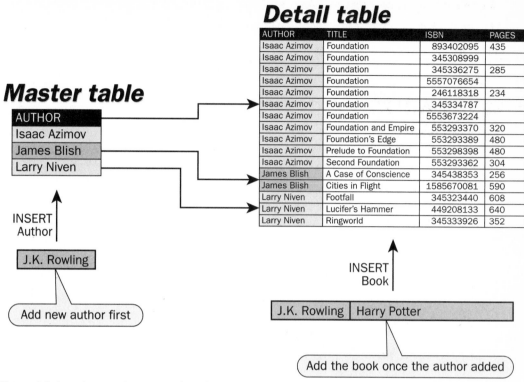

Master table

AUTHOR
Isaac Azimov
James Blish
Larry Niven

INSERT
Author

J.K. Rowling

(Add new author first)

Detail table

AUTHOR	TITLE	ISBN	PAGES
Isaac Azimov	Foundation	893402095	435
Isaac Azimov	Foundation	345308999	
Isaac Azimov	Foundation	345336275	285
Isaac Azimov	Foundation	5557076654	
Isaac Azimov	Foundation	246118318	234
Isaac Azimov	Foundation	345334787	
Isaac Azimov	Foundation	5553673224	
Isaac Azimov	Foundation and Empire	553293370	320
Isaac Azimov	Foundation's Edge	553293389	480
Isaac Azimov	Prelude to Foundation	553298398	480
Isaac Azimov	Second Foundation	553293362	304
James Blish	A Case of Conscience	345438353	256
James Blish	Cities in Flight	1585670081	590
Larry Niven	Footfall	345323440	608
Larry Niven	Lucifer's Hammer	449208133	640
Larry Niven	Ringworld	345333926	352

INSERT
Book

| J.K. Rowling | Harry Potter |

(Add the book once the author added)

Figure 4-1: Insert anomaly occurs when detail record added with no master record.

❑ *Delete anomaly* — Caused when a record is deleted from a master table, without first deleting all sibling records, in a detail table. The exception is a *cascade deletion*, occurring when deletion of a master record automatically deletes all child records in all related detail tables, before deleting the parent record in the master table. For example, referring to Figure 4-2, deleting an author requires initial deletion of any books that an author might already have published. If an author was deleted and books were left in the database without corresponding parent authors, the BOOK table records would become known as orphaned records. The books become logically inaccessible within the bounds of the AUTHOR and BOOK table relationship.

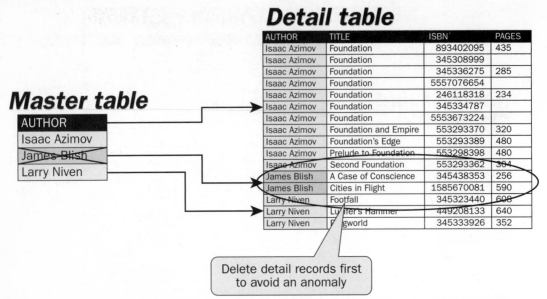

Detail table

AUTHOR	TITLE	ISBN	PAGES
Isaac Azimov	Foundation	893402095	435
Isaac Azimov	Foundation	345308999	
Isaac Azimov	Foundation	345336275	285
Isaac Azimov	Foundation	5557076654	
Isaac Azimov	Foundation	246118318	234
Isaac Azimov	Foundation	345334787	
Isaac Azimov	Foundation	5553673224	
Isaac Azimov	Foundation and Empire	553293370	320
Isaac Azimov	Foundation's Edge	553293389	480
Isaac Azimov	Prelude to Foundation	553298398	480
Isaac Azimov	Second Foundation	553293362	304
James Blish	A Case of Conscience	345438353	256
James Blish	Cities in Flight	1585670081	590
Larry Niven	Footfall	345323440	608
Larry Niven	Lucifer's Hammer	449208133	640
Larry Niven	Ringworld	345333926	352

Master table

AUTHOR
Isaac Azimov
~~James Blish~~
Larry Niven

Delete detail records first to avoid an anomaly

Figure 4-2: DELETE **anomaly occurs when detail records removed without deleting master record first.**

❑ *Update anomaly* — This anomaly is similar to deletion in that both master and detail records must be updated to avoid orphaned detail records. When cascading, ensure that any primary key updates are propagated to related child table foreign keys.

Dependency, Determinants, and Other Jargon

The following are some simple mathematical terms you should understand.

❑ *Functional dependency* — Y is functionally dependent on X if the value of Y is determined by X. In other words, if Y = X +1, the value of X will determine the resultant value of Y. Thus, Y is dependent on X as a function of the value of X. Figure 4-3 demonstrates functional dependency by showing that the currency being Pounds depends on the FXCODE value being GBP.

❑ *Determinant* — The determinant in the description of functional dependency in the previous point is X because X determines the value Y, at least partially because 1 is added to X as well. In Figure 4-3 the determinant of the currency being Deutsche Marks is that the value of FXCODE be DM. The determinant is thus FXCODE.

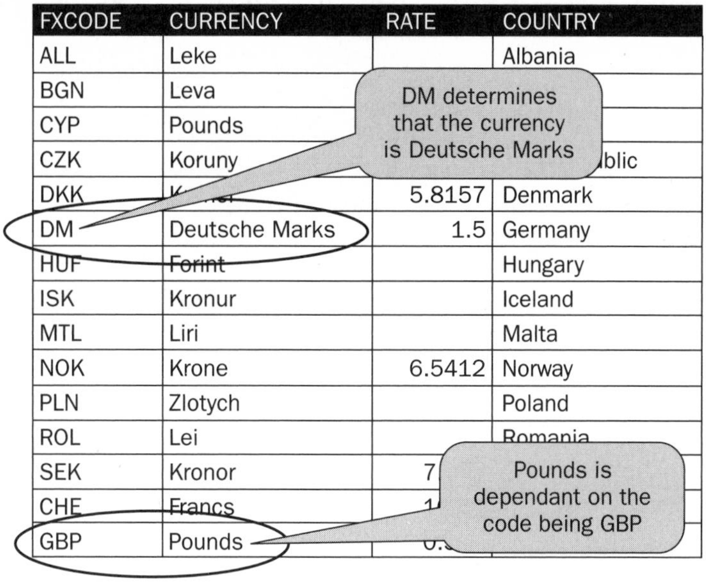

FXCODE	CURRENCY	RATE	COUNTRY
ALL	Leke		Albania
BGN	Leva		
CYP	Pounds		
CZK	Koruny		blic
DKK	K	5.8157	Denmark
DM	Deutsche Marks	1.5	Germany
HUF	Forint		Hungary
ISK	Kronur		Iceland
MTL	Liri		Malta
NOK	Krone	6.5412	Norway
PLN	Zlotych		Poland
ROL	Lei		Romania
SEK	Kronor	7	
CHE	Francs	1	
GBP	Pounds	0.	

(callout: DM determines that the currency is Deutsche Marks)

(callout: Pounds is dependant on the code being GBP)

Figure 4-3: Functional dependency and the determinant.

A determinant is the inversion or opposite of functional dependency.

❑ *Transitive dependence* — Z is transitively dependent on X when X determines Y and Y determines Z. Transitive dependence thus describes that Z is indirectly dependent on X through its relationship with Y. In Figure 4-3, the foreign exchange rates in the RATE field (against the US Dollar) are dependent on CURRENCY. The currency in turn is dependent on COUNTRY. Thus, the rate is dependent on the currency, which is in turn dependent on the country; therefore, RATE is transitively dependent on COUNTRY.

❑ *Candidate key* — A candidate key (potential or permissible key) is a field or combination of fields that can act as a primary key field for a table — thus uniquely identifying each record in the table. Figure 4-4 shows five different variations of one table, all of which have valid primary keys, both of one field and more than one field. The number of options displayed in Figure 4-4 is a little ridiculous, but demonstrates the concept.

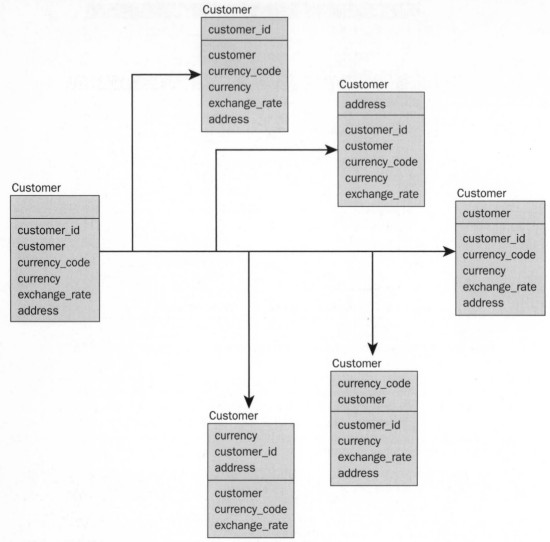

Figure 4-4: A table with five and possibly more candidate keys.

❑   *Full functional dependence* — This situation occurs where X determines Y, but X combined with Z does not determine Y. In other words, Y depends on X and X alone. If Y depends on X with anything else, there is not full functional dependence. Essentially X, the determinant, cannot be a composite key. A composite key contains more than one field (the equivalent of X with Z). Figure 4-5 shows that POPULATION is dependent on COUNTRY but not on the combination of RATE and COUNTRY. Therefore, there is full functional dependency between POPULATION and COUNTRY because RATE is irrelevant to POPULATION. Conversely, there is not full functional dependence between POPULATION and the combination of COUNTRY and RATE.

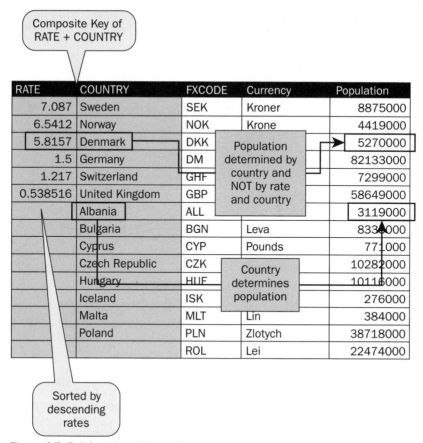

Figure 4-5: Full functional dependence.

❑ *Multiple valued dependency* — This is also known as a *multi-valued dependency*. A commonly used example of a multi-valued dependency is a field containing a comma-delimited list or collection of some kind. A *collection* could be an array of values of the same type. Those multiple values are dependent as a whole on the primary key, *as a whole* meaning the entire collection in the comma delimited list. More precisely, a *trivial multi-valued dependency* occurs between two fields when they are the only two fields in the table. One is the primary key and the other the multi-valued list. A *trivial multi-valued dependency* is shown in the lower-right of the diagram in Figure 4-6. A non-trivial, multi-valued dependency occurs when there are other fields in the table as shown by the top data diagram in the upper-right of Figure 4-6.

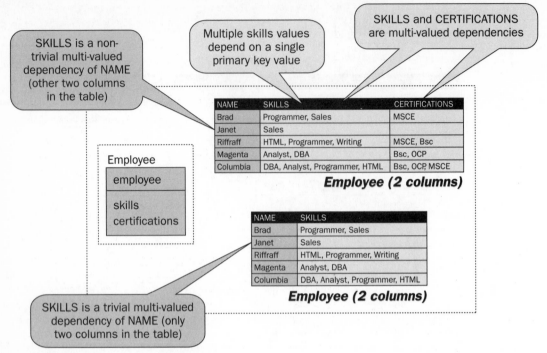

Figure 4-6: Multiple valued dependencies.

❑ *Cyclic dependency* — The meaning of the word "cyclic" is a circular pattern, recurrent, closed ring, or a circular chain structure. In the context of the relational database model, *cyclic dependence* means that X is dependent on Y, which in turn is also dependent on X, directly or indirectly. Cyclic dependence, therefore, indicates a logically circular pattern of interdependence. Cyclic dependence typically occurs with tables containing a composite primary key of three or more fields (for example, where three fields are related in pairs to each other). In other words, X relates to Y, Y relates to Z, and X relates to Z. Ultimately Z relates back to X.

Defining Normal Forms

Normal forms can be defined in two ways. One is the accepted academic approach. The other is my invention, a little unorthodox and much criticized for its lack of precision, but easier to grasp at first.

Defining Normal Forms the Academic Way

The following are the precise academic definitions of Normal Forms.

❑ *1st Normal Form* (1NF) — Eliminate repeating groups such that all records in all tables can be identified uniquely by a primary key in each table. In other words, all fields other than the primary key must depend on the primary key.

❑ *2nd Normal Form* (2NF) — All non-key values must be fully functionally dependent on the primary key. No partial dependencies are allowed. A partial dependency exists when a field is fully dependent on a part of a composite primary key.

- ❑ *3rd Normal Form (3NF)* — Eliminate transitive dependencies, meaning that a field is indirectly determined by the primary key. This is because the field is functionally dependent on another field, whereas the other field is dependent on the primary key.

- ❑ *Boyce-Codd Normal Form (BCNF)* — Every determinant in a table is a candidate key. If there is only one candidate key, 3NF and BCNF are one and the same.

- ❑ *4th Normal Form (4NF)* — Eliminate multiple sets of multivalued dependencies.

- ❑ *5th Normal Form (5NF)* — Eliminate cyclic dependencies. 5NF is also known as Projection Normal Form (PJNF).

- ❑ *Domain Key Normal Form (DKNF)* — DKNF is the ultimate application of normalization and is more a measurement of conceptual state, as opposed to a transformation process in itself.

The irritating thing about all this precise language is that it can be extremely confusing. Most of normalization is essentially common sense. For example, most experienced database modelers, architects, designers, programmers, whatever you want to call them — can actually figure out 1NFs, 2NFs, and 3NFs simply by looking at a set of data. Anything else is usually ignored. Experienced architects often have an understanding of how to apply common generic database modeling structures to often repetitive or classifiable business operational structures.

Maintenance of data with respect to accessing of individual records in a database can be more effectively and easily managed using "beyond 3NF." Any querying, however, is adversely affected by too many tables. In some cases, the performance factor can be completely debilitating, making a database useless. Additionally, even in highly accurate, single-record update environments, the extra functionality and accuracy given by beyond 3NF structures (BCNF, 4NF, 5NF, DKNF) can always be provided by application coding and SQL code to find those individual records.

Is "beyond 3NF" unnecessary? It might be, but probably in many commercial situations it is unnecessary. Remember that application SDKs are just as powerful as database engine structural and functional capabilities. Extreme implementation of normalization using layers beyond 3NF tends to place too much functionality into the database. Why not use the best of both worlds — both database and application capabilities? Use the database to store data and allow applications to manipulate and verify data to a certain extent.

Defining Normal Forms the Easy Way

Many modern-day commercial relational database implementations do not go beyond the implementation of 3NF. This is often true of OLTP databases and nearly always true in properly designed data warehouse databases. Application of Normal Forms beyond that of 3NF tends to produce too many tables, resulting in too many tables in SQL joins. Bigger joins result in poor performance. In general, good performance is much more important than granular perfection in relational database design.

How can normalization be made simple? Why is it easy? I like to offer a simplified interpretation of normalization just to get the novice started. In a perfect world, most relational database model designs are very similar. As a result, much of the basic database design for many applications from accounting to manufacturing (and anything else you can think of) is all more or less the same. Some of the common factors are separation of repeated fields in master-detail relationships using 1NF, pushing static data into new tables using 2NF, and doing various interesting things with 3NF (such as uniquely identifying repetitions between many-to-many relationships).

Normalization is, for the most part, easy and mostly common sense with some business knowledge thrown in. There are, of course, numerous exceptional circumstances and special cases where my basic interpretation of normalization does fill all needs 100 percent. In these situations, parts of the more refined academic interpretation can be used.

The following defines the Normal Forms in an easy to understand manner:

❑ *1st Normal Form (1NF)* — Removes repeating fields by creating a new table where the original and new table are linked together with a master-detail, one-to-many relationship. For example, a master table could contain parent records representing all the ships owned by a cruise line. A detail table would contain detail records, such as all the passengers on a cruise to the Caribbean. Create primary keys on both tables where the detail table will have a composite primary key containing the master table primary key field as the prefix field of its primary key. That prefix field is also a foreign key back to the master table.

❑ *2nd Normal Form (2NF)* — Performs a seemingly similar function to that of 1NF, but creates a table where repeating values (rather than repeating fields as for 1NF) are removed to a new table. The result is a many-to-one relationship rather than a one-to-many relationship, created between the original and the new tables. The new table gets a primary key consisting of a single field. The master table contains a foreign key pointing back to the primary key of the new table. That foreign key is not part of the primary key in the original table.

❑ *3rd Normal Form (3NF)* — It is difficult to explain 3NF without using a mind bogglingly confusing technical definition. Elimination of a transitive dependency implies creation of a new table for something indirectly dependent on the primary key in an existing table. There are a multitude of ways in which 3NF can be interpreted.

❑ *Beyond 3NF* — Many modern relational database models do not extend beyond 3NF. Sometimes 3NF is not used at all. The reason why is because of the generation of too many tables and the resulting complex SQL code joins, with resulting terrible database response times. One common case that bears mentioning is removal of potentially NULL valued fields into new tables, creating a one-to-one relationship. In modern high-end relational database engines with variable record lengths, this is largely irrelevant. Disk space is cheap and, as already stated, increased numbers of tables leads to bigger SQL joins and poorer performance.

Now let's examine 1NF in detail.

1st Normal Form (1NF)

The following sections define 1NF academically and then demonstrate an easier way.

1NF the Academic Way

1NF does the following.

❑ Eliminates repeating groups.

❑ Defines primary keys.

❑ All records must be identified uniquely with a primary key. A primary key is unique and thus no duplicate values are allowed.

❏ All fields other than the primary key must depend on the primary key, either directly or indirectly.

❏ All fields must contain a single value.

❏ All values in each field must be of the same datatype.

❏ Create a new table to move the repeating groups from the original table.

1NF the Easy Way

1NF removes repeating fields by creating a new table where the original and new table are linked in a master-detail, one-to-many relationship. Figure 4-7 shows a table in 0th Normal Form and exactly why 1NF is so essential. This is a classic master-detail relationship not yet split into two tables. There should be a split into two tables where each author can have multiple books published, including repeated books (repeating groups) in the same table because each individual author requires repetitions, for each book defined in each author record. Also, because one of the authors has 11 different titles, this author can't be included unless the AUTHORSBOOKS table is expanded with more repetitive fields.

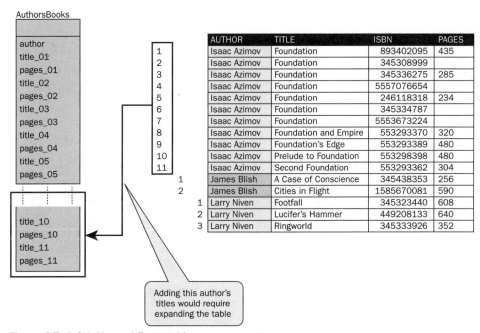

Figure 4-7: A 0th Normal Form table.

Figure 4-8 simply shows the detail of the AUTHORSBOOKS table shown in Figure 4-7, demonstrating that leaving a table with no Normal Forms applied at all is completely silly. In fact, by definition, 1NF is actually a requirement of a relational database being relational.

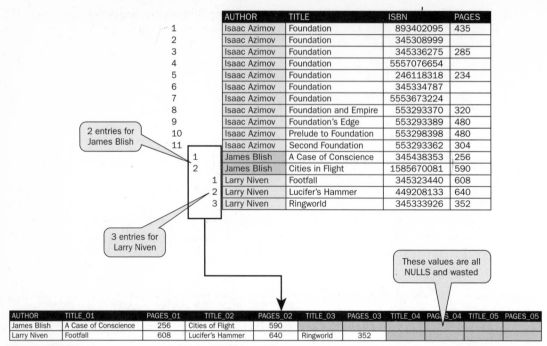

Figure 4-8: The `AUTHORSBOOKS` **table in 0th Normal Form.**

To alleviate any potential confusion, Figure 4-9 shows how comma-delimited lists are used as another common method of displaying 0th Normal Form data, including repeated groups. The data shown in Figure 4-9 is identical to the data shown in Figure 4-8, except with a slightly different structural representation.

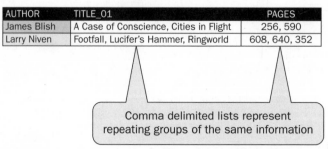

Figure 4-9: Using comma-delimited lists to represent 0th Normal Form.

Figure 4-10 shows the application of 1NF, removing repeating fields by creating a new table where the original and new table are linked in a master-detail, one-to-many relationship.

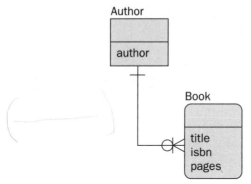

Figure 4-10: 1NF normalization master-detail tables for
AUTHORSBOOKS.

In Figure 4-11, primary keys are created on both tables where the detail table has a composite primary key. The composite primary key contains the master table primary key field as the prefix field of its primary key. Therefore, the prefix field AUTHOR on the BOOK table is the foreign key pointing back to the master table AUTHOR.

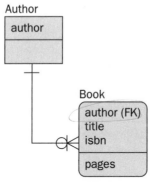

Figure 4-11: Primary keys and the foreign key pointer.

Figure 4-12 shows what the data looks like in the altered AUTHOR table and the new BOOK table, previously the AUTHORSBOOKS table. Notice how the introduction of the relationship between the two tables allows any number of books for each author to be catered for.

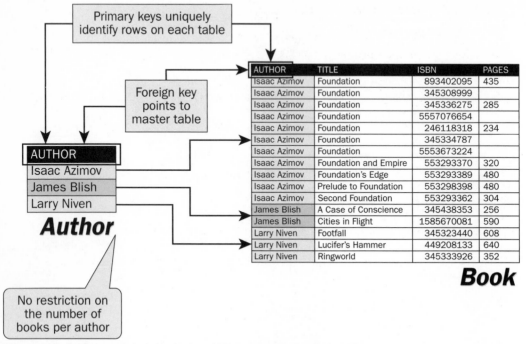

Figure 4-12: Authors and their books in a 1NF master-detail relationship.

Looking at Figure 4-12, it is apparent that applying 1NF to the AUTHORSBOOKS in Figure 4-7 has not actually saved any physical space. It has, however, saved on unused metadata slots for numerous TITLE_*nn* and PAGES_*nn* fields. Thus, each field across a record contains different information where titles and pages are not repeated a fixed number of times for each record. Also, there is no restriction on the number of books. Perhaps most importantly, the data is better organized in 1NF and it now is actually a relational database model.

Try It Out   1st Normal Form

Figure 4-13 shows a 0th Normal Form table:

1. Put the SALES table shown in Figure 4-13 into 1NF.

2. Create a new table with the appropriate fields.

3. Remove the appropriate fields from the original table.

4. Create primary keys in the original and new tables.

5. Create the one-to-many relationship between the original and new tables by defining the foreign key in the new table.

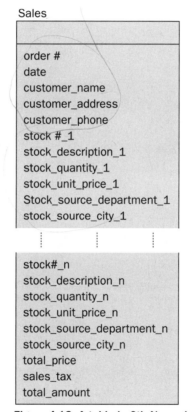

Figure 4-13: A table in 0th Normal Form.

How It Works

1NF requires removal of repeating groups into a new table.

1. The SALES table contains orders with lines on each order represented by each stock item on the order. It would help having the data in this situation, but previous examples and exercises have already shown data, so this is unnecessary. At this point, understanding of concepts is important.

2. Figure 4-14 shows the desired 1NF transformation.

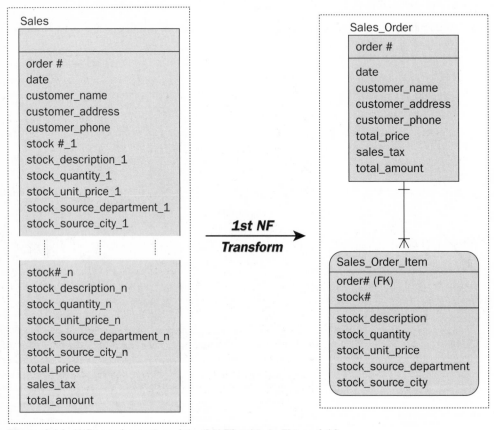

Figure 4-14: 1NF transformation of the SALES table in Figure 4-13.

Figure 4-14 shows repeated sales order item entries in the form of stock item entries removed to the SALE_ORDER_ITEM table, linking back to the renamed SALE_ORDER table, renamed from the original SALES table. The two tables are linked by a one-to-many relationship between the SALE_ORDER and SALE_ORDER_ITEM tables using the primary key on the SALE_ORDER table, duplicated to the SALE_ORDER_ITEM table as the ORDER# (FK) field, part of the SALE_ORDER_ITEM table primary key.

Now let's examine 2NF in detail.

2nd Normal Form (2NF)

This section defines 2NF academically and then demonstrates an easier way.

2NF the Academic Way

2NF does the following.

❑ The table must be in 1NF.

❑ All non-key values must be fully functionally dependent on the primary key. In other words, non-key fields not completely and individually dependent on the primary key are not allowed.

❑ Partial dependencies must be removed. A partial dependency is a special type of functional dependency that exists when a field is fully dependant on a part of a composite primary key.

Stating the previous two points in a different way, remove fields that are independent of the primary key.

❑ Create a new table to separate the partially dependent part of the primary key and its dependent fields.

2NF the Easy Way

2NF performs a seemingly similar function to that of 1NF, but creates a table where repeating values rather than repeating fields are removed to a new table. The result is a many-to-one relationship rather than a one-to-many relationship, created between the original and the new tables. The new table gets a primary key consisting of a single field. Typically, 2NF creates many-to-one relationships between dynamic and static data, removing static data from transactional tables into new tables. In Figure 4-15, the BOOK table is in 1NF after separation of repeating group books from the authors. The publisher and subject information are relatively static compared with books. In this situation, the BOOK table represents transactional or dynamic information where books are published, reprinted, discontinued, produced in different formats, among other options. All the while, publishers and subjects remain relatively the same—static.

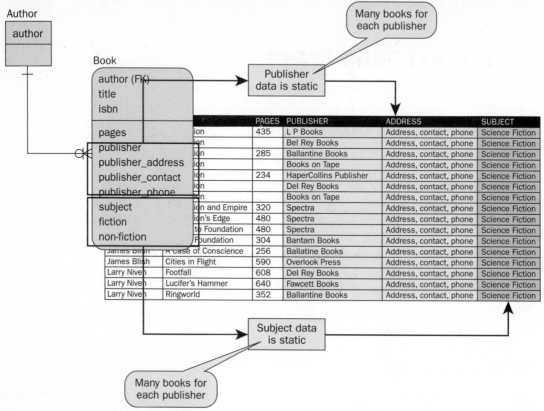

Figure 4-15: The BOOK table is in 1NF.

Figure 4-16 shows the initial stage of the application of 2NF, removing static publisher and subject information from the more dynamic BOOK transaction table.

In Figure 4-17, many-to-one relationships are established between dynamic and static tables, namely BOOK to PUBLISHER and BOOK to SUBJECT tables. When applying 1NF, one-to-many relationships are established between master and detail tables, as shown in Figure 4-10 and Figure 4-11. Application of 2NF establishes the same relationship, except it is easier to understand the slight difference by calling that relationship a many-to-one relationship. Mathematically, a one-to-many relationship is identical to a many-to-one relationship; however, 1NFs and 2NFs are completely different because the one-to-many relationship is established for a completely different reason.

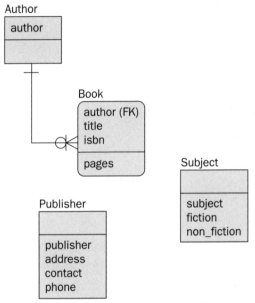

Figure 4-16: Using 2NF to separate static data from dynamic data.

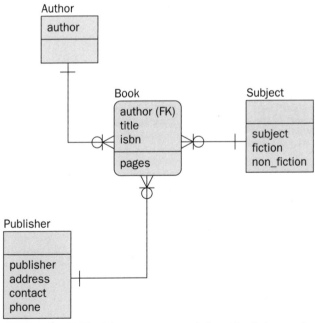

Figure 4-17: 2NF builds many-to-one relationships between dynamic and static tables.

In Figure 4-18, primary keys are created on both the PUBLISHER and SUBJECT tables to uniquely identify individual publishers and subjects within their two respective tables. Identifying relationships as BOOK related to PUBLISHER and BOOK related to SUBJECT causes the publisher and subject primary key values to be included in the composite primary key of the BOOK table.

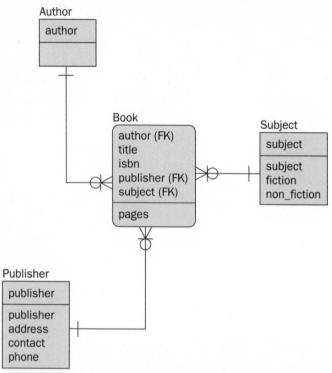

Figure 4-18: Primary keys in static tables are copied to the BOOK dynamic table as part of the dynamic table composite primary key.

Including the static table primary key fields into the composite primary key of the dynamic table is incorrect in this situation, as shown in Figure 4-18. This is corrected as shown in Figure 4-19 by changing the relationships between dynamic and static tables from identifying to non-identifying. This is because the existence of static data is not dependent on the existence of child dynamic data. In other words, a SUBJECT entry is not dependent on the existence of any books within that subject. It is permissible to add the Science Fiction genre to the SUBJECT table without having to have any Science Fiction BOOK entries. This is not always the case for 2NF but is often true. Figure 4-19 shows that by changing the relationships to non-identifying, primary keys for publishers and subjects are no longer part of the composite primary key for the BOOK table.

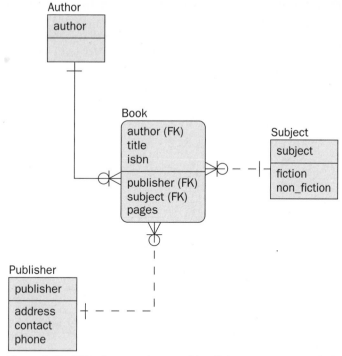

Figure 4-19: 2NF often requires non-identifying one-to-many relationships.

It is important to understand these 2NF relationships in the opposite direction such that BOOK entries depend on the existence of PUBLISHER and SUBJECT entries. Thus, publishers and subjects must exist for a book to exist — or every book must have a publisher and subject. Think about it; it makes perfect sense, exception could be a bankrupt publisher. On the contrary, the relationship between PUBLISHER and BOOK plus SUBJECT and BOOK are actually one-to-zero, one, or many. This means that not all publishers absolutely have to have any titles published at any specific time, and also that there is not always a book available covering each available subject.

Figure 4-20 shows what the data looks like in the altered BOOK table with the new PUBLISHER and SUBJECT tables shown as well. Multiple fields of publisher and subject field information previously duplicated on the BOOK table (as shown in Figure 4-15) is now separated into the two new PUBLISHER and SUBJECT tables, with duplicate publishers and subjects removed from the new tables.

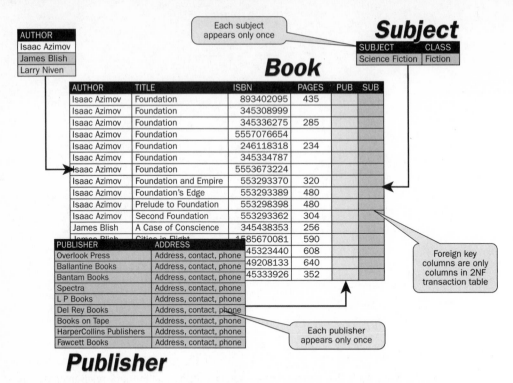

Figure 4-20: Books plus their respective publishers and subjects in a 2NF relationship.

It is readily apparent from Figure 4-20 that placing the BOOK table into 2NF has physically saved space. Duplication has been removed, as shown by there now being only a single SUBJECT record and far fewer PUBLISHER records. Once again, data has become better organized by the application of 2NF to the BOOK table.

Try It Out   2nd Normal Form

Figure 4-21 shows two tables in 1NF. Put the SALE_ORDER and SALE_ORDER_ITEM tables shown in Figure 4-21 into 2NF:

1. Create two new tables with the appropriate fields.

2. Remove the appropriate fields from the original tables.

3. Create primary keys in the new tables.

4. Create the many-to-one relationships between the original tables and the new tables, defining and placing foreign keys appropriately.

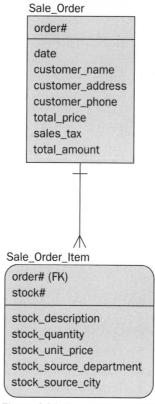

Figure 4-21: Two tables in 1NF.

How It Works

2NF requires removal to new tables of fields partially dependent on primary keys.

1. Create the CUSTOMER table to remove static data from the SALE_ORDER table.

2. Create the STOCK_ITEM table to remove static data from the SALE_ORDER_ITEM table.

3. Figure 4-22 shows all four tables after the 2NF transformation.

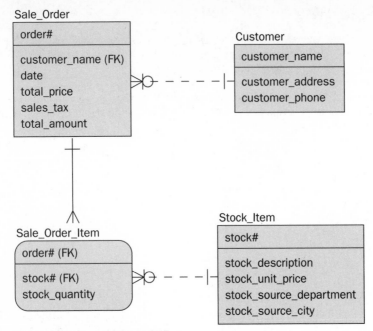

Figure 4-22: Four tables in 2NF.

Figure 4-22 shows creation of two new tables. Both new tables establish many-to-one, as opposed to one-to-many relationships when applying 1NF transformation. Another difference is that the foreign key fields appear in the original tables rather than the new tables, given the direction of the relationship between original and new tables.

Now let's examine 3NF in detail.

3rd Normal Form (3NF)

This section defines 3NF academically, and then demonstrates an easier way.

3NF the Academic Way

3NF does the following.

❑ The table must be in 2NF.

❑ Eliminate transitive dependencies. A *transitive dependency* is where a field is indirectly determined by the primary key because that field is functionally dependent on a second field, where that second field is dependent on the primary key.

❑ Create a new table to contain any separated fields.

3NF the Easy Way

3NF is an odd one and can often cause confusion. In basic terms, every field in a table that is not a key field must be directly dependent on the primary key. There are number of different ways to look at 3NF, and this section goes through them one by one.

Figure 4-23 shows one of the easiest interpretations of 3NF where a many-to-many relationship presents the possibility that more than one record will be returned using a query joining both tables.

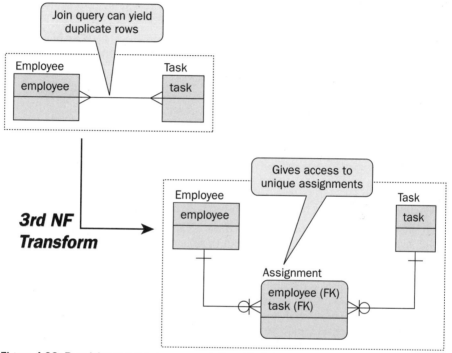

Figure 4-23: Resolving a many-to-many relationship into a new table.

Figure 4-24 shows employees and tasks from the 2NF version on the left of the diagram in Figure 4-23. Employees perform tasks in their daily routines, doing their jobs. If you were searching for the employee Columbia, three tasks would always be returned. Similarly, if searching for the third task shown in Figure 4-24, two employees would always be returned. A problem would arise with this situation when searching for an attribute specific to a particular assignment where an assignment is a single task assigned to a single employee. Without the new ASSIGNMENT table created by the 3NF transformation shown in Figure 4-23, finding an individual assignment would be impossible.

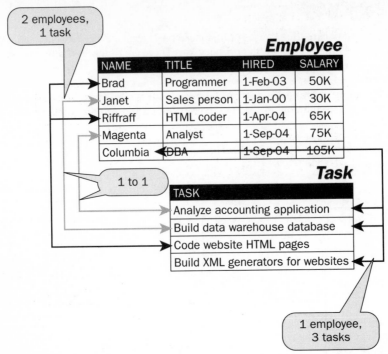

Figure 4-24: A many-to-many relationship finds duplicate records when unique records are sought.

Another way to look at 3NF is as displayed in Figure 4-25, where fields common to more than one table can be moved to a new table, as shown by the creation of the FOREIGN_EXCHANGE table. At first, this looks like a 2NF transformation because fields not dependent on the primary key are removed to the new table; however, currencies should be conceived as being dependent upon location. Both CUSTOMER and SUPPLIER have addresses and, thus, there are transitive dependencies between currencies, through addresses (location), ultimately to customers and suppliers. Customers and suppliers use specific currencies depending on what country they are located in. Figure 4-25 shows a 3NF transformation allowing removal of common information from the CUSTOMER and SUPPLIER tables for two reasons:

❑ Currency coding and rate information does not depend on CUSTOMER and SUPPLIER primary keys, even though which currency they use does depend on who the customer or supplier are, based on the country in which they do business.

❑ The CURRENCY and EXCHANGE_RATE fields in the pre-transformation tables are transitively dependant on CUSTOMER and SUPPLIER primary keys because they depend on the CURRENCY_CODE, which in turn does depends on addresses.

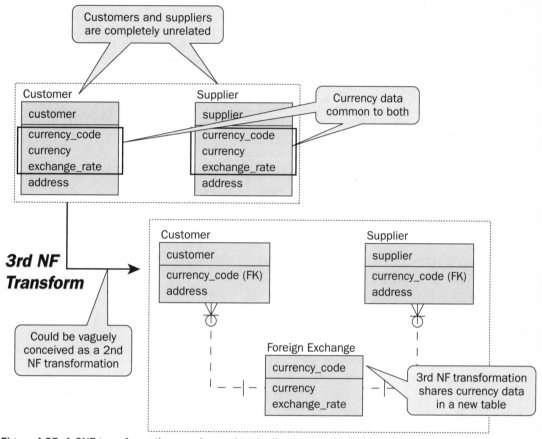

Figure 4-25: A 3NF transformation amalgamating duplication into a new table.

The transformation in Figure 4-25 could be conceived as being two 2NF transformations because a many-to-one relationship is creating a more static table by creating the FOREIGN_EXCHANGE *table.*

Obviously, the 3NF transformation shown in Figure 4-25 decreases the size of the database in general because repeated copies of CURRENCY and EXCHANGE_RATE fields have been normalized into the FOREIGN_EXCHANGE table and completely removed from the CUSTOMER and SUPPLIER tables. No data example is necessary in this case because the diagram in Figure 4-25 is self-explanatory.

Another commonly encountered version of 3NF is as shown in Figure 4-26. In this case, there is a very clear transitive dependency from CITY to DEPARTMENT and on to the EMPLOYEE primary key field.

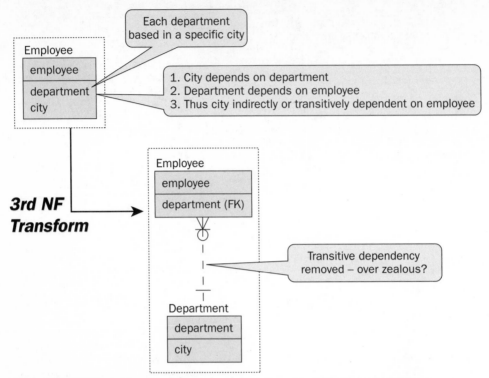

Figure 4-26: 3NF transitive dependency separation from one table to a new table.

A transitive dependency occurs where one field depends on another, which in turn depends on a third field — the third field typically being the primary key. A state of transitive dependency can also be interpreted as a field not being entirely dependent on the primary key.

In Figure 4-26, a transitive dependency exists because it is assumed that each employee is assigned to a particular department. Each department within a company is exclusively based in one specific city. In other words, any company in the database does not have single departments spread across more than a single city. As stated in Figure 4-26, this type of normalization might be getting a little over zealous in terms of creating too many tables, possibly resulting in slow queries having to join too many tables.

Another very typical 3NF candidate is as shown in Figure 4-27, where a calculated value is stored in a table. Also, the calculated value results from values in other fields within the same table. In this situation, the calculated field is actually non-fully dependent on the primary key (transitively dependent) and thus does not necessarily require a new table. Calculated fields are simply removed.

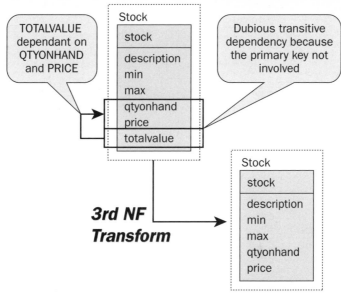

Figure 4-27: 3NF transformation to remove calculated fields.

There is usually a good reason for including calculated fields — usually performance denormalization. (Denormalization is explained as a concept in a later chapter.) In a data warehouse, calculated fields are sometimes stored in materialized views. Data warehouse database modeling is also covered in a later chapter.

Try It Out   3rd Normal Form

Figure 4-28 shows four tables:

1. Assume that any particular department within the company is located in only one city. Thus, assume that a city is always dependent upon which department a sales order occurred within.

2. Put the SALE_ORDER and STOCK_ITEM tables into 3NF.

3. Remove some calculated fields and create a new table.

4. Remove the appropriate fields from an original table to a new table.

5. Create a primary key in the new table.

6. Create a many-to-one relationship between the original table and the new table, defining and placing a foreign key appropriately.

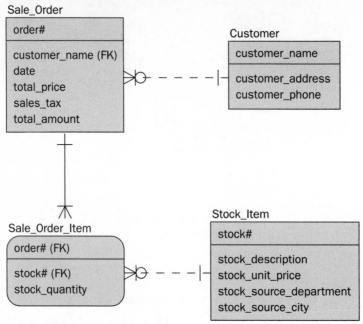

Figure 4-28: Four tables in 2NF.

How It Works

3NF requires elimination of transitive dependencies.

1. Create the STOCK_SOURCE_DEPARTMENT table as the city is dependent upon the department, which is in turn dependent on the primary key. This is a transitive dependency.

2. Remove the TOTAL_PRICE, and TOTAL_AMOUNT fields from the SALE_ORDER table because these fields are all transitively dependent on the sum of STOCK_QUANTITY and STOCK_UNIT_PRICE values from two other tables. The SALES_TAX field is changed to a percentage to allow for subsequent recalculation of the sales tax value.

3. Figure 4-29 shows the desired 3NF transformations.

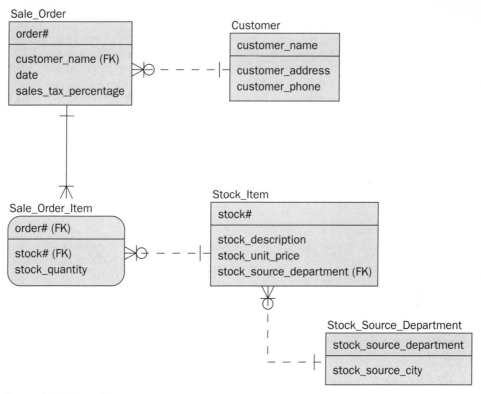

Figure 4-29: Five tables in 3NF, including removal of calculated fields.

Figure 4-29 shows creation of one new table and changes to three dependent fields from the SALE_ORDER table. The new table has its primary key placed into the STOCK_ITEM table as a foreign key.

Let's take a look at some examples with 3NF.

Beyond 3rd Normal Form (3NF)

As stated earlier in this chapter, many modern relational database models do not extend beyond 3NF. Sometimes 3NF is not used at all. The reason why is because of the generation of too many tables and the resulting complex SQL code joins, with resulting terrible database response times.

Why Go Beyond 3NF?

The objective of naming this section "Beyond 3rd Normal Form [3NF"] is to, in a small way, show the possible folly of using Normal Forms beyond 3NF. The biggest problems with going beyond 3NF are complexity and performance issues. Too much granularity actually introduces complexity, especially in a relational database. After all, a relational structure is not an object structure. Object structures become more simplistic as they are further reduced. Object database reduction is equivalent to the extremes of normalization in a relational database.

Extreme reduction in a relational database has the opposite effect to that of an object database where everything gets far to complex—even more complicated than is possible to manage. Extreme forms of reduction are not of benefit to the relational database model. Additionally, in a relational database the more normalization that is used then the greater the number of tables. The greater the number of tables, the larger SQL query joins become. The larger joins become the poorer database performance.

Extreme levels of granularity in relational database modeling are a form of mathematical perfection. These extremes rarely apply in fast-paced commercial environments. Commercial operations require that a job is done efficiently and cost effectively. Perfection in database model design is a side issue to that of making a profit.

Beyond 3NF the Easy Way

In this section, you begin with the easy way, and not the academic way, as previously. Beyond 3NF are Boyce-Codd normal form (BCNF), 4NF, 5NF, and Domain Key Normal Form (DKNF). Yoiks! That's just one or two Normal Forms to deal with. It always seems so inconceivable that relational database models can become so horribly complicated. After all, the essentials are by and large covered by 1NF and 2NF, with occasional need for 3NF transformations.

The specifics of Boyce-Codd normal form (BCNF), 4NF, 5NF, and DKNF will be covered later in this chapter.

One-to-One NULL Tables

Figure 4-30 shows removal of two often to be NULL valued fields from a table called EDITION, creating the new table called RANK. The result is a zero or one-to-one relationship between the RANK and EDITION tables. This implies that if a RANK record exists, then a corresponding EDITION record must exist as well. In the opposite case, however, an EDITION record can exist where a RANK record does not have to exist. This opposite case, accounts for an edition of a publication having no RANK and INGRAM_UNITS values. A recently published publication will rarely have any statistical information.

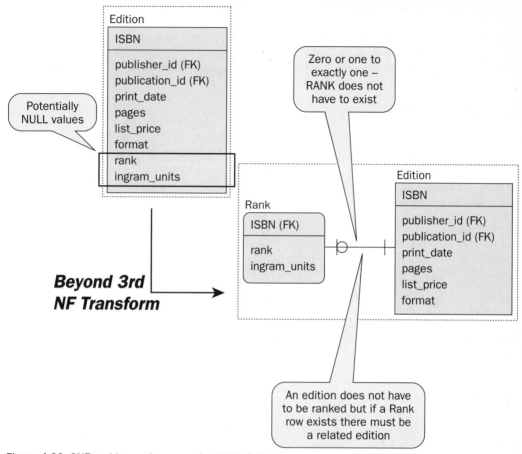

Figure 4-30: 3NF and beyond — removing NULL fields to new tables.

Figure 4-31 shows a data picture of the normalized structure shown at the lower-right of the diagram in Figure 4-30. What has effectively happened is that potentially NULL valued fields are moved into a new table, creating a one-to-one or zero relationship.

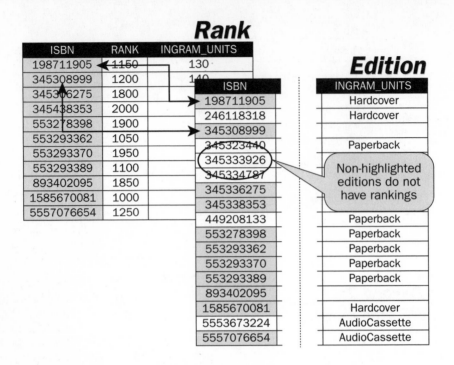

Figure 4-31: 3NF and beyond — separating NULL **valued fields.**

In the case of the tables shown in Figure 4-30 and Figure 4-31, it should be made apparent that the RANK and INGRAM_UNITS fields are not co-dependent. They do not depend on each other and are completely unrelated. It is quite possible that one field may be NULL valued and the other not. In the extreme, the data model could include two new tables, as shown in Figure 4-32. This level of normalization is completely absurd and seriously overzealous. In modern high-end relational database engines with variable record lengths, this is largely irrelevant. Once again disk space is cheap, plus increased numbers of tables leads to bigger SQL joins and poorer performance.

This level of normalization separating NULL valued fields into separate tables is simply going much too far, making too many little-bitty pieces and introducing too much granularity. This practice is not recommended; however, it is common. If normalization of this depth can be undone without destroying applications, do so — especially if there is a performance problem with SQL code joins.

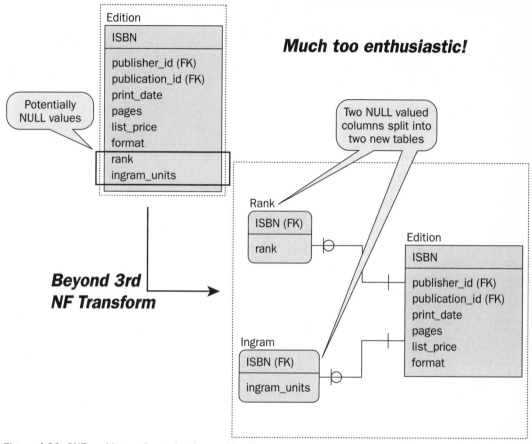

Figure 4-32: 3NF and beyond — going beyond too far.

Beyond 3NF the Academic Way

As you recall from the beginning of this chapter, academic definitions of layers beyond 3NF are as follows:

❑ *BCNF or Boyce-Codd Normal Form (BCNF)* — Every determinant in a table is a candidate key. If there is only one candidate key, then 3NF and BCNF are one and the same.

❑ *4th Normal Form (4NF)* — Eliminate multiple sets of multi-valued dependencies.

❑ *5th Normal Form (5NF)* — Eliminate cyclic dependencies. 5NF is also known as Projection normal form (PJNF).

❑ *Domain Key normal form (DKNF)* — DKNF is the ultimate application of normalization and is more of a measurement of conceptual state as opposed to a transformation process in itself.

Boyce-Codd Normal Form (BCNF)

BCNF does the following.

- ❑ A table must be in 3NF.

- ❑ A table can have only one candidate key.

A candidate key has potential for being a table's primary key. A table is not allowed more than one primary key because referential integrity requires it as such. It would be impossible to check foreign keys against more than one primary key. Referential integrity would be automatically invalid, unenforceable, and, thus, there would be no relational database model.

BCNF is an odd one because it is a little like a special case of 3NF. BCNF requires that every determinant in a table is a candidate key. If there is only one candidate key, 3NF and BCNF are the same. What does this mean? A *determinant* is a field whose value may depend other fields for their values. And some tables can be uniquely identified by more than one field or combination of fields. Each one of these is a potential primary key that can uniquely identify records in a table, and, thus, they are candidate keys, or potential primary keys.

This is where BCNF gets interesting because most examples of BCNF (and, in fact, any level of normalization beyond 3NF) utilize generally highly complex, multiple table, multiple many-to-many join resolution issues. You will get to those nasty, horribly complicated examples — just not yet.

The left side of the diagram in Figure 4-33 shows an example of a table with both a surrogate key and a natural key. Surrogate keys are added to tables to replace natural keys because surrogate keys are more efficient and easier to manage than natural keys. The other problem is that the original primary key (the natural key) needs a unique qualifier on it to ensure that it is not duplicated. Two customers with the same name could cause a problem when it comes to sending them both an invoice at the end of the month. The right side of the diagram in Figure 4-33 shows a BCNF breakdown into an innumerate multiple of tables created from the original table, for any values that are potentially unique. This is what the purest form of BCNF essentially requires. It is a little bit ridiculous.

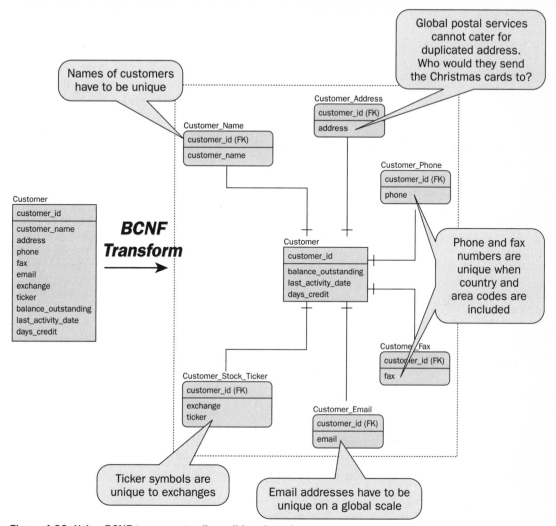

Figure 4-33: Using BCNF to separate all candidate keys into separate tables.

Unique key tables created on the right side of the diagram in Figure 4-33 all show quite conceivable possibilities of separating tables into individual units, accessible by the single primary key field CUSTOMER_ID, simply because the separated fields are unique.

> *Dividing tables up like that shown in Figure 4-33 can result in some serious inefficiency as a result of too many tables in SQL code join queries. Is BCNF folly in the case of Figure 4-33? That's an indefatigable yes!*

The usual type of example used to describe BCNF and other "beyond 3NF" transformations is often similar to the example shown in Figure 4-34, which is much more complicated than that shown in Figure 4-33; however, the usefulness of the transformation shown in Figure 4-33 is dubious to say the least.

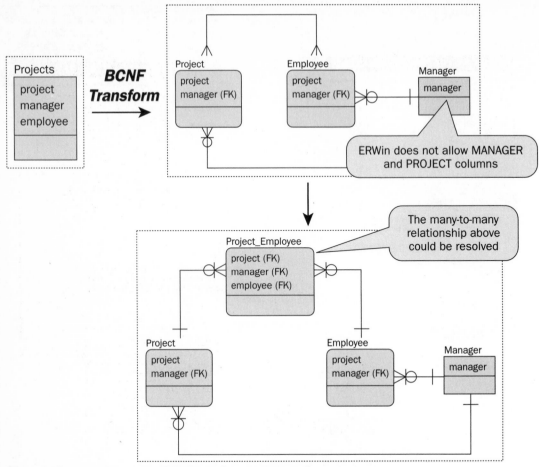

Figure 4-34: A common type of BCNF transformation example.

Data for Figure 4-34 is shown in Figure 4-35 to attempt to make this picture clearer.

The point about BCNF is that a candidate key is, by definition, a unique key, and thus a potential primary key. If a table contains more than one candidate key (primary key), it has a problem according to BCNF. I disagree! BCNF divides a table up into multiple tables to ensure that no single table has more than one potential primary key. This is my understanding of BCNF. In my opinion, BCNF is overzealous for a commercial environment. Essentially, BCNF prohibits a table from having two possible primary keys. Why? And so what! This is not a hard-and-fast rule commercially, but more of a purist requirement from a mathematical perspective. In other words, it's nice, but it's not cool commercially.

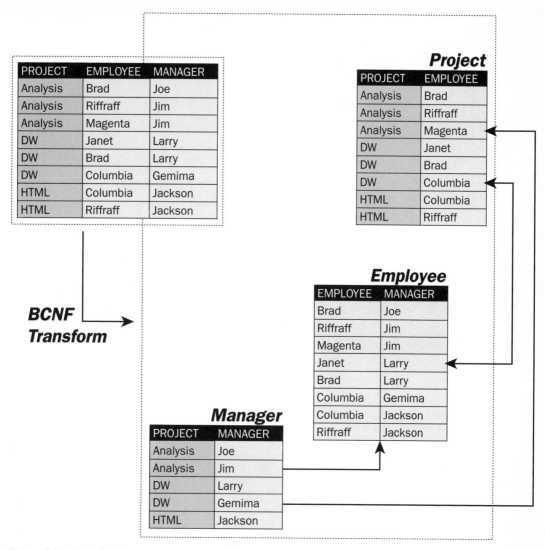

Figure 4-35: Data for the common type of BCNF transformation example shown in Figure 4-34.

4th Normal Form (4NF)

4NF does the following.

- ❑ A table must be in 3NF or BCNF with 3NF.

- ❑ Multi-valued dependencies must be transformed into functional dependencies. This implies that one value and not multiple values are dependent on a primary key.

- ❑ Eliminate multiple sets of multiple valued or multi-valued dependencies, sometimes described as non-trivial multi-valued dependencies.

A *multiple valued set* is a field containing a comma-delimited list or collections of some kind. A collection could be an array of values of the same type. Those multiple values are dependent as a whole on the primary key (the "whole" meaning the entire collection in each record).

4NF is similar to 5NF in that both attempt to minimize the number of fields in composite keys.

Figure 4-36 shows employees with variable numbers of both skills and certifications where those skills and certifications are not only unrelated to each other, but are stored as comma-delimited list arrays in single fields (*take a breath*) in the EMPLOYEE table.

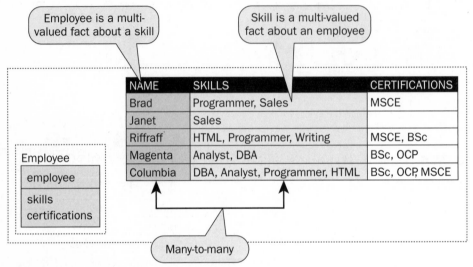

Figure 4-36: Multi-valued lists not in 4NF.

Figure 4-37 shows a non-4NF transformation essentially only spreading the comma-delimited lists into separate records, using the same existing EMPLOYEE table.

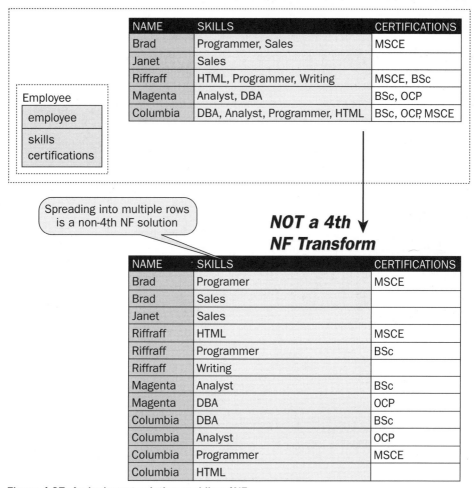

Figure 4-37: An inelegant solution avoiding 4NF.

Figure 4-38 performs a partial 4NF transformation by splitting skills and certifications from the EMPLOYEE table into SKILL and CERTIFICATION tables. This is only a partial transformation, however, because there are still many-to-many relationships between EMPLOYEE to SKILL tables, and EMPLOYEE to CERTIFICATION tables.

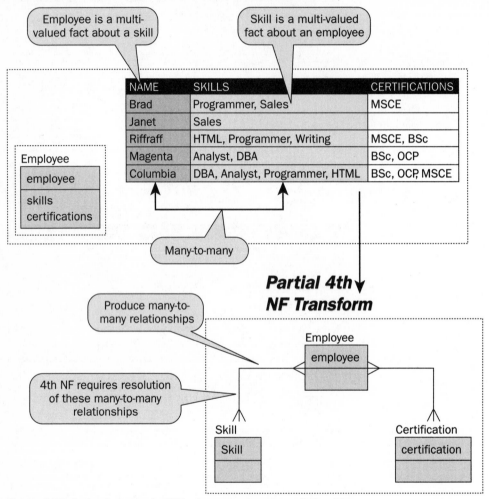

Figure 4-38: A classic example 4NF using many-to-many relationships.

Figure 4-39 shows a more simplistic example where every FATHER table entry is unique because fathers can have multiple children, but each child has only one father.

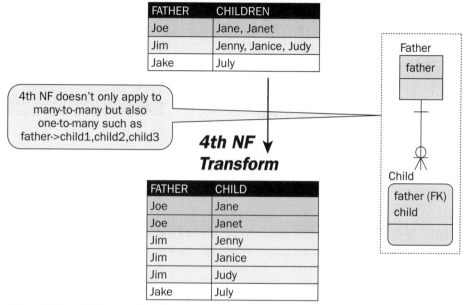

Figure 4-39: A 4NF example using a one-to-many relationship.

Figure 4-40 resolves the many-to-many relationships into EMPLOYEE_SKILL and EMPLOYEE_CERTIFI-CATION tables, shown as many-to-many relationships in Figure 4-38. The many-to-many relationships resolved into one-to-many relationships in Figure 4-40 contain composites of employee names, original skills and certifications arrays, with arrays spread into separate records.

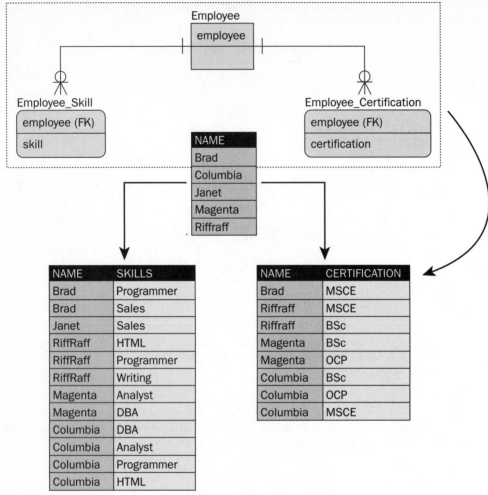

Figure 4-40: Data for the classic example 4NF as shown in Figure 4-36.

Essentially, 4NF attempts to generate sets or arrays spread into separate records in separate tables, making each individual record perhaps easier to access when doing exact match searching.

5th Normal Form (5NF)

5NF does the following.

❑   A table must be in 4NF.

❑   Cyclic dependencies must be eliminated. A *cyclic dependency* is simply something that depends on one thing, where that one thing is either directly in indirectly dependent on itself.

5NF is also known as Projection Normal Form (PJNF). The term "projection" is used to describe new tables containing subsets of data from the original table. A cyclic dependency is a form of circular dependency where three pairs result as a combination of a single three-field composite primary key table, those three pairs being field 1 with field 2, field 2 with field 3, and field 1 with field 3. The cyclic dependency is that everything is related to everything else, including itself. In other words, there is a combination or a permutation excluding repetitions. If tables are joined again using a three-table join, the resulting records will be the same as that present in the original table. It is a stated requirement of the validity of 5NF that the post-transformation join must match records for a query on the pre-transformation table.

5NF is similar to 4NF in that both attempt to minimize the number of fields in composite keys.

5NF can be demonstrated as follows. You begin by creating a three-field composite primary key table:

```
CREATE TABLE Employees
(
        project VARCHAR2(32) NOT NULL,
        employee VARCHAR2(32) NOT NULL,
        manager VARCHAR2(32) NOT NULL,
        PRIMARY KEY (project,employee,manager)
);
```

Note the composite primary key on all three fields present in the table. Now, add some records to the table (shown also in the graphic in Figure 4-41):

```
INSERT INTO Employees VALUES('Analysis','Brad','Joe');
INSERT INTO Employees VALUES('Analysis','Riffraff','Jim');
INSERT INTO Employees VALUES('Analysis','Magenta','Jim');
INSERT INTO Employees VALUES('DW','Janet','Larry');
INSERT INTO Employees VALUES('DW','Brad','Larry');
INSERT INTO Employees VALUES('DW','Columbia','Gemima');
INSERT INTO Employees VALUES('HTML','Columbia','Jackson');
INSERT INTO Employees VALUES('HTML','Riffraff','Jackson');
COMMIT;
```

PROJECT	EMPLOYEE	MANAGER
Analysis	Brad	Joe
Analysis	Riffraff	Jim
Analysis	Magenta	Jim
DW	Janet	Larry
DW	Brad	Larry
DW	Columbia	Gemima
HTML	Columbia	Jackson
HTML	Riffraff	Jackson

Figure 4-41: A pre-5NF three field composite primary key table.

Figure 4-42 shows the 5NF transformation from single three-field composite primary key table to three semi-related tables, each containing two-field composite primary keys. Why is the term *semi-related* used? Because the tool used in this book to draw ERDs does not actually allow creation of the ERD shown on the right side of the diagram in Figure 4-42. This is very interesting; however, all texts indicate that the 5NF transformation shown in Figure 4-42 as being true and correct. I still find this interesting, though, and harp back to my previous comments on anything beyond 3NF being commercially impractical and possibly overzealous in the application of design *features*.

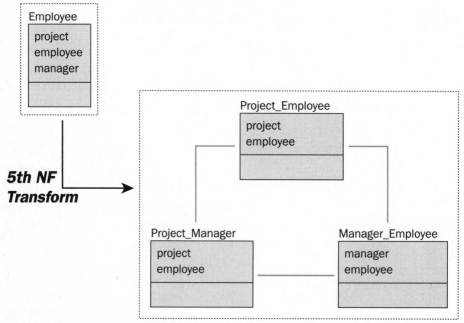

Figure 4-42: A 5NF transformation.

Figure 4-43 shows the actual data structures that reflect 5NF structure shown at the lower-right of the diagram shown in Figure 4-42.

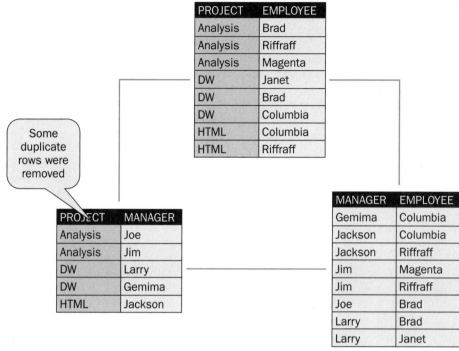

Figure 4-43: 5NF transformations sometimes remove duplicates.

Going further with the table-creation commands and record-insertion commands for each of the three separate 5NF tables, note that all records added are exactly the same as for adding to the pre-5NF table, with any duplicate records removed. Create the PROJECT_EMPLOYEE table and add records:

```
CREATE TABLE Project_Employee
(
        project VARCHAR2(32) NOT NULL,
        employee VARCHAR2(32) NOT NULL,
        PRIMARY KEY (project, employee)
);

INSERT INTO Project_Employee VALUES('Analysis','Brad');
INSERT INTO Project_Employee VALUES('Analysis','Riffraff');
INSERT INTO Project_Employee VALUES('Analysis','Magenta');
INSERT INTO Project_Employee VALUES('DW','Janet');
INSERT INTO Project_Employee VALUES('DW','Brad');
INSERT INTO Project_Employee VALUES('DW','Columbia');
INSERT INTO Project_Employee VALUES('HTML','Columbia');
INSERT INTO Project_Employee VALUES('HTML','Riffraff');
COMMIT;
```

Create the PROJECT_MANAGER table and add records:

```
CREATE TABLE Project_Manager
(
        project VARCHAR2(32) NOT NULL,
        manager VARCHAR2(32) NOT NULL,
        PRIMARY KEY (project, manager)
);

INSERT INTO Project_Manager VALUES('Analysis','Joe');
INSERT INTO Project_Manager VALUES('Analysis','Jim');
INSERT INTO Project_Manager VALUES('DW','Larry');
INSERT INTO Project_Manager VALUES('DW','Gemima');
INSERT INTO Project_Manager VALUES('HTML','Jackson');
COMMIT;
```

Create the MANAGER_EMPLOYEE table and add records:

```
CREATE TABLE Manager_Employee
(
        manager VARCHAR2(32) NOT NULL,
        employee VARCHAR2(32) NOT NULL,
        PRIMARY KEY (manager, employee)
);

INSERT INTO Manager_Employee VALUES('Gemima','Columbia');
INSERT INTO Manager_Employee VALUES('Jackson','Columbia');
INSERT INTO Manager_Employee VALUES('Jackson','Riffraff');
INSERT INTO Manager_Employee VALUES('Jim','Magenta');
INSERT INTO Manager_Employee VALUES('Jim','Riffraff');
INSERT INTO Manager_Employee VALUES('Joe','Brad');
INSERT INTO Manager_Employee VALUES('Larry','Brad');
INSERT INTO Manager_Employee VALUES('Larry','Janet');
COMMIT;
```

As previously stated, the one hard-and-fast rule with respect to 5NF is that the pre-5NF records must be identical to the 5NF divided up tables (as shown in Figure 4-44) when querying the database. In other words, the two queries must match — in this case, records from one table must match records from the three joined tables.

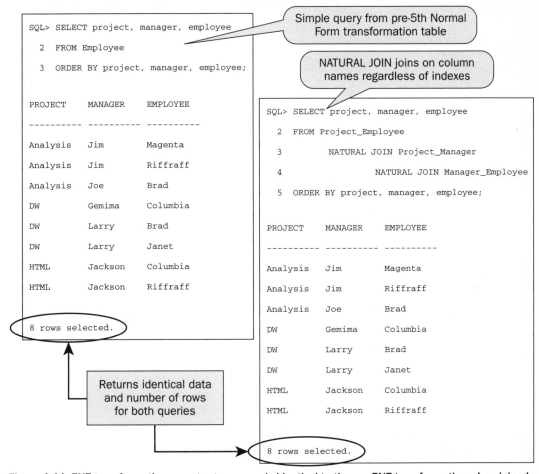

Figure 4-44: 5NF transformations must return records identical to the pre-5NF transformation when joined.

Domain Key Normal Form (DKNF)

Domain Key Normal Form (DKNF) is quite often a conceptual state of a relational database model as opposed to a final transformation process. DKNF is the ultimate normal form and essentially describes how a completely normalized database model should appear:

❑ There can be no insertion, change, or data removal anomalies. In other words, every record in the database must be directly accessible in all manners, such that no errors can result.

❑ Every record in every table must be uniquely identifiable and directly related to the primary key in its table. This means that every field in every table is directly determined by the primary key in its table.

❑ All validation of data is done within the database model. As far as application and database performance are concerned this is nearly always an extremely undesirable state in a commercial environment. It is better to split functionality between database and applications. Some may call this business rules. It is generally common knowledge that some business rule implementation is often most effectively divided up between database and applications.

DKNF is an ideal form and an ultimate or final form of relational database normalization. This level of normalization is more mathematically perfect and has beauty in its granular simplicity. In an object database model, this approach is perfectly suited where individual data items are only ever accessed as unique elements (primary keys) and records are never accessed in groups. In a relational database model where commercially most databases require not only exact matches but also range searching for reporting, this level of intensity in normalization nearly always has a seriously negative impact on general database and application performance, and thus a negative effect on end-user satisfaction. End-user satisfaction is the objective of any application. If it isn't, it should be because they usually pay the bills!

Summary

In this chapter, you learned about:

❑   What normalization is, its benefits and potential hazards

❑   A layman's method of understanding normalization

❑   A purist, academic definition of normalization

❑   How referential integrity is maintained using primary and foreign keys

❑   Normal Forms from 1st through to 5th, including Boyce-Codd Normal Form and Domain Key Normal Form

❑   Special terminology used in Normal Forms

The next chapter discusses some advanced relational database modeling techniques, including denormalization, special tricks used for different database model types, followed by introductions to the object database model and data warehouse database modeling.

Exercises

1.   Write five CREATE TABLE commands for the tables in Figure 4-29. Ensure that all primary key, foreign key, and any potentially necessary unique keys are included.

2.   Write CREATE INDEX commands to create all indexes on any foreign keys indicated in the CREATE TABLE commands written for the previous question.

Reading and Writing Data with SQL

"Any sufficiently advanced technology is indistinguishable from magic." (Arthur C. Clarke)

SQL helps to explain relational database modeling. None of this is magic, and is much easier to understand than you might think.

This chapter shows how the relational database model is used from an application perspective. There is little point in understanding something, such as relational database modeling, without seeing it applied in some way, no matter how simple. With that in mind, this chapter looks at how a database model is accessed when it contains data in a database. A relational database model contains tables, and the records in those tables are accessed using Structured Query Language (SQL). SQL is used to create the database access sections of applications. When a database model is correctly designed, creation of SQL code is a simple process. Great difficulties in coding of SQL queries in particular can often indicate serious database model design flaws.

This book is all about relational database modeling; therefore, it is necessary to explain only the basis of SQL in this book as pertaining directly to helping in the understanding of relational database modeling. How can describing the basic details of SQL help with the understanding of relational database modeling? The answer to this question is very simple. SQL uses a relational database model to change data in a database, and to retrieve data from that database. SQL essentially applies all the structures created by the relational database modeling process. SQL — and particularly SQL queries and their simplicity — is a direct result of the underlying structure of a database model. In other words, the better and more appropriate a database model is, the easier building SQL code for applications will be. Another way to look at this is that a database model is most easily utilized by applications, when matching application structure. It makes perfect sense to describe the basics of using SQL because it demonstrates the use of a relational database model in action.

In this chapter, you learn about the following:

❑   What SQL is

❑   The origins of SQL

❑   Many types of queries

❑   Changing data in tables

❑   Changing table structure

Defining SQL

SQL is a non-procedural language used for accessing field and record values in relational database tables.

A procedural programming language is a language where there can be dependencies between sequential commands. For example, when setting a variable X = 1 on a line, that variable X can be used to reference the value 1, as the variable X in subsequent lines of programming code. A non-procedural programming language does not allow communication between different lines of programming code. Non-procedural languages also do not allow use of procedures. A procedure allows intra-program communication by passing values in and out of procedures.

Keep in mind the following when considering what SQL is.

❑   SQL is structured in the sense that it is used to access structured data, in a structured manner, or retrieve data from organized structures. Those organized structures are tables.

❑   Use of the word "language" implies a computer programming language. Computer programming languages are often used to get information from a computer.

❑   A *non-procedural language* essentially submits a single command, with a questioning or querying type nature. SQL is a non-procedural language consisting of single commands, where the database itself does a lot of the work in deciding how to get that information. On the other hand, a *procedural language* contains blocks of commands. Those blocks of commands are sequences of distinct steps, typically where each successive step is dependent on the result of the previous command in the sequence.

❑   In most relational databases, SQL does have the capability to function in a limited procedural fashion, allowing the programmer to determine partially how a database is accessed. Traditionally, SQL procedural code is used to write what are called *stored procedures, triggers, database events,* or *database procedures*. There are other names for these code blocks, depending on the database in use. Procedural SQL code is generally simplistic and can sometimes allow the inclusion of basic programming constructs such as `IF` statements, `CASE` statements, and so on.

So, SQL is a simple non-procedural programming language allowing single line commands. These single-line commands are used to access data stored in database table structures.

The Origins of SQL

IBM created the original relational database technology. SQL was created as an uncomplicated, non-procedural way of accessing data from an IBM-created relational database. SQL was initially called "Sequel." Thus, SQL is often pronounced as "sequel." For some other databases, SQL is pronounced by representing each letter, as in "ess-queue-ell." The meaning of the two pronunciations is identical.

> *The query language used to access an object database is called Object Database Query Language (ODQL). The acronym "QL" thus means "query language," a language used to query a database.*

In its most primitive form, SQL stems from the idea of a reporting language, devised in theory by the inventor of the relational database model. The roots of SQL lie in retrieval of sets of data. What this means is that SQL is intended as a language to retrieve many records from one or many tables at once, yielding a result set. SQL was not originally intended to retrieve individual records from a relational database, as exact record matches, common in transactional and OLTP databases. However, SQL can now be used to do precisely just that, and with excellent efficiency. SQL is now used in modern-day relational database engines to retrieve both sets of records, and individual records, in transactional, OLTP, and data warehouse databases.

What does all this mean without using a plethora of nasty long words? In short, SQL was developed as a shorthand method of retrieving information from relational databases. SQL has become the industry standard over the last 20 years. The following is an example of a *query* (a request or question put to the database) written in SQL, in this case all the records in the AUTHOR table will be retrieved:

```
SELECT AUTHOR_ID, NAME FROM AUTHOR;

AUTHOR_ID NAME
---------- --------------------------------
         1 Orson Scott Card
         2 James Blish
         3 Isaac Azimov
         4 Larry Niven
         5 Jerry Pournelle
         6 William Shakespeare
         7 Kurt Vonnegut
```

SQL for Different Databases

SQL as implemented in different database engines is not standardized. Each database vendor developed a unique relational database, and relational database management system (database management toolkit). The result was different relational databases having different strengths. The vendors often altered and extended the standard form of SQL to take advantage of the way in which their individual products were written. The result is that relational database products from different vendors, although similar in nature, and even appearance, are often very different internally. Additionally, the different relational databases are different both in internal structural characteristics, and in the way they are used. And that's only the database engine itself. There is also use of different computer hardware platforms and operating systems. The larger database vendors service multiple operating systems, with completely different versions of the database software, applicable to different operating systems, even down to different flavors of Unix.

Many of the smaller-scale database engines such as dBase and MSAccess are only written for a single platform and operating system. In the case of dBase and MSAccess, that system is PC-based, running the Windows operating system.

So, what are the basics of SQL?

The Basics of SQL

The basics of SQL consist of a number of parts. This section briefly introduces what simple SQL can do. As you read through this chapter, each is explained individually by example.

❑ *Query commands* — Querying a database is performed with a single command called the SELECT command. The SELECT command creates queries, and has various optional clauses that include performing functions such as filtering and sorting. Queries are used to retrieve data from tables in a database. There are various ways in which data can be retrieved from tables:

Some database engines refer to SQL commands as SQL statements. Don't get confused. The two terms mean exactly the same thing. I prefer the term "command." This is merely a personal preference on my part. The term "clause" is usually applied to subset parts of commands.

   ❑ *Basic query* — The most simple of queries retrieves all records from a single table.

   ❑ *Filtered query* — A filtered query uses a WHERE clause to include or exclude specific records.

   ❑ *Sorted query* — Sorting uses the ORDER BY clause to retrieve records in a specific sorted order.

   ❑ *Aggregated query* — The GROUP BY clause allows summarizing, grouping, or aggregating of records into summarized record sets. Typically, aggregated queries contain fewer records than the query would produce, if the GROUP BY clause were not used. A HAVING clause can be used to filter in, or filter out, records in the resulting summarized aggregated record set. In other words, the HAVING clause filters the results of the GROUP BY clause, and not the records retrieved before aggregation.

   ❑ *Join query* — A join query joins tables together, returning records from multiple tables. Joins can be performed in various ways, including inner joins and outer joins.

   ❑ *Nested queries* — A nested query is also known as a *subquery*, which is a query contained within another query (a *parent* or *calling query*). Nesting implies that subqueries can be nested in multiple layers and thus a subquery itself can also be a calling query of another subquery.

   ❑ *Composite queries* — A composite query is a query that merges multiple query results together, most often using the UNION keyword.

❑ *Data change commands* — The following commands are used to change data in tables in a database.

   ❑ INSERT — The INSERT command is used to add new records to a table.

   ❑ UPDATE — The UPDATE command allows changes to one or more records in a table, at once.

   ❑ DELETE — The DELETE command allows deletion of one or more records from a table, at once.

❑   *Database structure change commands* — These commands allow alterations to metadata (the data about the data). Metadata in a simple relational database comprises tables and indexes. Table metadata change commands allow creation of new tables, changes to existing tables, and destruction of existing tables, among other more obscure types of operations — too obscure for this book. Table metadata commands are CREATE TABLE, ALTER TABLE, and DROP TABLE commands.

Querying a Database Using SELECT

The following sections examine database queries using the SELECT command in detail, as well as by example.

Basic Queries

The following syntax shows the structure of the SELECT statement and the FROM clause. The SELECT list is the list of fields, or otherwise, usually retrieved from tables. The FROM clause specifies one or more tables from which to retrieve data.

```
SELECT { [alias.]field | expression | [alias.]* [,the rest of the list of fields] }
FROM table [alias] [ , ... ];
```

> **Please see the Introduction to this book for syntax conventions, known as Backus-Naur Form syntax notation.**

The easiest way to understand SQL is by example. Retrieve all fields from the AUTHOR table using the * (star or asterisk) character. The * character tells the query to retrieve all fields in all tables in the FROM clause:

```
SELECT * FROM AUTHOR;

AUTHOR_ID NAME
---------- -----------------------------------
        1 Orson Scott Card
        2 James Blish
        3 Isaac Azimov
        4 Larry Niven
        5 Jerry Pournelle
        6 William Shakespeare
        7 Kurt Vonnegut
```

A semi-colon and carriage return is used to end the query command, submitting the query to the query engine. Not all relational databases execute on a semi-colon. Some databases use a different character; others just a carriage-return.

Specify an individual field by retrieving only the name of the author from the AUTHOR table:

```
SELECT NAME FROM AUTHOR;

NAME
--------------------------------
Orson Scott Card
```

```
James Blish
Isaac Azimov
Larry Niven
Jerry Pournelle
William Shakespeare
Kurt Vonnegut
```

> **Retrieving specific field names is very slightly more efficient than retrieving all fields using the * character. The * character requires the added overhead of metadata interpretation lookups into the metadata dictionary — to find the fields in the table. In highly concurrent, very busy databases, continual data dictionary lookups can stress out database concurrency handling capacity.**

Execute an expression on a single field of the AUTHOR table, returning a small section of the author's name:

```
SELECT AUTHOR_ID, SUBSTR(NAME,1,10) FROM AUTHOR;

AUTHOR_ID SUBSTR(NAM
---------- ----------
         1 Orson Scot
         2 James Blis
         3 Isaac Azim
         4 Larry Nive
         5 Jerry Pour
         6 William Sh
         7 Kurt Vonne
```

Execute an expression, but this time involving more than a single field:

```
SELECT E.ISBN, (E.LIST_PRICE * R.RANK) + R.INGRAM_UNITS
FROM EDITION E JOIN RANK R ON (R.ISBN = E.ISBN);

      ISBN (E.LIST_PRICE*R.RANK)+R.INGRAM_UNITS
---------- -----------------------------------
 198711905                             46072.5
 345308999                                9728
 345336275                               11860
 345438353                               24200
 553278398                               14430
 553293362                                7985
 553293370                               14815
 553293389                                8370
 893402095                             14026.5
1585670081                               34600
5557076654                             37632.5
```

Use aliases as substitutes for table names:

```
SELECT A.NAME, P.TITLE, E.ISBN
FROM AUTHOR A JOIN PUBLICATION P USING (AUTHOR_ID)
```

```
   JOIN EDITION E USING (PUBLICATION_ID);

   NAME                  TITLE                                      ISBN
   ------------------    --------------------------------------    ----------
   William Shakespeare   The Complete Works of Shakespeare          198711905
   Isaac Azimov          Foundation                                 246118318
   Isaac Azimov          Foundation                                 345308999
   Larry Niven           Footfall                                   345323440
   Larry Niven           Ringworld                                  345333926
   Isaac Azimov          Foundation                                 345334787
   Isaac Azimov          Foundation                                 345336275
   James Blish           A Case of Conscience                       345438353
   Larry Niven           Lucifer's Hammer                           449208133
   Isaac Azimov          Prelude to Foundation                      553278398
   Isaac Azimov          Second Foundation                          553293362
   Isaac Azimov          Foundation and Empire                      553293370
   Isaac Azimov          Foundation's Edge                          553293389
   Isaac Azimov          Foundation                                 893402095
   James Blish           Cities in Flight                          1585670081
   Isaac Azimov          Foundation                                5553673224
   Isaac Azimov          Foundation                                5557076654
```

The USING clause in join syntax allows a vague specification of a join field. This assumes that the two joined tables have the required relationship on the field of the required field name. In the previous query, both the AUTHOR and PUBLICATION tables have the field PUBLICATION_ID, and in both tables the same values, one being a primary key, and the other a directly related foreign key.

Without the alias, the query would simply have table names, much longer strings, making the query a little more difficult to read and code:

```
SELECT AUTHOR.NAME, PUBLICATION.TITLE, EDITION.ISBN
FROM AUTHOR JOIN PUBLICATION USING (AUTHOR_ID)
   JOIN EDITION USING (PUBLICATION_ID);

   NAME                  TITLE                                      ISBN
   ------------------    --------------------------------------    ----------
   William Shakespeare   The Complete Works of Shakespeare          198711905
   Isaac Azimov          Foundation                                 246118318
   Isaac Azimov          Foundation                                 345308999
   Larry Niven           Footfall                                   345323440
   Larry Niven           Ringworld                                  345333926
   Isaac Azimov          Foundation                                 345334787
   Isaac Azimov          Foundation                                 345336275
   James Blish           A Case of Conscience                       345438353
   Larry Niven           Lucifer's Hammer                           449208133
   Isaac Azimov          Prelude to Foundation                      553278398
   Isaac Azimov          Second Foundation                          553293362
   Isaac Azimov          Foundation and Empire                      553293370
   Isaac Azimov          Foundation's Edge                          553293389
   Isaac Azimov          Foundation                                 893402095
   James Blish           Cities in Flight                          1585670081
   Isaac Azimov          Foundation                                5553673224
   Isaac Azimov          Foundation                                5557076654
```

> Using shorter alias names can help to keep SQL code more easily readable, particularly for programmers in the future having to make changes. Maintainable code is less prone to error and much easier to tune properly.

Filtering with the WHERE Clause

A filtered query uses the WHERE clause to include, or exclude, specific records. The following syntax adds the syntax for the WHERE clause to the SELECT command:

```
SELECT ...
FROM table [alias] [, ... ]
[ WHERE [table.|alias.] { field | expression } comparison { ... }
  [ { AND | OR } [ NOT ] ... ] ];
```

The WHERE clause is optional.

Begin with filtering by retrieving the author whose primary key values is equal to 5:

```
SELECT * FROM AUTHOR WHERE AUTHOR_ID = 5;

AUTHOR_ID NAME
---------- --------------------
        5 Jerry Pournelle
```

> This filter is efficient because a single record is found using the primary key. A fast index search can be used to find a single record very quickly, even in an extremely large table.

Now find everything other than authors whose primary key value is 5:

```
SELECT * FROM AUTHOR WHERE AUTHOR_ID != 5;

AUTHOR_ID NAME
---------- --------------------
        1 Orson Scott Card
        2 James Blish
        3 Isaac Azimov
        4 Larry Niven
        6 William Shakespeare
        7 Kurt Vonnegut
```

Filtering using a negative such as NOT or != forces a full table scan and ignores all indexes altogether. Searching for something on the premise that it does not exist is extremely inefficient, especially for a very large table. A full table scan is a physical input/output (I/O) read of all the records in a table. Reading an entire table containing billions of records can take a week. Not many programmers have that long to test their queries.

Some small tables are more efficiently read using only the table (a full table scan) and ignoring indexes.

How about authors whose primary key value is less than or equal to 5:

```
SELECT * FROM AUTHOR WHERE AUTHOR_ID <= 5;

AUTHOR_ID NAME
---------- --------------------
        1 Orson Scott Card
        2 James Blish
        3 Isaac Azimov
        4 Larry Niven
        5 Jerry Pournelle
```

A range search is more efficient than a full table scan for large tables because certain types of indexes, such as BTree indexes, are read efficiently using range scans. A BTree index is built like an upside down tree and searching requires traversal up and down the tree structure. Therefore, both single record and multiple record range scans are efficient using BTree indexes.

This one finds a range:

```
SELECT * FROM AUTHOR WHERE AUTHOR_ID >= 3 AND AUTHOR_ID <= 5;

AUTHOR_ID NAME
---------- --------------------
        3 Isaac Azimov
        4 Larry Niven
        5 Jerry Pournelle
```

Many relational databases use a special operator called BETWEEN, which retrieves between a range inclusive of the end points:

```
SELECT * FROM AUTHOR WHERE AUTHOR_ID BETWEEN 3 AND 5;

AUTHOR_ID NAME
---------- --------------------
        3 Isaac Azimov
        4 Larry Niven
        5 Jerry Pournelle
```

There are other ways of filtering (common to many relational databases), such as the LIKE operator. The LIKE operator is somewhat similar to a very simple string pattern matcher. The following query finds all authors with the vowel "a" in their names:

```
SELECT * FROM AUTHOR WHERE NAME LIKE "%a%";

AUTHOR_ID NAME
---------- --------------------
        3 Isaac Azimov
        2 James Blish
        4 Larry Niven
        1 Orson Scott Card
        6 William Shakespeare
```

> The LIKE **operator is generally not efficient. Simple string pattern matching tends to full-table scan entire tables, no matter how the string is structured.**

IN can be used as set membership operator:

```
SELECT * FROM AUTHOR WHERE AUTHOR_ID IN (1,2,3,4,5);

AUTHOR_ID NAME
---------- --------------------
        1 Orson Scott Card
        2 James Blish
        3 Isaac Azimov
        4 Larry Niven
        5 Jerry Pournelle
```

Traditionally, the IN operator is most efficient when testing against a list of literal values.

The NOT, AND, and OR operators are known as *logical operators*, or sometimes as *logical conditions*. This depends on the database in use. Logical operators allow for Boolean logic in WHERE clause filtering and various other SQL code commands and clauses. Mathematically, the sequence of precedence is NOT, followed by AND, and finally OR. Precedence, covered in the next section, can be altered using parentheses.

Precedence

Precedence is the order of resolution of an expression and generally acts from left to right, across an expression. In other words, in the following expression, each of the first, second, and third expressions are evaluated one after the other:

```
<expression1> AND <expression2> AND <expression3>
```

> An expression is a mathematical term representing any part of a larger mathematical expression. Thus, an expression is an expression in itself, can contain other expressions, and can be a subset part of other expressions. So in the expression (((5 + 3) * 23) – 50), (5 + 3) is an expression, so is (5 + 3) * 23, so is ((5 + 3) * 23), and even the number 50 is an expression, in this context.

In the following expression, however, the conjunction of the second and third expressions is evaluated first; then the result is evaluated against the first expression using the OR logical operator. This is because the AND operator has higher precedence than the OR operator:

```
<expression1> OR <expression2> AND <expression3>
```

Higher precedence implies "executed first."

The precedence of evaluation of expressions in the next expression is changed by using the parentheses. Therefore, use of parentheses as in () has higher precedence than NOT, AND, and OR.

```
(<expression1> OR <expression2>) AND <expression3>
```

Aside from logical operator precedence, there is also the factor of *arithmetical precedence*. Basic arithmetic is something we all learned in grade school mathematics. This is to refresh your memory, rather than to insult your intelligence, by explaining the completely obvious. Addition and subtraction have the lowest level of precedence, but they are equal to each other:

```
5 + 4 - 3 = 6
```

It should be plain to see why addition and subtraction have equal precedence because no matter what order in which the numbers are added and subtracted, the result will always be the same. Try it out yourself in your head, and you will understand better. Asking you to do an exercise like this in your head is once again not intended as an intellectual insult; however, just try it and you will understand how simplicity can be used to explain so many things. Perhaps even the answers to life itself could be answered so easily, by breaking all questions into their constituent little pieces.

The ability to break things into small parts to solve small problems is very important when building anything with computers, including relational database models. Object-oriented design is the most modern of software design methodologies. Breaking things into small things is what object- oriented design using programming languages such as Java are all about — breaking things into smaller constituent parts to make the complexity of the whole much easier to implement. In some respects, relational database modeling has some striking similarities in term of breaking down complexity to introduce simplicity. There is beauty in simplicity because it is easy to understand!

Multiplication and division have higher precedence than addition and subtraction but once again are equal in precedence to each other:

```
3 + 4 * 5 = 23 and not 35
```

Remember that parenthesizing a part of an expression changes precedence, giving priority to the parenthesized section:

```
( 3 + 4 ) * 5 = 35
```

Any function such as raising a number to a power, or using a SUBSTR function, has the highest level of precedence. Apart from the parenthesized section of course:

```
3 + 4² * 5 = 83
3 * 4 + LENGTH(SUBSTR(NAME, 1, 10)) = 22
```

> *Some databases and programming languages may represent raising a number to a power in different ways, such as* 4^2, 4^^2, EXP(4,2), POWER(4,2). *This depends on the database in use.*

So now go back to the WHERE clause and utilize the rules of precedence. The following query has precedence executed from left to right. It finds all Hardcover editions, of all books, regardless of the page count or list price. After PAGES and LIST_PRICE are checked, the query also allows any hard cover edition. The OR operator simply overrides the effect of the filters against PAGES and LIST_PRICE:

```
SELECT ISBN, PRINT_DATE, PAGES, LIST_PRICE, FORMAT FROM EDITION

WHERE PAGES < 300 AND LIST_PRICE < 50 OR FORMAT = "Hardcover";

      ISBN PRINT_DAT     PAGES LIST_PRICE FORMAT
---------- ---------- ---------- ---------- --------------
1585670081                 590       34.5 Hardcover
 345438353                 256         12 Paperback
 198711905                1232      39.95 Hardcover
 345336275 31-JUL-86       285        6.5
 246118318 28-APR-83       234       9.44 Hardcover
```

The next query changes the precedence of the WHERE clause filter, from the previous query, preventing the OR operator from simply overriding what has already been selected by the filter on the PAGES filter (now page counts are all under 300 pages):

```
SELECT ISBN, PRINT_DATE, PAGES, LIST_PRICE, FORMAT FROM EDITION
WHERE PAGES < 300 AND (LIST_PRICE < 50 OR FORMAT = 'Hardcover');

      ISBN PRINT_DAT     PAGES LIST_PRICE FORMAT
---------- ---------- ---------- ---------- -------------------------------
 345438353                 256         12 Paperback
 345336275 31-JUL-86       285        6.5
 246118318 28-APR-83       234       9.44 Hardcover
```

Sorting with the ORDER BY Clause

Sorting records in a query requires use of the ORDER BY clause, whose syntax is as follows:

```
SELECT ...
FROM table [alias] [, ... ]
[ WHERE ... ]
[ ORDER BY { field | expression [ASC| DESC] [ , ... ] } ];
```

The ORDER BY *clause is optional.*

Sorting with the ORDER BY clause allows resorting into an order other than the natural physical order that records were originally added into a table. This example sorts by AUTHOR_ID, contained within the name of the author (the NAME field):

```
SELECT * FROM AUTHOR ORDER BY NAME, AUTHOR_ID;

AUTHOR_ID NAME
---------- --------------------
        3 Isaac Azimov
        2 James Blish
        5 Jerry Pournelle
        7 Kurt Vonnegut
        4 Larry Niven
        1 Orson Scott Card
        6 William Shakespeare
```

> **Some queries, depending on data retrieved, whether tables or indexes are read, which clause are used — can be sorted without use of the** ORDER BY **clause. It is rare but it is possible. Using the** ORDER BY **clause in all situations can be inefficient.**

Different databases allow different formats for ORDER BY clause syntax. Some formats are more restrictive than others.

Aggregating with the GROUP BY Clause

An aggregated query uses the GROUP BY clause to summarize repeating groups of records into aggregations of those groups. The following syntax adds the syntax for the GROUP BY clause:

```
SELECT ...
FROM table [alias] [, ... ]
 [ WHERE ... ]
[ GROUP BY expression [, ... ] [ HAVING condition ] ]
[ ORDER BY ... ];
```

The GROUP BY *clause is optional.*

Some databases allow special expansions to the GROUP BY *clause, allowing creation of rollup and cubic query output, even to the point of creating highly complex spreadsheet or On-Line Analytical process (OLAP) type analytical output rollups create rollup totals, such as subtotals for each grouping in a nested groups query. Cubic output allows for reporting such as cross-tabbing and similar cross sections of data. Lookup OLAP, rollup and cubic data on the Internet for more information. OLAP is an immense topic in itself and detailed explanation does not belong in this book.*

> Note the sequence of the different clauses in the previous syntax. The WHERE clause is always executed first, and the ORDER BY clause is always executed last. It follows that the GROUP BY clause always appears after a WHERE clause, and always before an ORDER BY clause.

A simple application of the GROUP BY clause is to create a summary, as in the following example, creating an average price for all editions, printed by each publisher:

```
SELECT P.NAME AS PUBLISHER, AVG(E.LIST_PRICE)
FROM PUBLISHER P JOIN EDITION E USING (PUBLISHER_ID)
GROUP BY P.NAME;

PUBLISHER                        AVG(E.LIST_PRICE)
-------------------------------- -----------------
Ballantine Books                        8.49666667
Bantam Books                                   7.5
Books on Tape                                29.97
Del Rey Books                                 6.99
Fawcett Books                                 6.99
HarperCollins Publishers                      9.44
L P Books                                     7.49
Overlook Press                                34.5
Oxford University Press                      39.95
Spectra                                        7.5
```

In this example, an average price is returned for each publisher. Individual editions of books are summarized into each average, for each publisher; therefore, individual editions of each book are not returned as separate records because they are summarized into the averages.

The next example selects only the averages for publishers, where that average is greater than 10:

```
SELECT P.NAME AS PUBLISHER, AVG(E.LIST_PRICE)
FROM PUBLISHER P JOIN EDITION E USING (PUBLISHER_ID)
GROUP BY P.NAME
HAVING AVG(E.LIST_PRICE) > 10;

PUBLISHER                        AVG(E.LIST_PRICE)
-------------------------------- -----------------
Books on Tape                                29.97
Overlook Press                                34.5
Oxford University Press                      39.95
```

The AS clause in the preceding query renames a field in a query.

The above example filters out aggregated records.

A common programming error is to get the purpose of the WHERE and HAVING clause filters mixed up. The WHERE clause filters records as they are read (as I/O activity takes place) from the database. The HAVING clause filters aggregated groups, after all database I/O activity has completed. Don't use the HAVING clause when the WHERE clause should be used, and visa versa.

Join Queries

A *join query* is a query retrieving records from more than one table. Records from different tables are usually joined on related key field values. The most efficient and effective forms of join are those between directly related primary and foreign key fields. There are a number of different types of joins:

❑ *Inner Join* — An intersection between two tables using matching field values, returning records common to both tables only. Inner join syntax is as follows:

```
SELECT ...
FROM table [alias] [, ... ]
[
   INNER JOIN table [alias]
[
     USING (field [, ... ])
   | ON (field = field [{AND | OR} [NOT] [ ... ])
   ]
]
[ WHERE ... ] [ GROUP BY ... ] [ ORDER BY ... ];
```

The following query is an inner join because it finds all publishers and related published editions. The two tables are linked based on the established primary key to foreign key relationship. The primary key is in the PUBLISHER table on the one side of the one-to-many relationship, between the PUBLISHER and EDITION tables. The foreign key is precisely where it should be, on the "many" side of the one-to-many relationship.

```
SELECT P.NAME AS PUBLISHER, E.ISBN
FROM PUBLISHER P JOIN EDITION E USING (PUBLISHER_ID);

PUBLISHER                            ISBN
----------------------------------   ----------
Overlook Press                       1585670081
Ballantine Books                      345333926
Ballantine Books                      345336275
Ballantine Books                      345438353
Bantam Books                          553293362
Spectra                               553278398
Spectra                               553293370
Spectra                               553293389
Oxford University Press               198711905
L P Books                             893402095
Del Rey Books                         345308999
Del Rey Books                         345334787
Del Rey Books                         345323440
Books on Tape                        5553673224
Books on Tape                        5557076654
```

```
HarperCollins Publishers          246118318
Fawcett Books                     449208133
```

❑ *Cross join* — This is also known mathematically as a *Cartesian product*. A cross join merges all records in one table with all records in another table, regardless of any matching values. Cross join syntax is as follows:

```
SELECT ...
FROM table [alias] [, ... ]
[ CROSS JOIN table [alias] ]
[ WHERE ... ] [ GROUP BY ... ] [ ORDER BY ... ];
```

A cross-join simply joins two tables regardless of any relationship. The result is a query where each record in the first table is joined to each record in the second table (a little like a merge):

```
SELECT P.NAME AS PUBLISHER, E.ISBN
FROM PUBLISHER P CROSS JOIN EDITION E;

PUBLISHER                              ISBN
------------------------------    ----------
Overlook Press                     198711905
Overlook Press                     246118318
Overlook Press                     345308999
Overlook Press                    1585670081
Overlook Press                    5553673224
Overlook Press                    5557076654
Overlook Press                    9999999999
...
Ballantine Books                   198711905
Ballantine Books                   246118318
Ballantine Books                   345308999
...
```

The previous record output has been edited. Some Overlook Press records have been removed, as well as all records returned after the last Ballantine Books record shown.

❑ *Outer join* — Returns records from two tables as with an inner join, including both the intersection between the two tables, plus records in one table that are not in the other. Any missing values are typically replaced with NULL values. Outer joins can be of three forms:

   ❑ *Left outer join* — All records from the left side table plus the intersection of the two tables. Values missing from the right side table are replaced with NULL values. Left outer join syntax is as follows:

```
SELECT ...
FROM table [alias] [, ... ]
[
  LEFT OUTER JOIN table [alias]
  [
    USING (field [, ... ])
  | ON (field = field [{AND | OR} [NOT] [ ... ])
  ]
]
[ WHERE ... ] [ GROUP BY ... ] [ ORDER BY ... ];
```

This query finds the intersection between publishers and editions, plus all publishers currently with no titles in print:

```
SELECT P.NAME AS PUBLISHER, E.ISBN
FROM PUBLISHER P LEFT OUTER JOIN EDITION E USING (PUBLISHER_ID);


PUBLISHER                           ISBN
------------------------------ ----------
Overlook Press                  1585670081
Ballantine Books                 345333926
Ballantine Books                 345336275
Ballantine Books                 345438353
Bantam Books                     553293362
Spectra                          553278398
Spectra                          553293370
Spectra                          553293389
Oxford University Press          198711905
Bt Bound
L P Books                        893402095
Del Rey Books                    345308999
Del Rey Books                    345334787
Del Rey Books                    345323440
Books on Tape                   5553673224
Books on Tape                   5557076654
HarperCollins Publishers         246118318
Fawcett Books                    449208133
Berkley Publishing Group
```

In this example, any publishers with no titles currently in print have NULL valued ISBN numbers.

❑ *Right outer join* — All records from the right side table plus the intersection of the two tables. Values missing from the left side table are replaced with NULL values. Right outer join syntax is as follows:

```
SELECT ...
FROM table [alias] [, ... ]
[
  RIGHT OUTER JOIN table [alias]
  [
    USING (field [, ... ])
  | ON (field = field [{AND | OR} [NOT] [ ... ])
  ]
]
[ WHERE ... ] [ GROUP BY ... ] [ ORDER BY ... ];
```

Now, find the intersection between publishers and editions, plus all self-published titles (no publisher):

```
SELECT P.NAME AS PUBLISHER, E.ISBN
FROM PUBLISHER P RIGHT OUTER JOIN EDITION E USING (PUBLISHER_ID);


PUBLISHER                           ISBN
------------------------------ ----------
Overlook Press                  1585670081
Ballantine Books                 345333926
Ballantine Books                 345336275
Ballantine Books                 345438353
```

```
Bantam Books                        553293362
Spectra                             553278398
Spectra                             553293389
Spectra                             553293370
Oxford University Press             198711905
L P Books                          893402095
Del Rey Books                      345323440
Del Rey Books                      345334787
Del Rey Books                      345308999
Books on Tape                     5553673224
Books on Tape                     5557076654
HarperCollins Publishers           246118318
Fawcett Books                      449208133
                                  9999999999
```

In this example, books without a publisher would have NULL valued publishing house entries.

❑ *Full outer join* — The intersection plus all records from the right side table not in the left side table, in addition to all records from the left side table not in the right side table. Full outer join syntax is as follows:

```
SELECT ...
FROM table [alias] [, ... ]
[
  FULL OUTER JOIN table [alias]
  [
    USING (field [, ... ])
  | ON (field = field [{AND | OR} [NOT] [ ... ])
  ]
]
[ WHERE ... ] [ GROUP BY ... ] [ ORDER BY ... ];
```

This query finds the full outer join, effectively both the left and the right outer joins at the same time:

```
SELECT P.NAME AS PUBLISHER, E.ISBN
FROM PUBLISHER P FULL OUTER JOIN EDITION E USING (PUBLISHER_ID);

PUBLISHER                              ISBN
--------------------------------  ----------
Overlook Press                    1585670081
Ballantine Books                   345333926
Ballantine Books                   345336275
Ballantine Books                   345438353
Bantam Books                       553293362
Spectra                            553278398
Spectra                            553293370
Spectra                            553293389
Oxford University Press            198711905
Bt Bound
L P Books                          893402095
Del Rey Books                      345308999
Del Rey Books                      345334787
Del Rey Books                      345323440
Books on Tape                     5553673224
```

```
Books on Tape               5557076654
HarperCollins Publishers     246118318
Fawcett Books                449208133
Berkley Publishing Group

                             9999999999
```

In this example, missing entries of both publishers and editions are replaced with NULL values.

❑ *Self Join* — A self join simply joins a table to itself, and is commonly used with a table containing a hierarchy of records (a denormalized one-to-many relationship). A self join does not require any explicit syntax other than including the same table in the FROM clause twice, as in the following example:

```
SELECT P.NAME AS PARENT, C.NAME
FROM SUBJECT P JOIN SUBJECT C ON (C.PARENT_ID = P.SUBJECT_ID);

PARENT              NAME
----------------    ----------------------
Non-Fiction         Self Help
Non-Fiction         Esoteric
Non-Fiction         Metaphysics
Non-Fiction         Computers
Fiction             Science Fiction
Fiction             Fantasy
Fiction             Drama
Fiction             Whodunnit
Fiction             Suspense
Fiction             Literature
Literature          Poetry
Literature          Victorian
Literature          Shakespearian
Literature          Modern American
Literature          19th Century American
```

Nested Queries

A *nested query* is a query containing other subqueries or queries contained within other queries. It is important to note that use of the term "nested" means that a query can be nested within a query, within a query, and so on — more or less *ad infinitum*, or as much as your patience and willingness to deal with complexity allows. Some databases use the IN set operator to nest one query within another, where one value is checked for membership in a list of values. The following query finds all authors, where each author has a publication, each publication has an edition, and each edition has a publisher:

```
SELECT * FROM AUTHOR WHERE AUTHOR_ID IN
  (SELECT AUTHOR_ID FROM PUBLICATION WHERE PUBLICATION_ID IN
   (SELECT PUBLICATION_ID FROM EDITION WHERE PUBLISHER_ID IN
      (SELECT PUBLISHER_ID FROM PUBLISHER)));

AUTHOR_ID NAME
---------- --------------------
        2 James Blish
        3 Isaac Azimov
        4 Larry Niven
        6 William Shakespeare
```

Some databases also allow use of the EXISTS keyword. The EXISTS keyword returns a Boolean True result if the result is positive (it exists), or False otherwise. Where the IN operator includes expressions on both sides, the EXISTS operator has an expression only on the right side of the comparison. The next query finds all authors where the author exists as a foreign key AUTHOR_ID value in the PUBLISHER table:

```
SELECT * FROM AUTHOR WHERE EXISTS
  (SELECT AUTHOR_ID FROM PUBLICATION);

AUTHOR_ID NAME
---------- --------------------
        1 Orson Scott Card
        2 James Blish
        3 Isaac Azimov
        4 Larry Niven
        5 Jerry Pournelle
        6 William Shakespeare
        7 Kurt Vonnegut
```

It is often also possible to pass a cross checking or correlation value into a subquery, such as in the following case using EXISTS. The query is a slightly more complex variation on the previous one where the AUTHOR_ID value, for each record found in the AUTHOR table, is passed to the subquery, and used by the subquery, to match with a PUBLISHER record:

A correlation between a calling query and a subquery is a link where variables in calling query and subquery are expected to contain the same values. The correlation link is usually a primary key to foreign key link — but it doesn't have to be.

```
SELECT * FROM AUTHOR WHERE EXISTS
  (SELECT AUTHOR_ID FROM PUBLICATION WHERE AUTHOR_ID = AUTHOR.AUTHOR_ID);

AUTHOR_ID NAME
---------- --------------------
        2 James Blish
        3 Isaac Azimov
        4 Larry Niven
        6 William Shakespeare
        7 Kurt Vonnegut
```

Sometimes a correlation can be established between the calling query and subquery, using the IN operator as well as the EXISTS operator, although this is not as common. The next query is almost identical to the previous query, except that it uses the IN operator:

```
SELECT * FROM AUTHOR WHERE AUTHOR_ID IN
  (SELECT AUTHOR_ID FROM PUBLICATION WHERE AUTHOR_ID = AUTHOR.AUTHOR_ID);

AUTHOR_ID NAME
---------- --------------------
        2 James Blish
        3 Isaac Azimov
        4 Larry Niven
        6 William Shakespeare
        7 Kurt Vonnegut
```

Subqueries can produce single scalar values. In this query, the subquery passes the AUTHOR_ID value for the filtered author, back to the query on the PUBLICATION table — it passes a single AUTHOR_ID value (a single value is a scalar value):

```
SELECT AUTHOR_ID, TITLE FROM PUBLICATION WHERE AUTHOR_ID =
  (SELECT AUTHOR_ID FROM AUTHOR WHERE NAME = 'James Blish');


AUTHOR_ID TITLE
---------- ---------------------------
        2 Cities in Flight
```

The DISTINCT clause is used to return only the unique records in a set of returned records.

> **Traditionally, the IN set membership operator is regarded as more efficient when testing against a list of literal values. The EXISTS set membership operator is regarded a being better than IN when checking against a subquery, in particular a correlated subquery. A correlated subquery creates a semi-join between the calling query and the subquery, by passing a key value from calling to subquery, allowing a join between calling query and subquery. This may not be true for all relational databases. A semi-join is called a semi-join because it effectively joins two tables but does not necessarily return any field values to the calling query, for return to the user, by the calling query.**

Subqueries can also produce and be verified as multiple fields (this query returns no records):

```
SELECT * FROM COAUTHOR WHERE (COAUTHOR_ID, PUBLICATION_ID) IN
  (SELECT A.AUTHOR_ID, P.PUBLICATION_ID
   FROM AUTHOR A JOIN PUBLICATION P
     ON (P.AUTHOR_ID = A.AUTHOR_ID));
```

The ON clause in join syntax allows specification of two fields from different tables to join on. The ON clause is used when join fields in the two joined tables have different names, or in this case, when the complexity of the query, and use of aliases, forces explicit join field specification.

Composite Queries

Set merge operators can be used to combine two separate queries into a merged *composite query*. Both queries must have the same data types for each field, all in the same sequence. The term *set merge* implies a merge or sticking together of two separate sets of data. In the case of the following query, all records from two different tables are merged into a single set of records:

```
SELECT AUTHOR_ID AS ID, NAME FROM AUTHOR
UNION
SELECT PUBLISHER_ID AS ID, NAME FROM PUBLISHER;


ID NAME
---------- ------------------------------
        1 Orson Scott Card
        1 Overlook Press
        2 Ballantine Books
```

```
    2 James Blish
    3 Bantam Books
    3 Isaac Azimov
    4 Larry Niven
    4 Spectra
    5 Jerry Pournelle
    5 Oxford University Press
    6 Bt Bound
    6 William Shakespeare
    7 Kurt Vonnegut
    7 L P Books
    8 Del Rey Books
    9 Books on Tape
   10 HarperCollins Publishers
   11 Fawcett Books
   12 Berkley Publishing Group
   41 Gavin Powell
```

Changing Data in a Database

Changes to a database can be performed using the INSERT, UPDATE, and DELETE commands. Some database have variations on these commands, such as multiple table INSERT commands, MERGE commands to merge current and historical records, among others. These other types of commands are far too advanced for this book.

The INSERT command allows additions to tables in a database. Its syntax is generally as follows:

```
INSERT INTO table [ ( field [, ... ] ) ] VALUES ( expression [ , ... ] );
```

The UPDATE command has the following syntax. The WHERE clause allows targeting of one or more records:

```
UPDATE table SET field = expression [, ... ] [ WHERE ... ];
```

The DELETE command is similar in syntax to the UPDATE command. Again the WHERE clause allows targeting of one or more records for deletion from a table:

```
DELETE FROM table [ WHERE ... ];
```

Understanding Transactions

In a relational database, a *transaction* allows you to temporarily store changes. At a later point, you can choose to store the changes permanently using a COMMIT command. Or, you can completely remove all changes you have made since the last COMMIT command, by using a ROLLBACK command. It is that simple!

You can execute multiple database change commands, storing the changes to the database, localized for your connected session (no other connected users can see your changes until you commit them using the COMMIT command). If you were to execute a ROLLBACK command, rather than a COMMIT command, all new records would be removed from the database. For example, in the following script, the first two new authors are added to the AUTHOR table (they are committed), and the third author is not added (it is rolled back):

```
INSERT INTO AUTHOR(AUTHOR_ID, NAME) VALUES(100, 'Jim Jones');
INSERT INTO AUTHOR(AUTHOR_ID, NAME) VALUES(100, 'Jack Smith');
COMMIT;
INSERT INTO AUTHOR(AUTHOR_ID, NAME) VALUES(100, 'Jenny Brown');
ROLLBACK;
```

Blocks of commands can be executed within a single transaction, where all commands can be committed at once (by a single COMMIT command), or removed from the database at once (by a single ROLLBACK command). The following script introduces the concept of a block of code in a database. Blocks are used to compartmentalize sections of code, not only for the purposes of transaction control (controlling how transactions are executed) but also to create blocks of independently executable code, such as for stored procedures.

```
BEGIN
  INSERT INTO AUTHOR(AUTHOR_ID, NAME) VALUES(100, 'Jim Jones');
  INSERT INTO AUTHOR(AUTHOR_ID, NAME) VALUES(100, 'Jack Smith');
  INSERT INTO AUTHOR(AUTHOR_ID, NAME) VALUES(100, 'Jenny Brown');
  COMMIT;
TRAP ERROR
  ROLLBACK;
END;
```

> The preceding script includes an *error trap*. The error trap is active for all commands between the BEGIN and END commands. Any error occurring between the BEGIN and END commands reroutes execution to the TRAP ERROR section, executing the ROLL-BACK command, instead of the COMMIT command. The error trap section aborts the entire block of code, aborting any changes made so far. Any of the INSERT commands can trigger the error trap condition, if an error occurs.

Changing Database Metadata

Database objects such as tables define how data is stored in a database; therefore, database objects are known as *metadata*, which is the data about the data. In general, all databases include CREATE, ALTER, and DROP commands for all object types, with some exceptions. Exceptions are usually related to the nature of the object type, which is, of course, beside the point for this book. The intention in this chapter is to keep everything simple because SQL is not the focus of this book. Relational database modeling is the focus of this book.

The following command creates the AUTHOR table:

```
CREATE TABLE AUTHOR(
        AUTHOR_ID INTEGER NULL,
        NAME VARCHAR(32) NULL);
```

Use the ALTER TABLE command to set the AUTHOR_ID field as non-nullable:

```
ALTER TABLE AUTHOR MODIFY(AUTHOR_ID NOT NULL);
```

Use the DROP TABLE and CREATE TABLE commands to recreate the AUTHOR table with two constraints:

```
DROP TABLE AUTHOR;
CREATE TABLE AUTHOR (
        AUTHOR_ID INTEGER PRIMARY KEY NOT NULL,
        NAME VARCHAR(32) UNIQUE NOT NULL);
```

This CREATE TABLE command creates the PUBLICATION table, including a foreign key (REFERENCES AUTHOR), pointing back to the primary key field on the AUTHOR table:

```
CREATE TABLE PUBLICATION(
        PUBLICATION_ID INTEGER PRIMARY KEY NOT NULL,
        AUTHOR_ID INTEGER REFERENCES AUTHOR NOT NULL,
        TITLE VARCHAR(64) UNIQUE NOT NULL);
```

A relational database should automatically create an index for a primary key and a unique key field. The reason is simple to understand. When adding a new record, a primary key or unique key must be checked for uniqueness. What better way to maintain unique key values than an index? However, foreign key fields by their very nature can be both NULL valued and duplicated in a child table. Duplicates can occur because, in its most simple form, a foreign key field is usually on the "many" side of a one-to-many relationship. In other words, there are potentially many different publications for each author. Many authors often write more than one book. Additionally, a foreign key value could potentially be NULL valued. An author does not necessarily have to have any publications, currently in print. Creating an index on a foreign key field is not automatically controlled by a relational database. If an index is required for a foreign key field, that index should be manually created:

```
CREATE INDEX XFK_PUBLICATION_AUTHOR ON PUBLICATION (AUTHOR_ID);
```

Indexes can also be altered and dropped using the ALTER INDEX and DROP INDEX commands, respectively.

In general, database metadata change commands are a lot more comprehensive than just creating, altering, and dropping simple tables and indexes. Then again, it is not necessary to bombard you with too much scripting in this book.

Try It Out   Creating Tables and Constraints

Figure 5-1 shows the tables of the online bookstore database model. Create all tables, including primary and foreign key constraints:

1. It is important to create the table in the correct sequence because some tables depend on the existence of others.

2. The PUBLISHER, AUTHOR, and SUBJECT tables can be created first because they are at the top of dependency hierarchies.

3. Next, create the PUBLICATION table.

4. Then create the EDITION, REVIEW, and COAUTHOR tables.

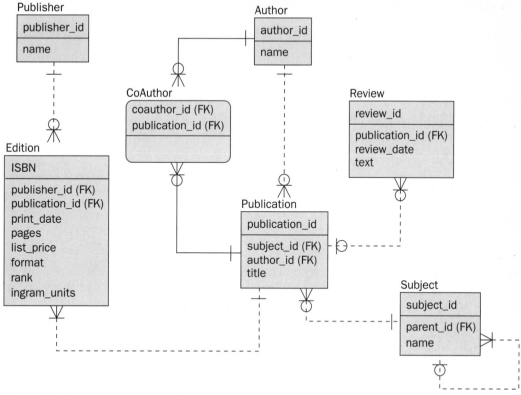

Figure 5-1: The online bookstore relational database model.

How It Works

Create tables as follows:

1. Create the PUBLISHER, AUTHOR, and SUBJECT tables:

```
CREATE TABLE PUBLISHER(
  PUBLISHER_ID INTEGER PRIMARY KEY NOT NULL,
  NAME VARCHAR(32) UNIQUE NOT NULL);

CREATE TABLE AUTHOR(
  AUTHOR_ID INTEGER PRIMARY KEY NOT NULL,
  NAME VARCHAR(32) UNIQUE NOT NULL);

CREATE TABLE SUBJECT(
  SUBJECT_ID INTEGER PRIMARY KEY NOT NULL,
  PARENT_ID INTEGER REFERENCES SUBJECT NULL,
  NAME VARCHAR(32) UNIQUE NOT NULL);
```

2. Create the PUBLICATION table (indexes can be created on foreign key fields):

```
CREATE TABLE PUBLICATION(
  PUBLICATION_ID INTEGER PRIMARY KEY NOT NULL,
  SUBJECT_ID INTEGER REFERENCES SUBJECT NOT NULL,
```

```
    AUTHOR_ID INTEGER REFERENCES AUTHOR NOT NULL,
    TITLE VARCHAR(64) UNIQUE NOT NULL);

CREATE INDEX XFK_P_AUTHOR ON PUBLICATION(AUTHOR_ID);
CREATE INDEX XFK_P_PUBLISHER ON PUBLICATION(SUBJECT_ID);
```

3.   Create the EDITION, REVIEW, and COAUTHOR tables (indexes can be created on foreign key fields):

```
CREATE TABLE EDITION(
   ISBN INTEGER PRIMARY KEY NOT NULL,
   PUBLISHER_ID INTEGER REFERENCES PUBLISHER NOT NULL,
   PUBLICATION_ID INTEGER REFERENCES PUBLICATION NOT NULL,
   PRINT_DATE DATE NULL,
   PAGES INTEGER NULL,
   LIST_PRICE INTEGER NULL,
   FORMAT VARCHAR(32) NULL,
   RANK INTEGER NULL,
   INGRAM_UNITS INTEGER NULL);

CREATE INDEX XFK_E_PUBLICATION ON EDITION(PUBLICATION_ID);
CREATE INDEX XFK_E_PUBLISHER ON EDITION(PUBLISHER_ID);

CREATE TABLE REVIEW(
   REVIEW_ID INTEGER PRIMARY KEY NOT NULL,
   PUBLICATION_ID INTEGER REFERENCES PUBLICATION NOT NULL,
   REVIEW_DATE DATE NOT NULL,
   TEXT VARCHAR(4000) NULL);

CREATE TABLE COAUTHOR(
   COAUTHOR_ID INTEGER REFERENCES AUTHOR NOT NULL,
   PUBLICATION_ID INTEGER REFERENCES PUBLICATION NOT NULL);
   CONSTRAINT PRIMARY KEY (COAUTHOR_ID, PUBLICATION_ID);

CREATE INDEX XFK_CA_PUBLICATION ON COAUTHOR(COAUTHOR_ID);
CREATE INDEX XFK_CA_AUTHOR ON COAUTHOR(PUBLICATION_ID);
```

Summary

In this chapter, you learned about:

❑   What SQL is, why it is used, and how and why it originated

❑   SQL is a reporting language for relational databases

❑   SQL is primarily designed to retrieve sets or groups of related records

❑   SQL was not originally intended for retrieving unique records but does this fairly well in modern relational databases

❏ There are many different types of queries used for extracting and presenting information to the user in different ways

❏ There are three specific commands (INSERT, UPDATE, and DELETE) used for changing records in tables

❏ Tables and indexes can themselves be changed using table and index database metadata changing commands

❏ There are some simple ways of building better written, more maintainable, and faster performing SQL code commands

Above all, this chapter has shown how the relational database model is used from an application perspective. There is little point in understanding something such as relational database modeling without seeing it applied in some way, no matter how simple.

The next chapter returns to the topic of relational database modeling by presenting some advanced relational database modeling techniques.

Exercises

Use the ERD in Figure 5-1 to help you answer these questions.

1. Find all records and fields in the EDITION table.

2. Find all ISBN values in the EDITION table, for all FORMAT='Hardcover' books.

3. Do the same query, but sort records by LIST_PRICE contained within FORMAT.

4. Which of the two expressions 3 + 4 * 5, and (3 + 4) * 5 yields the greater value?

5. Find the sum of all LIST_PRICE values in the EDITION table, for each publisher.

6. Join the SUBJECT and PUBLICATION tables on the SUBJECT_ID field, as an intersection.

7. Find the intersection of subjects and publications, where subjects do not necessarily have to have publications.

8. Find subjects with publications, using a semi-join, in two different ways.

Advanced Relational Database Modeling

"A computer lets you make more mistakes faster than any invention in human history — with the possible exceptions of hand guns and tequila." (Mitch Ratliffe)

Acts of overzealousness in application of normalization techniques can sometimes be partially rectified by using denormalization, aspects of the object-relational database model, and maybe even a data warehouse.

Remember your first job? The first thing your new boss said to you might have been something of this nature. "Forget everything you learned in college. Here we do what's necessary to get the job done. Sometimes we have to break the rules."

This chapter expands on the concepts of relational database modeling, normalization, and Normal Forms. This chapter introduces denormalization, the object database model, and data warehousing. These topics are all related to normalization in one way or another.

Understanding how to build normalized table structures is all well and good; however, without knowledge of how to undo those granular structures through denormalization, you will not be able to understand other essential topics of database modeling, such as data warehousing.

This chapter bridges the gap between creating properly normalized table structures, and ultimately creating adequately performing table structures. Good performance services applications in a usable manner. Usability is all important. Modern-day applications are often built using object-oriented SDKs; therefore, this chapter includes a brief introduction to object modeling theory. Additionally, data warehouses are essential to maintaining performance of active OLTP databases, to providing good projections and forecasting facilities for end-users. An introduction to data warehousing is included here as a primer for further detail later on in this book.

In this chapter, you learn about the following:

- ❑ Denormalization
- ❑ Denormalization by reversing of Normal Forms
- ❑ Denormalization using specialized database objects

❑   The object database model

❑   The data warehouse database model

Let's begin this chapter by examining the topic of denormalization.

Understanding Denormalization

Denormalization is often (but not always) the opposite of normalization. (See Chapter 4 for a discussion of normalization.) Denormalization can be applied to a database model to create data warehouse or reporting only type tables. Denormalization is also sometimes required as a solution to reviving dying OLTP applications that exhibit dreadful performance. This can be a result of past profligate use of normalization in the development of database models and applications. Too much granularity in normalization can cause as many problems as it solves. So, denormalization often attempts to reverse granularity, created by over-application of Normal Forms during the normalization process.

Reversing Normal Forms

Denormalization is often a reversal of the processing performed by normalization; therefore, it is essential when describing denormalization to understand the steps (Normal Forms) contained within normalization. Take a look at the definitions of normalization once again, as a reminder:

❑   *1st Normal Form (1NF)* — Remove repeating fields by creating a new table. The original and new tables are linked together with a master-detail, one-to-many relationship. Also create primary keys on both tables. 1NF does not require definition of the detail table primary key, but so what? The detail table has a composite primary key containing the master table primary key field, as the prefix field of its primary key. That prefix field is also a foreign key back to the master table.

❑   *2nd Normal Form (2NF)* — Perform a seemingly similar function to that of 1NF; however, create a table where repeating values rather than repeating fields are removed to a new table. The result is a many-to-one relationship, rather than a one-to-many relationship as for 1NF, created between the original and the new tables. The new table gets a primary key consisting of a single field. The master table contains a foreign key pointing back to the primary key of the new table. That foreign key is not part of the primary key in the original table.

❑   *3rd Normal Form (3NF)* — Eliminate transitive dependencies. A field is transitively dependent on the primary key if it is indirectly determined by the primary key. In other words, the field is functionally dependent on another field, where the other field is dependent on the primary key. In some cases, elimination of a transitive dependency implies creation of a new table for something indirectly dependent on the primary key in an existing table. There are numerous methods of interpreting 3NF.

❑   *Beyond 3rd Normal Form* — Many modern relational database models do not extend beyond 3NF. Sometimes 3NF is not used at all. The reason why is because of the generation of too many tables and the resulting complex SQL code joins, with resulting dreadful database response times. Disk space is cheap and, as already stated, increased numbers of tables leads to bigger SQL joins and poorer performance. The other point to note about Boyce-Codd Normal Form (BCNF), 4th Normal Form (4NF), 5th Normal Form (5NF), and Domain Key Normal Form (DKNF) levels of normalization is that they tend to place a lot of business functionality (business rules) into database tables. This is often unnecessary because modern day application SDKs are more than capable of dealing with this type of complex processing. Let applications do the number crunching and leave the database to storing data, not processing data or applying too many rules to data.

It makes perfect sense to begin by demonstrating denormalization from the highest Normal Form downward.

Denormalizing Beyond 3NF

Figure 6-1 shows reversal of the normalization processing applied in Figure 4-28, Figure 4-29, and Figure 4-30. Removing nullable fields to separate tables is a common method of saving space, particularly in databases with fixed record lengths. Many modern databases allow variable record lengths. If variable length records are allowed, removal of NULL valued fields is pointless because the space saved is either none, or completely negligible.

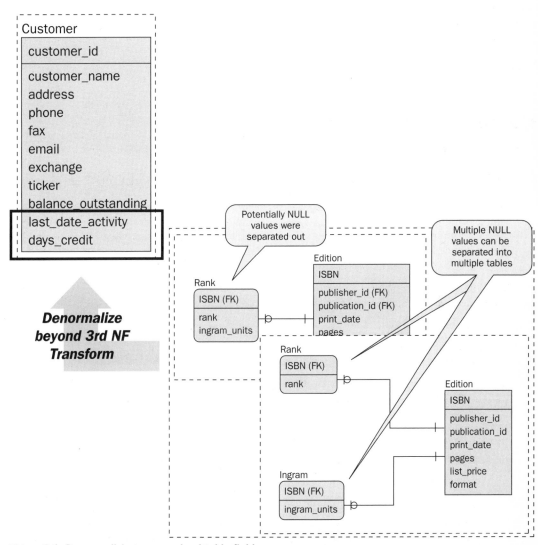

Figure 6-1: Denormalizing NULL valued table fields.

A fixed-length record is where each record always occupies the same number of characters. In other words, all string and number values are a fixed length. For example, a string value of 30 characters, can never be NULL, *but will contain 30 space characters. It follows that a 30-character string with a 10-character name contains the name followed by 20 trailing space characters.*

Figure 6-2 shows reversal of normalization processing applied in Figure 4-31. Figure 6-2 shows a particularly upsetting application of BCNF where all candidate keys are separated into separate tables. A *candidate key* is any field that potentially can be used as a primary key (unique identifier) for the original entity, in this case a customer (the CUSTOMER table). Applying this type of normalization in a commercial environment would result in incredibly poor performance and is more of a mathematical nicety rather than a commercial necessity.

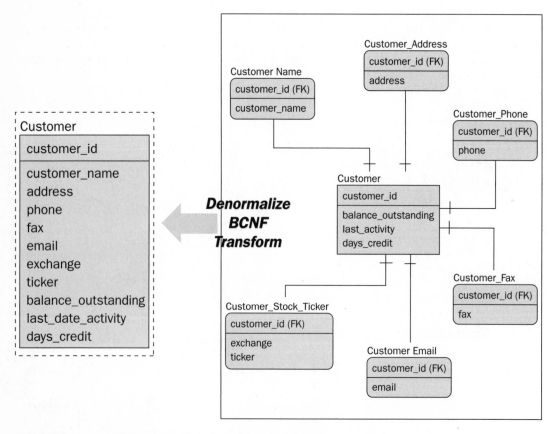

Figure 6-2: Denormalizing separation of candidate keys into separate tables.

Once again Figure 6-3 shows another application of the reversal of BCNF. Application of BCNF in Figure 4-32 and Figure 4-33 created three tables, each with unique combinations of unique values from the PROJECTS table on the left. Accessing of unique records in the PROJECT table can be handled with application coding more effectively, without the downside of creating too much granularity in table structures.

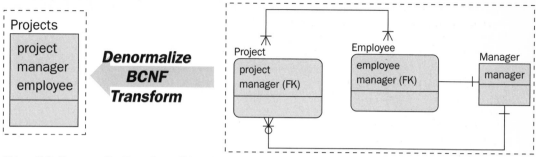

Figure 6-3: Denormalization of candidate keys, created for the sake of uniqueness in tables.

It is interesting to note that the relational database modeling tool, ERWin, would not allow the MANAGER table to have more than the MANAGER field in its primary key. For 5NF, the MANAGER table could contain either the PROJECT or EMPLOYEE field as a subset part of the primary key. ERWin perhaps "thinks" that 5NF in this case is excessive, useless, or invalid.

Figure 4-34, Figure 4-35, Figure 4-36, and Figure 4-38 show a typical 4NF transformation where multiple valued lists in individual fields are separated out into separate tables. This type of denormalization is shown in Figure 6-4.

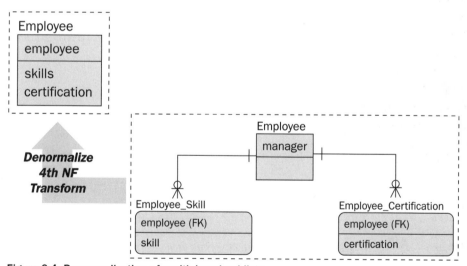

Figure 6-4: Denormalization of multiple valued lists.

The problem with denormalizing the structure shown in Figure 6-4 is that the relationships between EMPLOYEE and SKILL tables, plus EMPLOYEE and CERTIFICATIONS tables, are many-to-many, and not one-to-many. Even in a denormalized state, each EMPLOYEE record must have some kind of collection of SKILLS and CERTIFICATIONS values. A better solution might be a combination of collection arrays in the EMPLOYEE table, and 2NF static tables for skills and certifications as shown in Figure 6-5.

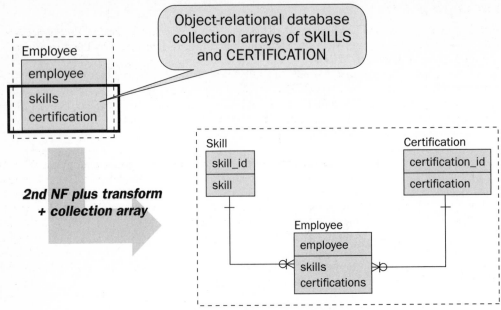

Figure 6-5: Denormalization of multiple valued lists using collections and 2NF.

Figure 4-39 to Figure 4-42 shows a 5NF transformation. As already noted, ERWin does not appear to allow construction of 5NF table structures of this nature. The reason is suspect! Once again, as shown in Figure 6-6, application of this type of normalization is overkill. It is better to place this type of layering into application coding, leaving the EMPLOYEE table as it is, shown in the upper left of the diagram in Figure 6-6.

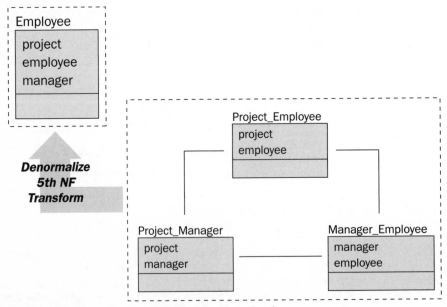

Figure 6-6: Denormalization of 5NF cyclic dependencies.

Denormalizing 3NF

The role of 3NF is to eliminate what are called transitive dependencies. A *transitive dependency* is where a field is not directly determined by the primary key, but indirectly determined by the primary key, through another field.

Most of the Normal Form layers beyond 3NF are often impractical in a commercial environment because applications can often do better at that level. What happens in reality is that 3NF occupies a gray area, fitting in between what should not be done in the database model (beyond 3NF), and what should done in the database model (1NF and 2NF).

There are a number of different ways of interpreting 3NF, as shown in Figure 4-21, Figure 4-23, Figure 4-24, and Figure 4-25. All of these example interpretations of 3NF are completely different. Figure 6-7 shows the denormalization of a many-to-many join resolution table. As a general rule, a many-to-many join resolution table is usually required by applications when it can be specifically named, as for the ASSIGNMENT table shown in Figure 6-7. If it was nonsensical to call the new table ASSIGNMENT, and it was called something such as EMPLOYEE_TASK, chances are that the extra table is unnecessary. Quite often these types of tables are created without forethought as to application requirements. If a table like this is not essential to application requirements, it is probably unnecessary. The result of too many new tables is more tables in joins and slower queries.

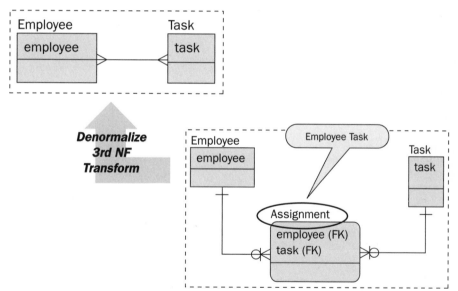

Figure 6-7: Denormalize unnecessary 3NF many-to-many join resolution tables.

Figure 6-8 shows another version of 3NF where common fields are extracted into a new table. Once again, this type of normalization is quite often more for mathematical precision and clarity, and quite contrary to commercial performance requirements. Of course, there is still a transitive dependency in the new FOREIGN_EXCHANGE link table itself, because EXCHANGE_RATE depends on CURRENCY, which in turn depends on CURRENCY_CODE. Normalizing further would complicate something even more than it is already.

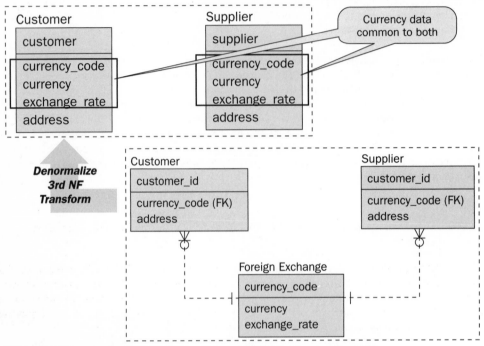

Figure 6-8: Denormalization of 3NF amalgamated fields into an extra table.

Figure 6-9 shows a classic 3NF transitive dependency resolution, or the creation of a new table. The 3NF transformation is providing mathematical precision; however, practical commercial value is dubious because a new table is created, containing potentially a very small number of fields and records. The benefit will very likely be severely outweighed by the loss in performance, as a result of bigger joins in queries.

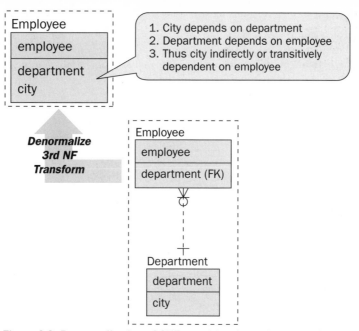

Figure 6-9: Denormalization of 3NF transitive dependence resolution table.

Figure 6-10 shows a 3NF transformation removing a total value of one field on the same table. The value of including the total amount on each record, containing the elements of the expression as well, is determined by how much a total value is used at the application level. If the constituents of the totaling expression are not required, perhaps only the total value should be stored. Again, this is a matter to be decided only from the perspective of application requirements.

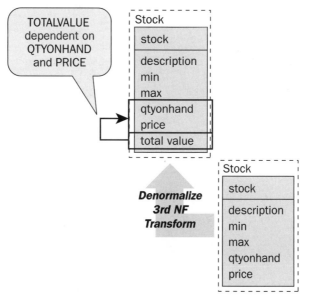

Figure 6-10: Denormalization of 3NF calculated fields.

Denormalizing 2NF

The role of 2NF is to separate static data into separate tables, removing repeated static values from transactional tables. Figure 6-11 shows an example of over-application of 2NF. The lower right of the diagram shows an extreme of four tables, created from what is essentially a more-than-adequately normalized COMPANY table at the upper left of the diagram.

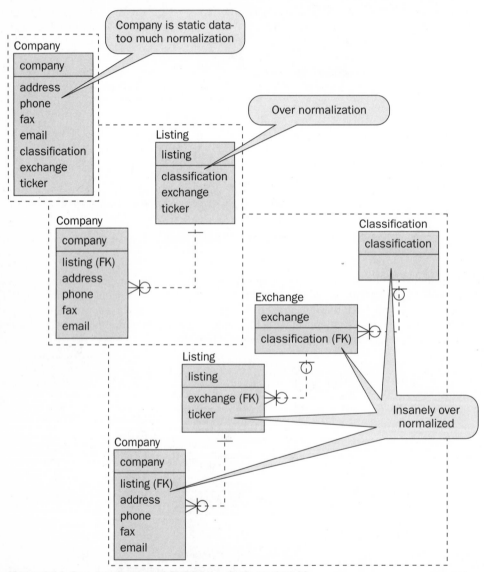

Figure 6-11: Denormalization of 2NF into a single static table.

Denormalizing 1NF

Just don't do it! Data warehouse fact tables can be interpreted as being in 0th Normal Form, but the connections to dimensions are 2NF. So, denormalization of 1NF is not advisable.

Denormalize to 2NF

Figure 6-12 shows a highly normalized table structure representing bands, their released CDs, tracks on the CDs, ranks of tracks, charts the tracks are listed on, plus the genres and regions of the country those charts are located in.

1. The RANK and TRACK tables are one-to-one related (TRACK to RANK: one-to-zero or one). This implies a BCNF or 4NF transformation, zero or one meaning a track does not have to be ranked. Thus, a track's rank can be NULL valued. Push the RANK column back into the TRACK table and remove the RANK table.

2. The three tables BAND_ADDRESS, BAND_PHONE, and BAND_EMAIL were created because of each prospective band attribute being a candidate primary key in itself. Reverse the BCNF transformation, pushing address, phone, and email details back into the BAND table.

3. The CHART, GENRE, and REGION tables are an absurd application of multiple layers of 2NF transformation, separating static information, from what is effectively parent static information. Chart, genre, and region details can all be pushed back into the TRACK table.

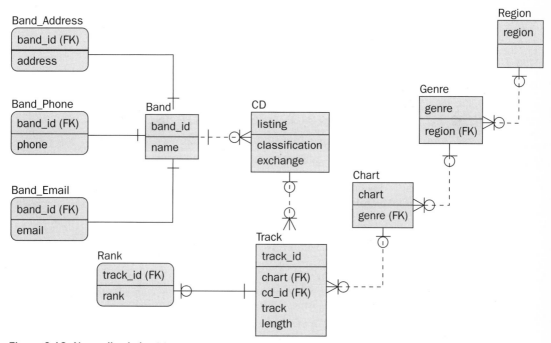

Figure 6-12: Normalized chart toppers.

How It Works

Figure 6-13 shows what the tables should look like in 2NF.

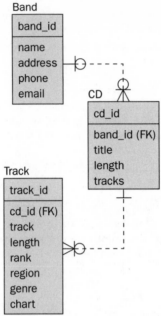

Figure 6-13: Denormalized chart toppers.

Denormalization Using Specialized Database Objects

Many databases have specialized database objects for certain types of tasks. Some specialized objects allow for physical copies of data, copying data into a denormalized form.

❑   *Materialized views* — Materialized views are allowed in many larger relational databases. These objects are commonly used in data warehouses for pre-calculated aggregation queries. Queries can be automatically switched to direct access of materialized views. The result is less I/O activity by direct access to aggregated data stored in materialized views. Typically, aggregated materialized views contain far fewer records than underlying tables, reducing I/O activity and thus increasing performance.

Views are not the same thing as materialized views. Views are overlays and not duplications of data and interfere with underlying source tables. Views often cause far more in the way of performance problems than application design issues they might ease.

❑   *Clusters* — These objects allow physical copies of heavily accessed fields and tables in join queries, allowing for faster access to data with more precise I/O.

❑   *Index-organized tables* — A table can be constructed, including both index and data fields in the same physical space. The table itself becomes both the index and the data because the table is constructed as a sorted index (usually as a BTree index), rather than just a heap or "pile" of unorganized "bits and pieces."

❏ *Temporary tables* — Temporary tables can be used on a temporary basis, either for a connected session or for a period of time. Typically, temporary tables perform intermediary functions, helping to eliminate duplication or processing, and reducing repetitive I/O activities.

Denormalization Tricks

There are many tricks to denormalizing data, not reversals of the steps of normalization. These are some ideas to consider:

❏ *Separate active and inactive data* — Data can be separated into separate physical tables, namely active and inactive tables. This is a factor often missed where inactive (historical) data can occupy sometimes as much as thousands of times more space than active data. This can drastically decrease performance to the most frequently needed data, the active data.

Separation of active and inactive data is the purpose of a data warehouse, the data warehouse being the inactive data.

❏ *Copy fields between tables* — Make copies of fields between tables not directly related to each other. This can help to avoid multiple table joins between two tables where other tables must be "passed through" to join the two desired tables. An example is shown in Figure 6-14 where the SUBJECT_ID field is duplicated into the EDITION table. The objective is to minimize the size of subsequent SQL code joins.

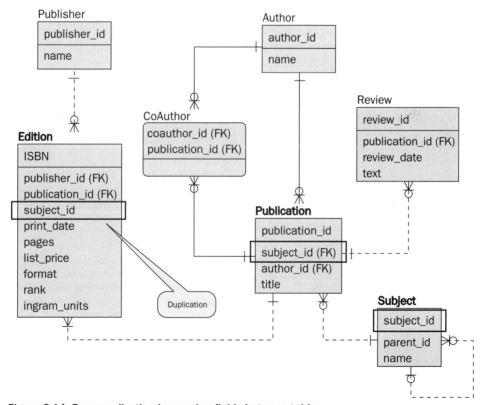

Figure 6-14: Denormalization by copying fields between tables.

❑ *Summary fields in parent tables* — This can help to avoid costly grouping joins, but real-time updates can cause serious problems with hot blocks. Examples are shown in Figure 6-15. Again, the objective is to minimize the size of subsequent SQL code joins, and to provide summary values without having to constantly add all the details, from multiple records in a detail table.

A hot block is a very busy part of the database accessed much too often by many different sessions.

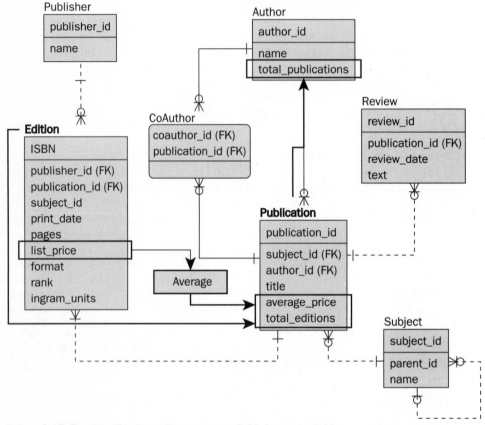

Figure 6-15: Denormalization using summary fields in parent tables.

❑ *Separate heavily and lightly accessed fields* — Much like separating inactive and active data at the table level, tables containing fields with vastly different rates of access can be separated. This avoids continual physical scanning of rarely used data field values, especially when those values do not contain NULLs. This is one potentially sensible use of 4NF in terms of separation of tables into two tables, related by one-to-one relationships.

Understanding the Object Model

Many modern relational databases are, in fact, object-relational databases. An *object-relational database* is by definition a relational database allowing certain object characteristics. To get a good understanding of what an object-relational database is, you must have a basic understanding of the object model.

The object database model is different from the relational model. An object database is more capable at handling complex issues. Following are the parts making up the object model:

❏ *Class* — A class is the equivalent of a table in a relational database.

❏ *Object* — An object is the iteration or copy of a class at run-time, such that multiple object instances can be created from a class.

The computer jargon term for the creation of an object from a class is instantiation or to instantiate.

❏ *Attribute* — An attribute is the equivalent of a relational database field.

❏ *Method* — A method is equivalent to a relational database stored procedure, except that it executes on the data contents of an object, within the bounds of that object.

In the relational database model, relationships are established using both table structures (metadata) and data values in fields, such as those between primary and foreign key values. On the contrary, in an object database, relationships are established solely through the structure of objects and the metadata relationships between objects, declared by the classes defining those objects. Class collections and inheritance define object database structure. Classes are defined as containing collections of pointers to other classes, as being inherited from other classes above in a hierarchy, or as being abstractions of other classes below in a hierarchy. A class can be specialized and abstracted. A *specialized class* is a specific form of a class, inheriting everything from its parent class, allowing local overriding changes and additions. An *abstracted class* is a generalized or generic form of a class, containing common aspects of inherited classes.

> It is important to reiterate a distinct difference between a class and an object. An object exists at run-time. A class is a metadata structure. Objects are created from classes at run-time. As a result, the structure of classes can often be different from the structure of objects created from a class hierarchy. Object database models are often designed incorrectly because the difference between a class and an object is misunderstood. In general, class structure never looks like an object structure. Class structure is an abstraction of object structure. Additionally, a class structure does not look anything like a relational database model table structure. If it does, you might be attempting to build a relational database structure into an object database model.

Figure 6-16 shows an object database class structure on the left and a relational database entity structure on the right. Note a number of differences:

❏ The object model has no types (SUBJECT). Subjects in the relational model are represented by both parent and child SUBJECT table records. The FICTION and NON-FICTION classes are representative of the SUBJECT.PARENT_ID fields. The SCIFI, ACTION, and FANTASY classes are genres, representing three different fiction type subjects. All of these new classes are specializations of the PUBLICATION class. More specifically, the FICTION and NON-FICTION classes are specializations of the PUBLICATION class. The SCIFI, ACTION, and FANTASY classes are specializations of the FICTION class.

❑ Inheritance is all about types and not collections.

In computer jargon, the undoing of types is known as type casting where one type is made to contain the behavior of another type.

❑ The previous point discussed types and how types are represented by the structure of an object model. Now let's briefly examine collections. The operational relationship between publications and editions is actually one publication containing a collection of many editions (of the same publication). Now, if you consider types, fiction and non-fiction are types of publications, and sci-fi (science fiction), action and fantasy are all specialized types of fiction publications. Editions *multiple inherit* from all publication specialized (inherited) types, including all the fiction types, plus the non-fiction type (non-fiction has no subtypes in this model). Effectively, there is no need for a relationship between publications and editions because it is inherent in the structure. Take note of the little circle on top of the edition class, indicating the many side of a collection.

❑ The relationships between the different classes in the object model are represented in the class structure itself, those relationships being both collection inclusion and inheritance between classes. During run-time, objects instantiated from classes contain objects containing pointers to other contained objects.

❑ An invisible difference is the power of self-contained (black-box) processing using methods in an object database. Relational database stored procedures can perform a similar function to methods, but always inadequately. Method processing can act on each class, within the scope of each class alone.

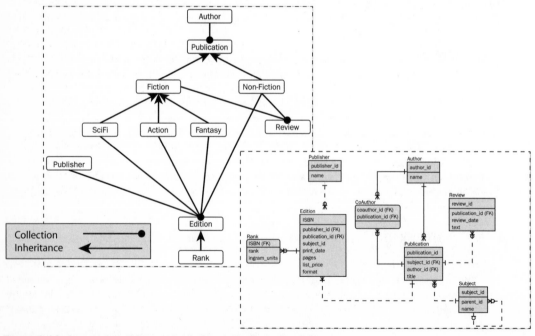

Figure 6-16: Comparing object and relational database models.

The object model and object methodologies are extreme. This section merely touches on it briefly, and is here only to give you a very short introduction to differences between relational and object modeling techniques (types and collections). If you really want to know more about the object model, there are a multitude of available texts.

Introducing the Data Warehouse Database Model

So far, this chapter has examined the topics of denormalization and the object model. The next logical step from these two subjects is the subject of data warehouses.

A data warehouse vaguely combines some of the aspects of the relational model and the object model. The relational model breaks data into mathematically precise, detailed structures. These structures are often difficult for the uninitiated to decipher from a business operational perspective. The object model also breaks everything down, not for the purposes of granularity, but to reduce the complexity of the whole. The process of breaking things into their simplest parts is a conceptual thing.

The result from the point of view of the uninitiated layman is startling, though. Where a relational database model appears cryptic and over-detailed, an object database model starts to look like a real-world picture of data, from the perspective of someone using databases and applications, as opposed to someone building the stuff. This perspective is apparent if you take another brief look at Figure 6-16. The names of structures in the object model (the left side of Figure 6-16) are much clearer than the names of structures in the equivalent relational model (the right side of Figure 6-16). The relational model in Figure 6-16 is abstract and cryptic. The object model, on the other hand, contains a structural break down of data, as an author, publisher, or a book retailer would understand books.

The point is that a data warehouse database model combines some aspects of the relational database model in its application of normalization, and the more easily understandable visual aspects of the object database model. There is a big difference with data warehouses, though, in that they are most effective when severely denormalized. The reason why data warehouse metadata (table) structures look more real-world is essentially as a result of severe denormalization, and has nothing to do with the object database model. The comparison is interesting, though, because it also helps to explain one part of why application SDKs are now largely object-oriented in approach. Objects are easier to understand because they mimic the real world much more closely than the set hierarchical structures of the relational model of data.

So, where does the data warehouse model really fit into the grand scheme of things? The truth is it doesn't. The data warehouse database model is essentially an animal unto itself, with very little relationship to either the relational or the object database models:

❑ *Data warehouses and the relational model* — The relational model is too granular. The relational model introduces granularity by removing duplication. The result is a database model nearly always highly effective for front-end application performance and OLTP databases. OLTP databases involve small amounts of data accessed frequently and concurrently by many users. On the other hand, data warehouses require throughput of huge amounts of data by a small user population. OLTP databases (the relational database model) need lightning-quick response to many people and small chunks of data. Data warehouses perform enormous amounts of I/O activity, over millions (if not billions) of records. It is acceptable for data warehouse reports to take hours to run.

❑ *Data warehouses and the object model* — The object model is even more granular than the relational model, just in a different way, even if it does appear more realistic to the naked eye. Highly granular normalized relations (the relational model), or uniquely autonomous objects (the object model), can cause serious inefficiencies in a data warehouse. Data warehouses perform lots of big queries, with lots of data in many records in many tables. The fewer tables there are in a data warehouse, the better! Query joins on large sets of records can become completely unmanageable and even totally useless.

The heart of the data warehouse database model, different to both the relational and object models, vaguely combines aspects of both relations and objects. A data warehouse database is effectively a highly denormalized structure, consisting of preferably only two distinct hierarchical layers. A central table contains highly denormalized transactional data. The second layer contains referential static data. This data warehouse database model is known as the *dimensional model* or the *fact-dimensional model*.

A data warehouse consists of facts and dimensions. *Facts* and *dimensions* are types of tables. Each data warehouse structure consists of a single fact table, surrounded by multiple dimensions. It is possible to have more than a single fact table but essentially different fact tables are likely to be related to the same set of dimension tables. Therefore, different fact tables represent an entire new set of tables, or a new modular structure. That entire new set of tables is essentially another subset data warehouse, also known as a *data mart*.

The term data mart is used to describe a self-contained, subsection of a data warehouse.

Fact and dimension tables contain different types of data. Where dimensions contain static data, and facts contain transactional data. Transactional data is the record of a company's activities, such as invoices sent to its customers. The dimensions describe the facts, such as the customer's name and address.

For example, an online retailer selling thousands of items per day could ship 20 items to each customer every year. Over the course of a number of years, each customer might be shipped hundreds of separate items.

The detail of a customer (such as the address) is static information. Static information does not change very often. The customer is a dimension. The customer dimension describes the fact, or the transactions (the invoices or details of every item shipped over many years). The active database (OLTP database) would likely have all records of transactions deleted from its active files on a periodical basis (annually, for example). Annual historical data could be archived into a data warehouse. The data warehouse data can then be used for forecasting (making guesses as to what customers might purchase over the next 10 years). The result of all this mishmash of complicated activities and other wonderful stuff is a table structure looking similar to that shown in Figure 6-17. Figure 6-17 shows a pseudo-table structure, describing graphically what is known as a *star schema* (a single fact table surrounded by a group of dimensions). Data warehouse database models are ideally made up of data mart, subset star schemas. Effectively, different schemas are also known as *data marts*. Each data mart is a single *fact table*, all linked to shared dimension tables (not necessarily all the same dimensions, but it is possible). Each fact-dimensional structure is a *star schema* (a data mart). Each star schema is likely to contain data for a different department of a company, or a different region (however a company may decide to split its data).

Some data warehouses are built using 3NF table structures, or even combine normalized structures with fact-dimensional structures in the same database.

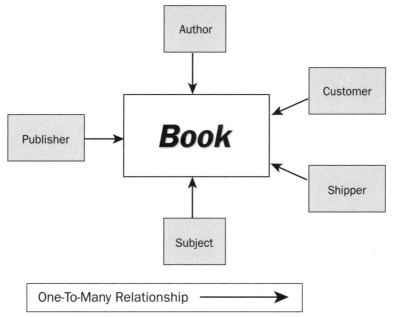

Figure 6-17: A data warehouse database model star schema.

A book can obviously have several authors or a primary author and co-author. This, however, is too much detail for the purposes of the diagram in Figure 6-17.

In Figure 6-17, dimensions are PUBLISHER, AUTHOR, SUBJECT, CUSTOMER, and SHIPPER tables. The single fact table is the BOOK table. A single fact table is surrounded in a star format (star schema) by multiple dimensions. Each dimension is related to the single fact table through a one-to-many relationship.

Summary

In this chapter, you learned about:

- ❑ Denormalization
- ❑ Denormalization using reversal of Normal Forms, from normalization
- ❑ Denormalization using specialized database objects such as materialized views
- ❑ Denormalizing each Normal Form, using the same examples from previous chapters
- ❑ The object database model and its significance
- ❑ The data warehouse database model, and its significance

This chapter has described some advanced database modeling topics, including denormalization, object database modeling, and data warehouse modeling. A brief grasp of object modeling is important to understanding the basics of object-relational databases. Denormalization is essential to understanding not only database performance but also the topic area of data warehousing database modeling. Data warehousing is very important to modern-day databases and is a large topic in itself. The next chapter covers data warehouse database modeling in detail.

Exercises

Use the ERD in Figure 6-12 to help you answer these questions.

1. Create a temporary table called BAND2, joining the four tables BAND, BAND_ADDRESS, BAND_PHONE, and BAND_EMAIL together. Use a CREATE TABLE command. In the same CREATE TABLE command, add the records from the four tables into the new BAND2 temporary table. Some databases allow this; others do not. A database not allowing insertion of records on table creation requires creation of the table, and subsequent population of the new table with INSERT commands, from selected records.

2. Drop the BAND table using a DROP TABLE command and rename the BAND2 table to BAND, using an ALTER TABLE . . . RENAME command. A database not allowing a table rename command would require that the BAND2 table be copied to the BAND table, including data, either included with the CREATE TABLE BAND command, or with INSERT commands. Afterward, the BAND2 temporary table can be dropped using a DROP TABLE command.

Understanding Data Warehouse Database Modeling

"Intuition becomes increasingly valuable in the new information society precisely because there is so much data." (John Naisbitt)

Data warehouses need special treatment and a special type of approach to database modeling, simply because they can get so unmanageably large.

Chapter 6 introduced the data warehouse database model, amongst other advanced relational database modeling techniques. Chapter 6 briefly compared data warehouse modeling relative to both the relational database model, and the object database model. In addition, a brief description covered star schemas. This chapter delves deeply into the details of the database warehouse database model.

Expanding the relational database model to include the data warehouse database model may seem a little obtuse; however, in the modern, computerized, commercial world, there is probably more physical disk space occupied by data warehouse database installations as a whole. Data warehouse databases are usually physically much larger on average. Something larger is generally much more expensive and likely just as important as OLTP databases, if not more so. A bigger database costs more money to build and maintain; therefore, data warehouse data modeling is just as important as relational database modeling for OLTP and transactional databases.

This chapter discusses data warehouse database modeling in detail, preferably without bombarding you with too much complexity all at once. Data warehouse data model design is a semi-normalization approach to relational database model design. Because many existing databases are data warehouses, inclusion of this chapter in this book, at this point, is critical.

In this chapter, you learn about the following:

- ❏ The origin of data warehouses
- ❏ How data warehouses require a specialized database model
- ❏ Star and snowflake schemas
- ❏ Facts and dimensions
- ❏ The fact-dimensional database model
- ❏ How to create a data warehouse database model
- ❏ The contents of a data warehouse database model

The Origin of Data Warehouses

Data warehouses were originally devised because existing databases were being subjected to conflicting requirements. Conflict arose between operational use and decision-support requirements as follows:

- ❏ *Operational use* — Operational use of a database requires a precise, accurate, and instant picture of data in a database. This includes all day-to-day operations in the functional running of a business. When a customer comes through the door, asks for a specific part, for a specific automobile, for a specific year, the part is searched for in a database. After the customer makes the purchase, they are invoiced. When the customer pays, the transaction is processed through bank accounts, and otherwise. All of this is operational-type activity. Response is instantaneous (or as near to instantaneous as possible) and it is all company to customer-direct trading activity. The operations aspect of a company is the heart of its business.

- ❏ *Decision-support use* — Where operational use divides data based on business function, decision-support requires division of database data based on subject matter. Operational use requires access to specific items such as a specific part for a specific automobile, for a specific customer. Decision-support use requirements might be a summary of which parts were ordered on which dates, not necessarily by whom. A decision-support database presents reports, such as all parts in stock, plus all parts ordered, over the period of a whole year. The result could be a projection of when new parts should be ordered. The report allows company employees to cater for restocking of popular items.

There is a big difference between requirements for operational and decision-support databases. Operational systems require instant responses on small amounts of information. Decision-support systems need access to large amounts of data (large portions of a database), allowing for good all-round estimates as to future prospects for a company. The invention of data warehouses was inevitable to reduce conflict between small transactional (OLTP databases) and large historical analytical reporting requirements (data warehouses).

The demands of the modern global economy and the Internet dictate that end user operational applications are required to be active 24/7, 365 days a year. There is no window for any type of batch activity because when people are asleep in Europe, others are awake down under in Australia. The global economy requires instant and acceptable servicing of the needs of a global user population.

In reality, the most significant difference between OLTP databases and data warehouses extends all the way down to the hardware layer. OLTP databases need highly efficient sharing of critical resources such as onboard memory (RAM), and have very small I/O requirements. Data warehouses are completely opposite. Data warehouses can consume large portions of RAM by transferring between disk and memory, in detriment to an OLTP database running on the same machine. Where OLTP databases need resource sharing, data warehouses need to hog those resources for extended periods of time. So, a data warehouse hogs machine resources. An OLTP database attempts to share those same resources. It is likely to have unacceptable response times because of a lack of basic I/O resources for both database types. The result, therefore, is a requirement for a complete separation between operational (OLTP) and decision-support (data warehouse) activity. This is why data warehouses exist!

The Relational Database Model and Data Warehouses

The traditional OLTP (transactional) type of relational database model does not cater for data warehouse requirements. The relational database model is too granular. "Granular" implies too many little pieces. Processing through all those little-bitty pieces is too time consuming for large transactions, joining all those pieces together. Similar to the object database model, the relational database model removes duplication and creates granularity. This type of database model is efficient for front-end application performance, involving small amounts of data that are accessed frequently and concurrently by many users at once. This is what an OLTP database does.

Data warehouses, on the other hand, need throughput of huge amounts of data by relatively very few users. Data warehouses process large quantities of data at once, mainly for reporting and analytical processing. Also, data warehouses are regularly updated, but usually in large batch operations. OLTP databases need lightning-quick response to many individual users. Data warehouses perform enormous amounts of I/O activity over copious quantities of data; therefore, the needs of OLTP and data warehouse databases are completely contrary to each other, down to the lowest layer of hardware resource usage.

Hardware resource usage is the most critical consideration. Software rests quite squarely on the shoulders of your hardware. Proper use of memory (RAM), disk storage, and CPU time to manage everything is the critical layer for all activity. OLTP and data warehouse database differences extend all the way down to this most critical of layers. OLTP databases require intensely sharable hardware structures (commonly known as *concurrency*), needing highly efficient use of memory and processor time allocations. Data warehouses need huge amounts of disk space, processing power as well, but all dedicated to long-running programs (commonly known as *batch operations* or *throughput*).

A data warehouse database simply cannot cope using a standard OLTP database relational database model. Something else is needed for a data warehouse.

Surrogate Keys in a Data Warehouse

Surrogate keys, as you already know, are replacement key values. A surrogate key makes database access more efficient — usually. In data warehouse databases, surrogate keys are possibly more important in terms of gluing together different data, even from different databases, perhaps even different database engines. Sometimes different databases could be keyed on different values, or even contain different key values, which in the non-computerized world are actually identical.

For example, a customer in a department of a company could be uniquely identified by the customer's name. In a second department, within the same company, the same customer could be identified by the name of a contact or even perhaps the phone number of that customer. A third department could identify the same customer by a fixed-length character coding system. All three definitions identify exactly the same customer. If this single company is to have meaningful data across all departments, it must identify the three separate formats, all representing the same customer as being the same customer in the data warehouse. A surrogate key is the perfect solution, using the same surrogate key value for each repetition of the same customer, across all departments. Surrogate key use is prominent in data warehouse database modeling.

Referential Integrity in a Data Warehouse

Data warehouse data modeling is essentially a form of relational database modeling, albeit a simplistic form. Referential integrity still applies to data warehouse databases; however, even though referential integrity applies, it is not essential to create primary keys, foreign keys, and their inter-table referential links (referential integrity). It is important to understand that a data warehouse database generally has two distinct activities. The first activity is updating with large numbers of records added at once, sometimes also with large numbers of records changed. It is always best to only add or remove data in a data warehouse. Changing existing data warehouse table records can be extremely inefficient simply because of the sheer size of data warehouses.

Referential integrity is best implemented and enforced when updating tables. The second activity of a data warehouse is the reading of data. When data is read, referential integrity does not need to be verified because no changes are occurring to records in tables. On the contrary, because referential integrity implies creation of primary and foreign keys, and because the best database model designs make profligate use of primary and foreign key fields in SQL code, leave referential integrity intact for a data warehouse.

So, now we know the origin of data warehouses and why they were devised. What is the data warehouse dimensional database model?

The Dimensional Database Model

A standard, normalized, relational database model is completely inappropriate to the requirements of a data warehouse. Even a denormalized relational database model doesn't make the cut. An entirely different modeling technique, called a *dimensional database model*, is needed for data warehouses. A dimensional model contains what are called facts and dimensions. A *fact table* contains historical transactions, such as all invoices issued to all customers for the last five years. That could be a lot of records. *Dimensions* describe facts.

The easiest way to describe the dimensional model is to demonstrate by example. Figure 7-1 shows a relational table structure for both static book data and dynamic (transactional) book data. The grayed out tables in Figure 7-1 are static data tables and others are tables containing data, which is in a constant state of change. Static tables are the equivalent of dimensions, describing facts (equivalent to transactions). So, in Figure 7-1, the dimensions are grayed out and the facts are not.

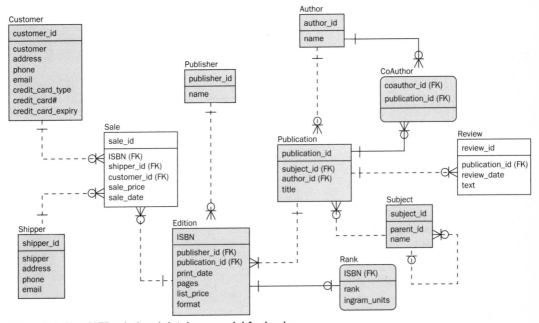

Figure 7-1: The OLTP relational database model for books.

What Is a Star Schema?

The most effective approach for a data warehouse database model (using dimensions and facts) is called a *star schema*. Figure 7-2 shows a simple star schema for the REVIEW fact table shown in Figure 7-1.

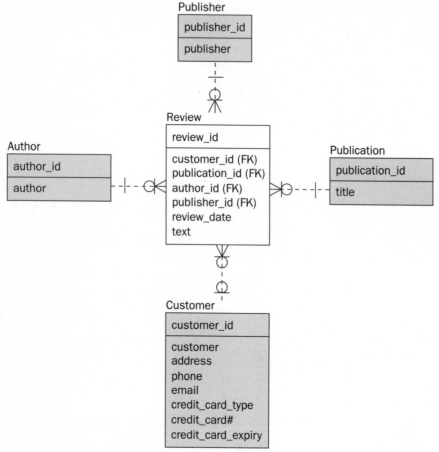

Figure 7-2: The REVIEW **table fact-dimensional structure.**

A more simplistic equivalent diagram to that of Figure 7-2 is shown by the star schema structure in Figure 7-3.

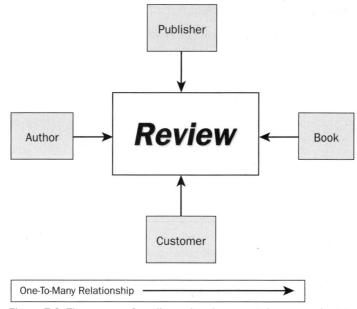

Figure 7-3: The REVIEW fact-dimensional structure is a star schema.

A star schema contains a single fact table plus a number of small dimensional tables. If there is more than one fact table, effectively there is more than one star schema. Fact tables contain transactional records, which over a period of time can come to contain very large numbers of records. Dimension tables on the other hand remain relatively constant in record numbers. The objective is to enhance SQL query join performance, where joins are executed between a single fact table and multiple dimensions, all on a single hierarchical level. So, a star schema is a single, very large, very changeable, fact table, connected directly to a single layer of multiple, static-sized dimensional tables.

What Is a Snowflake Schema?

A *snowflake schema* is shown in Figure 7-4. A snowflake schema is a normalized star schema, such that dimension entities are normalized (dimensions are separated into multiple tables). Normalized dimensions have all duplication removed from each dimension, such that the result is a single fact table, connected directly to some of the dimensions. Not all of the dimensions are directly connected to the fact table. In Figure 7-4, the dimensions are grayed out in two shades of gray. The lighter shade of gray represents dimensions connected directly to the fact table (BOOK, AUTHOR, SUBJECT, SHIPPER, and CUSTOMER). The darker-shaded gray dimensional tables, are normalized subset dimensional tables, not connected to the fact table directly (PUBLISHER, PUBLICATION, and CATEGORY).

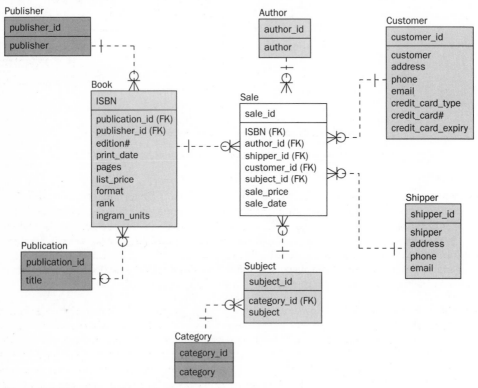

Figure 7-4: The SALE table fact-dimensional structure.

A more simplistic equivalent diagram to that of Figure 7-4 is shown by the snowflake schema in Figure 7-5.

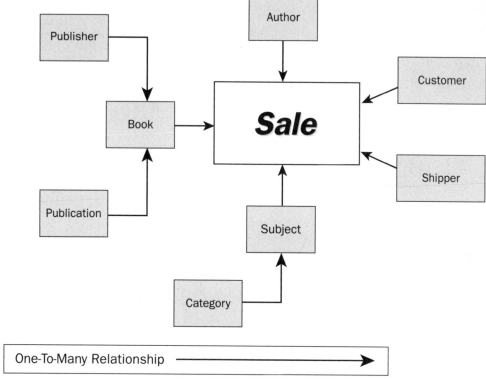

Figure 7-5: The SALE **fact-dimensional structure is a snowflake schema.**

The problem with snowflake schemas isn't too many tables but too many layers. Data warehouse fact tables can become incredibly large, even to millions, billions, even trillions of records. The critical factor in creating star and snowflake schemas, instead of using standard "nth" Normal Form layers, is decreasing the number of tables in SQL query joins. The more tables in a join, the more complex a query, the slower it will execute. When fact tables contain enormous record counts, reports can take hours and days, not minutes. Adding just one more table to a fact-dimensional query join at that level of database size could make the query run for weeks. That's no good!

The solution is an obvious one. Convert (denormalize) a normalized snowflake schema into a star schema, as shown in Figure 7-6. In Figure 7-6 the PUBLISHER and PUBLICATION tables have been denormalized into the BOOK table, plus the CATEGORY table has been denormalized into the SUBJECT table.

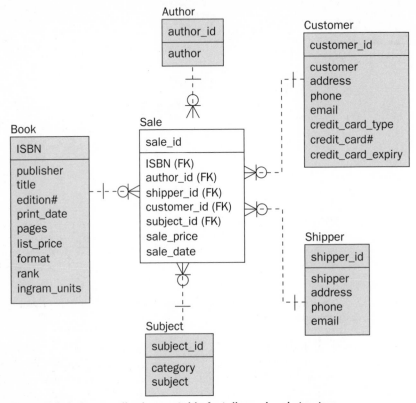

Figure 7-6: A denormalized SALE table fact-dimensional structure.

A more simplistic equivalent diagram to that of Figure 7-6 is shown by the star schema in Figure 7-7.

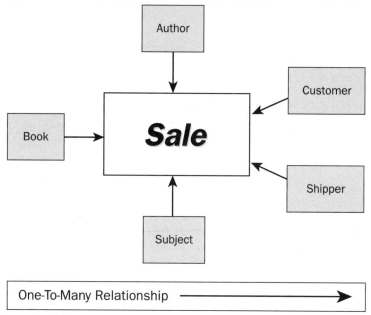

One-To-Many Relationship ————————————▶

Figure 7-7: The SALE **fact-dimensional structure denormalized into a star schema.**

What does all this prove? Not much, you might say. On the contrary, two things are achieved by using fact-dimensional structures and star schemas:

❑ Figure 7-1 shows a highly normalized table structure, useful for high-concurrency, precision record-searching databases (an OLTP database). Replacing this structure with a fact-dimensional structure (as shown in Figure 7-2, Figure 7-4, and Figure 7-6) reduces the number of tables. As you already know, reducing the number tables is critical to SQL query performance. Data warehouses consist of large quantities of data, batch updates, and incredibly complex queries. The fewer tables, the better. It just makes things so much easier with fewer tables, especially because there is so much data. The following code is a SQL join query for the snowflake schema, joining all nine tables in the snowflake schema shown in Figure 7-5.

```
SELECT * FROM SALE SAL JOIN AUTHOR AUT
      JOIN CUSTOMER CUS
           JOIN SHIPPER SHP
                JOIN SUBJECT SUB
                     JOIN CATEGORY CAT
                          JOIN BOOK BOO
                               JOIN PUBLISHER PBS
                                    JOIN PUBLICATION PBL
WHERE ...
GROUP BY ...

ORDER BY ... ;
```

❑ If the SALE fact table has 1 million records, and all dimensions contain 10 records each, a Cartesian product would return 10^6 multiplied by 10^9 records. That makes for 10^{15} records. That is a lot of records for any CPU to process.

A Cartesian product is a worse-case scenario.

❏   Now look at the next query.

```
SELECT * FROM SALE SAL JOIN AUTHOR AUT
      JOIN CUSTOMER CUS
           JOIN SHIPPER SHP
                JOIN SUBJECT SUB
                     JOIN BOOK BOO
WHERE ...
GROUP BY ...

ORDER BY ... ;
```

❏   Using the star schema from Figure 7-7, assuming the same number of records, a join occurs between one fact table and six dimensional tables. That is a Cartesian product of 10^6 multiple by 10^6, resulting in 10^{12} records returned. The difference between 10^{12} and 10^{15} is three decimals. Three decimals is not just three zeroes and thus 1,000 records. The difference is actually 1,000,000,000,000,000 − 1,000,000,000,000 = 999,000,000,000,000. That is effectively just a little less than 10^{15}. The difference between six dimensions and nine dimensions is more or less infinite, from the perspective of counting all those zeros. Fewer dimensions make for faster queries. That's why it is so essential to denormalize snowflake schemas into star schemas.

❏   Take another quick glance at the snowflake schema in Figure 7-4 and Figure 7-5. Then examine the equivalent denormalized star schema in Figure 7-6 and Figure 7-7. Now put yourself into the shoes of a hustled, harried and very busy executive — trying to get a quick report. Think as an end-user, one only interested in results. Which diagram is easier to decipher as to content and meaning? The diagram in Figure 7-7 is more complex than the diagram in Figure 7-5? After all, being an end-user, you are probably not too interested in understanding the complexities of how to build SQL join queries. You have bigger fish to fry. The point is this: The less complex the table structure, the easier it will be to use. This is because a star schema is more representative of the real world than a snowflake schema. Look at it this way. A snowflake schema is more deeply normalized than a star schema, and, therefore, by definition more mathematical. Something more mathematical is generally of more use to a mathematician than it is to an executive manager. The executive is trying to get a quick overall impression of whether his company will sell more cans of lima beans, or more cans of string beans, over the course of the next ten years. If you are a computer programmer, you will quite probably not agree with this analogy.

That tells us the very basics of data warehouse database modeling. How can a data warehouse database model be constructed?

How to Build a Data Warehouse Database Model

Now you know how to build star schemas for data warehouse database models. As you can see, a star schema is quite different from a standard relational database model (Figure 7-1). The next step is to examine the process, or the steps, by which a data warehouse database model can be built.

Data Warehouse Modeling Step by Step

The primary objective of a data warehouse (or any database) is to service end-users. The end-users are the people who read reports produced by data warehouse SQL queries. End-users utilize a data warehouse to search for patterns, and attempt to forecast trends from masses of historical information. From that perspective, there is a sequence of steps in approaching data warehouse database design, beginning with the end-user perspective. The end-user looks at a company from a business process, or operational perspective:

❑ *Business processes*—Establish the subject areas of a business. How can a business be divided up? The result is the fact tables. Fact tables contain records of historical transactions.

❑ *Granularity*—Granularity is the level of detail required. In other words, should a data warehouse store every single transaction? Should it summarize transactions as a single record for each day, month, year, and so on? The more granularity the data warehouse contains, the bigger fact tables are because the more records they contain. The safest option is include all historical data down to the lowest level of granularity. This ensures that any possible future requirements for detailed analysis can always be met, without needed data perhaps missing in the future. Missing data might make your executive managers a little irate in the future. They will be irate with you, and that's usually best avoided. There are specialized objects such as materialized views that can create summaries at a later stage. When you do not know the precise requirements for future use of your data warehouse, to be on the safe side, it is best to store all levels of detail (assuming hardware storage capacity allows it). If you miss a level of detail in any specific area and it is later requested, you won't be able to comply. In other words, store every transaction, if you have the physical disk space and general hardware-processing capacity.

❑ *Identify and build dimensions*—Dimensions contain static information. Dimensions describe facts by storing static details about transactions in fact tables. Dimensions must be built before facts because facts contain foreign key references to dimension tables.

❑ *Build facts*—As previously mentioned, facts are transactional records, going back even many years. Fact tables are built after all dimensions are decided upon because, as you already know, facts are dependent on dimensions.

How Long to Keep Data in a Data Warehouse?

The amount of time you keep data in a data warehouse depends on end-user requirements. Typically, when designing a data warehouse, at the point of creating table ERD diagrams, it is impossible to tell how detail is required. The best option is retain every single transaction without summarizing anything; however, that can chew up a humungous amount of disk space. If you have the space, why not use it. If you run out of space later, you can always begin summarizing and destroying detail level records at a later stage.

> *Be warned! Summarizing data warehouse records into aggregated records, and deleting detail records can be a seriously time- consuming effort if done when the data warehouse has grown to be extremely large.*

Data warehouses sometimes retain all data forever. When a data warehouse becomes too difficult to manage, there will have to be some deletion of older data, or summarizing (or both). It all depends on hardware storage capacity, the power of computers, and how much you can spend on continually expanding the capacity of existing hardware. Upgrading a large data warehouse to new hardware and software can also be very time-consuming.

Types of Dimension Tables

The data warehouse database models for the REVIEW and SALE tables, shown previously in this chapter, are actually inadequate. Many data warehouse databases have standard requirements based on how end-users need to analyze data. Typical additions to data warehouse databases are dimensions such as dates, locations, and products. These extra dimensions can be built from most types of transactional data.

Any types of transactions involving products or services are usually dated, such as orders, invoices, or payments. Therefore, every transaction can be placed (or dated) into specific periods. Locations can usually be assessed either generally or in detail from customers, suppliers, shippers, and other company's that contact is had with. The REVIEW and SALE fact tables shown in Figure 7-2 and Figure 7-4 both contain date fields (REVIEW.REVIEW_DATE and SALE.SALE_DATE). A date or timestamp dimension might look something similar to that shown in Figure 7-8. Date fields in the tables would be replaced with identifiers as shown in Figure 7-9. Note how the date values in the TIME table, as shown in Figure 7-8, are reconstituted in a specific time window period, such as MONTH, QUARTER, and YEAR.

Figure 7-8: A time dimension entity.

Figure 7-9 shows fact tables for both book reviews and sales, where the date fields have been replaced with foreign key links to the TIME table. The result of this is that facts can be analyzed by month, quarter, and year. In this case, removing the date fields from the fact tables has actually decreased the detail level. Now data can only be analyzed by month. Months are the lowest level of detail. To retain the ability to analyze on a daily basis, or with further detail such as hours and minutes, either the TIME table should be expanded to accommodate more detail periods, or the date fields should be retained in the fact tables.

Another commonly used dimension involves locations, which can be states, cities, countries, continents, regions, and others. Location details for review and sale facts can be gleaned from customer and shipper address details. The resulting LOCATION table would look something like that shown in Figure 7-10. Some silly fields have been added just to give this conversation a little color. The equivalent star schema changes are shown in Figure 7-11.

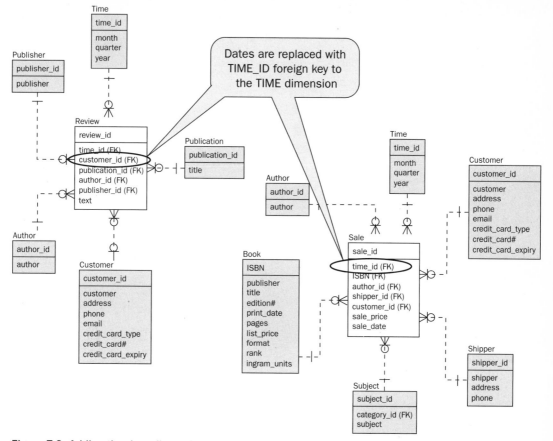

Figure 7-9: Adding the time dimension to the facts.

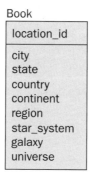

Figure 7-10: Location dimensions are commonly used to analyze data by region.

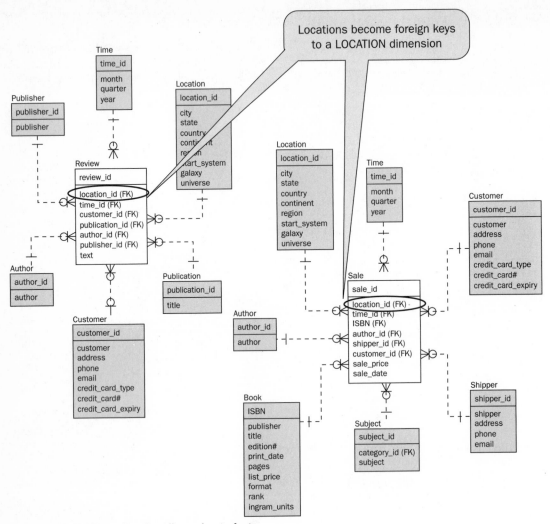

Figure 7-11: Adding a location dimension to facts.

Other types of dimensions, common to many data warehouses, cover topic areas such as products or product categories. There are many other possible dimensions. Dimensions typically depend on the data content of a data warehouse, and also how the data warehouse is used for analysis.

Try It Out   Creating a Data Warehouse Database Model

Figure 7-12 shows the tables of a database containing details of bands, their released CDs, tracks on each of those CDs, followed by three tables containing royalty amounts earned by each track, from radio plays, live performances, and recordings by other artists. Create an equivalent data warehouse snowflake schema. From the snowflake schema, denormalize into a star schema.

1.   Identify the fact tables. Facts are generally business processes of the day-to-day functions of a business. Transactional data is function.

2.   Granularity can be ignored in this case.

3.   What are the dimensions? Dimensions are the static tables in a data warehouse database model.

4.   Create the dimension tables, followed by the fact tables.

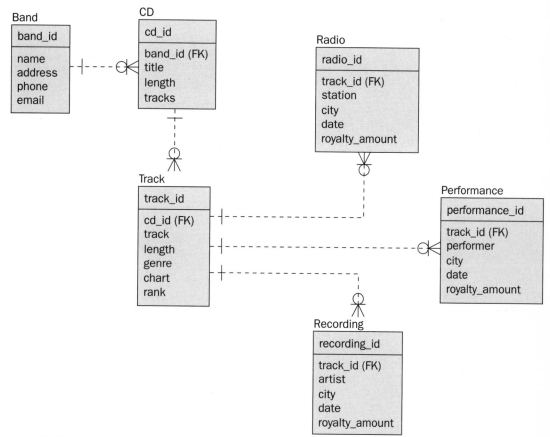

Figure 7-12: An OLTP relational database model.

How It Works

Go through the process as follows:

1. In Figure 7-12, you should be able to see that transactional tables, those constantly changing, in relation to static tables, which are the royalty tables. The royalty tables are the RADIO, PERFORMANCE, and RECORDING tables. These three tables are the only tables with amount and date values in them. This makes them transactional tables and thus fact tables.

2. In Figure 7-12, dimensions are all the tables containing static data, not previously assessed as being transactional facts. Dimension tables in Figure 7-12 are the BAND, CD, and TRACK tables.

3. The next step is to begin by building dimensions. Build facts after that. Figure 7-13 shows a simplistic picture of all static dimensions and facts, in the form of a dimensionally normalized snowflake schema.

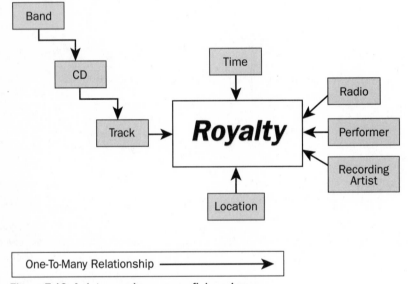

Figure 7-13: A data warehouse snowflake schema.

Figure 7-14 shows the ERD equivalent of the snowflake schema shown in Figure 7-13. Note how date and location values are replaced by dimensions TIME and LOCATION (shown both in Figure 7-13 and Figure 7-14).

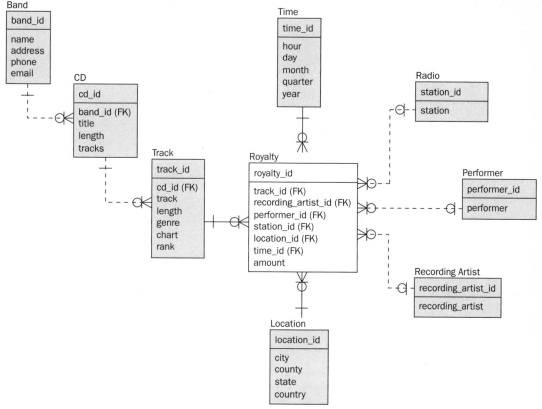

Figure 7-14: A data warehouse snowflake schema ERD.

4. Figure 7-15 and Figure 7-16 show a conversion of snowflake to star schema. The BAND, CD, and TRACK tables are all denormalized into the single table called TRACK. The result is a single-level hierarchy of dimensions.

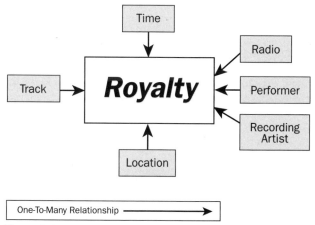

Figure 7-15: A data warehouse star schema.

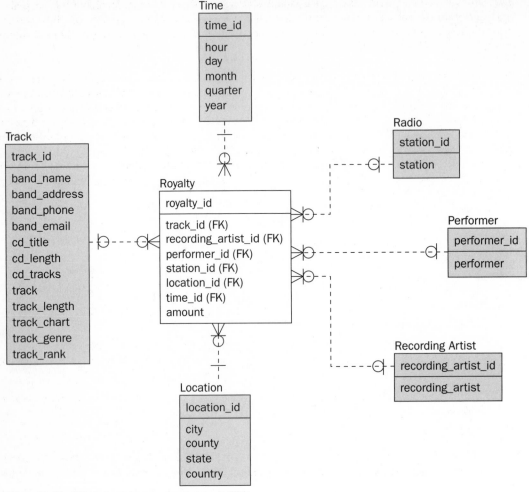

Figure 7-16: A data warehouse star schema ERD.

Understanding Fact Tables

Fact table fields contain the content and field types of fact tables; therefore, facts are not actually the tables themselves but the fields within those tables. Facts are generally numeric in nature, allowing aggregation of those numeric values into analytical data warehouse reporting structures.

Foreign keys in fact tables that point to dimensions are not facts. Fact table foreign keys (often surrogate keys) simply link to more descriptive dimension tables. Dimension tables contain detailed descriptions about fact values, such as the time and location details of when and where a particular transaction took place. There are other less commonly used dimensions, such as with whom and what (customers, authors, shippers, books).

Fact tables can contain detailed transactional histories, summaries (aggregations), or both. Details and aggregations can be separated into different fact tables. Many relational databases allow use of materialized views to contain fact table aggregations, containing less detailed aggregations of their underlying fact tables.

One of the most significant factors with fact tables, specifically because of their potentially enormous size, is how fact tables are changed. How is data changed in fact tables? Fact tables can be added to or changed, and even deleted from. The least obstructive changes to fact tables are done by adding new data, preferably during low end-user activity time windows. Deletion from fact tables is necessary when upgrading to more summarized details, or perhaps deletion of old data that is no longer useful. Fact tables are thus regarded as being additive, semi-additive, or non-additive. The most efficient data warehouses are those that never change, containing only non-additive fact tables. Additive tables are more practical because the more current data warehouse facts are, the more useful they should become for analysis.

Summary

In this chapter, you learned about:

- ❏ The importance of understanding the origin of data warehouses, especially why they were invented and how they are used
- ❏ The inadequacy of the transactional (OLTP) database model for producing forecasts and predictions from huge amounts of out of date data because an OLTP database model has too much granularity
- ❏ Specialized database modeling techniques required by data warehouses in the form of facts and dimensions
- ❏ Star schemas as single dimensional layers and how they provide best efficiency and clarity to end-users
- ❏ Snowflake schemas as normalized, less efficient forms of star schemas
- ❏ Variable data, the transactions or history of company transactional activities that compose facts
- ❏ How dimensions contain static, descriptive data; dimensional data describes fact data
- ❏ How dimensions describe the facts by normalizing only static (dimensional) data, preferably in a single dimensional layer
- ❏ How fact-dimensional or dimensional database modeling is either a star schema or a snowflake schema
- ❏ Data warehouses containing one or more fact tables, linked to the same dimensions, or a subset of the dimensions
- ❏ The various steps and processes used in the creation of a data warehouse database model
- ❏ The contents of a data warehouse database and model are both static and historical
- ❏ Static (dimensional) data changes infrequently
- ❏ Historical or archived data (factual) is continually added to, and can grow enormously over time

This chapter has described the specialized database modeling techniques required for the building of data warehouses. The next chapter examines one of the most important factors of database modeling — performance. If a database underperforms, a company can lose customers and, in extreme situations, lose all its customers. Guess what happens after that? Look, no job!

Exercises

Use the ERDs in Figure 7-14 and Figure 7-16 to help you answer these questions:

1. Create scripts to create tables for the snowflake schema in Figure 7-14.

2. Change the tables created for the previous question, converting the snowflake schema in Figure 7-14 to the star schema in Figure 7-16. Use CREATE TABLE and DROP TABLE commands.

Building Fast-Performing Database Models

"Man is a slow, sloppy, and brilliant thinker; the machine is fast, accurate, and stupid."
(William M. Kelly)

Man is ingenious. Only by instructing a database properly will it perform well.

Much of the information in this chapter has already been discussed, perhaps even analyzed, and often alluded to, in previous chapters of this book. This chapter is intended to take everything you have learned so far (all the theory) and begin the process of putting it into practice. This chapter describes various factors affecting database performance tuning, as applied to different database model types. Anything obviously repeated from a previous chapter should be considered as being doubly significant, with respect to database modeling. Database performance is the most important factor as far as any database or database model is concerned. If performance is not acceptable, your database model does not service the end-users in an acceptable manner. End-users are your clients and thus the most important people in your life—at least as far as your database is concerned.

> *A client can be a direct customer or an indirect customer. An indirect client could be someone else's customer—your customer's client.*

Previous chapters have explained database modeling theory. This chapter forms a bridge between database modeling and related theoretical concepts described in the previous chapters, and a large ongoing case study in chapters to follow this chapter. The following chapters dig into the practical aspects of database modeling by describing and demonstrating the full process of thinking about, analyzing, designing and building a database model in a real world environment.

By the end of this chapter, you should have a slightly less theoretical and slightly more real-world picture of database modeling techniques.

In this chapter, you learn about the following:

❏   Factors affecting tuning of different types of database models

❏   All the detail on writing efficient queries

❏   Helping database performance by using appropriate indexing

❏   Views

❏   Application caching

The Needs of Different Database Models

Performance tuning of different database model types depends solely on what the database is servicing, in terms of applications connected to that database. All the theory about tuning database models has been discussed in previous chapters. Essentially, everything needs to be tied together. All the theory you have so far been bombarded with is now explained from the point of view of why and how it used.

Different database model types are tuned in different ways. In general, a database model can be tuned based on what its dependant applications require. It comes down to what the end-users need. The two extreme ends of the scale are the OLTP database model and the data warehouse database model. The following sections break down the aspects of different types of databases based on the performance survival needs of the different database model types.

Factors Affecting OLTP Database Model Tuning

An OLTP database services the Internet. The primary characteristics of OLTP databases are as follows:

❏   *Large user population* — OLTP databases have an immeasurably large user population, all trying to get at the same information at once.

❏   *Very high concurrency* — Concurrency implies a very high degree of sharing of the same information.

❏   *Large database size* — OLTP databases have small to large databases, depending on application type and user population. A large globally available online book retailer might have a multitude of servers all over the world. A site advertising local night spots for only a single city, in a specific country, has local appeal and, thus, potentially far less information.

❏   *Reaction time* — Real-time, instantaneous reaction to database changes and activities are essential. If you withdraw cash from an ATM at your bank and then check your statement online in an hour or so, you would expect to see the transaction. Similarly, if you purchase something online, you would hope to see the transaction on your credit card account within minutes, if not seconds.

❏   *Small transactions* — Users retrieve single records or very small joins.

❏   *Granularity* — Many OLTP database models are highly normalized structures, but this is often a mistake. OLTP databases allow access to small chunks of data; however, the problem is that sometimes those small chunks of data can actually equate to large multiple table joins caused by excessive normalization. If a table structure is normalized to the point of catering for all business rules in the table structure, performance problems may well arise, even for users seeking to view

10 to 20 records on a single screen. A prime example of this is a user logging onto a bank account a getting bank statement. If all the information on a single sheet of paper (a short Web page) is in a multitude of tables, that user could become seriously irritated with all the data glued together (if it takes more than seven seconds for a response). Thousands of other users could be accessing the same data at the same time.

❑ *Manageability* — This is usually possible but quite often difficult. OLTP database user populations are generally globally based, round the clock and 365 days a year. This can make managing an OLTP database complex and awkward.

❑ *Service window* — As already stated, OLTP databases must be alert, awake, and ready for use permanently. This is an ideal, but many service providers sell themselves based on the ability to provide availability at slightly less than 100 percent. Less than 100 percent service time allows for small servicing windows of time.

Factors Affecting Client-Server Database Model Tuning

There are plenty of client-server environments servicing small numbers of users in the range of tens of users or even less. The primary characteristics of client-server databases are as follows:

❑ *Small user population* — A company can be small or large, on local- or wide-area networks. Predicting and measuring internal company use is much easier than trying to cater to OLTP database capacity requirements.

❑ *Low level of concurrency* — Company-wide client-server databases have measurable user populations. These populations can be extremely small or relatively large, but it is a quantifiable service requirement because of being a measurable user population. OLTP database requirements are actually quantifiable; however, for OLTP databases, user populations are immeasurably larger, but OLTP database use can often have sudden increases (or decreases), even occasional massive spikes (jumps in end-users). Client-server database concurrency levels are much more predictable than OLTP databases. Predictability implies the ability to prepare for and cater to application requirements more easily.

❑ *Database size* — Client-server databases are usually small in size. Anything too large, and a client-server architecture simply won't be able to cope with requirements. One solution to over use of client-server architectures is extremely costly hardware. At that stage, costs can probably be reduced by implementing OLTP and data warehouse architectural approaches.

❑ *Reaction time* — Client-server reaction times are generally acceptable as real-time for single record user interface actions, and perhaps minutes for reporting requirements.

❑ *Small and large transactions* — Client-server environments combine both small and large transactions in the form of user interface connectivity to data, plus reporting needs, which are small enough to manage at the same time. This type of service is possible because both user population numbers and concurrency requirement levels are low.

❑ *Granularity* — All items of data are often relatively small and table structures can be more mathematical in nature. Client-server databases can even incorporate large quantities of business rule structure into table structures by utilizing very high levels of normalization, beyond 3NFs.

Once again application of high-level normalization is, in my opinion, often more mathematical than practical. Let applications do the number crunching and leave the database to store the data. Don't put too much processing into the database. It is quite possible, but can become very complicated to manage, change, and administer. Modern application SDKs are more than capable of intense processing and number crunching. The purpose of a relational database is to store and apply structure to data. Object databases manage processing inside database objects well. Relational databases do not!

❑ *Manageability* — Data is fairly easily manageable not only because parameters are small and quantifiable but also because everyone goes home at night, giving plenty of down time for maintenance.

❑ *Service window* — See this same explanation in the previous section, "Factors Affecting OLTP Database Model Tuning."

Factors Affecting Data Warehouse Database Model Tuning

Data warehouses are all about seriously large amounts of data and a very few — often very technically challenging — application environments:

❑ *Minimal user population* — Administrators, developers, and analytical-type end-users typically access data warehouses. Those analytical end-users are usually knowledgeable and executive or middle-management level. One of the primary purposes of storing lots and lots of old data in a data warehouse is to help with forecasting for the future. This type of user population finds this type of information extremely useful.

❑ *Very low concurrency* — There is very little data sharing in a data warehouse. Most activity is read-only, or bulk updates to fact tables, when the database is not being used for reporting and analysis. Concurrency is not really an issue.

❑ *Frightening database size* — Data warehouses can become incredibly large. Administrators and developers must decide how much detail to retain, when to remove data, when to summarize, and what to summarize. A lot of these decisions are done during production when the data warehouse is in use. It is very difficult to predict what will be needed in design and development phases. Ad-hoc queries can cause serious problems if a data warehouse is very large. User education in relation to how to code proper joins may be essential; otherwise, provision of efficiency providing structures such as pre-built joins and aggregations in materialized views can help.

Materialized views copy data, allowing access to physical copies of data and avoiding underlying table access, expensive joins, and aggregations. A relational database allowing use of materialized views uses something called query rewrite. Query rewrite is where requested access to a table in a query, is potentially replaced with access to a much smaller, and more efficient materialized view. I/O and processing activity are substantially reduced. Query performance is helped enormously.

❑ *Reaction time* — Data warehouse reaction times are acceptable as hours and perhaps even longer. Reaction times depend on various factors, such as data warehouse database physical size, complexity of end-user reporting and analytical requests, granularity of data, and general end-user understanding of the scale of data warehouses.

❑ *Incredibly large transactions* — Users retrieve large amounts of data, using both simple reporting and highly complex analytical techniques. The fewer tables in joins, the better. Updates are best performed periodically in large batch operations.

❑ *Very low granularity* — A star schema is the best route to adopt for a data warehouse because it minimizes on the potential numbers of tables in joins. A star schema contains a single large fact table connected to a single layer of very small, descriptive, static dimensional tables. Very small tables can be joined with a single very large table fairly efficiently. When joins involve more than one very large table, serious performance problems can arise.

❑ *Very demanding manageability* — Because of their size, extremely large databases can become difficult to manage. The larger a database becomes, the more time and hardware resources needed to use and alter that data. Demanding manageability is gradually replaced with more sophisticated means of handling sheer database sized, such as hugely expensive hardware and special tricks (such as clustering, partitioning, parallel processing, and materialized views). Data warehouses are, more often than not, largely read-only structures. This gives far more flexibility, allowing for more available options to cope with a very demanding physical database size.

❑ *Service window* — Data warehouse service windows are generally not an issue because end-user usage is driven by occasional bursts of furious I/O activity, but generally not constant usage as with an OLTP database. Most I/O activity is read-only. This, of course, depends on the real-time capability of a data warehouse. Real-time reporting requirements in a data warehouse complicate everything substantially, requiring constant real-time updating.

One way to alleviate performance issues with data warehouses is the use of data marts. A data mart is a subsection of a larger single data warehouse. A large data warehouse can consist of a number of very large fact tables, linked to the same dimensions. A data mart can be pictured as a single large fact table (perhaps one or two fact table star schemas) linked to a single set of dimensions.

Understanding Database Model Tuning

The biggest problem with database model tuning is that it really must be done during the design phase, and preferably before any development is complete. This is the case as far as tables and their inter-relationships are concerned. Data warehouses are largely read-only and are not as restrictive with production-phase changes. Data warehouses are mostly read-only type environments. Read-only environments can take advantage of specialized database structures, which overlay, duplicate, and summarize data in tables. Materialized views are used extensively in data warehouses and even some OLTP databases. A materialized view allows for copying of table data, either as individual tables or joins. The result is a physical copy of data. Queries then execute against the materialized view copy, which is built based on the requirements of a single query or a group of queries. The result is better performance.

Tuning a database model is the most difficult and expensive option because SQL code depends on the structure of the underlying database model; extensive application code changes can result. The database model underpins and supports everything else. Changes to a database model can cause major application changes, obviously applying after development of application code. The point is that database model tuning changes (such as changes to underlying tables) can affect everything else. Changing everything from database model up is very expensive because everything is dependent on the database model. Everything must be changed. This is why it is so important to get the database model correct before development begins. Unfortunately, we don't live in an ideal world, but we can strive for it. Big changes to database model table structure can often result in what amounts to full rewrites of application software.

An effective way to performance-tune a database model after development is complete, is the creation of alternate indexing. Stored procedures can also help by compartmentalizing, speeding up and organizing what already exists.

When it comes to database model tuning, at the worst and most expensive end of the scale are normalization, denormalization, changes to referential integrity and table structure, and anything else that changes the basic table structure. At best, and with minimal intrusion on existing tables and relationships, alternate indexing, materialized views, clustering, and other such tricks, can help to enhance a database model, without messing around with critical underlying table structure. Database objects such as materialized views and clustering help to circumvent table changes by creating copies and overlays of existing table structures, without affecting those existing tables, and obviously avoiding changes to any dependent application coding already written, tested, debugged, and in general use in a production environment. The down side to overlaying and copying is that there is a limit to how many things such as materialized views that can be created. Too much can hinder rather than help performance.

So, now you know why OLTP databases need less granularity, some denormalization, and small quantities of data. The same applies with the other extreme in that data warehouses need highly denormalized (simple) table structures to minimize table numbers in join queries, thus not severely impeding data warehouse reporting performance.

Writing Efficient Queries

Efficient SQL code is primarily about efficient queries using the SELECT command. The SELECT command allows use of a WHERE clause, reducing the amount of data read. The WHERE clause is used to return (or not return) specific records. The UPDATE and DELETE commands can also have a WHERE clause and, thus, they can also be performance-tuned with respect to WHERE clause use, reducing the amount of data accessed.

> *Performance tuning of the INSERT command to add records to a database is often the job of both developers and administrators. This is because end-users usually add data to a database through the use of applications. Metadata change commands such as (CREATE TABLE and ALTER TABLE) are more database administration. Thus, INSERT commands and metadata commands and not relevant to this text.*

In an OLTP (transactional) database, small transactions and high concurrency are the most important aspects. Accuracy of SQL code and matching indexes is critical. In data warehouses, large queries and batch updates are prevalent. Therefore, in data warehouses, large complex queries are executed against as few tables as possible, minimizing on the number of tables in join queries. Joining too many tables at once in a query can have the most significant impact on query performance of all, in both OLTP and data warehouse databases. Data warehouses simply exacerbate problems because of huge data quantities.

There are some general philosophical rules of thumb to follow when performance-tuning SQL code:

❑ *Database model design supports SQL code*—The quality of SQL code depends completely on the quality of database model design, not only from a perspective of correct levels of normalization and denormalization, but also from the point of view of using appropriate structures. For example, a data warehouse database model design is needed for a data warehouse because over-normalized, granular, deep normal form tables, often used in OLTP databases, are completely inappropriate to the very large transactions, across many tables, required by data warehouses.

❑ *The KISS Rule (Keep It Simple and Stupid)* — Any type of program code broken into simple, (preferably independent) pieces is always easier "to wrap your head around." Simple SQL commands with simple clauses are easy to write and easy to tune. Longer and more complicated queries are more difficult to write, and it's more difficult to get them to produce the proper results. Performance tuning is an additional step. If you have to tune some big nasty queries because they are running too slow, well, what can I say? If you had kept it simple, making them run faster would probably be a lot easier, and a lot more possible. Simplify first if over-complexity is an issue. In the very least, simplicity can help you understand precisely what a query is doing, without giving you a headache just staring at lines of meaningless SQL code.

❑ *Good table structure allows for easy construction of SQL code* — Be aware of anything controlling the way or manner in which SQL code is constructed and written, other than, of course, the database model. In an ideal table structure, SQL code should be written directly from those table structures, or as subsets of it, not the other way around. Writing SQL code should not be difficult. You should not get a constant impression (a nagging doubt or hunch) that table structure doesn't quite fit. The structure of the database model should make for easy of SQL code construction. After all, SQL code supports applications. Don't forget that SQL code rests on the database table structure. If there is any kind of mismatch between application requirements and database structure, there is likely something wrong with the database model. Performance-tuning SQL code in a situation such as this will likely be a serious problem.

❑ *Breaking down into the smallest pieces* — Break down the construction of SQL code commands, such as queries and DML commands (INSERT, UPDATE, and DELETE). Do not break down non-query and non-DML type commands. For example, do not continually connect and disconnect from a database for every single code snippet of SQL database access executed. Either connect for a period of time, for each user, or connect at the start and end of sessions. On the other hand, make extensive use of subqueries if it helps to making coding easier. You can always merge sub-queries back into the parent query later on.

> The most important thing to remember is that the SQL code, and its potential to execute with acceptable speed, is completely dependant on the underlying structure of a database model. Queries are quite literally constructed from the tables and the relationships between those tables.

There are a set of specific ways in which the most basic elements of SQL code can be constructed to ensure good processing performance. There are a number of general areas that are important to the most basic rules of query performance tuning. Examine how each factor is affected by the underlying structure of the database model:

❑ *The SELECT command* — This includes how many tables are involved in SELECT commands. These factors have a highly significant impact on performance of queries. The more granular a database model, the more tables retrieved from at once. The manner in which fields are retrieved can also affect performance, but table numbers in joins are more significant, especially in larger databases.

❑ *The WHERE clause* — This includes how records are filtered. Comparison conditions dictate that a WHERE clause is applied to records, such as only to retrieve records with the vowel "a" in an author's name. A comparison condition is the main factor determining the construction of a WHERE clause. There are different types of comparison conditions. The manner in which records are filtered in a query can affect the way in which a query executes. The result is a highly signifi-cant impact on performance. Indexing has a very significant affect on how well WHERE clause fil-tering performs.

❏ *The* GROUP BY *clause* — The GROUP BY clause is used to aggregate records into summarized groups of records retrieved from a database. Groupings are best achieved as a direct mapping onto one-to-many relationships between tables. Materialized views are commonly used in data warehouse to pre-calculate and pre-store GROUP BY clause aggregations.

❏ *Joins* — A join query retrieves records from multiple tables, joining tables based on related field values between those tables. Typically, relationships are based on referential integrity established between primary and foreign keys, in two tables. Perhaps the most significant factor in making queries execute at an acceptable speed is how tables are joined, and how many tables are in joins (as stated previously). When considering a database model design, the more granular a database model is (the more tables you have and the more it is broken down into small pieces), the larger the number of tables will be in join queries. In a data warehouse, this is generally much more significant because data warehouses contain huge volumes of data; however, even in OTLP databases, with a multitude of miniscule-sized transactions, large joins with ten or more tables can kill performance just as effectively as more than two large tables for a join query in a data warehouse.

Joins are important to performance. The database model design can have a most profound effect on join query performance if the database model has too many little-bitty tables (too much granularity or normalization).

The SELECT *Command*

The SELECT command is used to query the database. There are a number of points to remember when intending to build efficient queries:

❏ *Querying all fields* — Retrieving specific field names is very slightly more efficient than retrieving all fields using the * character. The * character requires the added overhead of metadata interpret-ation lookups into the metadata dictionary — to find the fields in the table. In highly concurrent, very busy databases (OLTP databases), continual data dictionary lookups can stress out database concurrency handling capacity. Consider the following query:

```
SELECT NAME FROM AUTHOR;
```

This is faster than this query:

```
SELECT * FROM AUTHOR;
```

❏ *Reading indexes* — If there is an index, use it. Reading field values directly from an index without reading a table at all is faster because the index occupies less physical space. There is, therefore, less I/O activity. In the ERD snippet shown in Figure 8-1, reading the EDITION table, with the following query should be able to force a direct read of the index because primary keys are automatically indexed. The ISBN field is the primary key for the EDITION table.

```
SELECT ISBN FROM EDITION;
```

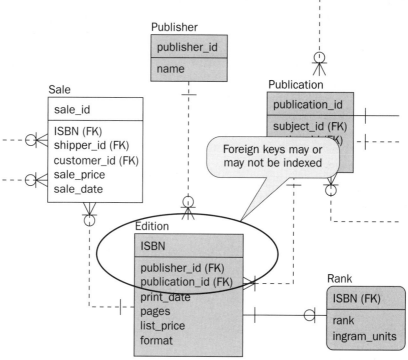

Figure 8-1: Reading indexes instead of tables.

Not all database engines allow direct index scans, even when a SELECT *command might encourage it.*

❑   *Simple aliases* — Shorter alias names can help to keep SQL code more easily readable, particularly for programmers in the future having to make changes. Maintainable code is less prone to error and much easier to tune properly. Consider the following query:

```
SELECT A.NAME, P.TITLE, E.ISBN
FROM AUTHOR A JOIN PUBLICATION P USING (AUTHOR_ID)
  JOIN EDITION E USING (PUBLICATION_ID);
```

This is much easier to deal with than this query:

```
SELECT AUTHOR.NAME, PUBLICATION.TITLE, EDITION.ISBN
FROM AUTHOR JOIN PUBLICATION USING (AUTHOR_ID)
  JOIN EDITION USING (PUBLICATION_ID);
```

Why? There is less code. Less code is easier to handle. Less is more in this case.

Filtering with the WHERE Clause

The WHERE clause can be used either to include wanted records or exclude unwanted records (or both). The WHERE clause can be built in specific ways, allowing for faster execution of SQL code. Use of the WHERE clause can be applied to tune SQL statements simply by attempting to match WHERE clause specifications to indexes, sorted orders, and physical ordering in tables. In other words, filter according to how the metadata is constructed.

> *The WHERE clause is used to filter records and can, therefore, be placed in all three of SELECT, UPDATE, and DELETE commands.*

There are numerous points to keep in mind when building efficient filtering:

❑ *Single record searches* — The best filters utilize a primary key on a single table, preferably finding a single record only, or a very small number of records. This query finds the only author with primary key identifier as 10:

```
SELECT * FROM AUTHOR WHERE AUTHOR_ID = 10;
```

❑ *Record range searches* — Using the >, >=, <, and <= operators executes range searching. Range searches are not as efficient as using equality with an = operator. A group of rows rather than a single row are targeted. Range searching can still use indexing and is fairly efficient. This query finds the range of all author records, with identifiers between 5 and 10, inclusive:

```
SELECT * FROM AUTHOR WHERE AUTHOR_ID >= 5 AND AUTHOR_ID <= 10;
```

❑ *Negative WHERE clauses* — Negative filters using NOT, !=, or <> (an operator that is different in different databases) try to find something that is not there. Indexes are ignored and the entire table is read. This query reads all records, excluding only the record with author identifier as 10:

```
SELECT * FROM AUTHOR WHERE AUTHOR_ID != 10;
```

❑ *The LIKE operator* — Beware of the LIKE operator. It usually involves a full scan of a table and ignores indexing. If searching for a small number of records, this could be extremely inefficient. When searching for 10 records in 10 million, it is best to find those 10 records only using something like equality, and not pull them from all 10 million records, because all those 10 million records are read. The following query finds all authors with the vowel "a" in their names, reading the entire table:

```
SELECT * FROM AUTHOR WHERE NAME LIKE '%a%';
```

❑ *Functions in the WHERE clause* — Any type of functional expression used in a WHERE clause must be used carefully. Functions are best not to be used where you expect a SQL statement to use an index. In the following query, the function will prohibit use on an index created on the PRINT_DATE field:

```
SELECT * FROM EDITION WHERE TO_CHAR(PRINT_DATE,'DD-MON-YYYY')='01-JAN-2005';
```

Utilize the index by not applying the function to a field in a table, but using the literal value on the opposite side of the expression:

```
SELECT * FROM EDITION WHERE PRINT_DATE=TO_DATE('01-JAN-2005','DD-MON-YYYY');
```

❑ *Small and large tables* — Very small tables are often more efficiently read by reading only the table, and not the index plus the table. The same applies when large portions of a single table are read. If enough of the table is read at once, the index may as well be ignored. Reading an index involves scanning an index and then passing pointers through to a table, scanning the table with index values found. When enough of the table is read, index scanning activity to find table records can become more time-consuming than reading only the table (ignoring the index).

❑ *Composite index field sequence* — In many databases, the sequence of fields in a WHERE clause can determine if an index is matched or missed. For example, create a composite index with three fields, indexed as follows:

```
CREATE INDEX CAK_EDITION_1 ON EDITION (PUBLISHER_ID, PUBLICATION_ID, ISBN);
```

When a table is accessed with the following WHERE clause, the index will be used because all fields are included, and in the indexed field sequence:

```
SELECT ... WHERE PUBLISHER_ID=1 AND PUBLICATION=10 AND ISBN='1555583059';
```

When a table is accessed with the following WHERE clauses, the composite index may not be used (depending on the database):

```
SELECT ... WHERE ISBN='1555583059' AND PUBLISHER_ID=1 AND PUBLICATION=10;
SELECT ... WHERE ISBN='1555583059';
SELECT ... WHERE PUBLISHER_ID=1;
```

Some databases may allow index use of composite indexes for the previous queries, but it is unusual.

The first query above does not match the sequence of indexed fields. The second query contains only the last field in the index. The last query contains only the first field in the index.

❑ IN *and* EXISTS *set operators* — IN is often used to test a single value against a list of literal values, as in the following query:

```
SELECT * FROM AUTHOR WHERE AUTHOR_ID IN (1,2,3,4,5);
```

EXISTS is used to check against a dynamic set of values, such as that produced by a subquery, as in the following example:

```
SELECT * FROM AUTHOR WHERE EXISTS
  (SELECT AUTHOR_ID FROM PUBLICATION);
```

IN and EXISTS can be efficient, depending on how they are used. In other words, performing an IN check against a non-indexed field forces a full table scan. The IN operator query above checks literal values against a primary key and, thus, uses an index. The EXISTS operator full scans two tables. This can be made more efficient by incorporating a WHERE clause in both queries and by using a correlation between the calling query and subquery.

❑   *Using* AND *and* OR — AND and OR allow logical combination of multiple expressions, such as in a WHERE clause:

```
SELECT * FROM AUTHOR
```

```
WHERE NAME LIKE '%a%' OR (AUTHOR_ID >= 5 AND AUTHOR_ID <= 10);
```

Matching indexes where AND and OR operators are used is important because anything missing in an index field use could result in a full table scan.

Some databases allow for use of specialized built-in functions, very similar to regular programming CASE statements. Sometimes these CASE statement, much like functions, can be used to more efficiently replace expressions logically joined with AND and OR operators. The UNION clause is another option to consider. UNION merges two separate queries into a single set of records and can be equivalent to an OR logical operation.

The HAVING *and* WHERE *Clauses*

A common programming error is to get the purposes of the WHERE and HAVING clause filters mixed up. The WHERE clause filters records as they are read from the database (as I/O activity takes place). The HAVING clause (part of the GROUP BY clause) filters aggregated groups, after all database I/O activity has completed. Don't use the HAVING clause when the WHERE clause could be used more efficiently, and visa versa. In the following example, the PUBLISHER_ID restriction in the HAVING clause can be moved to the WHERE clause:

```
SELECT ISBN, PUBLISHER_ID, AVG(LIST_PRICE)
FROM EDITION
GROUP BY ISBN
HAVING PUBLISHER_ID > 5 AND AVG(LIST_PRICE) > 10;
```

Move the PUBLISHER_ID restriction from the HAVING clause, to the WHERE clause, as shown by the following altered query:

```
SELECT ISBN, PUBLISHER_ID, AVG(LIST_PRICE)
FROM EDITION
WHERE PUBLISHER_ID > 5
GROUP BY ISBN
HAVING AVG(LIST_PRICE) > 10;
```

Why move the condition from the HAVING clause to the WHERE clause? As already stated, the WHERE clause executes filtering at the time that I/O activity occurs. In other words, WHERE clause filtering using the second query above, should under ideal circumstances, not even read records with PUBLISHER_ID less than or equal to 5. Leaving the PUBLISHER_ID filter in the HAVING clause will not limit I/O activity because the HAVING clause is only applied after all WHERE clause filtering, and thus I/O activity has been completed. Ensuring that any filtering that can be placed into the WHERE clause — is in the WHERE clause, and not in the HAVING clause — ensures best execution efficiency, in most cases.

Joins

Chapter 5 provided a large quantity of information on joins. This section briefly examines joins, purely from a performance-tuning perspective. There are various different types of joins. Some join types can be classified with inherently good performance. Some join types might need a little manual help. Some join types can be stubbornly difficult to tune. Different join types and their tuning attributes can be described as follows:

- ❑ *Inner join* — An inner join is an intersection between two tables. The join is usually performed between two referential integrity keys in those two tables. Intersections are the most efficient types of joins because they match records between two tables based on equality (an = sign). The following query joins the PUBLISHER and EDITION tables, based on the primary and foreign key link between the two tables (one-to-many relationship). The tables are shown in Figure 8-1.

```
SELECT P.NAME AS Publisher, E.ISBN
FROM PUBLISHER P JOIN EDITION E USING (PUBLISHER_ID);
```

A self-join is a special type of intersection where records on multiple hierarchical levels, stored in a single table, are returned as a hierarchical structure.

- ❑ *Outer join* — An inner join returns an intersection between two tables. An outer join returns the opposite of an inner join. An outer join returns all records in one table, which are excluded from the other table. Profligate use of outer joins in queries could indicate a possibly over-granular database model. Tuning outer joins is inherently more difficult than tuning inner joins because outer joins are more complex to write. The following query returns the intersection between PUBLISHER and EDITION, as well as all publishers currently with no titles in print (the outer part of the outer join):

```
SELECT P.NAME AS Publisher, E.ISBN
FROM PUBLISHER P LEFT OUTER JOIN EDITION E USING (PUBLISHER_ID);
```

- ❑ *Cross join* — A cross join is a Cartesian product, joining every record in one table to every record in another table, regardless of any meaningful referential integrity connection of keys between the two tables, or any other field connection. Obviously, cross joins will be slow, depending on the number of records in both tables, relative to each other, and in total number of records. The following query returns all publishers with all editions regardless of any PUBLICATION to EDITION relationship. In other words, every book is returned with every publisher, regardless of who published the book. Even if a particular publisher did not publish a particular book, a record is still returned containing completely unrelated publishers and books (those books belonging to other publishers, or perhaps even no publisher whatsoever — self-published books).

```
SELECT P.NAME AS Publisher, E.ISBN
FROM PUBLISHER P CROSS JOIN EDITION E;
```

The most important factor for performance tuning joins is minimizing the number of tables in a join, in all types of database models

Any poorly coded join will likely be inefficient. In data warehouses, inefficient joins can easily have disastrous performance effects because of the sheer quantities of data. OLTP databases can also be crippled to the point of uselessness, but it is less likely because of smaller physical database size. One particular project I contracted on in the past, however, had a miniscule 10 GB database and joins composed of 15 tables or more in each query. Short Web page listings of 10 records were taking 30 seconds to return a response to their customers. After I spent two months persuading developers how to speed up their software, they took about a week to fix. The Web site subsequently turned those 30-second waits into less than a half a second. Internet surfers typically lose interest in Web sites taking longer than seven seconds to react.

There are some basic rules when attempting to tune SQL code joins:

❑ *Apply largest filters first* — Filter from largest tables first to reduce records joined. Retrieve tables in order from the most highly filtered table downward, preferably the largest table has the most filtering applied. It is essential to reduce record numbers from large tables as much as possible before joining them to other tables. The most highly filtered table is the table having the smallest percentage of its records retrieved; preferably, the largest table is filtered the most.

❑ *Use indexes* — Try to write code to utilize indexes wherever possible, except for very small tables. Small tables can sometimes be more efficiently read, ignoring any indexing on the small table. Small tables are often read by ignoring indexes. Sometimes even large tables are best read by ignoring indexing, especially in cases where a larger percentage of the bigger table is read.

❑ *Nested subquery semi-joins* — It is possible to tune or merely simplify joins (for easier tuning) by using nested layers of subqueries. This type of tuning is much more applicable to highly normalized OLTP database models, and does not apply to denormalized data warehouse database models.

Auto Counters

Many relational databases have some kind of automated counter or *auto counter*. An auto counter is a specific database object used to count integer values, usually from 1 upwards. Auto counters are often used by a database to fill primary key surrogate key integer values. In the old and dirty days, before the invention of auto counters, items such as unique surrogate keys were either not used or stored in a single central system metadata table. A single central system data table is potentially disastrous in highly concurrent environments, resulting in a serious hot block problem on that system data table. A *hot block problem* is where enormous quantities of queries access the same physical area of the disk, all at the same time (concurrently). Multiple operations compete for the same resources. Eventually resources become scarce and performance suffers.

This section expanded on details provided in Chapter 5 by going into detail of performance tuning of SQL code, queries in particular. Poorly designed table structures ultimately equate to queries, which are quite likely impossible to tune up to an acceptable level of performance. Well-designed table structures propagate into high-performance queries. Indexing is also important to query performance, and overall database model performance.

Efficient Indexing for Performance

Most important, always be more circumspect about creating an index rather than not creating an index. Many databases get so convoluted and mixed up with over-indexing that, after long periods of time, no one knows who created what — and why. Never be afraid of not creating an index. It follows that you should not always assume that an existing index should exist, simply because it does exist.

Types of Indexes

Some databases allow different types of indexing. In relational databases, one index type is most commonly used. That index type is usually some form of binary tree index (BTree). Other index types are nearly always rare and only applicable in specialized cases. Be aware of the needs of, and consequences for, using special types of indexing such as ISAM, hash, or bitmap indexing.

> *Different database engines use index structures and methods in different ways. Some examples are warranted here. Where one database engine allows creation of separate physical ISAM indexes, another database may use an ISAM algorithm to access a BTree index. Some databases allow creation of hash indexes as separate physical structures; others only allow application of hashing algorithms to all fields in an entire table. Some database engines allow creation of BTree indexes both as an index, and as a sorting sequence on an entire table. The table itself, and all its fields, become a BTree index (known as a clustered index or an index organized table).*

They have very specialized applications and are not commonly used. Also, be aware that these less commonly used index types are often subject to overflow when changes are made to source tables. In reality, unusual types of indexes can often be subject to performance-crippling forms of overflow. *Overflow* is where an index has its performance created index structure completely diverted from and partially undone, by data changes to tables. Most of these unusual types of indexes are more often that not for read-only type environments, and should generally be implemented and applied with great care and forethought beforehand.

Database administrators should always keep a watchful eye on indexing in a database. Of course, there is never really available time, but when an application is released it is always best to re-examine all indexing. Quite often, developers will create many indexes, sometimes each creating their own sets of indexes, for the same application. The result is over-indexing. Too many indexes on a table create a performance problem. Effectively, executing a table change command (INSERT, UPDATE, or DELETE) on a table executes the same command on all of its indexes in addition to just the table. For example, inserting a single record into a table with four indexes comprises five changes to the database.

How to Apply Indexes in the Real World

There are various ways in which indexes can be applied, generally dependent on the function of the table for which an index is created:

❑   *No index* — Data in a table is heap structured (in a heap or disorganized pile). Both small and large tables can benefit from having no indexing. Small tables may be best accessed as a whole, rather than with table and index, because they access a small amount of physical space. Large tables could very well only be read in their entirety based on application requirements. Why index a table when indexes are never used? It is even sometimes beneficial to drop referential integrity keys and indexes.

❑   *Static data* — Small static data tables are often better off without indexing. Be aware of two potential problems: removing foreign key indexes can cause serious locking problems that can drastically hamper performance; and highly complex joins with many tables usually benefit from all tables having indexes, particularly unique primary key indexes, even on small static tables.

❑ *Dynamic data*—*Dynamic data* is data that changes all the time (*transactional data*). These indexes are changed frequently, are subject to overflow, and require frequent refreshing. Be acutely aware of the type of index used for dynamic data. The default index type for a particular database is usually the best option for dynamic data. This index type is usually some form of binary tree indexing structure. Other index types involving pre-calculated structures such as ISAM, hash tables, and bitmaps will overflow almost immediately when subject to change.

Overflow of an index is seriously ugly for performance. Index overflow happens to certain types of indexes where any changes to data in tables cannot be slotted into the proper physical point in the original structure of the index. This is because of the way in which certain index types are constructed. The result of overflow and a lot of data changes could be query I/O quite literally bouncing all over disk storage trying to find data. This can cause serious performance problems.

❑ *Read only reporting index*—Unlike dynamic data indexing, read-only data is much more flexible with respect to index types, because data is not subject to change. Read-only indexing is specially designed for read only queries, often in data warehouses. Types of indexing in this category are pre-built structures subject to overflow but highly efficient when used for read only I/O activity. Index types proficient as read-only indexes (bitmaps, clusters, hash tables) are ineffective in highly dynamic environments.

❑ *Unique and non-unique indexes*—A *unique index* is an index allowing only a single value in a table. Be careful when creating unique indexes because every insertion or update to a uniquely indexed field (or fields) requires a scan of the entire index space (to verify a value as unique). A *non-unique index* allows more than one record with the same value and is typical of foreign key indexes. Unique indexing is better for performance and is typical of primary keys. A unique index is better for performance because subset index searching can be used to find single records, in theory making for less I/O, and less traversal through index structures.

❑ *Single field versus multiple field indexes*—*Multiple field indexes* are generally known as *composite field indexes*. *Single field indexes* are more efficient than composite multiple field indexes. The simple fact is the fewer fields, the less to search through. Also, fewer fields means the index is relatively much smaller than its parent table. The bigger the relative difference in size between table and index, the more effective the index is at reducing I/O, especially for larger tables.

❑ *Datatypes to index*—Integers are always best. An *integer* is a whole number with no digits to the right of the decimal point. Any other datatypes are nearly always flexible in terms of both length and content. Fixed-length strings are not quite as efficient as integers but they can be good options for index construction if the strings are a few characters, such as with use of codes. Quite often, codes are used to represent structures, such as code names for states in the United States. For example, NY represents the state of New York and CA represents California. Numbers are still better because there are 10 possible digits. Character strings have 26 different variations for the letters of the alphabet, plus 10 possible digits (strings are alphanumeric and can contain numerals as well), plus all sorts of punctuation and other odd characters.

❑ *Sacrificing referential integrity for performance*—Sometimes this is a good idea, but most often it is not. Dropping of foreign key indexing can cause serious locking issues. Referential integrity uses primary and foreign keys to validate relationships between records in related tables. If there is a lot of validation occurring, and a table containing a foreign key has no foreign key index, the child table could be frequently fully scanned, resulting in huge competition for the entire table rather than just the index.

❑ *Optimizing with alternate indexes* — *Alternate indexing* is often referred to as *secondary indexing*. Alternate indexing includes any indexes created against tables in a database model, which are not part of referential integrity constraints. Quite often, the need for alternate indexing is a mismatch between the database model and functionality required by applications. Excessive alternate indexing could indicate the database model not catering to application needs. Reporting or data warehousing application requirements will usually cause further demand for alternate indexing.

When Not to Use Indexes

Possibly the most important question is when should an index not be created? There are some circumstances where indexes can be detrimental to performance and sometimes those indexes should not exist. Sometimes (in fact, quite frequently), it is better for query performance for indexes to be ignored, and the entire table be read. The following explains when indexes should be avoided.

❑ A table with a small number of fields may not benefit from an index if a large percentage of its records are always retrieved from it. Creating an index will not prevent full table scans. Note that removing primary key or foreign keys is not a good idea.

❑ Small static data tables are often small enough to be read as a table scan rather than an index scan, plus a point into a table. Let's explain by example. Underlying I/O activity in the operating system (UNIX, Windows, Linux, and many others) is read in what are sometimes called *blocks* or *pages*. These pages can be many sizes, but usually at the database level the pages become 2 KB, 4 KB, 8 KB, 16 KB, and sometimes even 32 KB pages. The point to understand is that if a table has a small enough number of records, to occupy a single physical page, why read an index and point to a table? Reading the index and the table is reading two pages, when reading the table only constitutes an I/O on a single page only.

❑ Often, tables created for reporting or during data warehouse periodical appending (batch updates) may already be in the required physical order.

❑ Indexes should usually be created on a small percentage of the fields in a table. Large composite indexes may be relatively large compared with the table. The relative size between index and table is important. The larger the ratio of index to table physical size, the less helpful the index will be in terms of decreasing physical space to be read. Fields containing NULL values may exacerbate this effect. It may be faster to read the entire table, rather than a large composite field index, containing a lot of NULL values. Why create indexes with every field for a composite? It is, of course, acceptable to create a duplicate valued index on less than all the fields desired by the composite field structure. Sometimes a partial index is more efficient than no index, and also more efficient than the complete field set for a composite field index.

That's indexing. Indexes are important to database modeling and overall database performance as a whole, even to the point of not using indexing under certain circumstances. Overuse of indexing can hinder performance just as easily as not using indexing where indexing should be used.

What about using views?

Using Views

Quite contrary to popular belief, views can actually hurt performance—not necessarily because they exist, but because of the ways in which they are commonly used in commercial environments. Why should views not be implemented as a performance tuning tool, when in the database model design phase? This book is after all, all about database modeling.

> *Views are not the same thing as materialized views. A view creates a logical overlay without copying data from tables. Query a view and you query the underlying tables directly. Materialized views are physical copies of data. Query a materialized view and you query the materialized view, and not the underlying tables.*

Views are not conducive to performance. In other words, they can make your applications run a whole heck of a lot slower. Being the author of this book, I have to try to impress on you that I am not biased when it comes to views. How can I convince you of this? Well to begin with, I have worked as both a database administrator and an applications developer. What this means is that I have used views from both the perspective of building new software (development), and that of maintaining existing software (administration).

Views are usually used by administrators to implement security, down to the record and field levels. In other words, a view can be used to restrict specific users to access only specific records in a table. This is because a view contains a query. That query can have a WHERE clause filter, restricting the records returned from underlying tables:

```
CREATE VIEW BooksStartingWithA AS SELECT * FROM EDITION WHERE TITLE LIKE 'A%';
```

When querying this view, you will find only books with titles beginning with the letter A. The next query restricts access to fields in a table, as opposed to restricting access to records:

```
CREATE VIEW BooksWithoutRankings AS SELECT ISBN,PUBLISHER_ID,PUBLICATION_ID
    ,PRINT_DATE,PAGES,LIST_PRICE,FORMAT FROM EDITION WHERE TITLE LIKE 'A%';
```

The table from which this view retrieves records is shown in Figure 8-2.

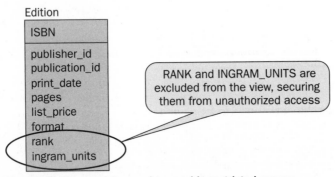

Figure 8-2: Views can be used to provide restricted access.

The only way to access the RANK and INGRAM_UNITS field is by accessing the table directly in the following query:

```
SELECT * FROM EDITION;
```

Obviously, if you do not want particular users accessing ranks and Ingram numbers, you can restrict access to the table, allowing general access to the view only. End-users can only access the view.

Different types of security access are required by different users. End-users only get to access data from the views that are specifically built for them; therefore, an executive-level manager can see all fields, for all records, in tables a non-management employee would be prohibited from looking at (such as employee salaries). Employees seeing each other's salaries can cause morale problems. Then again, an executive may simply access different information, perhaps wanting factual business-applicable information, avoiding technical details.

The problem with views is that they slow things down because they are often used by developers, or administrators, to make application coding easier. So, the issue is that there is absolutely nothing wrong with using views. The real problem is that views are very often inappropriately used. This is a highly significant consideration. You can never, ever assume that everyone having access to a database knows and understands everything about everything. And you, as a database modeler, cannot expect it even of yourself. Look at it this way. If executive managers use data warehouse reporting, they probably know as much about the internal workings of your database as you know about executive management — Nothing!

Views are database objects even if they are only logical overlays. If they are used in a database, they do effectively become a part of the database model because they tend to break things down, even if only in a logical and not a physical sense. When considering views and database model performance, keep an eye on use of views. The more you allow the use of views by developers and the general user population, the more you must monitor and performance-tune those views. If managing those views becomes an overwhelming task you may eventually be faced with a difficult task to resolve performance problem.

In my 20 years of development and administration experience, I've found that the best way to avoid abuse, misuse, and misunderstood use of views is to avoid using views altogether. That is my philosophical approach and is by no means an absolute rule.

Be careful using views. Views have very specific roles and the biggest danger is misuse of views.

Another interesting topic to discuss is application caching.

Application Caching

Application caching is where data can be stored in the memory of a client computer. That client computer can even be on the other side of the world, using an Internet browser. Application caching is significant to database model performance because the best things to cache are static tables.

In any database, it can sometimes be an effective performance-tuning method to cache static data, or even index structures, even dynamic table indexes. This caching process can be implemented on the database server, within the server, on an application server, and even in the application itself, even as far as a front-end application passed to a multitude of unknown users over the Internet (in a browser).

211

For OLTP databases, just the static data tables can be cached, even perhaps some dynamic table indexes as well. Caching makes perfect sense for OLTP databases because very high levels of sharing are prevalent (high concurrency). For example, an online bookstore might perform much better for a user buying books if all recently accessed static files, by that specific user, were cached as soon as the user logged in. Sometimes, even partially static files can be preloaded into an application such as an online bookstore. Common types of structures in this category for online bookstores as likely candidates for online browser caching are wish lists, the contents of a shopping cart, previously purchased items, and the list goes on.

Caching of any form is completely useless in data warehouses because fact tables are usually so incredibly huge in comparison with dimensions. Also, tables are accessed infrequently and by very few users at once. For data warehouses, quantities of data in each table have much more significant impact. Caching large data warehouse tables in memory would fill hardware resource capacities rapidly. Data warehouses are simply I/O intensive and that is all there is to it.

Summary

In this chapter, you learned about:

- ❑ Factors affecting tuning of OLTP database models
- ❑ Factors affecting tuning of client-server database models
- ❑ Factors affecting tuning of data warehouse database models
- ❑ Writing efficient queries using the SELECT command, the WHERE clause and joins
- ❑ Auto counters and surrogate keys
- ❑ The type of indexes useful for performance
- ❑ Index types and how they apply in reality
- ❑ When not to use indexing
- ❑ Performance problems caused by views down the road
- ❑ Application caching used to reduce database demand and network activity

This chapter linked the theory presented in previous chapters with case study and database modeling in practice, to be presented in chapters to follow this chapter. This linking process has been done using the most critical factor to all database installations—performance. If the database and its attached applications do not perform up to scratch, end-users will not be happy, and will probably go elsewhere, or find another employee to replace you. Performance tuning is a highly complex topic and this chapter has barely scratched the surface. The intention of this chapter has been to attempt to give a very brief mental impression of how database modeling theory might be applied in the real world, perhaps attempting to tweak a subconscious change in your train of thought, as you read through this book. In other words, the approach in this chapter is changing the direction of this book from theory into practice, in small steps. The idea is to make it all a little easier to absorb.

Exercises

Answer the following questions:

1. Which of these apply to OLTP databases?

  a. Large transactions

  b. High concurrency

  c. Frequent servicing opportunities

  d. Real-time response to end-users

2. Which of these apply to data warehouse databases?

  a. Lots of users

  b. High concurrency

  c. Very large database

  d. High granularity

3. Which aspect of a query affects performance most profoundly? Select the most appropriate answer.

  a. WHERE clause filtering

  b. Sorting with the ORDER BY clause

  c. Aggregating with the GROUP BY clause

  d. The number of tables in join queries

  e. The number of fields in join queries

4. Assume that there 1,000,000 records in a table. One record has AUTHOR_ID = 50. AUTHOR_ID as the primary key. Which is the fastest query?

  a. SELECT * FROM AUTHOR WHERE AUTHOR_ID != 50;

  b. SELECT * FROM AUTHOR WHERE AUTHOR_ID = 50;

Part III
A Case Study in Relational Database Modeling

In this Part:

Planning and Preparation Through Analysis

"The temptation to form premature theories upon insufficient data is the bane of our profession." (Sherlock Holmes)

"It almost looks like analysis were the third of those impossible professions in which one can be quite sure of unsatisfying results. The other two, much older-established, are the bringing up of children and the government of nations." (Sigmund Freud)

Rocket science is an exact science. Analysis is by no means an exact science.

In planning this book, I thought of just that—planning. Where would the human race be without planning? Probably still up in the trees hanging from gnarly branches, shouting "Aaark!" every now and again. Previous chapters in this book have examined not only the theory of how to create a relational database model but also some other interesting topics, such as the history of it all, and why these things came about.

At this stage, why the relational database model was devised should make some sense. Additionally, different applications cause a need for different variations on the same theme, leading to the invention of specialized data warehouse database models. A data warehouse database model is denormalized to the point of being more or less totally unrecognizable when compared to an OLTP (transactional) type relational database model structure. ERDs for OLTP and data warehouse database models only appear similar. The two are completely different in structure because the data warehouse database model is completely denormalized. This is why it is so important to present both OLTP and data warehouse database models in this book. Both are relevant, and both require intensive planning and preparation to ensure useful results.

This chapter begins a case study where theoretical information (absorbed from previous chapters) is applied in a practical real-world scenario. This chapter (and the next three following chapters) uses practice to apply theory presented in the first seven chapters. Why? Theory and practice are two completely different things. Theory describes and expounds on a set of rules, attempting to quantify and explain the real world in a formal manner, with formal methods. Formal methods are essentially a precise mathematical expression as a methodology. A methodology is an approach as applied to a real-world scenario. In this book, the desired result is usable underlying *structure*—a relational database model.

Without placing a set of rules into practice, in a recognizable form, from start to finish, understanding of theory is often lost through memorization. In other words, there is no point learning something by heart without actually having a clear understanding of what you are learning, and why you are learning it. Using a case study helps to teach by application of theory.

This might all seem a little silly, but I have always found that a little understanding lends itself to not requiring my conscious mind to mindlessly memorize everything about a topic. I prefer to understand rather than memorize. I find that understanding makes me much more capable of applying what I have learned in not-yet-encountered scenarios. By understanding a multiple-chapter case study, you should learn how everything fits together.

So far, you have read about history, some practical application, and lots and lots of theory. Even some advanced stuff (such as data warehousing and performance) has been skimmed over briefly. What's the point of all this information, crammed into your head, without any kind of demonstration? The act of demonstrating is exactly how this book proceeds from here on in with a progressive, fictitious case study example. There are plenty of examples in previous chapters, but it's all been little pieces. This chapter starts the development of a larger case study example. The idea is to demonstrate and describe the process of creating a database model for an entire application. And it starts at the very beginning. The only assumptions made are that everyone knows how to work the mouse, and we all know what a computer is. This chapter begins the process of creating appropriate database models for an OLTP database and a data warehouse. The specific company type will be an online auctioning Web site. Online auctions have high concurrent activity (OLTP activity), and a large amount of potential historical trans-actions (data warehouse activity).

This chapter begins with the very basics. The very basics are not getting out a piece of paper and drawing table structures, or installing your favorite ERD tool and getting to it. The very beginning of database model design (and any software project for that matter) is drawing up a specific analysis of what is actually needed. You should talk to people and analyze what software should be built, if any. There are, of course, other important factors. How much is it going to cost? How long will it take? The intention of this chapter is to subliminally give a message of focusing on how to obtain the correct information, from the right people. The goal is to present information as *structure*.

By the time you have completed reading this chapter, you should have a good understanding of the analytical process, not only for database modeling, but also as applicable for any software development process. More importantly, you should get a grip on the importance of planning. It is possible to build a bridge without drawing, designing, and architecting. An engineer could avoid doing lots of nasty complicated mathematical civil engineering calculations. What about planning that bridge? Imagine a bridge that is built from the ground up with no planning. Whoever pays the engineer to build the bridge is probably prudent to ask the builder to be the first to walk across it.

In this chapter, you learn about the following:

- ❏ The basics of analysis and design
- ❏ The steps in the analysis process
- ❏ Common problem areas and misconceptions associated with analysis
- ❏ The value of following a paper trail

❑   How to create a database model to cover objectives

❑   How to refine a database model using business rules

❑   How to apply everything learned so far with a comprehensive case study

Steps to Creating a Database Model

Before beginning in earnest with the case study example, you need to sidestep a little over the course of this and the next few chapters. There is an abundance of information covering the systematized process (the "what and how") of building a database model.

The building of a database model can be divided up into distinct steps (as can any software development process). These steps can be loosely defined as follows:

1.   Analysis

2.   Design

3.   Construction

4.   Implementation

Take a brief look at each of these in a bit more detail.

Step 1: Analysis

Analyzing a situation or company is a process of initial fact-finding through interviews with end-users. If there are technical computer staff members on hand, with the added bonus of inside company operational knowledge, interview them as well.

A proper analysis cannot be achieved by interviewing just the technical people. An all-around picture of a client or scenario is required. End-users are those who will eventually use what you are building. The end-users are more important! A database system is built for applications. Technical people program the applications. End-users are the ultimate recipients of whatever you are providing as the database designer or modeler.

As stated previously, analysis is more about what is required, not how it will be provided. What will the database model do to fulfill requirements? How it will fulfill requirements is a different issue. Analysis essentially describes a business. What does the company do to earn its keep? If a company manufactures tires for automobiles, it very likely does such things as buying rubber, steel, and nylon for reinforcement, purchasing valves, advertising its tires, and selling tires, among a myriad of other things. Analysis helps to establish what a company does to get from raw materials to finished product. In the case of the tire manufacturer, the raw materials are rubber, steel, nylon, and valves. The finished products are the tires.

Analysis is all about what a company does for a living? This equates to analyzing what are the tables in the database? And what are the most basic and essential relationships between those tables?

Analysis defines general table structure. An auction Web site might contain a seller table and a bidder table. You must know what tables should generally contain in terms of information content. Should both the seller and bidder tables contain addresses of sellers and bidders respectively? Analysis merely defines. Analysis does not describe how many fields should be used for an address, or what datatypes those fields should be. Analysis simply determines that an address field actually exists, and, obviously, which table or tables require address information.

Step 2: Design

Design involves using what was discovered during analysis, and figuring out how those analyzed things can be catered for, with the software tools available. The analysis stage decided what should be created. The design stage applies more precision by deciding how tables should be created. This includes the tables, their fields, and datatypes. Most importantly, it includes how everything is linked together.

Analysis defines tables, information in tables, and basic relationships between tables. The linking together aspect of the design stage is, in its most basic form, the precise definition of referential integrity. *Referential integrity* is a design process because it enforces relationships between tables. The initial establishment of inter-table relationships is an analysis process, not one of designs.

In other words, analysis defines what is to be done; design organizes how it's done. The design stage introduces database modeling refinement processing, such as normalization and denormalization. In terms of application construction, the design stage begins to define front-end user "bits and pieces" such as reports and graphical user interface (GUI) screens.

> *Build the tables graphically, add fields, define datatypes, and apply referential integrity. Refine through use of processes such as normalization and denormalization.*

Step 3: Construction

In this stage, you build and test code. For a database model, you build scripts to create tables, referential integrity keys, indexes, and anything else such as stored procedures. In other words, with this step, you build scripts to create tables and execute them.

Step 4: Implementation

This is the final step in the process. Here you create a production database. In other words, it is at this stage of the process that you actually put it all into practice.

> This book is primarily concerned with the *analysis stage* but partially with the *design stage* as well. As already stated, *construction* is all about testing and verification. *Implementation* is putting it into production. This book is about database modeling — analysis and design. The construction and implementation phases are largely irrelevant to this text; however, it is important to understand that analysis and design do not complete the entire building process. Physical construction and implementation are required to achieve an end result.

The case study example introduced later in this chapter is all about analyzing what is needed for a database model — the analysis stage of the process. Let's turn our attention to analysis. What is analysis and how can you go about the process of analyzing for a database model?

Understanding Analysis

As you have learned, analysis is the beginning point in the building of a good relational database model. Analysis is about the operational factors of a company, the business of a company. It is not about the technical aspects of the computer system. It is not about the database model, or what the administrators, or programmers want, and would like to see. The analyst must understand the business. Participation from people in the business — the company employees, both technical and non-technical (end-users), even up to and including executive management level — is critical to success. On the other hand, complete control cannot be passed to the company. Some companies develop software using only temporarily hired staff, with no in-house technical involvement whatsoever. This can result in an entirely end-user oriented database model. There needs to be a balance between both technical and non-technical input.

It is important to understand that the analysis stage is a requirements activity. What is needed? When building a database model, an application or a software product, it is important to understand that there is a process to figuring what is in a database. What tables do you need? In computer jargon, these processes are often called *methodologies* (a set of rules) by which a builder of computer systems gets from A to B (from doodles on scrap paper, to a useful computer system) A lot of people have spent many years mulling over these sets of rules, refining and redefining, giving anyone and everyone a series of sometimes easy or sometimes incredibly complex steps to follow, in getting from A to B.

> *Normalization is a methodology. Normalization is a complex set of rules for refining relational database table structures. Dividing up the database model design process into separate steps of analysis, design, construction, and implementation, is also a methodology.*

The best database models are produced by paying attention to detail in the analysis stage. It is important to understand exactly what is needed before jumping in and "just getting to it." If changes are required at a later stage of development, changes can be added at a later stage; however, making changes to a database model used in a production system can be extremely problematic, so much so as to not be an option. This is because applications are usually dependent on a database and therefore usually dependent on the database model.

Analysis is planning. It is doubly important to plan for a database model. The reason is that the database model forms the basis of all database-driven applications, quite often for an entire company. In the case of an off-the-shelf product, that database model could drive duplicated and semi-customized applications for hundreds and even thousands of companies. Getting the database model right in the first place is critical. The more that is understood about requirements in the analysis stage, the better a database model and product will ultimately be produced.

Some database modeling and design tools allow generation of table scripts into different database engines. The tool used for database modeling in this book is called ERWin. ERWin can be used to generate table creation scripts for a number of database engines. Microsoft Access has its own built-in ERD modeling tool. Database models can generally be designed using pretty pictures in a graphical database modeling tool, such as ERWin. Building a database model using pretty pictures and fancy graphics packages allows for an analytical mindset and approach, ignoring some of the more technical details when performing analysis. Deep-level technical aspects (such as field datatypes and precise composition) can actually muddy the perspective of analysis by including too much complexity at the outset.

Analysis is about what is needed. Design is about how to provide what is needed by an already completed analysis.

In the case of a rewrite of an existing system (reconstruction of an existing database model), analysis simply includes the old system in interviews and discussions with end-users and technical staff. If a system is being rewritten, it is likely that the original system is inadequate, for one or more reasons. The analysis process should be partially performed to enlighten as to exactly what is missing, incorrect, or inadequate.

End-users are likely to tell you what they cannot do with the existing system. End-users are also likely to have a long list of what they would like. A conservative approach on the part of the analyst is to assess what enhancements and new features are most important. This is because one of the most important features of the analysis stage is how much it is all going to cost. The more work that is done, the more it will cost.

Technical staffers, such as programmers and administrators, are likely to tell you what is wrong. They can also tell you how they "got around" inadequacies, such as what "kludges" they used.

A "kludge" is a term often used by computer programmers to describe a clumsy or inelegant solution to a problem. The result is often a computer system consisting of a number of poorly matched elements.

Analysis Considerations

Because the analysis stage is a process of establishing and quantifying what is needed, you should keep in mind several factors and considerations, including the following:

❑ *Overall objectives* — These include the objectives of a company when creating a database model What should be in the database model? What is the expected result? What should be achieved? For example, is it a new application or a rewrite?

❑ *Company operations* — These include the operations of a company in terms of what the company does to make its keep. How can all this be computerized?

❑ *Business rules* — This is the heart of the analysis stage, describing what has been analyzed and what needs to be created to design the database model. What tables are needed and what are the basic relationships between those tables?

❑ *Planning and timelines* — A project plan and timeline are useful for larger projects. Project plans typically include who does what and when. More sophisticated plans integrate multiple tasks, sharing them among many people, and ensuring that dependencies are catered for. For example, if task B requires completion of task A, the same person can do both tasks A and B. If there is no dependency, two people can do both tasks A an B at the same time.

❑ *Budgeting* — How much will it cost? Is it cost effective? Is it actually worth it? Is it affordable? Will it give the company an edge over the competition without bankrupting the company before being able to bring that competitive edge to market? This includes the following considerations:

  ❑ *Hiring help costs money* — Do you need hired help? Help is expensive. Are skilled personnel available? Is recruitment required? Are expensive consultants required?

  ❑ *Hardware costs* — Hardware requirements in terms of speed and capacity should be assessed. Concurrency in terms of number and size of processors, on-board RAM, specialized hardware (RAID arrays), and network bandwidth are important factors for OLTP databases. Storage space projections and I/O performance are very significant for data warehouses.

  ❑ *Maintenance* — Ease of future maintenance implies lower long-term costs.

  ❑ *Training* — End-users and programmers must know how to use what is being created. Otherwise, it may be difficult at best to apply, if not completely useless. If a database designer introduces a new database engine such as Oracle Database into a company, training is a requirement, and must be budgeted for. Technical training can be extremely expensive and time-consuming.

❑ *Other factors* — Other less-noticed (but not less-relevant) factors include the following:

  ❑ *Duplication of data* — Avoid duplication of data (if performance is not sacrificed) and excessive granularity. Excessive granularity is often a result of over-normalization. Over-normalization can make SQL code much more complex to write, more difficult to make it perform acceptably, and much more problematic and expensive to maintain.

Excessive application of normalization removes potential for error in data (referential integrity violations). It also makes for ERDs with hundreds of tables and a lot of head-scratching on the part of programmers. Over-normalization is perfection to a database designer, and a programmer's nightmare. Relational database model design is a means to an end, not a process in itself. In other words, build a database model for programmers and end-users. Don't build a database model based on a mathematical precept of perfection because ultimately only the database modeler can understand it. Keep the objective in mind. That objective is to service application requirements and give the company an edge, but not to make life difficult for everyone involved.

  ❑ *Read-only or read-write* — Is a database read-only or is full read-write access required? Data warehouse databases are often partially read-only. Some parts of OLTP databases are can be somewhat read only, usually only where static data is concerned. Specialized methods can be applied to static tables, allowing for more flexibility in OLTP databases.

Not surprising, the considerations for the overall objectives, company operations, business rules, planning and timeliness, and budgeting all can serve as an outline for the analysis process. In fact, later in this chapter, the development of the case study example incorporates each of these considerations. Before you get to the case study example, see what potential problems lurk in the darkness when analyzing a company database model.

The "Other Factors" mentioned in the previous list are covered in detail in this chapter. These factors relate to topics already covered in previous chapters of this book.

Potential Problem Areas and Misconceptions

There are a number of negative factors worth considering and remembering, when analyzing a company database model. These include the following:

- ❑ Normalization and data integrity
- ❑ More normalization leads to better queries
- ❑ Performance
- ❑ Generic and standardized database models

Let's take a closer look.

Normalization and Data Integrity

Many analysts put forward the opinion that applying all levels of normalization through use of all available normal forms ensures no lost data (redundancy), and no referential integrity mismatches (orphaned records). A database is an information repository. Poor application programming or poor database use produces problematic data. Highly normalized database models can help ensure better data integrity, but the database model itself does not produce the problem. Application programmers and end-users cause the problem by making coding errors and incorrect changes in a database.

More Normalization Leads to Better Queries

This is another opinion put forward by many analysts. Some statements that might be made could be of the following forms:

- ❑ "Problem queries are often the result of an inadequate (denormalized) database structure."
- ❑ "It is much easier to write faster queries and updates against a normalized database structure."

My opinion is completely opposite on both counts. Denormalized structures lead to faster queries and they are easier for end-users to write. Denormalized tables tend to match a business more accurately from an operational perspective. In other words, the busy executives writing those ad-hoc queries can understand the tables and how tables relate to each other.

Building queries with lots of tables results in huge join queries. Join queries can be very complicated not only to write, but also to make them execute in less than a week (sarcasm intended). For the database novice end-user, writing highly complex join queries is really too much to expect. It simply isn't fair. Even for experienced programmers, building a join query against a DKNF level normalized database model often borders on the ridiculous. For example, 15 tables in a single join query against a database containing a paltry 1 GB taking 30 seconds is completely unacceptable. I have seen this in the past.

> *Database modeling should not be approached as an expression of mathematical perfection, but more as a means to an end. The means is the database model. The end is to service the users. The end is not to produce the most granularly perfect database model if it does not service the required needs.*

Performance

Some analysts state that the performance of a computer, its applications, and its database model are irrelevant to the analysis of a business. I disagree with this approach completely. I have seen applications and entire server environments thrown on the garbage pile of history because they were not built with performance foremost in mind, from the very beginning. Performance is always important. Analyzing a database model without performance in mind is like buying a new boat when you can't afford it—a hole in the water for throwing money into.

All SQL code depends on underlying table structure and table contents, even back to table identification and table information content. All this stuff is decided on in the analysis phase. Decisions made during analysis absolutely affect performance in the long term. Database and application performance is far from unimportant.

Generic and Standardized Database Models

Beware of generic database models or a model that is accepted as a standard for a particular industry or application. Generic database models are often present in purchased, perhaps semi-customizable applications. Generic models cater to a large variety of applications. If you are investing in a database model of your own, you may as well build a company-specific database model. Generic models often have a lot of scope that does not apply to the requirements of a specific company. In other words, your database might have many empty, useless tables. Unused tables are not really a problem technically, but they can cause serious confusion for programmers and end-users. The other downside to a generic model is that it may not cater exactly to all your needs, and will very likely require modification anyway.

Standardized database models, particular to a specific industry and perhaps accepted as the norm, are also dangerous because they are likely to be very out of date. As for generic models, standardized models are also likely to contain superfluous tables, with all the possible problems and inadequacies that go with it. Once again, if you are building a database model, you may as well invest in the real thing and custom build it for your company and your specific applications; however, narrowing of scope could build inflexibility and ultimately limitations into the system. It's all about achieving a good balance.

It's now time to get to the business of why you are here, why I am writing this book, and why you are so busily reading this chapter. How do you begin to put theory into practice? Start by analyzing.

Putting Theory into Practice

For the remainder of this chapter (and much of what is in the three chapters that follow), you build upon a case study example in an effort to put theory into practice. Recall from the beginning of this chapter that the case study involves a fictitious online auction house. This chapter performs the analysis stage of the case study. What does a database model need? What is in it?

Putting Analysis into Practice

As you learned at the beginning of this chapter, the first step in putting the database modeling process into practice is analysis. Discover and quantify what exactly it is that the company does to make ends meet. Remember that to perform a proper analysis, you must keep the following in mind:

- ❏ Company objectives
- ❏ Company operations
- ❏ Business rules

❑   Planning and timelines

❑   Budgeting

You perform the analysis stage for your case study by examining each of the items in the list. The following discussion begins with an examination of company objectives for the online auction house; however, once you have established what those objectives are, you then branch off a bit. You examine company operations and business rules in two separate contexts: one for an OLTP database, and one for a data warehouse model. By the end of the chapter, however, you'll converge back into a discussion of planning, timelines, and budgeting for your overall case study example.

So, let's find out exactly what the objectives of our online auction house really are.

Company Objectives

The most important objective is that the company actually turns a profit. After all, without profit, you have no company! In addition, the overall objective of software is always to provide a service to customers. For your online auction house, the customers are the *sellers* and *bidders*. Sellers list items for auction. Bidders place bids on listed items, hoping to win the auction.

After users are serviced adequately, if the business idea is a viable possibility, it has a better chance of succeeding in the commercial marketplace. A computer system would give a company an edge over its competition. Using the Internet, an online auction house is extremely likely to reach far more potential customers than an offline auction house. This would make it possible for the auction house to market far less expensive products, in very much larger quantities. Obviously, commissions would be lower. After all, world-famous auction houses such as Sotheby's auction only multimillion-dollar items, such as rare works of art. An online auction house can make good profitability, however, out of much higher quantities, all the while auctioning much cheaper items.

So, an online auction house has a very large potential market of sellers and buyers. Technically, this makes the usage capacity of this database highly shareable (concurrent) between thousands of users, if not more. An OLTP database model structure is, therefore, desirable. Also, it is valuable to the auction house (and perhaps many of its selling clientele) to understand trends. Trends and forecasting can be established using forecasts and projects into archived data sets. Archived data can be stored conveniently and efficiently using a specialized data warehouse database.

Technical objectives for this company would be to provide a data model for a highly concurrent OLTP database, plus an I/O intense data warehouse data model as well.

One additional factor concerns already existing software and database modeling, already used by the online auction house, for example. If the company is already computerized, already existing software and models can be used as a basis for creating new software.

> *Once again, a word of warning: If software is being rewritten, is the existing software inadequate? If so, why? Would using characteristics of existing software simply propagate existing problems into new software?*

Before tackling the two different database models, take a moment to think about how you can define the operations of your online auction house.

Following the Paper Trail and Talking to People

There are a couple of ways to analyze the operations of a company: look at its existing systems, (computerized or otherwise) and talk to its employees.

In the mean old days when most companies were not computerized, there was immense value in the simple pieces of paper that people in a company spent some (or even most) of the day writing on, stapling together, and pushing across their desks. Some of those pieces of paper can provide you with the inside scoop on a company's operations — even down to the tables and fields, datatypes, and defaulted values on specific fields, in specific tables. Take, for example, the invoice shown in Figure 9-1.

```
INVOICE NUMBER z0061843     04/06/05
   SHIP TO:
     MY STUFF
     MY Address
     Somewhere in Florida
QTY              DESCRIPTION                     AMOUNT
*********************************************************
   1             D'ADDARIO ECB81-5 BASS FLATWOOD  29.99
                                     *************
                              PRODUCT   29.99
                                  TAX    0.00
                    POSTAGE & HANDLING    4.04
                                     *************
                    PAY METHOD TOTAL $   34.03
```

Figure 9-1: A simple paper invoice can speak volumes about a company's activities.

Figure 9-1 is an invoice for something purchased from an online retailer. This particular invoice is very basic and was delivered to the buyer using email. Obviously, if the invoice was printed on a printer, it would become the namesake of its caption (a paper invoice). What can be analyzed from this invoice?

1. Each invoice is numbered.

2. The invoice number is not numeric. It might consist of two separate codes, the first a letter, and the second a sequential number.

3. The item is shipped to someone at a specified address (blacked out in Figure 9-1). This is the address of the customer who purchased the item.

4. The QTY column indicates that each invoice can be for multiples of the same item, purchased at the same point in time. It follows logically that each invoice could probably include multiples of many different items on the same invoice as well.

5. Each item line of one or more QTY entries has a total amount.

6. Sales tax or value-added tax (VAT) is not always applicable, but it does imply international trading and shipping, or shipping between any two states in the U.S.

7. POSTAGE & HANDLING means that the seller ships items. The seller probably makes a small profit on shipping charges as well, but that is beside the point.

8. A quick search of the Web for the item name "D'ADDARIO ECB81-5 BASS FLATWOUND" indicates that the online retailer sells replacement parts for musical instruments. This particular retailer could, of course, sell all sorts of other things, but this particular item is a set of flat wound strings for a five-string, electric bass guitar.

The invoice by itself, as shown in Figure 9-1, told me exactly eight things about the company concerned. It even told me what the company did, or very likely did as its primary source of revenue. This company sells musical instruments. The point is that simply by having the invoice, I can make a fairly good guess at what this company's business is, and I have not talked to any employees, visited the company, or even as much as looked them up the Internet to find out what they do.

The pieces of paper are important. So is interviewing people. Quite often, those interviews turn into long talks on the part of the company employee telling you all about their job. Get them talking and they will tell you everything about what they do, what everyone else does, even down to office politics and gossip (which you probably don't want to hear anyway, but it could all be useful someday). Talking to all these people might also get you a lot more pieces of paper, like the one shown in Figure 9-2. Figure 9-2 is a different invoice but this time with two items instead of a single item.

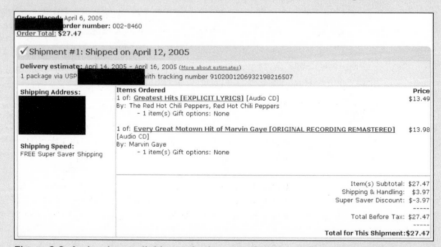

Figure 9-2: An invoice available on the Internet, from an online retailer, when purchasing.

Case Study: The OLTP Database Model

Begin by analyzing and presenting the OLTP database model for the online auction house.

Establishing Company Operations

Establishing the operational functions of a company is a process of understanding what a company does as a reason for its existence. For example, a paper mill harvests wood from mature forests. That wood is shipped to a nearby mill. The mill then processes the wood into pulp, ultimately producing paper.

Auction House Categories

An online auction house is more of a go-between in that it does not produce anything but acts as an agent for a seller. A seller sells an item by offering it up for auction to any number of potential buyers. Buyers make bids until a specified time period has passed, at which point the auction winning bidder is decided. The auction house makes its revenue by charging the seller a commission for listing the item up for auction.

The intention at this point in the analysis is to simply establish what goes on operationally within the online auction house. What pieces of information make up the database model (static data), and what pieces of information are moving through the database model (transactional data)? Note the use of the word "information" at this stage (that is, the word "data" is not used).

Examine the operational aspects for an online auction house database model. There are a number of category layers:

❑   The *primary category layer* divides all listed items into primary categories, such as musical instruments, books, antiques, collectibles, toys, hobbies. There are others that will be detailed at a later stage.

   You are not as yet concerned with detail. In other words, don't get bogged down in detail. Concentrate on the facts.

❑   The *secondary category* layer is effectively a subcategory within each of the primary categories. For example, the category for musical instruments can contain secondary category items, such as brass instruments, woodwind instruments, and stringed instruments.

❑   A *third* or *tertiary category* layer would be a potential subcategory within the secondary category layer. For example, the brass instruments secondary category could contain items such as trumpets, trombones, and French horns.

Figure 9-3 shows a simple diagram of the structure of the category information for our online auction house. Note how each tertiary category element has a secondary category element parent, and each secondary has a primary category parent. Also note that secondary category elements do not have to have any contained tertiary items.

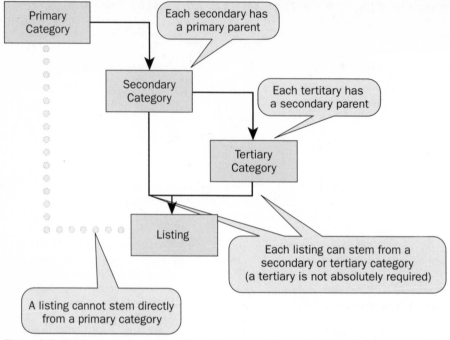

Figure 9-3: Static categories information placed as static parts of the database model.

Auction House Seller Listings

Auction *listings* are essentially an item a seller is selling, listed on the auction site for sale. Each listing must be contained within a secondary or tertiary category:

❑ Each auction listing contains a link through to details about the seller (the person or organization selling the item), such as the seller's name and address, the starting price of the item, and shipping details (shipping is required for an online auction house to determine who and where an item should be sent to, upon auction listing completion).

❑ An auction listing must have a seller, but not necessarily a final buyer. If there are no bids placed on the item, no buyer buys the auctioned item — there is no buyer.

❑ Auction listings have links to other subsets, which are one-to-many master-detail sets of information:

    ❑ Each auction can have a link to a history about the seller. Is the seller a reputable seller? This section consists of reviews of how past buyers have felt about dealing with a particular seller.

    ❑ Each auction item can have a link to a history of bids on a particular auction item. Both sellers and buyers could then examine all past bids made on an auctioned item, over the life of each auction listing.

Figure 9-4 shows the relationships between a seller and their auction listings, and their history of past dealings with buyers. Sellers can have more than one listing, not only over a period of time, but can list more than one item at the same time. There are also special types of auctions where a single listing can list multiple items for sale to multiple possible bidders, depending on how many items a bidder wishes to buy.

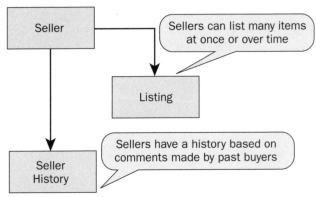

Figure 9-4: Sellers, listings, and seller history (dynamic information moving through the database model).

Auction House Buyers

Buyers have various items of information:

❏ Buyers should have bidding records so that sellers can verify they are dealing with a reputable buyer. It is prudent for sellers to avoid accepting bids on items for buyers who have, for example, placed bids in the past without making payment.

❏ The auction site needs to store buyer information such as names, addresses, credit card information, and credit worthiness.

Figure 9-5 shows the relationships between a buyer, bids made on existing listings, and a history of past dealings with buyers. Any listing can have more than one bid made on it during the life of the listing. When the auction is complete and there is an auction winner, no more bids are allowed. A listing may have no bids at all, at which stage it can be listed again.

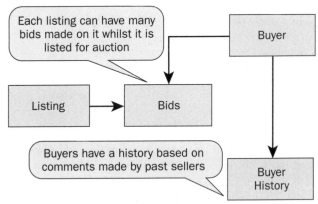

Figure 9-5: Buyers, listings, bids, and buyer history (dynamic information moving through the database model).

Any person or organization listing items for sale at auction could also buy items. In other words, a person or organization can list items for sale (as a seller), and also make bids on items for sale (as a buyer). The database model, however, should not allow sellers to make bids on their own items.

Auction House General Structure

Figure 9-6 shows an overall picture of the entire operational structure for the company, as discovered so far.

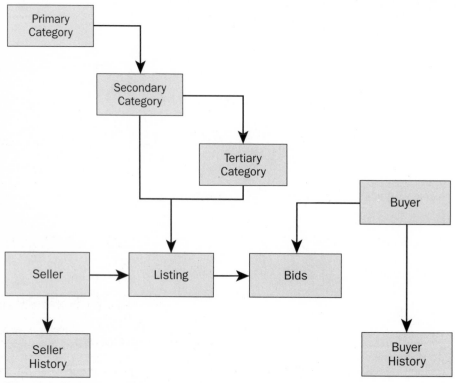

Figure 9-6: The entire operational structure for a simple online auction house.

As a final note, bear in mind that this brief analysis of company operational activities for an online auction house is by no means necessarily complete. One of the main points to remember in any software development project is that the steps in methodologies are iterative, and even the sequence in which the steps are executed is not necessarily strictly applied. For example, in the middle of analyzing and defining in the business rule stage, you can always go back and rework the company operations section, as shown in Figure 9-7.

Discovering Business Rules

So, begin an application of business rules by first examining what a business rule is. In short, *business rules* for a business are a set of functional rules that can be used to describe a business and how it operates, essentially a semi-mathematical interpretation of how a business functions. Business rules are essentially a more precise interpretation of a company's operational activities, as established for the online auction house in the previous section.

The business rules of a company, when applied to a database model, become that database model. The business rules are the tables, relationships between those tables, and even the constraint rules (in addition to referential integrity constraints) in a database. In fact, the application of normalization to a set of initial company data tables is a more and more complex application of business rules to that company data environment. Normalization is the application of business rules.

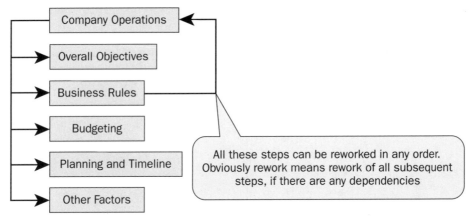

Figure 9-7: Iterative steps in the analysis methodology.

Figure 9-8 shows some very simple example business rules. In Figure 9-8, there are many categories of instruments listed for auction. Each separate category of instruments (such as brass instruments, or the brass section) has numerous instruments (such as a trumpet, trombone, or sousaphone).

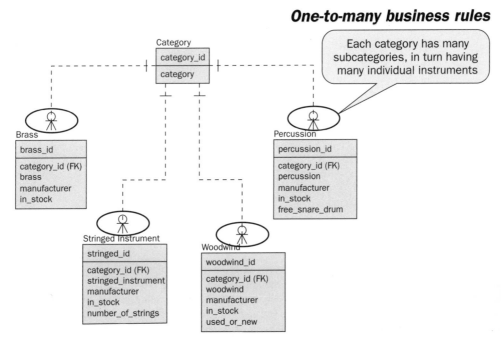

Figure 9-8: A one-to-many relationship is a business rule.

In Figure 9-8, the very act of separating each of multiple instrument sections into separate tables is a very simplistic form of creating business rule representations, using tables and the relationships between them. The ERD in Figure 9-8 is not standard normalization, but is shown to demonstrate clearly how the relationships created between different tables actually create the business rules, or operational functionality of a company. In this case, the company is the online auction company that allows auction listings for sales of musical instruments, for sale at auctions online.

Auction House Categories

Figure 9-9 shows a data picture of some of the structural table elements shown in Figure 9-8. The Guitar category has two instruments: Acoustic Guitar and Electric Guitar. The Wind category has numerous instruments.

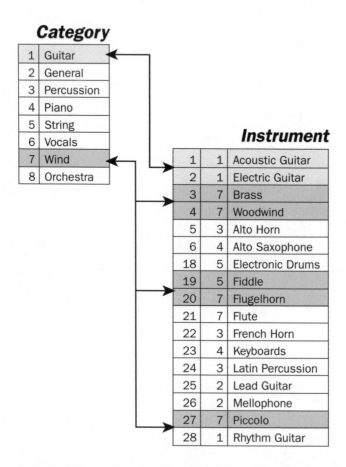

Figure 9-9: Some of the data in Figure 9-8.

At this stage, you can take the operations of the online auction house, established previously in Figure 9-3 to Figure 9-6, and create ERDs for those structures. As already stated previously in this chapter, business rules are at the heart of the analysis stage, describing what has been analyzed and what must be created to design the database model. The business rules part of the analysis of a database model entails creation of tables, and the basic relationships between those tables.

The overall aim of analysis is merely to define rather than specify with precision; therefore, analysis does not describe how many fields should be used for an address, for example, or what datatypes those fields should be. Analysis simply determines that an address field actually exists, and obviously which table or tables address information is required within.

Starting with the categories static structures in Figure 9-3, the ERD section in Figure 9-10 caters effectively to the category hierarchical structure, and the link to the table containing auction listings. The LISTING table has all the details for the master side of a master — detail table that depicts table design, including a description, listing table number reference (LISTING#), dates, prices, bids, and winning bidder details.

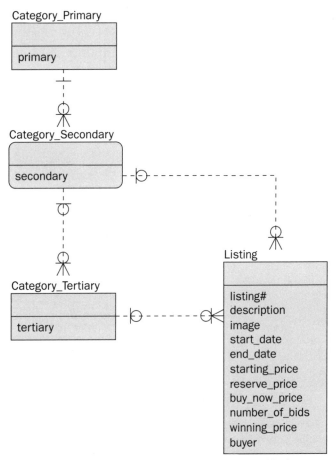

Figure 9-10: An ERD version of the category hierarchical structure of Figure 9-3.

As can be seen in Figure 9-10, the process of analysis is beginning to become one of partial definition, without specifics, of course, where individual fields are defined for different attributes of specific operations. Figure 9-11 and Figure 9-12 show some sample data (including surrogate key fields), to be represented by the ERD in Figure 9-10.

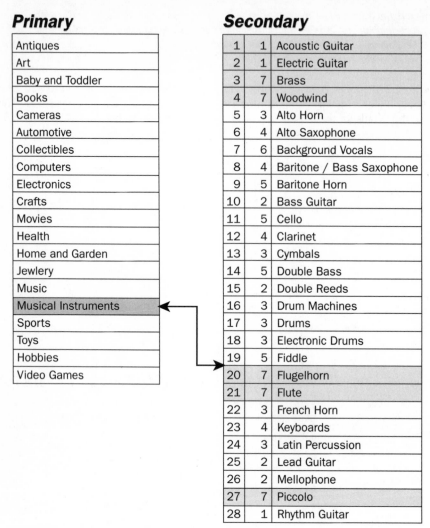

Figure 9-11: A simple picture of data from the ERD of Figure 9-10.

Figure 9-11 shows a list of primary categories on the left, including items such as Automotive, Collectibles, and Musical Instruments. Only the secondary category for Musical Instruments has been expanded, with vague highlights on secondary categories described in more detail in Figure 9-12.

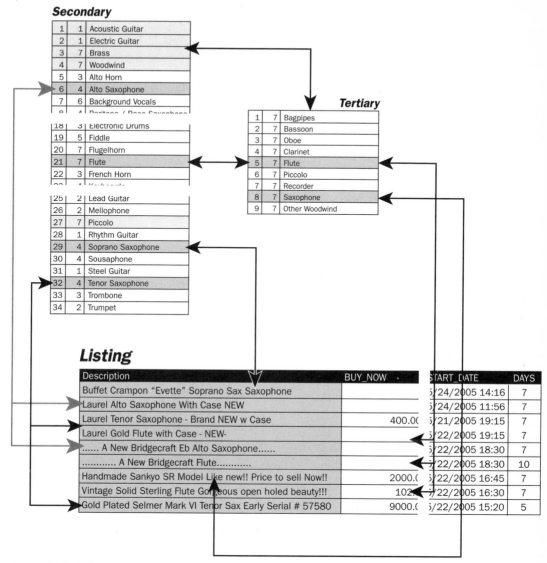

Figure 9-12: A simple picture of data from the ERD of Figure 9-10.

Figure 9-12 shows some of the secondary category listings shown in Figure 9-11, where highlighted items are linked through the tertiary categories and auction listing entries.

Chapter 9

Auction House Seller Listings

Figure 9-13 shows basic table structure as related to auction listings — the sellers of the listings (the person or organization selling something at auction). Note how indexing is not yet incorporated in this chapter. Indexing is more a design than analysis issue. All that is needed in the analysis stage is basic tables and relationships, including a preliminary field structure for each table. Primary keys, foreign keys, and alternate indexing are not required at this early point in the process of database model creation.

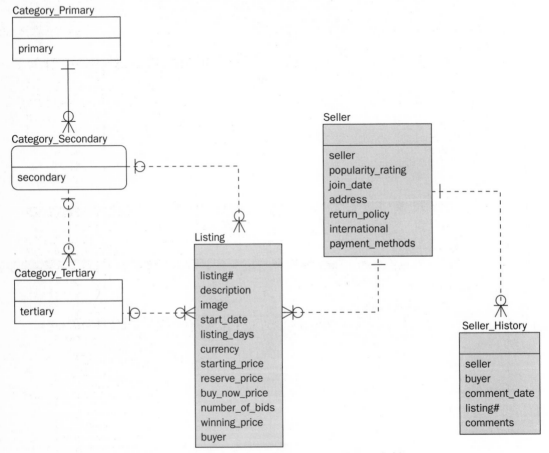

Figure 9-13: Adding seller information to the category structure in Figure 9-10.

In Figure 9-13, the seller and seller history information has been added with various field items to represent details of both. Figure 9-14 shows a brief view of seller and seller history data. You can see what it looks like in the real world. Figure 9-14 shows the seller and links to various listings, including details such as the name of the seller, popularity with buyers, when the seller joined the online auction house as a seller (when a seller created his or her first auction listing), plus various other bits and pieces of relevant information.

Figure 9-15 expands on seller information by adding in a picture of what seller history details would look like. Seller history information would include details such as who the buyer was, what was purchased (the auction item listing number), and what the buyer had to say about the seller (comments), among other details.

Listing

Description	BUY_NOW	START_PRICE	BIDS	START_DATE	DAYS
Buffet Crampon "Evette" Soprano Sax Saxophone		699.00	10	5/24/2005 14:16	7
Laurel Alto Saxophone With Case NEW		99.99		5/24/2005 11:56	7
Laurel Tenor Saxophone - Brand NEW w Case	400.00			5/21/2005 19:15	7
Laurel Gold Flute with Case - NEW-		99.99	4	5/22/2005 19:15	7
...... A New Bridgecraft Eb Alto Saxophone......		239.95		5/22/2005 18:30	7
.... A New Bridgecraft Flute............		109.95	25	5/22/2005 18:30	10
Handmade Sankyo SR Model Like new!! Price to sell Now!!	2000.00	4800.00	2	5/22/2005 16:45	7
Vintage Solid Sterling Flute Gorgeous open holed beauty!!!	102.50	600.00	3	5/22/2005 16:30	7
Gold Plated Selmer Mark VI Tenor Sax Early Serial # 57580	9000.00	12500.00		5/22/2005 15:20	5

Seller

SELLER	POPULARITY	JOINED	ADDRESS	RETURNS	INTERNATIONAL	PAYMENTS
Sax Man	100%	21-May-1999		Yes	US only	Pay online
Musicians Buddy	98%	14-Mar-2000		Yes	UK only	Personal cheque, MO
Instruments Inc.	85%	12-Sep-2004		No	Europe	Cashiers cheque, MO
Big Traders	100%	1-Jan-2005		Undamaged	Global	PayOnline
A&C Co	100%	12-Jun-1998		In original packaging	US only	ALL
KellysStuff	100%	18-Feb-2001		No	US only	ALL

Figure 9-14: A simple picture of seller details data shown in Figure 9-13.

Seller

SELLER	POPULARITY	JOINED	ADDRESS	RETURNS	INTERNATIONAL	PAYMENTS
Sax Man	100%	21-May-1999		Yes	US only	Pay online
Musicians Buddy	98%	14-Mar-2000		Yes	UK only	Personal cheque, MO
Instruments Inc.	85%	12-Sep-2004		No	Europe	Cashiers cheque, MO
Big Traders	100%	1-Jan-2005		Undamaged	Global	PayOnline
A&C Co	100%	12-Jun-1998		In original packaging	US only	ALL
KellysStuff	100%	18-Feb-2001		No	US only	ALL

Seller History

SELLER	BUYER	DATE	LISTING#	COMMENTS
Musicians Buddy	Jim Jones	21-Mar-2000	73178497	Very fine item makes me happy. Thanks
Musician's Buddy	Joe Bloggs	31-Dec-2003	34999234	I bought a great Tenor Sax that arrived sooner than I had expected!
Sax Man	Jake Smith	24-May-1999	34593445	Unbeatable price, fast shipping, well packaged
Sax Man	Jack the Wack	28-May-1999	67463564	Great shipping - very positive experience. Hope to shop with you again.
Sax Man	Saxophonist	14-Jun-1999	45645645	Great seller, Honest, Courteous and Prompt. Will do business again!
Sax Man	Slow Joe	21-Jul-2000	45345234	Nobody beats Kessler. GREAT MOUTHPIECE.
A&C Co	Slim Jim	15-Jul-1999	69784561	Item arrived well packed and exactly as described. Great transaction.
A&C Co	Slim Jim	21-Aug-2001	34554343	first class service, thanks Dave
A &C Co	Mark	24-Aug-2001	33455355	good saxophone
A&C Co	Eric	15-Sep-2004	33453457	Terrific sax

Figure 9-15: A simple picture of seller history details data shown in Figure 9-13.

Historical information allows the auction house to give a popularity rating to a seller, and also allows any future buyers to assess the reputation of a buyer that the sellers may or may not wish to deal with.

Auction House Buyers

Figure 9-16 adds the buyers to the table structure established so far. A buyer details table and a buyer history table are added. The buyer table has three fewer information fields than the seller details table. Removed fields cover return policies, international sales and shipping, and payment methods. Buyer history is the same as seller history field information.

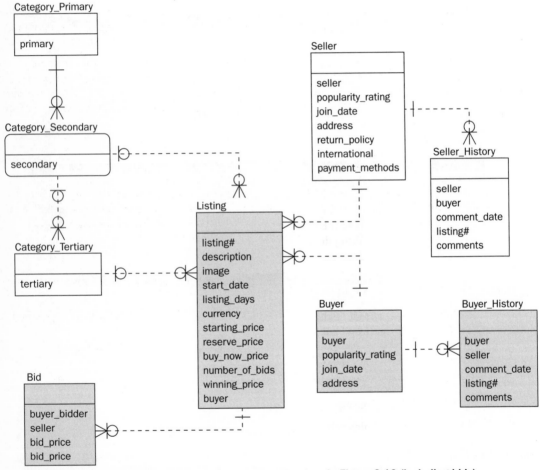

Figure 9-16: Adding buyer information to the category structure in Figure 9-10 (including bids).

Information in the two buyer tables would appear much the same as the structural pictures shown in Figure 9-14 and Figure 9-15; however, having built simple ERDs for all tables discovered so far, there are a few important points to note and recount:

❑ *Separating buyers and sellers* — In any auction model, a buyer can actually also be a seller (bidding on their own items should be prohibited). It might seem sensible to merge the buyer and seller tables, and also merge the two history tables together. Traditionally, in many database models, any types of customer and supplier details are generally separated. This is usually because they are not one and the same, from the perspective of content, as opposed to a structural point of view. In an auctioning database model, separating buyers from sellers is likely to be the most sensible option, simply because it is probably the norm (not always the case) that the buyers are unlikely to be sellers, and visa versa. Obviously, with normalization applied during the design phase (discussed in Chapter 10), it may make sense to separate buyers, sellers, and buyer-sellers (auctioneers who both buy and sell), all into three separate tables.

❑ *Referential integrity keys* — All the most basic relationships have been established between the different tables. Identifying appropriate primary and foreign keys is more a design issue than an analysis issue. Keys will be established in Chapter 10, which covers design.

❑ *Category hierarchy* — In some situations, separating static tables (such as the three category tables) may not be the most efficient option. There may be a case for merging all categories into a single table. The single table would contain all three category levels using specialized parent and child fields, for each category record. Because this is once again a design issue and not an analysis issue, it is covered in Chapter 10.

> Just in case you are wondering where all this stuff is going (the three points just mentioned), these factors are all design issues, not analysis issues. This chapter deals with the analytical process of discovering basic contents of the auctioning database model. Chapter 10 deals with design issues. The objective of these case study directed chapters is to introduce a data model in a manner that covers each concept step-by-step, making details easy to understand and absorb.

Try It Out   Analyzing an OLTP Database Model

Create a simple analytical-level OLTP database model for a Web site. This Web site allows creation of free classified ads for musicians and bands. Here's a simplistic approach:

1. Identify the operations of the company.

2. Draw up a picture of basic tables.

3. Establish simple relationships.

4. Create basic fields within each table.

How It Works

Figure 9-17 shows some basic information categories, both static and transactional in nature. Instruments and skills statically describe relatively static musicians (musicians come and go, skills and instrument classifications do not). This probably makes musicians dynamic transactional information. A band has a specific genre such as playing rock music, punk, classic rock, and so on. Thus, the band is dynamic and the genre is static. The classified advertisement itself is most certainly dynamic in nature.

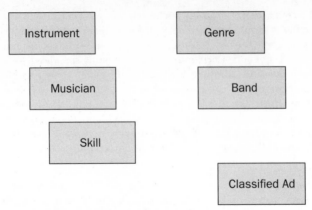

Figure 9-17: Identifying basic operations.

Figure 9-18 goes just a little further by establishing relationships between the different operations described in Figure 9-17. In other words, musicians play instruments and have skills. Bands are usually of a specific genre. Both musicians and bands can place classified ads to advertise themselves.

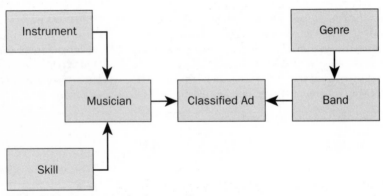

Figure 9-18: Linking the basic operations.

Figure 9-19 shows a briefly constructed ERD as an application of business rules to the operational diagram shown in Figure 9-18. There are a number of important points to note:

❑ Musicians can play multiple instruments.

❑ Musicians can be multi-skilled.

❑ A band can have multiple genres.

❑ The MEMBERS field in the band table takes into account the one-to-many relationship between BAND and MUSICIAN. In other words, there is usually more than one musician in a band; however, a musician doesn't necessarily have to be in a band, a band may be broken up and have no musicians, and both bands and musicians can advertise.

❑ Musicians and bands can place advertisements.

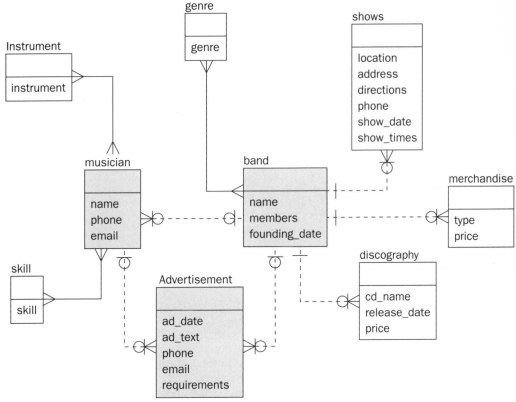

Figure 9-19: Creating a basic analytical ERD of business rules

Case Study: The Data Warehouse Model

Planning and analyzing a data warehouse database model is all about separation of static and transactional information. The *static information* consists of the little bits and pieces describing the facts. The *facts* are the variable or dynamic details that are commonly destroyed or archived when no longer useful. For the online auction house all the buyer and seller details, such as their addresses, is all static information, in that it does not change much.

The *transactional information* consists of what is added to the database and then removed from the database after a period of time. Transactional information is removed from a database to ensure that the database simply doesn't get too large to manage; however, all that historical information (such as past bids, and past listings) is valuable when trying to perform forecasting reporting. For example, the online auction house may want to promote and advertise. If auctions selling toys is 100 times more prevalent than selling old LP records from the 1950s, perhaps marketing to toy sellers is a better use of advertising funds. Executing forecasting reports, extrapolating from information over the last five years, could be very useful indeed in discovering which markets to target specifically. Old, out-of-date, and archived data can be extremely useful.

A data warehouse is used to contain archived information, separated from the OLTP database, thus not causing performance problems with the OLTP database.

Establishing Company Operations

Company operations have already been established when analyzing the database model for the OLTP database structure. All that needs to be done for a data warehouse database model is to establish what are the facts (transactional information), and what are the dimensions (static data). This can be done in a number of stages, as shown in Figure 9-20, Figure 9-21, and Figure 9-22.

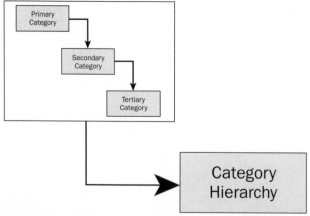

Figure 9-20: Data warehouse data modeling denormalizes multiple hierarchical static tables into single static structures.

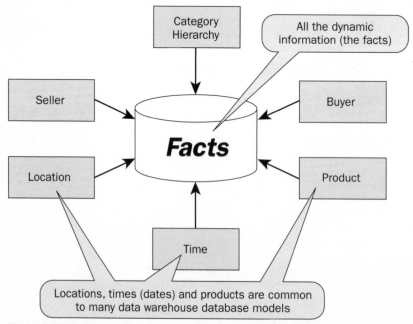

Figure 9-21: A data warehouse star schema database model for the online auction house.

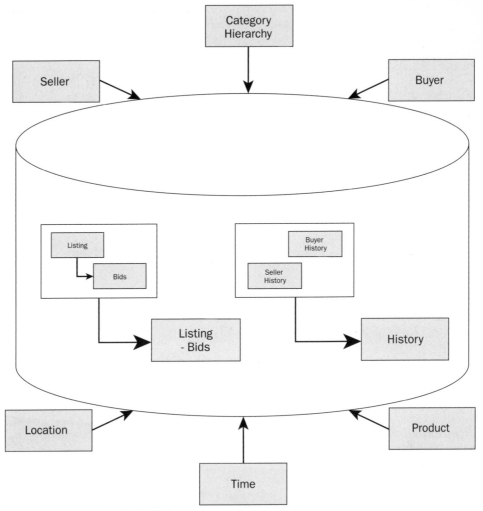

Figure 9-22: Analyzing the facts in a data warehouse database model.

In Figure 9-20, the three categories in the OLTP database model can be amalgamated into a single hierarchical category table. The merge of the three tables is done by including a parent reference in the new category table, allowing a direct link from tertiary to secondary, and from secondary to primary. A primary category has no parent category. Also, a secondary category may contain no tertiary categories (it has no child tertiary categories). Those tertiary category records simply will not exist if they are not required.

Figure 9-21 shows a developing star schema for the online auction company data warehouse database model. All the dimensions (static information containers) surround the facts (transactional information) in the form of a star schema.

Figure 9-21 also shows three newly added dimensions: LOCATION, TIME, and PRODUCT. Many data warehouse database models include extra dimensions containing information gleaned from the fact tables themselves, and sometimes the dimensions as well. These extra data warehouse-specific type dimensions allow for a better and more efficient structure when separating information in a data warehouse database model:

❑ *Locations* — Locations are usually built from address details, establishing locations for bidders and sellers (for the online auction house) as being in a specific city, state, country, continent, planet, star system, galaxy, and universe. That may seem silly, but you get the point. A location dimension allows analysis of data warehouse information into reports, based on regions. For example, what sells well, in what city, what region, and so on.

❑ *Time stamps* — Time stamp information allows dimensional division of information into time periods. The result is data warehouse reporting that can assess how a company performed in specific periods. For example, reporting could compare profitability in different years, across the same months or quarters. This type of reporting can help to assess the health of a business, among many other things (such as when business should be expected to pick up). If a company has a Christmas rush of trading, they might be able to prepare better for what types of products sell at Christmas, how much they need to manufacture, and where specific products need to be distributed to.

❑ *Products* — Product dimensional information allows division of reporting based on different products, similar to how information and reporting can be divided up into locations and time stamps.

There are numerous other data warehouse-specific static information structures. Locations, times, and products are probably the most commonly additional dimensions.

Essentially, commonly used dimensions in data warehouse database models (such as locations, times, and products) are generally used all at the same time, in the same reports. Also, data warehouse databases can be become so humongous that serious performance gains can be found by applying reporting filtering using information such as locations, times, and products.

Figure 9-22 shows a more detailed star schema for the online auction company data warehouse database model. In Figure 9-22, you can see that the dimensions are still pointing directly, and individually, at all the facts (transactional information). Typically, in a data warehouse, database dimension tables have very few records, relative to the size of fact tables. Fact tables can often rise into the millions, and even billions and trillions of records. Dimension tables containing tens, hundreds, or even thousands of records, and contain relatively much smaller numbers of records than fact tables. This is the idea!

> Data warehouse fact tables are relatively much larger than dimension tables (in record numbers). This is the objective of star schemas in making an efficient data warehouse database model. SQL code join queries between very small tables (dimensions with few records) and very large tables (facts with gazillions of records) are the most efficient types of joins. Joining two large tables, or even equally sized tables (assuming both tables contain more than thousands of records) is much less efficient.

Note in Figure 9-22 how LISTING and BID tables can be merged into a single LISTING_BIDS table. Also, the two SELLER_HISTORY and BIDDER_HISTORY tables can be merged into a single HISTORY table. Figure 9-23 shows the resulting structure of a data warehouse database model for the online auction company. The data warehouse model shown in Figure 9-23 actually contains two star schemas.

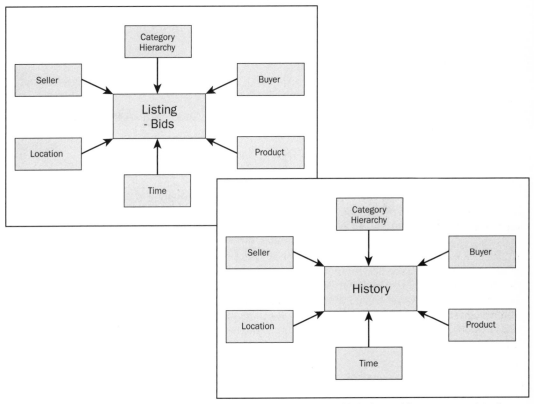

Figure 9-23: A data warehouse can have multiple star schemas (multiple fact tables, connected to the same dimensions).

Data warehouse database models can have more than one star schema (more than one fact table). Fact tables are not linked together. If multiple fact tables need to be joined by SQL code queries, multiple fact tables should be constructed as a single fact table (single star schema), as shown in Figure 9-24.

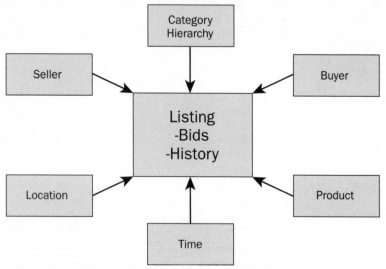

Figure 9-24: Multiple star schemas (fact tables) can all be merged into a single fact table.

Discovering Business Rules

At this stage, the data warehouse model is ready for business rule analysis and application. As previously described in this chapter, business rule application entails the building of tables, establishing the most basic of relationships between those tables, and adding sketchy ideas of table field content.

Previously in this chapter, the online auction house OLTP database model already went through the basic business rules application, ERD construction process. All that is needed for the data warehouse model is a simple ERD to begin the process of representing that data warehouse database model in a mathematical fashion. Figure 9-25 shows such an ERD.

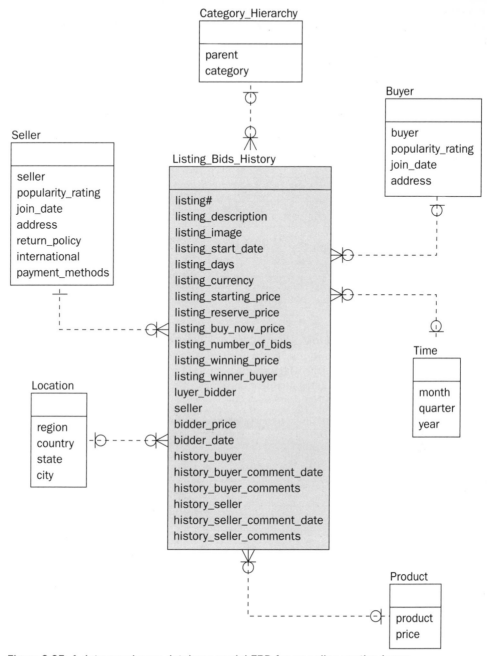

Category_Hierarchy

parent
category

Seller

seller
popularity_rating
join_date
address
return_policy
international
payment_methods

Buyer

buyer
popularity_rating
join_date
address

Listing_Bids_History

listing#
listing_description
listing_image
listing_start_date
listing_days
listing_currency
listing_starting_price
listing_reserve_price
listing_buy_now_price
listing_number_of_bids
listing_winning_price
listing_winner_buyer
luyer_bidder
seller
bidder_price
bidder_date
history_buyer
history_buyer_comment_date
history_buyer_comments
history_seller
history_seller_comment_date
history_seller_comments

Location

region
country
state
city

Time

month
quarter
year

Product

product
price

Figure 9-25: A data warehouse database model ERD for an online auction house.

Most of the fields in the tables shown in Figure 9-25 have already been discussed for the OLTP database model analysis. The only fields not covered are the additional locations, time stamp, and product content dimensions:

❑　*Locations* — Locations are a hierarchy of region, country, state, and city, as shown ion Figure 9-26.

Locations

REGION	COUNTRY	STATE	CITY
North America	Canada	NS	Halifax
North America	Canada	QB	Montreal
North America	Canada	ON	Ottawa
North America	Canada	QB	Quebec City
North America	Canada	ON	Toronto
North America	Canada	BC	Vancouver
North America	United States	NY	Albany
North America	United States	NM	Albuquerque
North America	United States	IA	Ames
North America	United States	AK	Anchorage
North America	United States	NC	Asheville
North America	United States	GA	Atlanta
North America	United States	ME	Augusta
North America	United States	TX	Austin

Figure 9-26: Some example locations records.

❑　*Times* — Times are month, quarter, and year, as shown in Figure 9-27. Time stamp dimensions can contain days, hours, and possibly even minutes; however, that level of detail can generate a very large time dimension, and is probably not worth it in general. There would be too many records to maintain SQL code join query efficiency.

Time Stamp Elements

MONTH	QUARTER	YEAR
1	1	1995
1	1	1996
1	1	1997
1	1	1998
1	1	1999
1	1	2000
1	1	2001
1	1	2002
1	1	2003
1	1	2004
1	1	2005
1	1	2006
2	1	1995
2	1	1996

Figure 9-27: Some example time stamp records.

❑　*Products* — Products are a bit of a misfit in the online auction house data warehouse database model. Products are essentially the same as the online auction house categories. Also, the price PRODUCT table PRICE field is irrelevant because there are no fixed prices for each listing category. Prices are flexible, determined by a multitude of different sellers, and ultimately the buyers making the bids. The PRODUCT table is, therefore, irrelevant to the data warehouse database model for the online auction house. The ERD in Figure 9-25 would be adjusted as shown in Figure 9-28.

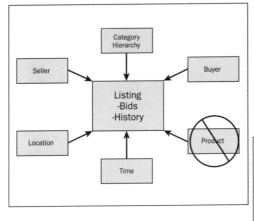

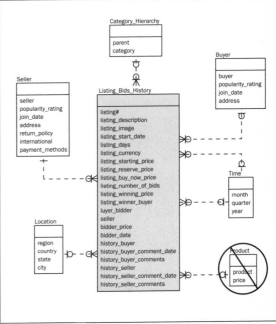

Figure 9-28: Adjusting the data warehouse database model ERD for an online auction house.

Figure 9-24 described the analysis and design process of database modeling as being an iterative one. Steps can be repeated, in any order, and adjustments can be made during the entire process. It is better to make adjustments, particularly at the database modeling stage, during analysis and design. Make changes before any application code is written, preferably before any reworking with methodologies (such as normalization and denormalization) have been applied to database models.

Chapter 9

Try It Out   Analyzing a Data Warehouse Database Model

Create a simple analytical level data warehouse database model, for the same Web site, as shown in Figure 9-19. Once again, use a simple approach for a simple problem:

1. Identify dimensions (static stuff).

2. Identify facts (dynamic stuff).

3. Establish simple relationships.

4. Create basic fields within each table.

How It Works

All the detail was covered for the "Try It Out" section discussed for the OLTP database model. All this "Try It Out" needs is a basic picture of the data warehouse database model, as shown in Figure 9-29.

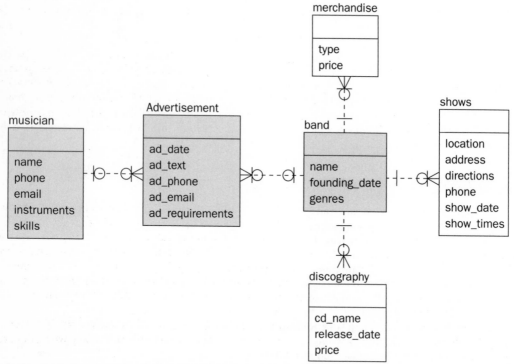

Figure 9-29: A basic data warehouse ERD business rules database model.

The ADVERTISEMENT table is decided on being the fact table. The MUSICIAN table is a single layer fact table. The BAND, MERCHANDISE, SHOWS, and DISCOGRAPHY tables constitute a two-layer dimensional hierarchy.

There are some gray areas between static and dynamic information in this situation. There are other ways of building this data warehouse database model.

Project Management

When it comes to planning and establishing timelines, there are some remarkably good project-planning software tools available. When planning any software project, including a database model design, there is often more than one person involved in a project. This excludes the planner. If not using a software tool, and multiple people are to perform multiple overlapping, interdependent tasks, you could end up with lots of drawings, and an awfully full garbage can. These things change. Plans can change. People get sick and go on vacation. They find new jobs. Sometimes people simply don't show up at all! In other words, expect things to change.

The fact is when it comes to planning, establishing timelines, and budgeting there is no enforceable or reasonably useful applicable set of rules and steps. It just doesn't exist. In any planning process (including budgeting), for any type of project, there is no way to accurately predict to any degree of mathematical certainty. None of us can really read the future. Planning, establishing timelines, and budgeting entail a flexible process, which is almost entirely dependant on the expertise, and past experience, of the planner. And then again, if changes and unexpected snags or events are not anticipated, a project can very quickly spiral out of control.

Project Planning and Timelines

A software development company can meet with its financial demise by not allowing enough time in project plans. It is quite common in the software development field for project-tender budgets from multiple companies to be as much as 50 times different. In other words, the difference in dollar estimates between the lowest and highest bidders can be enormous. This indicates guesswork. It is often the case that the most inexperienced companies put in the lowest bids. The highest bids are probably greedy. Those between the average and the highest are probably the most realistic. Also, they are likely to make a profit, and thus be around to support very expensive software tools, say, 5 to 10 years from now.

As already stated, there is much research into project planning in general. Unfortunately, few, if any quantifiable and useful results have been obtained. Expert level assessment based on past experience of experts, is usually the best measure of possibilities.

There is an International Standards Institute (ISO) model called the "ISO 9000-3 Model." This model is used more to give a method of quality assurance against the final product, of, say, an analysis of a database model. This ISO model does not give a set of instructions as to how to go about performing analysis process itself, but rather presents a method of validation after the fact.

The accuracy of a planned budget is dependent on the experience of the planner. Database designers, administrators, and programmers think that their project managers and planners do nothing. They are wrong. The planners take all the risk, make all the wild guesses; the programmers get to write all that mathematically precise programming code. So, the next time you see your project manager in a cold sweat, you know why. It's not your job on the line—it's theirs.

Here are some interesting—and sometimes amusing—terms, often used to describe planning, budgeting, and project management:

❑ *"Why did the chicken cross the road?"*—This is a well-known quotation about a now unfortunately discontinued software development consultancy company. This company was famous for producing enormous amounts of paper. Lots of paper can help to make more profit for the software development company. The more paper produced, the more useless waffle. However, the more paper produced, the less likely something has been overlooked, and the more likely the plan and budget are accurate. The other problem with lots of paper is no one has time to read it, and doesn't really want to either.

❑ *"Get someone with a great, big, long signature and a serious title to sign off on it ASAP."*—This one is also called "passing the buck." That buck has to stop somewhere, and the higher up, the better, and preferably not with the planner. The planner has enough things to think about without worrying about whether their wildest guesses will bear fruit, or simply crash and burn.

❑ *"Don't break it if it's already fixed."*—If something is working properly, why change it?

❑ *"Use information in existing systems, be they computerized or on paper."*—Existing structures can usually tell more about a company that its people can. There is, however, a danger that if a system is being replaced, there is probably something very wrong with the older system.

❑ *"Try not to reinvent the wheel."*—When planning on building software or a new database model, use other people's ideas if they are appropriate. Of course, beware of outdated ideas. Do thorough research. The Internet is an excellent source of freely available ideas, both old and new.

❑ *"More resources do not mean faster work."*—The more people involved in a project, the more confusion. Throwing more bodies at a project can just as likely make a project impossible to manage, as it can make it go faster.

Figure 9-30 shows a pretty picture of what a project timeline might look like, containing multiple people, multiple skills levels, multiple tasks (both overlapping and interdependent). Project timelines can become incredibly complicated. Simplify, if possible. Too much interdependency can lead to problems if one area overruns on time limitations. Keep something spare in terms of people, available hours, and otherwise. Expect changes. Plan with some resources in reserve.

Figure 9-30 shows five separate tasks in a simplistic project-timeline Gantt chart. Task 1 is assigned to Jim. There is no time conflict between Task 2 and Task 3, and can both be assigned to Joe (one person). Task 3 and Task 4 overlap between both Janet and Joe, in more ways than one. Joe is going to be very busy indeed. A project manager would allow overlap where the person doing the assigned tasks is known to be capable of multiple concurrent activities.

Gantt charts were invented as a graphical tool for project management. Gantt charts allow for a pictorial illustration of a schedule, thus helping with the planning, coordination between, and tracking of multiple tasks. Tasks can be independent or interdependent. Many off-the-shelf software tools allow computerized project management with Gantt charts (and otherwise), such as Microsoft Project, Excel spreadsheet plug-ins, and even Visio.

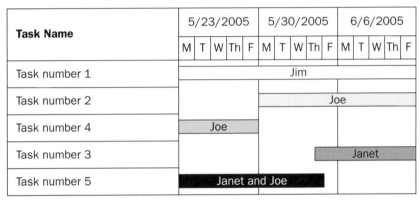

Figure 9-30: An example project timeline Gantt chart.

Budgeting

When it comes to budgeting for a project, budgeting is part of planning, and is thus open to expert interpretation. Once again, there is research on how to apply formal methods to budgeting. Much of that research is unsuccessful. In the commercial world, most observations offer a lot of guesswork based on experience. Also, there is an intense reluctance on the part of the experts to justify and quantify the how and why of the results they come up with. Budgeting is, as already stated, just like planning. It is educated guesswork. There is nothing to really present in a book such as this one, telling someone like you, the reader, how to go about budgeting a project, such as a database modeling project.

One big problem with software development (including database model development and design) is its *intangibility*. Software projects are difficult to quantify, partially because they are unpredictable, they can change drastically during development. The sheer *complexity* of software is another factor. Complexity is not only within each separate unit and step. One step could be the database model analysis and design. Another step could be writing of front-end application code. There is a complexity issue simply because of the need to account for all possibilities. There is also complexity because of the heavy interdependence between all parts of software development. This interdependence stems from the highest level (comparing, for example, database model and application coding) even down to the smallest piece (comparing two different fields in a single table, in a database model).

In short, database model analysis and design is extremely difficult to budget for. The most common and probably successful practice is to guess at an estimated cost based on estimated time to be spent (work hours). Then take the result and add a percentage, even as much as 50 percent, and sometimes multiplying the first conservative estimate by much more.

A number of detail areas already have been discussed previously in this chapter:

❑ *Hiring help costs money* — Hired help in the form of software development expertise can be astronomically expensive.

❑ *Hardware costs* — Hardware can be cheap to incredibly expensive. Generally, more expensive hardware leads to the following scenarios:

  ❑ Expensive hardware can help to alleviate software costs, but usually in the form of hiding performance problems. Sloppy database design and software development can be overcome by upgrading hardware. If growth is expected, and the hardware selected is ever outgrown, costly problems could be the result. The temptation when using expensive hardware is to not worry too much about building database and software applications properly. Fast-performing hardware lets you get away with a lot of things.

  ❑ Expensive hardware is complicated. Hiring people to set up and maintain that complexity can be extremely expensive. Simplistic and cheap hardware requires less training and lower skills levels. Less-skilled labor is much cheaper.

❑ *Maintenance* — Maintenance is all about complexity and quality. The more complex something is, the more difficult it is to maintain. Somewhat unrelated, but just as important, poor quality results in a lot more maintenance. Indirectly, maintenance is related to the life of a database model, and ultimately applications. How long will they last, how long will something be useful, and help to turn a profit? There is a point where constant maintenance is outweighed by doing a complete rewrite. In other words, sometimes rebuilding databases and software applications from scratch can save money, rather than continuing to maintain older software that has seen so many changes that it is no longer cost-effective to maintain.

❑ *Training* — Training affects all levels, from technical staff to unknown huge quantities of end-users on the Internet. Obviously, you don't want to have to train Internet users located at far-flung parts of the globe. Attempting to train Internet users is pointless. People lose interest in applications that are difficult to use. You might as well start again in this case. Training in-house staff is different. The higher the complexity, the more training is involved. Training costs money — sometimes a lot of money!

Summary

In this chapter, you learned about:

❑ The basics of analysis and design of a database model

❑ A usable set of semi-formal steps, for the database modeling analysis process

❑ Some common problem areas and misconceptions that can arise

❑ How talking, listening, and following a paper trail can be of immense value

❑ How to create a database model to cover objectives for both an OLTP and a data warehouse database model

- ❏ How to refine a database model using the application of business rules, through basic analysis, creating both an OLTP and a data warehouse database model

- ❏ How to apply everything learned so far with a comprehensive case study, creating both an OLTP and a data warehouse database model

This chapter has attempted to apply everything learned in previous chapters, by going through the motions of beginning with the process of creating a database model. An online auction company has been used as the case study example.

Chapter 10 expands on the analysis process (simplistic in this chapter at best) and design with more detail provided for the OLTP and database warehouse database models, as presented analytically in this chapter. The idea is to build things step-by-step, with as much planning as possible. This chapter has begun that database model building process, as the first little step in the right direction.

Exercises

Use the ERDs in Figure 9-19 and Figure 9-29 to help you answer these questions.

1. Create scripts to create tables for the OLTP database model Figure 9-19. Create the tables in the proper order by understanding the relationships between the tables.

2. Create scripts to create tables for the data warehouse database model Figure 9-29. Once again, create the tables in the proper order by understanding the relationships between the tables.

10

Creating and Refining Tables During the Design Phase

"Everything in the world must have design or the human mind rejects it. But in addition, it must have purpose or the human conscience shies away from it." (John Steinbeck)

Analysis is all about what needs to done. Design does it!

This chapter builds on and expands on the basic analytical process and structure discovered during the case study approach in Chapter 9, which covered analysis. Analysis is the process of discovering what needs to be done. Analysis is all about the operations of a company, what it does to make a living. Design is all about how to implement that which was analyzed into a useful database model.

This chapter passes from the analysis phase into the design phase by discovering through a case study example how to build and relate tables in a relational database model.

By the end of this chapter, you will have a much deeper understanding of how database models are created and designed. This chapter teaches you how to begin the implementation of what was analyzed (discovered) in Chapter 9. In short, implementation is the process of creating tables, and sticking those tables together with appropriate relationships.

In this chapter, you learn about the following:

❑   Database model design

❑   The difference between analysis and design

❑   Creating tables

❑   Enforcing inter-table relationships and referential integrity

❑   Normalization without going too far

❑   Denormalization without going too far

A Little More About Design

When designing a database model, the intention is to refine database model structure for reasons of maintaining data integrity, good performance, and adaptations to specific types of applications, such as a data warehouse. A data warehouse database model requires a different basic table structure than an OLTP database model, mostly for reasons of acceptable reporting performance.

Performance is not exclusively a programming or implementation construction or even a testing or "wait until it's in production" activity. Performance should be included at the outset in both analysis and design stages. This is particularly important for database model analysis and design for two reasons:

- ❑ Redesigning a database model after applications are written will change applications (a little like a rewrite—a complete waste of time and money).

- ❑ There is simply no earthly reason or excuse to not build for performance right from the beginning of the development process. If this is not possible, you might want additional expertise in the form of specialized personnel. Hiring a short-term consultant at the outset of a development project could save enormous amounts of maintenance, rewriting, redevelopment costs, and time in the future.

Business events and operations discovered in the analysis stage should be utilized to drive the design process, which consists of refining table pictures and ERDs already drawn. For larger projects, the design stage can also consist of detailed technical specifications. *Technical specifications* are used by programmers and administrators to create databases and programming code.

Essentially, the beginning of the design process marks the point where the thought processes of analysts and programmers begin to mix. In the analysis stage, the approach was one of a business operation (a business-wide view) of a company. In the design stage, it starts to get more technical.

When designing a database model, you should begin thinking about a database model from the perspective of how applications will use that database model. In other words, when considering how to build fact and dimensional table structures in a data warehouse database model, consider how reports will be structured. Consider how long those reports will take to run. For a data warehouse, not only are the table contents and relationships important, but factors such as reconstruction of data using materialized views and alternate indexing can help with the building and performance of data warehouse reporting.

Relational database model design includes the following:

- ❑ *Refine Database Models*—At this stage of the game, most of this is about normalization and denormalization.

- ❑ *Finalization and Approval*—This includes finalization (and most especially, approval) of business and technical design issues. You need to get it signed off for two reasons:

  - ❑ Software development involves large amounts of investment in both money and time. Management, and probably even executive management approval and responsibility, is required. A designer does not need this level of worry, but may need some powerful clout to back up the development process. Other departments and managers getting in the way of the development process could throw your schedule and budget for a complete loop.

Every project needs a sponsor and champion; otherwise, there is no point in progressing.

❑ You need to cover your back. You also need to be sure that you are going in the right direction because you may very well not be. There is usually a good reason why your boss is your boss, and it usually has a lot do with him or her having a lot more experience. Experience is always valuable. It is extremely likely that this person will help you get things moving when you need, such as when you need information and help from other departments.

So, it's not really about passing the buck up the ladder. It's really about getting a job done. The stronger approval and support for a project, the better the chance of success — unless, of course, it's your money. In that case, it's your problem! So, pinch those pennies. Of course, some entrepreneurs say that the secrets to making money are all about cash flow, spending it, and not stashing it in the bank for a rainy day. Be warned, however, that software development is a very expensive and risky venture!

So, the design stage is the next stage following the analysis stage. Design is a process of figuring out how to implement what was discovered during the analysis stage. As described in Chapter 9, analysis is about what needs to be done. Design is about how it should be done. The design stage deals with the following aspects of database model creation:

❑ More precise tables, including practical application of normalization.

❑ Establishment of primary and foreign key fields.

❑ Enforcement of referential integrity by establishing and quantifying precise relationships between tables, using primary and foreign key fields.

❑ Denormalization in the design stage (the sooner the better), particularly in the case of data warehouse table structures.

❑ Alternate and extra indexing in addition to that of referential integrity, primary and foreign keys; however, alternate indexing is more advanced (detailed) design, and is discussed in Chapter 11.

❑ Advanced database structures, such as materialized views, and some specialized types of indexing. Similar to alternate indexing, this is also more advanced (detailed) design, and is discussed in Chapter 11.

❑ Precise field definitions, structure, and their respective datatypes (again advanced design).

The intention of this chapter is to focus on the firm and proper establishment of inter-table relationships, through the application of normalization and denormalization for both OLTP and data warehouse database models. This process is performed as a case study, continuing with the use of the online auction company introduced in Chapter 9.

Let's create some tables.

Case Study: Creating Tables

In Chapter 9, tables were created on an analytical level, creating basic pictures. Following the basic pictures, simple ERDs were constructed. In this section, basic commands are used to create the initial simple tables, as shown in the analytical process of Chapter 9. The idea is to retain the step-by-step instruction of each concept layer, in the database modeling design process, for both OLTP and data warehouse database models. These models are created for the online auction house case study database models.

The OLTP Database Model

Figure 10-1 shows a simple analytical diagram, covering the various operational aspects of the online auction house, OLTP database model. Notice how the BIDS table is connected to both the LISTING and BUYER tables. This is the only table in this database structure that is connected to more than one table and not as part of a hierarchy. Category tables are part of a hierarchy.

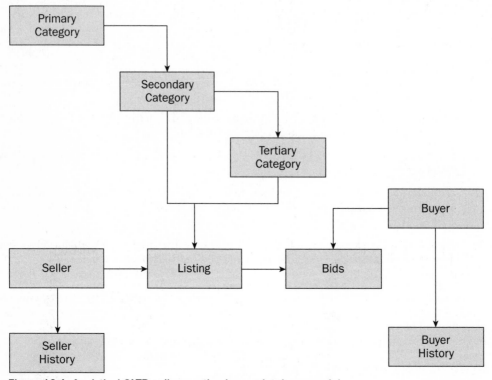

Figure 10-1: Analytical OLTP online auction house database model.

Figure 10-2 shows the application of business rules to the simple analytical diagram shown in Figure 10-1. Once again, notice the dual links for the BID table (now called BID for technical accuracy because each record represents a single bid), to both the LISTING and the BUYER tables. This double link represents a many-to-many relationship. The BID table is in actuality a resolution of the many-to-many relationship between the LISTING and BUYER tables. In other words, each buyer can place many bids on a single item listed for auction; however, each auction listed item can also have many buyers making those many bids.

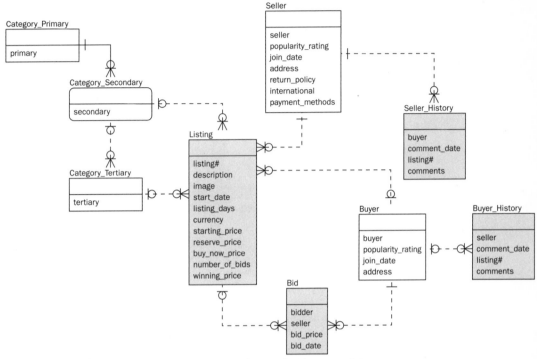

Figure 10-2: Business rules OLTP online auction house database model.

The easiest way to create tables in a database model is to create them in a top-down fashion, from static to dynamic tables, gradually introducing more and more dependent detail. In others words, information that does not change very often is created first. Information changing frequently is created after static tables. Technically speaking, it's all about catering to dependencies first. The first tables created are those with no dependencies. Subsequent tables are created when tables depended on have already been created. Begin by creating the three category static tables. The SECONDARY table depends on the PRIMARY table, and the TERTIARY table depends on both the SECONDARY, and thus the PRIMARY table as well; therefore you need to create PRIMARY, then SECONDARY, followed by TERTIARY tables:

```
CREATE TABLE CATEGORY_PRIMARY(PRIMARY STRING);
CREATE TABLE CATEGORY_SECONDARY(SECONDARY STRING);
CREATE TABLE CATEGORY_TERTIARY(TERTIARY STRING);
```

Some databases (if not many databases) do not allow use of keywords, such as PRIMARY, or even SECONDARY. PRIMARY could be reserved to represent a primary key and SECONDARY could be reserved to represent secondary (alternate) indexing. If you get an error, simply use another name.

The SELLER and BUYER tables are also static. According to the ERD shown in Figure 10-2 they are not dependencies. So you can create the SELLER and BUYER tables next:

```
CREATE TABLE SELLER
(
        SELLER STRING,
        POPULARITY_RATING INTEGER,
        JOIN_DATE DATE,
        ADDRESS STRING,
        RETURN_POLICY STRING,
        INTERNATIONAL STRING,
        PAYMENT_METHODS STRING
);

CREATE TABLE BUYER
(
        BUYER STRING,
        POPULARITY_RATING INTEGER,
        JOIN_DATE DATE,
        ADDRESS STRING
);
```

In these table creation script sections, I have begun to use de-formalized datatypes, such as STRING (representing text strings of any length), plus DATE for dates, and INTEGER for whole numbers.

Next, you can create the two history tables because the SELLER and BUYER tables are now available. Note how the SELLER_HISTORY table does not have a SELLER field, because this is implied by the direct parent relationship to the SELLER table. The same applies to the BUYER_HISTORY table, containing the SELLER field only.

```
CREATE TABLE SELLER_HISTORY
(
        BUYER STRING,
        COMMENT_DATE DATE,
        LISTING# STRING,
        COMMENTS STRING
);

CREATE TABLE BUYER_HISTORY
(
        SELLER STRING,
        COMMENT_DATE DATE,
        LISTING# STRING,
        COMMENTS STRING
);
```

Next, create the LISTING table:

```
CREATE TABLE LISTING
(
        LISTING# STRING,
        DESCRIPTION STRING,
        IMAGE BINARY,
        START_DATE DATE,
        LISTING_DAYS INTEGER,
        CURRENCY STRING,
        STARTING_PRICE MONEY,
        RESERVE_PRICE MONEY,
        BUY_NOW_PRICE MONEY,
        NUMBER_OF_BIDS INTEGER,
        WINNING_PRICE MONEY
);
```

This table introduces a new generic datatype called BINARY, *used to store an image. That image could be a JPG, BMP, or any other type of graphic file format. Binary object datatypes allow storage of binary formatted data inside relational databases. The* BINARY *datatype is not really important to this book; however, storing images into text strings is awkward.*

Lastly, create the BID table (the BID table is dependent on the LISTING table):

```
CREATE TABLE BID
(
        BIDDER STRING,
        SELLER STRING,
        BID_PRICE MONEY,
        BID_DATE DATE
);
```

These two tables introduce a new generic datatype called MONEY. *You can assume that the* MONEY *datatype, for most currencies, will have two fixed decimal places. Therefore, $100 will be represented as 100.00. There is a* CURRENCY *field in the* LISTING *table. Online auction companies can operate internationally, implying international sales and international bids from buyers in other countries. Different currencies may be involved. A few unusual currencies (such as some of the Arabian Peninsula currencies) actually use three rather than two decimal places. Thus, 100 "whatever's" would be stored as 100.000.*

The Data Warehouse Database Model

The previous section created very basic tables for the online auction house OLTP database model. Now do exactly the same thing for the data warehouse database model of the online auction house. Figure 10-3 shows a simple analytical diagram displaying the various operational sections for the online auction house data warehouse database model. All the fact information is shoved into a single table. Later on in this chapter, this information will be separated into separate fact tables (or separate star schemas).

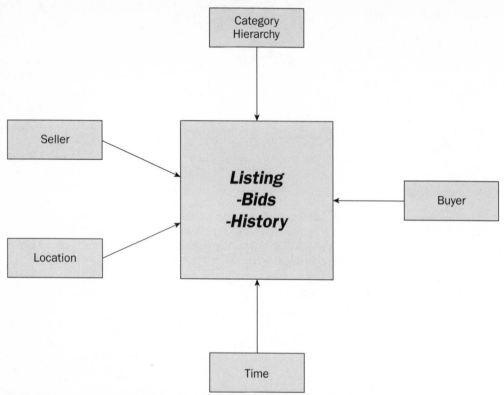

Figure 10-3: Analytical data warehouse online auction house database model.

Multiple star schemas within a single data warehouse are sometimes known as individual data marts.

Figure 10-4 shows the application of business rules to the simple analytical diagram shown in Figure 10-3 for the data warehouse database model. Once again, you must take table dependencies into account.

It is significant to observe how the three category tables, shown in Figure 10-2 (the OLTP database model), have been merged into a single hierarchical category table (CATEGORY_HIERARCHY) in the data warehouse model shown in Figure 10-4. This is a form of denormalization, used especially in data warehouse databases to simplify and compress dimensional information use.

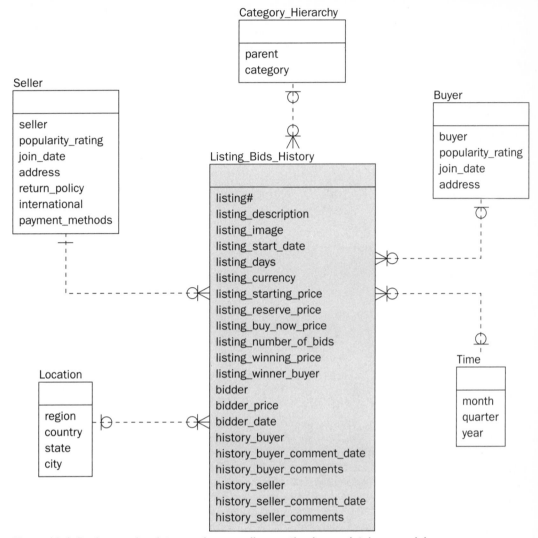

Figure 10-4: Business rules data warehouse online auction house database model.

Now you create the tables for the data warehouse model shown in Figure 10-4. In a well-designed data warehouse star schema, there is only one layer of dependence between a single layer of unrelated dimensions and a single fact table. Create the dimensions:

```
CREATE TABLE LOCATION
(
        REGION STRING,
        COUNTRY STRING,
        STATE STRING,
        CITY STRING
);

CREATE TABLE TIME
```

```
(
        MONTH INTEGER,
        QUARTER INTEGER,
        YEAR INTEGER
);

CREATE TABLE CATEGORY_HIERARCHY
(
        PARENT STRING,
        CATEGORY STRING
);

CREATE TABLE BUYER
(
        BUYER STRING,
        POPULARITY_RATING INTEGER,
        JOIN_DATE DATE,
        ADDRESS BIGSTRING
);

CREATE TABLE SELLER
(
        SELLER STRING,
        POPULARITY_RATING INTEGER,
        JOIN_DATE DATE,
        ADDRESS BIGSTRING,
        RETURN_POLICY BIGSTRING,
        INTERNATIONAL STRING,
        PAYMENT_METHODS BIGSTRING
);
```

In this table script, yet another datatype called BIGSTRING has been introduced. A BIGSTRING datatype is used to represent fields that may become multiple fields, or even a subsidiary table at a later stage, through normalization. For example, ADDRESS represents an address. An address can consist of many fields, such as STREET, ZIPCODE, CITY, STATE, and so on. The field PAYMENT_METHODS is named with plurality to indicate multiple possible acceptable methods of payment. Different sellers are likely to accept a number of a group of acceptable payment methods. Thus, the BIGSTRING datatype applies to the PAYMENT_METHODS field. For example, one seller may be willing to accept personal checks and cash. Another seller might only accept cash and credit cards, but not personal checks.

Now, let's create the fact table:

```
CREATE TABLE LISTING_BIDS_HISTORY
(
        LISTING# STRING,
        LISTING_DESCRIPTION STRING,
        LISTING_IMAGE BINARY,
        LISTING_START_DATE DATE,
        LISTING_DAYS INTEGER,
        LISTING_CURRENCY STRING,
        LISTING_STARTING_PRICE MONEY,
        LISTING_RESERVE_PRICE MONEY,
        LISTING_BUY_NOW_PRICE MONEY,
        LISTING_NUMBER_OF_BIDS INTEGER,
```

```
        LISTING_WINNING_PRICE MONEY,
        LISTING_WINNER_BUYER STRING,
        BIDDER MONEY,
        BIDDER_PRICE MONEY,
        BIDDER_DATE DATE,
        HISTORY_BUYER STRING,
        HISTORY_BUYER_COMMENT_DATE DATE,
        HISTORY_BUYER_COMMENTS BIGSTRING,
        HISTORY_SELLER STRING,
        HISTORY_SELLER_COMMENT_DATE DATE,
        HISTORY_SELLER_COMMENTS BIGSTRING
);
```

This fact table shows the source of all fields as being listing, bidder, buyer history, and seller history. Tables have been created for the OLTP and data warehouse database models for the online auction house. The next step is to establish and enforce referential integrity.

Case Study: Enforcing Table Relationships

Referential integrity maintains and enforces the data integrity of relationships between tables. In other words, referential integrity ensures that where a child table record exists, the parent table record exists as well.

Referential Integrity

In Figure 10-2, you cannot delete a SELLER record without deleting all the seller's listings first. If the seller is deleted, their listings become orphaned records. An *orphaned record* is term applied to a record not findable within the logical table structure of a database model. Essentially, the seller's name and address details are stored in the SELLER table and not in the LISTING table. If the seller record was deleted, any of their listings are useless because you don't know who is selling it. Similarly, if buyer information with winning bids were deleted, the seller wouldn't know who to mail it to. Referential integrity, through the use of primary and foreign keys, acts to ensure that the following activities are prohibited:

❑ INSERT *check* — A child record cannot be added to a child table unless the parent record exists in the parent table.

❑ UPDATE *check* — Parent and child table records cannot have their linking key field values changed, unless both are changed simultaneously ("simultaneously" implies within the same transaction).

❑ DELETE *check* — A parent table record cannot be deleted when a child table record exists, unless all related child table records are deleted first.

❑ DELETE CASCADE *check* — A parent table record can be deleted if all child records are deleted first. This is known as a *cascading delete*. Cascade deletion is rarely implemented because it can result in serious data loss (usually through operator or programmer error). Additionally, cascade deletions can cause serious locking conflicts because large numbers of child records could have to be deleted, when deleting a parent record. This type of locking problem can occur when a parent record has many records in child tables, through a multiple level table structure.

Primary and Foreign Keys

Primary and foreign keys are used to establish referential integrity relationships between parent and child tables. The parent table contains the primary key, and the child table the foreign key. The term *primary* implies most significant field for a table, and thus uniquely identifying. Each seller record would have a unique seller name (the name of the person or company selling the item at auction). Two sellers can't have the same name, leading to the obvious silly result. How would you dissimilate between two different sellers? Impossible. The term *foreign* implies a key that is foreign to a child table, whose uniquely identifying value lies in another table (the parent table containing the primary key).

Now demonstrate implementation of primary and foreign keys by re-creating the OLTP database model tables, as shown in Figure 10-2. The ERD in Figure 10-2 has been changed to the ERD shown in Figure 10-5.

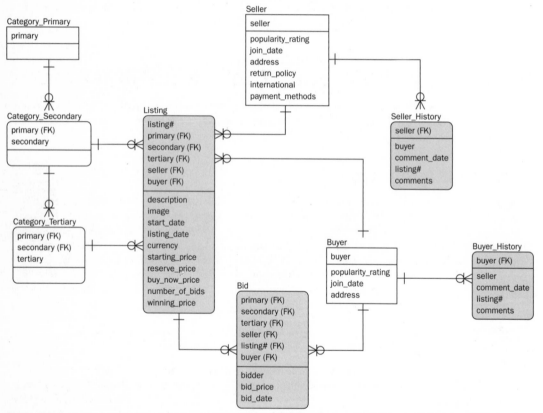

Figure 10-5: Defining primary and foreign keys for the OLTP online auction house database model.

The table contents in Figure 10-5 may appear somewhat confusing. All the dotted lines have changed to solid lines (non-identifying to identifying relationships) and the primary keys are largely composite key fields. Yuk! Use surrogate keys instead. Before explaining why relationships have been changed from non-identifying to identifying, first implement surrogate keys.

Using Surrogate Keys

Figure 10-6 shows the same model as shown in Figure 10-5, except with surrogate keys added. The only table without a surrogate primary key field is the LISTING table, still using the LISTING# field as its primary key. LISTING# is likely to be some type of auto counter anyway, and so a surrogate key is not necessary in this case. Figure 10-6 still has composite primary key fields.

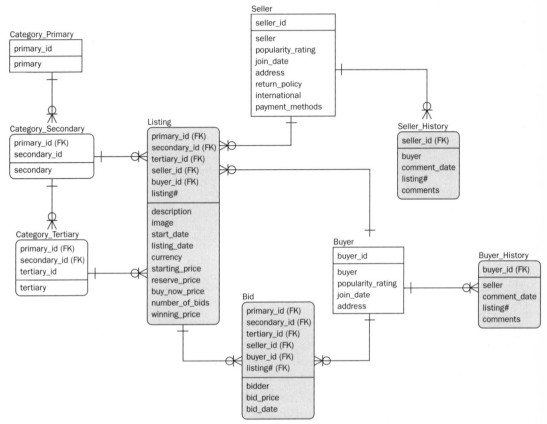

Figure 10-6: Using surrogate keys as primary keys with identifying relationships.

One important point about Figure 10-6 is that the three category tables, plus the buyer and seller table, have additional identifier fields as primary keys (for example, BUYER.BUYER_ID). However, these tables still have their original primary key fields, now no longer as the primary key (for example, BUYER.BUYER). The identifiers have become surrogates (replacements) for the original string datatype names.

Identifying relationships in Figure 10-6 imply that a child table record is specifically identified by a parent table record, through the connection between parent table primary key, and child table foreign key.

Identifying versus Non-Identifying Relationships

One more improvement that can be made is to change all the identifying relationships back to non-identifying relationships, where appropriate, as shown in Figure 10-7. Using non-identifying relationships (represented by dotted lines in Figure 10-7), child tables are no longer uniquely identified by parent table primary key values (by the parent table primary key). Notice how much simpler the ERD in Figure 10-7 has become. Also, notice how the BID, SELLER_HISTORY, and BUYER_HISTORY tables are still related to their parent tables using identifying relationships (solid, non-dotted lines in Figure 10-7). The two history tables do not have primary keys of their own. This means they can contain duplicated records for each. In other words, a buyer can contain many history entries, and, therefore, each buyer can have many BUYER_HISTORY records. The BID table does not have its own exclusive primary key field because it is a table resolving the many-to-many relationship between the LISTING and BID tables.

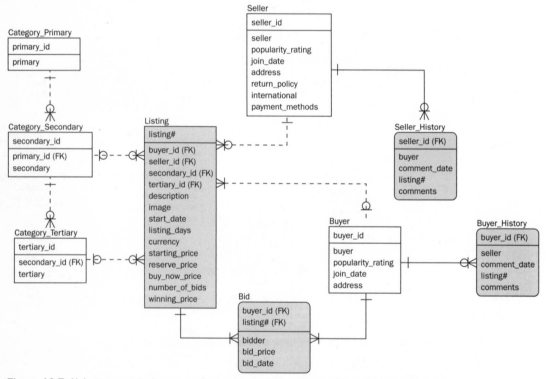

Figure 10-7: Using surrogate keys as primary keys with some non-identifying relationships.

Parent Records without Children

A parent record without children is where a parent table can have records, such that child related records are not required, within child tables. For example, there is no reason why a secondary category should always be created for a primary category. In other words, a primary category can be created where no secondary or tertiary categories exist for that primary category. For the online auction house, it depends on how categories are organized. It may be that some types of secondary and tertiary categories sell extremely well. This could perhaps make them primary categories as well. This particular complication is ignored.

In Figure 10-8, the relationship between the CATEGORY_PRIMARY and CATEGORY_SECONDARY tables is one-to-zero, one, or many. What this means is that a CATEGORY_PRIMARY record can exist with no related CATEGORY_SECONDARY records. On the contrary, a CATEGORY_SECONDARY record cannot exist unless it has a related parent CATEGORY_PRIMARY record. Similarly, a seller does not have to have any history (SELLER_HISTORY records), but there will be no SELLER_HISTORY if there is no seller for that history to be entered against.

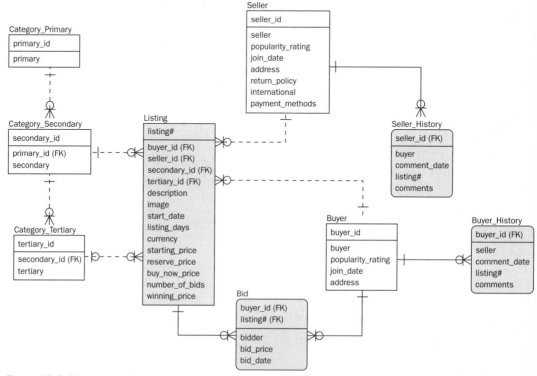

Figure 10-8: Parent records can exist and child records are not absolutely required (one-to-zero, one, or many).

Child Records with Optional Parents

A table containing child records with optional parent records is often typical of data warehouse fact tables, such that not all dimensions need be defined for every fact. This is especially true where facts stem from differing sources, such as BID in Figure 10-8. The result is some fact records with one or more NULL valued foreign keys. In Figure 10-8, a LISTING table record can be set as either being a secondary or a tertiary category. Thus, the relationship between both CATEGORY_SECONDARY and CATEGORY_TERTIARY tables to that of LISTING, is zero or one-to-zero, one, or zero. In other words, a listing can be specified as a secondary or a tertiary category (not both). The result is that for every LISTING record, that either the SECONDARY_ID, or the TERTIARY_ID fields can be NULL valued. Thus, LISTING table records can be said to have *optional parents*.

Optional parents are technically and more commonly known as NULL valued foreign keys.

The OLTP Database Model with Referential Integrity

The final step in this section on enforcing table relationships is to create the tables. In this version, all the primary and foreign keys to enforce referential integrity relationships are included. This is a sample script for creating tables for the OLTP database model of the online auction house. In this version, all primary and foreign key definitions are included, to enforce referential integrity:

```
CREATE TABLE CATEGORY_PRIMARY
(
        PRIMARY_ID INTEGER PRIMARY KEY,
        PRIMARY STRING
);

CREATE TABLE CATEGORY_SECONDARY
(
        SECONDARY_ID INTEGER PRIMARY KEY,
        PRIMARY_ID INTEGER FOREIGN KEY REFERENCES CATEGORY_PRIMARY,
        SECONDARY STRING
);

CREATE TABLE CATEGORY_TERTIARY
(
        TERTIARY_ID INTEGER PRIMARY KEY,
        SECONDARY_ID INTEGER FOREIGN KEY REFERENCES CATEGORY_SECONDARY,
        TERTIARY STRING
);
```

The CATEGORY_ PRIMARY *table has no foreign keys. The* CATEGORY_TERTIARY *table has no link to the* CATEGORY_PRIMARY *table, as a result of surrogate key use, and non-identifying relationships. A foreign key specification references the parent table, not the parent table primary key. The parent table already "knows" what its primary key field is.*

```
CREATE TABLE SELLER
(
        SELLER_ID INTEGER PRIMARY KEY,
        SELLER STRING,
        POPULARITY_RATING INTEGER,
        JOIN_DATE DATE,
        ADDRESS STRING,
        RETURN_POLICY STRING,
        INTERNATIONAL STRING,
        PAYMENT_METHODS STRING
);

CREATE TABLE BUYER
(
        BUYER_ID INTEGER PRIMARY KEY,
        BUYER STRING,
        POPULARITY_RATING INTEGER,
        JOIN_DATE DATE,
        ADDRESS STRING
);
```

The SELLER *and* BUYER *tables are at the top of the hierarchy, so they have no foreign keys.*

The SELLER_HISTORY and BUYER_HISTORY tables are incorrect as shown in Figure 10-8 because the lone foreign key is also the primary key. With the structure as it is in Figure 10-8, each seller and buyer would be restricted to a single history record each. A primary key value must also be unique across all records for an entire table. One solution is shown in Figure 10-9, with the script following it. In Figure 10-9, the primary key becomes a composite of the non-unique SELLER_ID or BUYER_ID, plus a subsidiary SEQ# (*counting sequence number*). The counting sequence number counts upwards from 1, for each seller and buyer (with history records). So, if one buyer has 10 history entries, that buyers history SEQ values would be 1 to 10, for those 10 records. Similarly, a second buyer with 25 history records would have SEQ# fields values valued at 1 to 25.

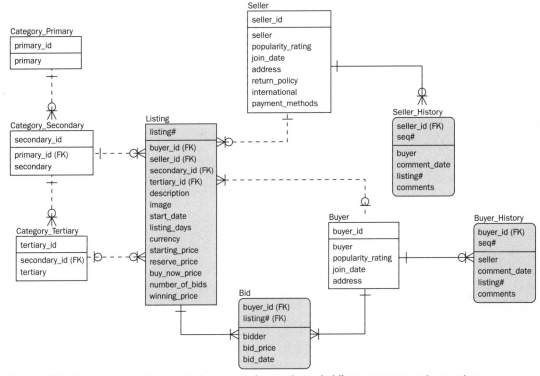

Figure 10-9: Non-unique table records become unique using subsidiary sequence auto counters.

Following is the script for Figure 10-9:

```
CREATE TABLE SELLER_HISTORY
(
        SELLER_ID INTEGER FOREIGN KEY REFERENCES SELLER NOT NULL,
        SEQ# INTEGER NOT NULL,
        BUYER STRING,
        COMMENT_DATE DATE,
        LISTING# STRING,
        COMMENTS STRING,
        CONSTRAINT PRIMARY KEY(SELLER_ID, SEQ#)
);

CREATE TABLE BUYER_HISTORY
```

```
(
        BUYER_ID INTEGER FOREIGN KEY REFERENCES BUYER NOT NULL,
        SEQ# INTEGER NOT NULL
        SELLER STRING,
        COMMENT_DATE DATE,
        LISTING# STRING,
        COMMENTS STRING,
        CONSTRAINT PRIMARY KEY(BUYER_ID, SEQ#)
);
```

The SELLER_ID, BUYER_ID *and* SEQ# *fields have all been specifically declared as being* NOT NULL. *This means that a value must be entered into these fields for the creation of a new record (or a change to an existing record). All the fields in a composite (multiple field) primary key must be declared as* NOT NULL. *This ensures uniqueness of the resulting composite primary key.*

A primary key declared on more than one field (a composite key) cannot be specified inline with that specific field definition. This is because there is more than one field. The primary key is declared out-of-line to field definitions, as a specific constraint. This forces the requirement for the NOT NULL *specifications of all the primary key fields.*

Another more elegant but perhaps more mathematical and somewhat confusing solution is to create a surrogate key for the BUYER_HISTORY and SELLER_HISTORY tables as well. The result is shown in Figure 10-10. The result is non-identifying relationships from SELLER to SELLER_HISTORY, and BUYER to BUYER_HISTORY tables.

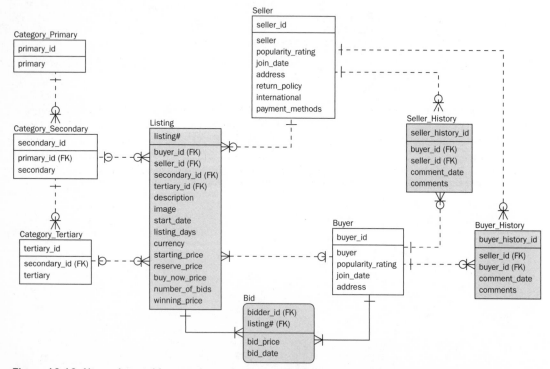

Figure 10-10: Non-unique table records can become unique by using surrogate key auto counters.

As a reminder, a non-identifying relationship is when the parent table primary key is not part of the primary key in the child table. A child table record is not specifically or uniquely identified by a child table record.

Further changes in Figure 10-10 are as follows:

❏ The addition of the relationships between SELLER to BUYER_HISTORY tables, and BUYER to SELLER_HISTORY tables. Every history record of seller activity is related to something purchased from that seller (by a buyer). The same applies to buyers.

❏ A buyer can be a seller as well, and visa versa. This database model is beginning to look a little messy.

Following is the script for changes introduced in Figure 10-10:

```
CREATE TABLE SELLER_HISTORY
(
        SELLER_HISTORY_ID INTEGER PRIMARY KEY,
        SELLER_ID INTEGER FOREIGN KEY REFERENCES SELLER,
        BUYER_ID INTEGER FOREIGN KEY REFERENCES BUYER,
        COMMENT_DATE DATE,
        COMMENTS STRING
);

CREATE TABLE BUYER_HISTORY
(
        BUYER_HISTORY_ID INTEGER PRIMARY KEY,
        BUYER_ID INTEGER FOREIGN KEY REFERENCES BUYER,
        SELLER_ID INTEGER FOREIGN KEY REFERENCES SELLER,
        COMMENT_DATE DATE,
        COMMENTS STRING
);
```

Figure 10-11 shows further refinement for the BID table. Essentially, this section has included some specific analysis-design reworking. Some things can't be assessed accurately by simple analysis. Don't mistake the fiddling with relationships, and specific fields, for primary and foreign keys as normalization or denormalization. Note, however, that some extensive normalization has occurred merely by the establishment of one-to-many relationships. This normalization activity has actually been performed from an analytical perspective.

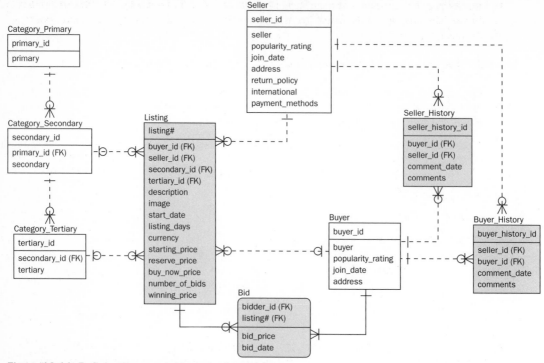

Figure 10-11: Refining the `BID` **table and related tables.**

> You don't actually have to apply the rules of normalization, using Normal Forms, to create a first pass of a database model. So far, it's all been common sense. This is one of the reasons why these final chapters are presented as a case study example. This case study is not an application of theory, by applying normalization and Normal Forms, to a bucket of information. A bucket of information implies a whole pile of things thrown into a heap, on the floor in front of you.

Figure 10-11 has essentially redefined the `BID` table and made a few other small necessary changes. These changes all make analytical sense and don't need normalization. Potential buyers place bids on auction listings, but do not necessarily win the auction; however, the history of all bids for a listing needs to be retained. The `BID` table, therefore, contains all bids for a listing, including all losing bids and the final winning bid. The final winning bid is recorded as the winning bid, by setting the `BUYER_ID` field in the `LISTING` table. As a result, a losing buyer is not stored in the `LISTING` table as a buyer because he or she is only a bidder (a *buyer* is only a bidder who wins the listing). The results are as follows:

❑   `LISTING` *to* `BID` *is one-to-zero, one, or many* — A listing that has just been listed is likely to have no bids. Also, an unpopular listing may have no bids placed over the life of the auction listing. It is still a listing, but it has no bids.

❑   `BUYER` *to* `LISTING` *is zero or one to zero, one, or many* — A losing buyer is only a bidder and not the winning bidder. Losing bidders are not entered into the `LISTING` table as buyers because they lost the auction.

❑ BUYER *to* BID *is one-to-one or many (zero is not allowed)* — A bid cannot exist without a potential buyer. This item is not a change, but listed as a reinforcing explanation of said relationships between BID, BUYER, and LISTING tables.

The result is the following script for creating the LISTING and BID tables:

```
CREATE TABLE LISTING
(
        LISTING# STRING PRIMARY KEY,
        BUYER_ID INTEGER FOREIGN KEY REFERENCES BUYER WITH NULL,
        SELLER_ID INTEGER FOREIGN KEY REFERENCES SELLER,
        SECONDARY_ID INTEGER FOREIGN KEY REFERENCES CATEGORY_SECONDARY WITH NULL,
        TERTIARY_ID INTEGER FOREIGN KEY REFERENCES CATEGORY_TERTIARY WITH NULL,
        DESCRIPTION STRING,
        IMAGE BINARY,
        START_DATE DATE,
        LISTING_DAYS INTEGER,
        CURRENCY STRING,
        STARTING_PRICE MONEY,
        RESERVE_PRICE MONEY,
        BUY_NOW_PRICE MONEY,
        NUMBER_OF_BIDS INTEGER,
        WINNING_PRICE MONEY
);
```

The BUYER_ID *field is specified as a* WITH NULL *foreign key, indicating that* LISTING *records only contain the* BUYER_ID *for the winning bidder. If no one bids, then a* LISTING *record will never have a* BUYER_ID *value. The* SECONDARY_ID *and* TERTIARY_ID *category fields are also listed as* WITH NULL *foreign key fields because either is allowed (not both).*

```
CREATE TABLE BID
(
        BIDDER_ID INTEGER FOREIGN KEY REFERENCES BIDDER,
        LISTING# INTEGER FOREIGN KEY REFERENCES LISTING,
        BID_PRICE MONEY,
        BID_DATE DATE,
        CONSTRAINT PRIMARY KEY(BIDDER_ID, LISTING#)
);
```

CREATE TABLE *commands would have to be preceded by* DROP TABLE *commands for all tables, preferably in reverse order to that of creation. Some databases will allow changes to primary and foreign keys using* ALTER TABLE *commands. Some databases even allow these changes directly into an ERD GUI tool. Microsoft Access allows these changes to be made very easily, using a GUI.*

The Data Warehouse Database Model with Referential Integrity

The data warehouse database model for the online auction house is altered slightly in Figure 10-12, including addition of surrogate primary keys to all tables. All of the dimensional-fact table relationships are zero or one, to zero, one, or many. This indicates that the fact table contains a mixture of multiple fact sources (multiple transaction types, including listings, bids, and histories). Essentially, a fact table does not absolutely have to contain all fields from all records, for all facts. In other words, fact records do not always have to contain location (`LOCATION` table) information, for example. The `LOCATION` table `LOCATION_ID` foreign key in the fact table can contain `NULL` values.

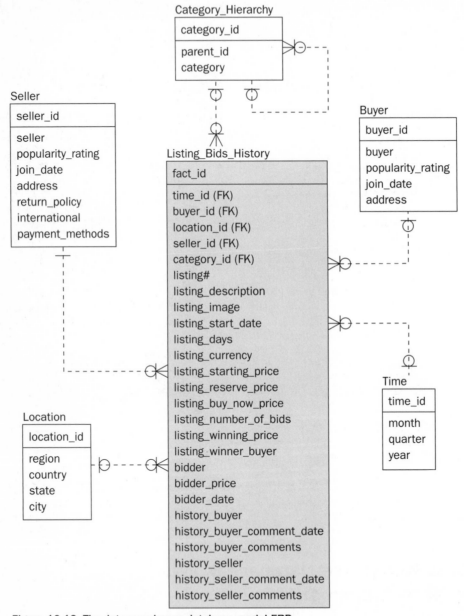

Figure 10-12: The data warehouse database model ERD.

A script to create the tables shown in Figure 10-12 is as follows:

```
CREATE TABLE CATEGORY_HIERARCHY
(
        CATEGORY_ID INTEGER PRIMARY KEY,
        PARENT_ID INTEGER FOREIGN KEY REFERENCES CATEGORY_HIERARCHY WITH NULL,
        CATEGORY STRING
);
```

The PARENT_ID *field points at a possible parent category. If there is no parent, then the* PARENT_ID *is* NULL *valued (*WITH NULL*). Primary categories will have* NULL *valued* PARENT_ID *fields.*

Data warehouse database model SELLER and BUYER tables are the same as for the OLTP database model:

```
CREATE TABLE SELLER
(
        SELLER_ID INTEGER PRIMARY KEY,
        SELLER STRING,
        POPULARITY_RATING INTEGER,
        JOIN_DATE DATE,
        ADDRESS STRING,
        RETURN_POLICY STRING,
        INTERNATIONAL STRING,
        PAYMENT_METHODS STRING
);

CREATE TABLE BUYER
(
        BUYER_ID INTEGER PRIMARY KEY,
        BUYER STRING,
        POPULARITY_RATING INTEGER,
        JOIN_DATE DATE,
        ADDRESS STRING
);
```

The LOCATION and TIME tables are as follows:

```
CREATE TABLE LOCATION
(
        LOCATION_ID INTEGER PRIMARY KEY,
        REGION STRING,
        COUNTRY STRING,
        STATE STRING,
        CITY STRING
);

CREATE TABLE TIME
(
        TIME_ID INTEGER PRIMARY KEY,
        MONTH STRING,
        QUARTER STRING,
        YEAR STRING
);
```

Finally, the single fact table has optional dimensions for all but sellers, and thus all foreign keys (except the SELLER_ID foreign key) are declared as WITH NULL fields:

```
CREATE TABLE LISTING_BIDS_HISTORY
(
        FACT_ID INTEGER PRIMARY KEY,
        CATEGORY_ID INTEGER FOREIGN KEY REFERENCES CATEGORY_HIERARCHY WITH NULL,
        TIME_ID INTEGER FOREIGN KEY REFERENCES TIME WITH NULL,
        LOCATION_ID INTEGER FOREIGN KEY REFERENCES LOCATION WITH NULL,
        BUYER_ID INTEGER FOREIGN KEY REFERENCES BUYER WITH NULL,
        SELLER_ID INTEGER FOREIGN KEY REFERENCES SELLER,
        ...
);
```

That is how referential integrity is enforced using primary and foreign keys. There are other ways of enforcing referential integrity, such as using stored procedures, event triggers, or even application code. These methods are, of course, not necessarily built in database model business rules. Even so, primary and foreign keys are a direct application of business rules in the database model and thus are the only relevant topic.

So, where do normalization and denormalization come in here?

Normalization and Denormalization

Normalization divides things up into smaller pieces. Denormalization does the opposite of normalization by reconstituting those *little-bitty* pieces back into larger pieces. When implementing normalization and denormalization, there are a number of general conceptual approaches to consider:

❑   Don't go overboard with normalization for an OLTP database model.

❑   Don't be afraid to denormalize, even in an OLTP database model.

❑   Generally, an OLTP database model is normalized and a data warehouse model is denormalized. Doing the opposite to each database model is usually secondary, and usually as a result of going too far initially, in the opposite direction.

❑   An OLTP database model should be normalized and a data warehouse database model should be denormalized, where appropriate.

At this stage, to maintain the case study approach, it makes sense to continue with use of the online auction company to go through the normalization and denormalization process in detail. Use of the term "detail" implies going through the whole process from scratch once again, as for analysis in Chapter 9, but executing the process using the mathematical approach (normalization), rather than the analytical approach.

Case Study: Normalizing an OLTP Database Model

Figure 10-11 shows the most recent version of the OLTP database model for the online auction house. From an operational perspective, you identified categories, sellers, buyers, listings, bids, seller histories, and buyer histories. Where do you go from here? The most sensible approach would not be to begin from scratch but perhaps to identify mathematically (using normalization) which Normal Forms were applied to create the OLTP database model shown in Figure 10-11. Figure 10-13 identifies the different layers of normalization applied to create the OLTP database model shown in Figure 10-11.

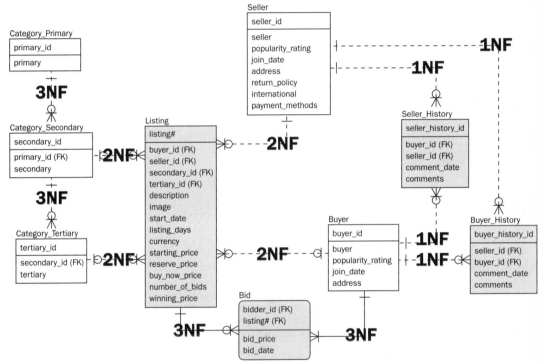

Figure 10-13: Identifying normalization Normal Form layers for the online auction house OLTP database model.

Essentially, it is probably easier to identify the different normal form implementations, after the operational analysis identification and design process has been applied; however, it might help in understanding of normalization from this perspective. Figure 10-13 simply quantifies the different Normal Forms from a more precise mathematical perspective. First of all, the following reiterates the rules of normalization, covering the 1NF, 2NF, and 3NF Normal Forms:

> ❏ *1st Normal Form (1NF)*—Eliminate repeating groups, such that all records in all tables can be identified uniquely by a primary key in each table. In other words, all fields other than the primary key must depend on the primary key.
>
> ### 1NF the Easy Way
>
> Remove repeating fields by creating a new table where the original and new table, are linked together, with a master-detail, one-to-many relationship. Create primary keys on both tables where the detail table will have a composite primary key, containing the master table primary key field as the prefix field, of its primary key. That prefix field is also a foreign key back to the master table.
>
> ❏ *2nd Normal Form (2NF)*—All non-key values must be fully functionally dependent on the primary key. No partial dependencies are allowed. A partial dependency exists when a field is fully dependent on a part of a composite primary key. A composite primary key is a primary key of more than one field.
>
> ### 2NF the Easy Way
>
> Perform a seemingly similar function to that of 1NF, but create a table where repeating values, rather than repeating fields, are removed to a new table. The result is a many-to-one relationship, rather than a one-to-many relationship, created between the original and new tables. The new table gets a primary key consisting of a single field. The master table contains a foreign key pointing back to the primary key of the new table. That foreign key is not part of the primary key in the original table.
>
> ❏ *3rd Normal Form (3NF)*—Eliminate transitive dependencies. What this means is that a field is indirectly determined by the primary key. This is because the field is functionally dependent on an intermediary field, where the intermediary field is dependent on the primary key.
>
> ### 3NF the Easy Way
>
> It is difficult to explain 3NF without using a mind-bogglingly, confusing, technical definition. Elimination of a transitive dependency implies creation of a new table, for something indirectly dependent on the primary key, in an existing table. There are a multitude of ways in which 3NF can be interpreted.

The following describes the Normal Form layers applied in Figure 10-13, in the order in which they have been applied, by the analysis process from Chapter 9.

Denormalizing 2NF

When performing analysis in Chapter 9, the initial operations decided upon were essentially that a listing is auctioned by a seller, in turn purchased by a buyer, and that all listings had extensive category layers. 2NF states that all non-key values must be fully functionally dependent on the primary key. No partial dependencies are allowed. A partial dependency exists when a field is fully dependent on a part of a composite primary key. In other words, seller, buyer, and category information is not dependent on the existence of a listing:

❑ A seller can exist in the database, without having any current listings. This assumes a seller registers with the auction house, even if never having listed something for sale. The seller is simply not ready yet.

❑ A buyer can exist, also without any current listings, by registering as a user.

❑ Category hierarchies are created, but there do not have to be any listings within those specific categories, at any specific point in time. The auction company would be wasting energy by creating unused categories.

The new tables and relationships created at this stage are as shown in Figure 10-14, including LISTING to SELLER, LISTING to BUYER, and LISTING to CATEGORY inter-table relationships. The LISTING table is essentially divided up into four different tables: LISTING, SELLER, BUYER, and CATEGORY.

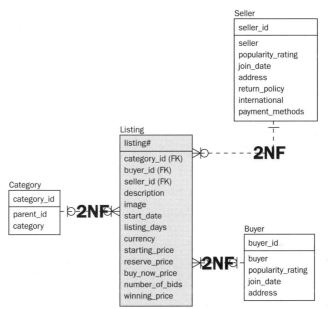

Figure 10-14: Identifying 2NF normalization for the online auction house OLTP database model.

Denormalizing 3NF

The next thing decided on in analysis was that there were multiple category layers. The CATEGORY table shown in Figure 10-14 vaguely demonstrates a transitive dependency. The parent of a category is dependent on the name of the category, and the category name is dependent on the primary key. Thus, PARENT_ID is dependent on CATEGORY, which is in turn dependent on CATEGORY_ID. Therefore, PARENT_ID is transitively dependent on CATEGORY_ID.

3NF requires that all transitive dependencies be removed by creating a new table. The resulting three-table structure is obviously not a direct application of 3NF, but the transitive dependency is removed, as shown by the three-level hierarchical structure, of the three category tables shown in Figure 10-15 (CATEGORY_PRIMARY, CATEGORY_SECONDARY, and CATEGORY_TERTIARY). The two relationships of CATEGORY_SECONDARY to LISTING, and CATEGORY_TERTIARY to LISTING, are somewhat cosmetic because for some listings, not all category layers are required. Another way to put it is that not all categories have three levels; some have only two levels. The analytical facts are as follows:

❑ There are three category layers: primary, secondary, and tertiary. Tertiary is contained within secondary, and secondary is contained within primary.

❑ A category structure with only two layers warrants the one-to-many relationship between the secondary category and the listings.

❑ A category structure with three layers warrants the one-to-many relationship between the tertiary category and the listings.

❑ Secondary and tertiary category entries do not have to both exist, and thus the tertiary category is related as zero or one to zero, one, or many, to the listings. Previously, the same relationship did not exist between secondary categories and listings because in the least, a secondary category must be used for every listing.

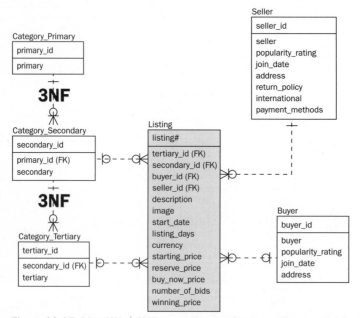

Figure 10-15: Identifying 3NF normalization for the online auction house OLTP database model.

The relationship between SECONDARY_CATEGORY and LISTING can be changed according to the last depiction of this relationship in analysis. This would be a refinement on analysis of the previous structure. It would imply that a listing must have at least a secondary category. Listings can have both secondary and tertiary categories. Essentially, this is a poor application of 3NF because the single self-joining CATEGORY table, as shown in Figure 10-14, is probably the better, and perhaps even more easily usable and understandable option.

Denormalizing 1NF

Applying 1NF is always the easiest and most obvious step to take. Technically, 1NF eliminates repeating groups, such that all records in all tables can be identified uniquely by a primary key in each table. In other words all fields (other than the primary key) must depend on the primary key. More simply put, 1NF creates master-detail relationships. The master table contains reference information and the detail table contains information, repeated over and over again, for each individual master reference record. From an analytical and operational perspective, the following details apply:

❑ All these relationships concern one-to-many, master-detail relationships. The master table contains individual reference records. References records are linked to multiple possible detail records, such as sellers (master records) are linked to multiple listings (a seller can auction more than one item at once).

❑ Sellers and buyers can have both have histories of their past auctioning and purchasing activities.

❑ Sellers can also be buyers, and visa versa; therefore, sellers and buyers and are both linked to both buyer and seller histories. This is getting messy, isn't it?

As shown in Figure 10-16, the relationships between the SELLER table to the two history tables, and the BUYER table to the two history tables, is one-to-many, and very much a master-to-detail relationship. The history tables contain histories of past activities for both buyers and sellers. The relationships are SELLER to SELLER_HISTORY, SELLER to BUYER_HISTORY, BUYER to BUYER_HISTORY, and BUYER to SELLER_HISTORY. These relationships are also a little messy. There is too much complexity perhaps.

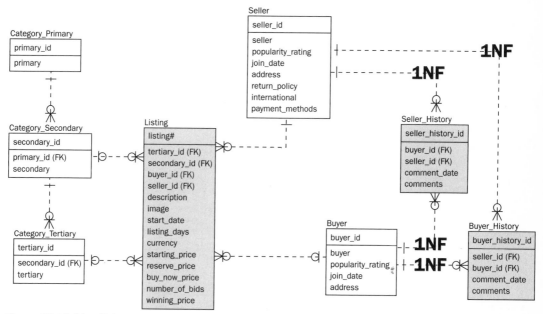

Figure 10-16: Identifying more 1NF normalization for the online auction house OLTP database model.

Denormalizing 3NF Again

The special case of 3NF shown in Figure 10-17 is actually quite a common occurrence. By definition, 3NF specifies that every field in a table that is not a key field must be directly dependent on the primary key. Without the presence of the BID table in Figure 10-16, there is actually a many-to-many relationship between the LISTING and BUYER tables. Why?

❑ Figure 10-16 combines winning and losing bidders into the BUYER table.

❑ A listing can have more than one potential buyer, be they winning or losing bidders.

❑ Each buyer can place bids on more than one listing at the same time.

One of the easiest interpretations of 3NF is where a many-to-many relationship presents the possibility that more than one record is returned using a query that joins the two tables (the two tables connected by the many-to-many relationship). The result of the application of 3NF to the relationship between LISTING and BUYER, is LISTING to BID, and BUYER to BID. This effectively allows the access to individual bids (regardless of winning or losing buyer).

Figure 10-17 shows the normalization of the relationship between LISTING and BUYER by the application of 3NF. Without the BID table, when searching for a single LISTING, all BUYER records for that listing are returned (both winning and losing bidders). The same is true for retrieving a BUYER record (returns all LISTINGS for that buyer). When a single bid entry is sought, the structure in Figure 10-16 does not permit that single record query return.

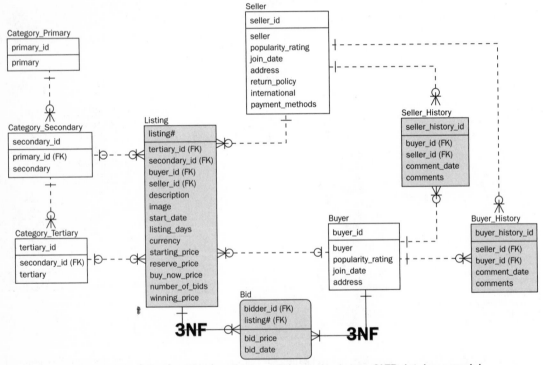

Figure 10-17: Identifying 3NF normalization for the online auction house OLTP database model.

> Normal Forms are not necessarily applied as 1NF, 2NF 3NF, but could be iterative, such as 1NF, 2NF, 3NF, 1NF, 3NF. Purists will state this is not the way to perform normalization and are likely to go completely *squint* at a comment like this. In reality, the thought processes of experienced designers rarely apply each Normal Form layer successively, without repeating already previously applied Normal Forms. This is likely because the sequential application of Normal Form layers applies more to individual tables (or small groupings of tables). On the contrary normalization is not typically applied to an entire database model — at least not for all tables at the same time.

Deeper Normalization Layers

Now examine various cases for applying beyond 3NFs to the current structure as represented in Figure 10-18.

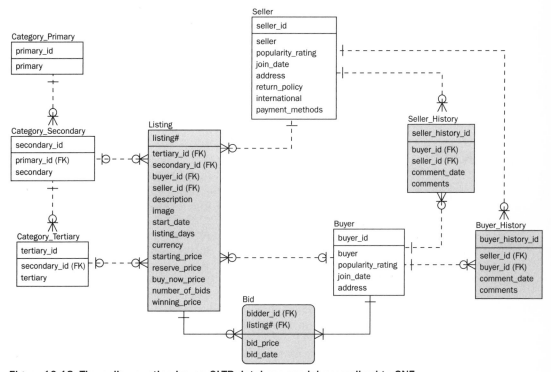

Figure 10-18: The online auction house OLTP database model normalized to 3NF.

> ### BCNF
>
> *Boyce-Codd Normal Form (BCNF)* — Every determinant in a table is a candidate key. If there is only one candidate key, 3NF and Boyce-Codd normal form are one and the same.

4NF

4th Normal Form (4NF) — Eliminate multiple sets of multi-valued dependencies.

SNF

5th Normal Form (5NF) — Eliminate cyclic dependencies. 5NF is also known as *projection normal form* (PJNF).

DKNF

Domain Key Normal Form (DKNF) — This is the ultimate application of normalization and is more a measurement of conceptual state, as opposed to a transformation process in itself. DKNF will, therefore, be ignored for the purposes of the online auction house case study example.

Beyond 3NF the Easy Way

Many commercial relational database models do not extend beyond 3NF. Sometimes 3NF is not used. The simple rule is not to make a rule out of it. Commerce requires flexibility, not rigidity. The reason why is because of the generation of too many tables, and the resulting complex SQL code joins, with resulting terrible database response times. One common case that bears mentioning is removal of potentially NULL valued fields into new tables, creating a one-to-one relationship. In modern high-end relational database engines, with variable record lengths, separating often times NULL valued fields from more actively used fields is largely irrelevant. Disk space is cheap and, as already stated, increased numbers of tables leads to bigger SQL joins and poorer performance.

Denormalizing BCNF

A table is allowed to have only one possible candidate key. A candidate key is a candidate to be a primary key. Personally, I have found BCNF a bit of an odd one, even a little obsessive. Go back to Chapter 4 and take a quick peek at Figure 4-33. In Figure 4-33, it should be clear if you read the callouts in the graphic that any field which is potentially unique for each record, that field can be a primary key. This is quite a common occurrence. In fact, quite often when replacing a traditional primary key with a surrogate key auto counter, one instantly violates BCNF. I have never seen a relational database that physically allows Data Definition Language (DDL) commands that permits the creation of a table with more than one primary key per table. Using a CREATE TABLE command or even a table-design GUI (such as in Microsoft Access) more than one primary key is simply not an option. In other words, your Microsoft Access table-modeling GUI and your Oracle or SQL Server database DDL commands will not allow creation of a table violating BCNF, with more than one primary key.

Looking at Figure 10-18 again, for the online auction house OLTP database model, you could apply BCNF to all of the SELLER, BUYER, LISTING, and both the history tables as shown in Figure 10-19.

Figure 10-19 provokes the following commentary:

❑   Separating out sellers and buyers, as well as names and addresses, is sensible from a mathematical perspective; however, from a practically applicable commercial perspective, it simply creates lots of tables to join. Additionally, the possibility of having two people or companies with the same name is unlikely, but it is possible. From a mathematical and data integrity perspective, allowing duplicate names is a problem, such as the wrong data going to the wrong person. For a bank, that would be libelous.

❑ Separating comments from the history tables is a correct application of BCNF; however, many applications use standardized comments. Some applications use commentary from pick lists. Sometimes data entry people are lazy. What about testing? When testing, programmers are likely to create the same comments. From the perspective of repetitious commentary, perhaps there should be a one-to-many relationship between a COMMENT table and the two history tables. Go figure!

❑ Listing descriptions could suffer the same potential standardization duplication problems, as would commentary in the history tables, for all the same reasons.

❑ From a mathematical perspective, images of listed items up for auction (binary encoded, stored pictures), should be unique and thus BCNF applies; however, from the point of view of the content of a field called IMAGE, it is unlikely that BCNF even remotely makes sense.

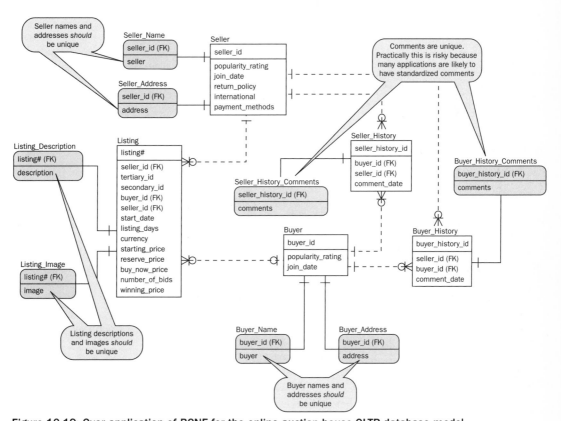

Figure 10-19: Over application of BCNF for the online auction house OLTP database model.

The items shown in Figure 10-19 are obviously all very extreme applications of BCNF, and normalization in general. Perhaps it would suffice to say that the various Normal Forms, and particularly those beyond 3NF, are not the be-all and end-all of database model design.

The extremes of application of BCNF are unnecessary and perhaps even going way too far in a commercial environment. Certainly this is very likely the case for the online auction house OLTP database model, as shown in Figure 10-19; however, it does look good from a mathematical perspective. Let's demonstrate by building a simple query to return all sellers of specific popularity rating, for all their listings and histories, listed on a particular date. Using the database model depicted in Figure 10-18, the query could look similar to the following:

```
SELECT *
FROM SELLER S JOIN SELLER_HISTORY SH USING (SELLER_ID)
    JOIN LISTING L USING (SELLER_ID)
WHERE S.POPULARITY_RATING BETWEEN 5 AND 8
AND L.START_DATE = '12-DEC-2004';
```

This query joins three tables. Query optimization procedures in any database has a much easier task of deciding how best to execute the query, joining only three tables, than it has trying to figure out an efficient method of joining the eight tables shown in the following query (based on the BCNF normalized database model shown in Figure 10-19):

```
SELECT *
FROM SELLER S JOIN SELLER_NAME SN USING (SELLER_ID)
    JOIN SELLER_ADDRESS SA USING (SELLER_ID)
      JOIN SELLER_HISTORY SH USING (SELLER_ID)
        JOIN SELLER_HISTORY_COMMENTS USING (SELLER_ID)
          JOIN LISTING L USING (SELLER_ID)
            JOIN LISTING_DESCRIPTION LD USING (LISTING#)
              JOIN LISTING_IMAGE LI USING (LISTING#)
WHERE S.POPULARITY_RATING BETWEEN 5 AND 8
AND L.START_DATE = '12-DEC-2004';
```

Additionally, the second query shown here (from Figure 10-19) is far more difficult to tune. It is much easier for a query programmer to understand the goings on in the first query than in the second query. The first query is less code and therefore easier to deal with. Programmers are usually very busy, very harried people. You can't expect programmers to solve every problem if you make their lives difficult in the first place. Give them simplicity.

Denormalizing 4NF

4NF is described as elimination of multiple sets of multi-valued dependencies or sets (in other words, multiple values being dependent on a primary key). In simple terms, a multi-valued set is a field containing a comma-delimited list, or a collection (object methodology parlance) of some kind. To see good examples and detail of 4NF transaction and application, briefly glance back to Chapter 4, at Figure 4-36 through Figure 4-40.

A candidate for being a multi-valued list in the online auction house OLTP database model is the PAYMENT_METHODS field, on the SELLER table. The PAYMENT_METHODS field has a plural name; however, plurality is not a deciding factor. Other fields, such as integers, can have plural names. For example, the LISTING_DAYS and NUMBER_OF_BIDS are both named as plural, but both are integers, and thus appropriately plural. A number can be defined as having a value of 1 or many (many is still a single value). A string, on the other hand, when being many, has many separate string values. For example, payment methods could be one or a combination of the following:

❑ Personal Check

❑ Cashier's Check

❑ Paypal

- ❏ Western Union

- ❏ Cash

- ❏ Visa

- ❏ MasterCard

- ❏ American Express

So, the PAYMENT_METHODS field for a specific listing could be something like this:

```
Cashier's Check, Western Union, Visa, MasterCard
```

This string is a comma-delimited list. A *comma-delimited list* is by definition a multi-valued set. A *multi-valued set* is thus a set, or a single item containing more than one possible value. 4NF demands that comma delimited strings should be split up. In the case of an online auction house, it is likely that the PAYMENT_METHODS field would only be used for online display. Then again, the list could be split in applications. For example, the string value Visa determines that a specific type of credit card is acceptable, perhaps processing payment through an online credit card payment service for Visa credit cards. 4NF would change the OLTP database model in Figure 10-18 to that shown in Figure 10-20.

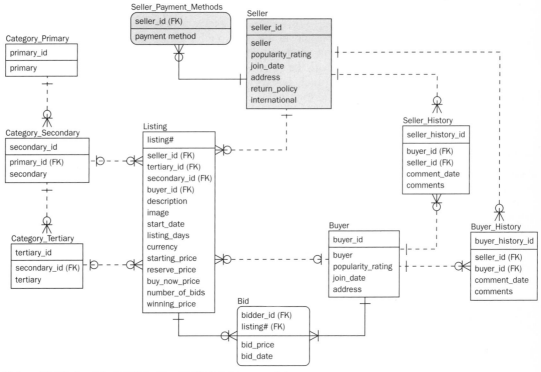

Figure 10-20: Applying 4NF to the OLTP database model.

The sensibility of the application of 4NF, as shown in Figure 10-20, depends on applications. Once again, increasing the number of tables in a database model leads to more tables in query joins. The more tables there are in query joins, the more performance is adversely affected. Using the 4NF application shown in Figure 10-20, a seller could allow four payment methods as follows:

```
Cashier's Check, Western Union, Visa, MasterCard
```

That seller would have four records as shown in Figure 10-21.

SELLER_ID	PAYMENT_METHOD
1	Cashier's Check
1	Western Union
1	Visa
1	Mastercard

Figure 10-21: Dividing a comma delimited list into separate records using 4NF.

Reading SELLER records using the database model shown in Figure 10-20 would require a two-table join of the SELLER and SELLER_PAYMENT_METHODS tables. On the contrary, without the 4NF application, as for the database model shown in Figure 10-18, only a single table would be read. Querying a single table is better and easier than a two table join; however, two-table joins perform perfectly adequately between a few tables, with no significant effect on performance, unless one of the tables has a huge number of records. The only problem with the database model structure in Figure 10-20 is that the SELLER_PAYMENT_METHODS table potentially has very few records for each SELLER record. Is there any point in dividing up multi-valued strings in this case? Splitting comma-delimited strings in programming languages for applications, is one of the easiest things in the world, and is extremely unlikely to cause performance problems in applications. Doing this type of normalization at the database model level using 4NF, on this scale, is a little overzealous—to say the least!

Denormalizing 5NF

5NF can be used, and not necessarily should be used, to eliminate cyclic dependencies. A *cyclic dependency* is something that depends on one thing, such that the one thing is either directly or indirectly dependent upon itself. Thus, a cyclic dependency is a form of *circular dependency*, where three pairs result, as a combination of a single three-field composite primary key table. For example, the three pairs could be field 1 with field 2, field 2 with field 3, and field 1 with field 3. In other words, the cyclic dependency means that everything is related to everything else, including itself. There is a combination or a permutation, which excludes repetitions. If tables are joined, again using a three-table join, the resulting records will be the same as that present in the original table. It is a stated requirement of the validity of 5NF that the post-transformation join must match the number of records for a query on the pre-transformation table. Effectively, 5NF is similar to 4NF, in that both attempt to minimize the number of fields in composite keys.

Figure 10-18 has no composite primary keys, because surrogate keys are used. At this stage, using 5NF is thus a little pointless; however, take a quick look at Figure 10-5 (earlier in this chapter) where surrogate keys were not yet implemented into the online auction house OLTP database model. The structure of the category tables in Figure 10-5 looks similar to that shown in Figure 10-22.

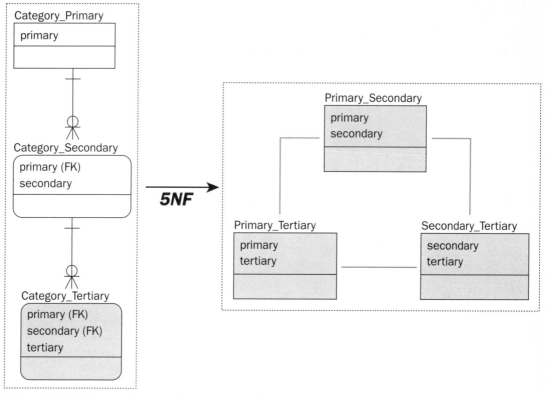

Figure 10-22: 5NF can help to break down composite primary keys.

Does the end justify the means? Commercially, probably not! As you can see in Figure 10-22, the 5NF implementation starts to look a little like the hierarchical structure shown on the left of Figure 10-22.

Case Study: Backtracking and Refining an OLTP Database Model

This is the part where you get to ignore the deep-layer normalization applied in the previous section, and go back to the OLTP database model shown in Figure 10-18. And, yes, the database model in Figure 10-18 can be denormalized.

Essentially, there are no rules or any kind of process with respect to performing denormalization. Denormalization is mostly common sense. In this case, common sense is the equivalent of experience. Figure 10-18 is repeated here again, in Figure 10-23, for convenience.

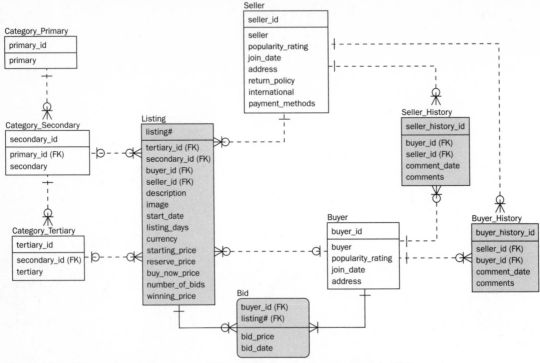

Figure 10-23: The online auction house OLTP database model normalized to 3NF.

What can and should be denormalized in the database model shown in Figure 10-23?

❑   The three category tables should be merged into a single self-joining table. Not only does this make management of categories easier, it also allows any number of layers in the category hierarchy, rather than restricting to the three of primary, secondary, and tertiary categories.

❑   Seller and buyer histories could benefit by being a single table, not only because fields are the same but also because a seller can also be a buyer and visa versa. Merging the two tables could make group search of historical information a little slower; however, proper indexing might even improve performance in general (for all applications). Also, because buyers can be sellers, and sellers can be buyers, it makes no logical sense to store historical records in two separate tables. If sellers and buyers are merged, it might be expedient to remove fields exclusive to the SELLER table, into a 4NF, one-to-one subset table, to remove NULL values from the merged table. These fields are the RETURN_POLICY, INTERNATIONAL, and the PAYMENT_METHODS fields.

❑   Depending on the relative numbers of buyers, sellers, and buyer-sellers (those who do both buying and selling), it might be expedient to even merge the sellers and buyers into a single table, as well as merging histories. Once again, fields are largely the same. The number of buyer-sellers in operation might preempt the merge as well.

The resulting OLTP database model could look similar to that shown in Figure 10-24.

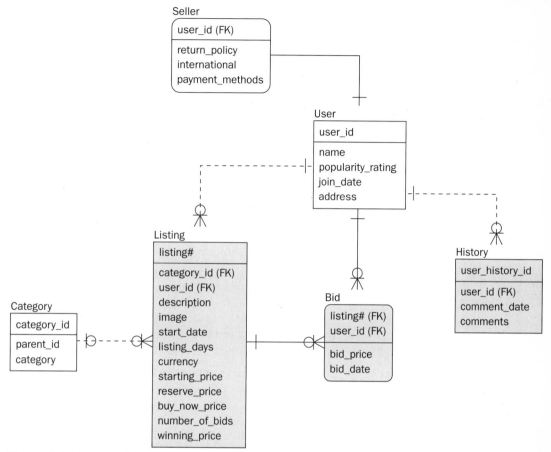

Figure 10-24: Denormalizing the online auction house OLTP database model.

Denormalization is, in general, far more significant for data warehouse database models than it is for OLTP database models. One of the problems with predicting what and how to denormalize is that in the analysis and design phases of database modeling and design, denormalization is a little like a Shakespearian *undiscovered country*. If you don't denormalize beyond 3NF, your system design could meet its maker. And then if you do denormalize an OLTP database model, you could kill the simplicity of the very structure you have just created.

In general, denormalization is not quantifiable because no one has really thought up a formal approach for it, like many have devised for normalization. Denormalization, therefore, might be somewhat akin to guesswork. Guesswork is always dangerous, but if analysis is all about expert subconscious knowledge through experience, don't let the lack of formal methods in denormalization scare you away from it.

The biggest problem with denormalization is that it requires extensive application knowledge. Typically, this kind of foresight is available only when a system has been analyzed, designed, implemented, and placed into production. Generally, when in production, any further database modeling changes are not possible. So, when hoping to denormalize a database model for efficiency and ease of use by developers, try to learn as much about how applications use tables, in terms of record quantities, how many records are accessed at once on GUI screens, how large reports will be, and so on. And do that learning process as part of analysis and design. It might be impossible to rectify in production and even in development.

Denormalization requires as much applications knowledge as possible.

Example Application Queries

The following state the obvious:

❑   The database model is the backbone of any application that uses data of any kind. That data is most likely stored in some kind of database. That database is likely to be a relational database of one form or another.

❑   Better designed database models tend to lend themselves to clearer and easier construction of SQL code queries. The ease of construction of, and the ultimate performance of queries, depends largely on the soundness of the underlying database model. The database model is the backbone of applications.

The better the database model design, the better queries are produced, the better applications will ultimately be and the happier your end-users will be. A good application often easily built by programmers is often not also easily usable by end-users. Similar to database modelers, programmers often write code for themselves, in an elegant fashion. Elegant solutions are not always going to produce the most end-user happy-smiley face result. Applications must run fast enough. Applications must not encourage end-users to become frustrated. Do not let elegant modeling and coding ultimately drive away your customers. No customer—no business. No business—no company. No company—no job! And, if your end-user happens to be your boss, well, you know the rest.

So, you must be able to build good queries. The soundness of those queries, and ultimately applications, are dependent upon the soundness of the underlying database model. A highly normalized database model is likely to be unsound because there are too many tables, too much complexity, and too many tables in joins. Lots of tables and lots of complex inter-table relationships confuse people, especially the query programmers. Denormalize for successful applications. And preferably perform denormalization of database models in the analysis and design phases, not after the fact in production. Changing database model structure for production systems is generally problematic, extremely expensive, and disruptive to end-users (applications go down for maintenance). After all, the objective is to turn a profit. This means keeping your end-users interested. If the database is an in-house thing, you need to keep your job. Denormalize, denormalize, denormalize!

Once again, the efficiency of queries comes down to how many tables are joined in a single query. Figure 10-23 shows the original normalized OLTP database model for the online auction house. In Figure 10-24, the following denormalization has occurred:

❑   *Categories*—Categories were denormalized from three tables down to a single table. A query against the three category tables would look similar to this:

```
SELECT *
FROM CATEGORY_PRIMARY CP JOIN CATEGORY_SECONDARY CS USING (PRIMARY_ID)
    JOIN CATEGORY_TERTIARY CT USING (SECONDARY_ID);
```

A query against the single category table could be constructed as follows:

```
SELECT *
FROM CATEGORY;
```

If the single category table was required to display a hierarchy, a self join could be used (some database engines have special syntax for single-table hierarchical queries):

```
SELECT P.CATEGORY, C.CATEGORY
FROM CATEGORY P JOIN CATEGORY C ON(P.CATEGORY_ID = C.CATEGORY_ID)
ORDER BY P.CATEGORY, C.CATEGORY;
```

Denormalizing categories in this way is probably a very sensible idea for the OLTP database model of the online auction house.

❑ *Users* — Sellers and buyers were partially denormalized into users, where 4NF normalization was used to separate seller details from buyers. Using the normalized database model in Figure 10-23 to find all listings for a specific seller, the following query applies (joining two tables and applying a WHERE clause to the SELLER table):

```
SELECT *
FROM SELLER S JOIN LISTING L USING (SELLER_ID)
WHERE S.SELLER = "Joe Soap";
```

Once again, using the normalized database model in Figure 10-23, the following query finds all existing bids, on all listings, for a particular buyer (joining three tables and applying a WHERE clause to the BUYER table):

```
SELECT *
FROM LISTING L JOIN BID BID USING (LISTING#)
    JOIN BUYER B USING (BUYER_ID)
WHERE B.BUYER = "Jim Smith";
```

Using the denormalized database model in Figure 10-24, this query finds all listings for a specific seller (the SELLER and USER tables are actually normalized):

```
SELECT *
FROM USER U JOIN SELLER S USING (SELLER_ID)
    JOIN LISTING L USING (USER_ID)
WHERE U.NAME = "Joe Soap";
```

This query is actually worse for the denormalized database model because it joins three tables instead of two. And again, using the denormalized database model in Figure 10-24, the following query finds all existing bids on all listings for a particular buyer:

```
SELECT *
FROM LISTING L JOIN BID BID USING (LISTING#)
    JOIN USER U USING (USER_ID)
WHERE U.NAME = "Jim Smith"
AND U.USER_ID NOT IN (SELECT USER_ID FROM SELLER);
```

This query is also worse for the denormalized version because not only does it join three tables, but additionally performs a semi-join (and an anti semi-join at that). An *anti semi-join* is a negative search. A negative search tries to find what is not in a table, and therefore must read all records in that table. Indexes can't be used at all and, thus, a full table scan results. Full table scans can be I/O heavy for larger tables.

It should be clear to conclude that denormalizing the BUYER and SELLER tables into the USER and normalized SELLER tables (as shown in Figure 10-24) is probably quite a bad idea! At least it appears that way from the perspective of query use; however, an extra field could be added to the USER table to dissimilate between users and buyers, in relation to bids and listings (a person performing both buying and selling will appear in both buyer and seller data sets). The extra field could be used as a base for very efficient indexing or even something as advanced as partitioning. *Partitioning* physically breaks tables into separate physical chunks. If the USER table were partitioned between users and sellers, reading only sellers from the USER table would only perform I/O against a partition containing sellers (not buyers). It is still not really very sensible to denormalize the BUYER and SELLER table into the USER table.

❑   *Histories* — The two history tables were denormalized into a single table, as shown in Figure 10-24. Executing a query using the normalized database model in Figure 10-23 to find the history for a specific seller, could be performed using a query like the following:

```
SELECT *
FROM SELLER S JOIN SELLER_HISTORY SH USING (SELLER_ID)
WHERE S.SELLER = "Joe Soap";
```

Finding a history for a specific seller using the denormalized database model shown in Figure 10-24 could use a query like this:

```
SELECT *
FROM USER U JOIN HISTORY H (USER_ID)
WHERE U.NAME = "Joe Soap"
AND U.USER_ID IN (SELECT USER_ID FROM SELLER);
```

Once again, as with denormalization of SELLER and BUYER tables into the USER table, denormalizing the SELLER_HISTORY and BUYER HISTORY tables into the HISTORY table, might actually be a bad idea. The first query above joins two tables. The second query also joins two tables, but also executes a semi-join. This semi-join is not as bad as for denormalization of users, which used an anti semi-join; however, this is still effectively a three-way join.

So, you have discovered that perhaps the most effective, descriptive, and potentially efficient database model for the OLTP online auction house is as shown in Figure 10-25. The only denormalization making sense at this stage is to merge the three separate category hierarchy tables into the single self-joining CATEGORY table. Buyer, seller, and history information is probably best left in separate tables.

Denormalization is rarely effective for OLTP database models for anything between 1NF and 3NF; however (and this very important), remember that previously in this chapter you read about layers of normalization beyond 3NF (BCNF, 4NF, 5NF and DKNF). None of these intensive Normal Forms have so far been applied to the OLTP database model for the online auction house. As of Figure 10-23, you began to attempt to backtrack on previously performed normalization, by denormalizing. You began with the 3NF database model as shown in Figure 10-23. In other words, any normalization beyond 3NF was simply ignored, having already been proved to be completely superfluous and over the top for this particular database model.

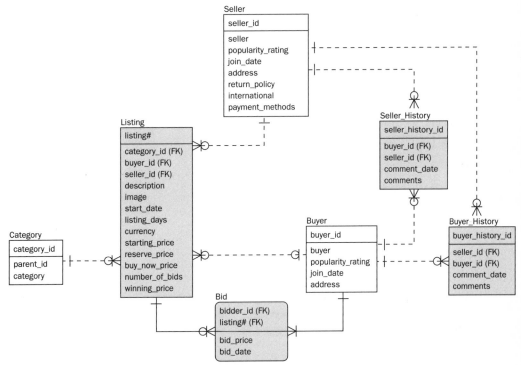

Figure 10-25: The online auction house OLTP database model, 3NF, partially denormalized.

The only obvious issue still with the database model as shown in Figure 10-25 is that the BUYER_HIS-TORY and SELLER_HISTORY tables have both BUYER_ID and SELLER_ID fields. In other words, both history tables are linked (related) to both of the BUYER and SELLER tables. It therefore could make perfect sense to denormalize not only the category tables, but the history tables as well, leave BUYER and SELLER tables normalized, and separate, as shown in Figure 10-26.

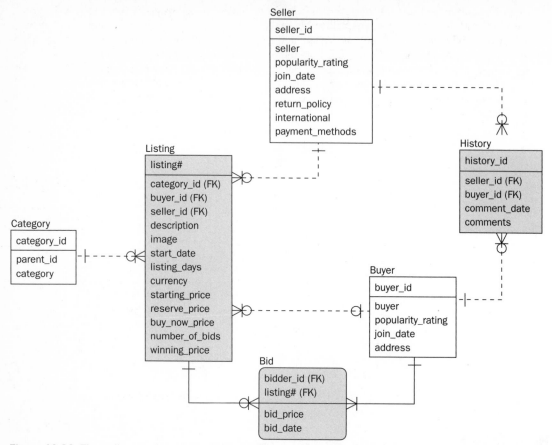

Figure 10-26: The online auction house OLTP database model, 3NF, slightly further denormalized.

The newly denormalized HISTORY table can be accessed efficiently by splitting the history records based on buyers and sellers, using indexing or something hairy fairy and sophisticated like physical partitioning.

Try It Out   Designing an OLTP Database Model

Create a simple design level OLTP database model for a Web site. This Web site allows creation of free classified ads for musicians and bands. Use the simple OLTP database model presented in Figure 10-27 (copied from Figure 9-19, in Chapter 9). Here's a basic approach:

1. Create surrogate primary keys for all tables.

2. Enforce referential integrity using appropriate primary keys, foreign keys, and inter-table relationships.

3. Refine inter-table relationships properly, according to requirements, as identifying, non-identifying relationships, and also be precise about whether each crow's foot allows zero.

4. Normalize as much as possible.

5. Denormalize for usability and performance.

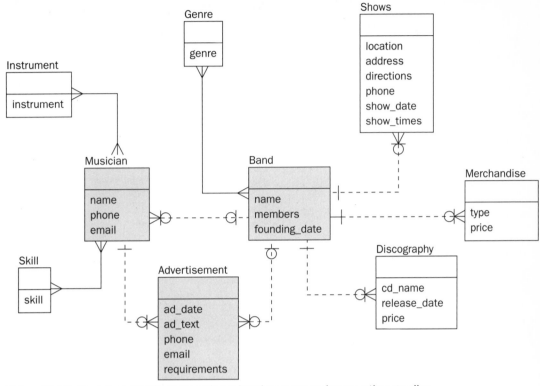

Figure 10-27: Musicians, bands, their online advertisements and some other goodies.

How It Works

Figure 10-27 shows the analyzed OLTP database model database model, for online musician and band advertisements. The database model in Figure 10-26 has the following basic requirements:

❑ Musicians can play multiple instruments.

❑ Musicians can be multi-skilled.

❑ A band can have multiple genres.

❑ The MEMBERS field in the band table takes into account the one-to-many relationship between BAND and MUSICIAN. In other words, there is more than one musician in a band (usually); however, a musician doesn't necessarily have to be in a band, a band may be broken up and have no musicians, and both bands and musicians can advertise.

❑ Musicians and bands can place advertisements.

❑ Bands and musicians perform shows.

❑ Bands and musicians sell merchandise, typically online.

❑ Discography contains all released CDs (albums).

Figure 10-28 shows the database model in Figure 10-27, with all primary keys as surrogate keys. The SHOWS table is renamed to SHOW (each record equals one show).

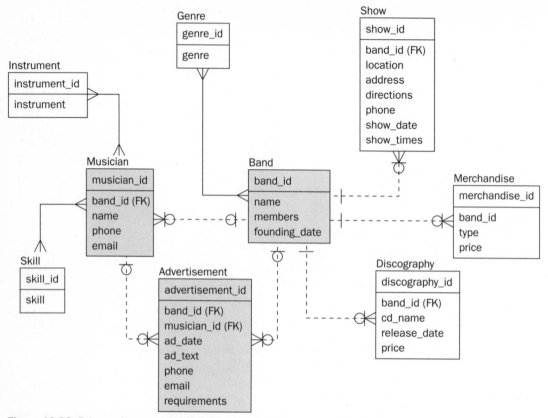

Figure 10-28: Primary keys as surrogate keys.

Figure 10-29 enforces referential integrity properly, between all primary and foreign keys, for all tables. This stage limited the many-to-many relationships between INSTRUMENT and MUSICIAN, SKILL and MUSICIAN, and GENRE and MUSICIAN.

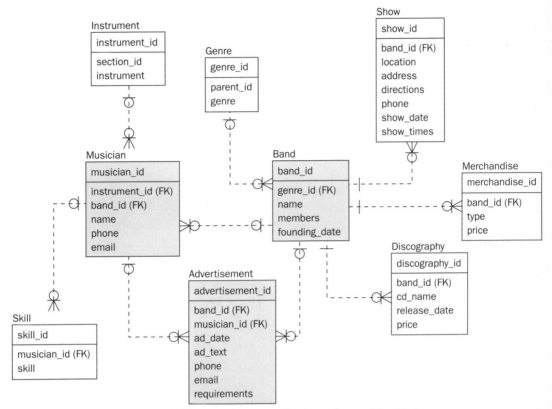

Figure 10-29: Enforcing referential integrity between all primary key and foreign keys.

Figure 10-30 refines relationships between tables as identifying, non-identifying, and NULL valued. The INSTRUMENT table contains a hierarchy, with instruments divided into sections (such as a strings section, or a percussion section). The GENRE table also contains a hierarchy of genres and sub-genres. For example, hard rock music is part of rock music, and rock music is part of modern music. Hard rock music could contain sub-genres as well, such as alternative rock. The INSTRUMENT and GENRE table has self join or fishhook join relationships added, to represent the hierarchies. A musician must play at least one instrument (voice is an instrument). Skills cannot exist without a musician.

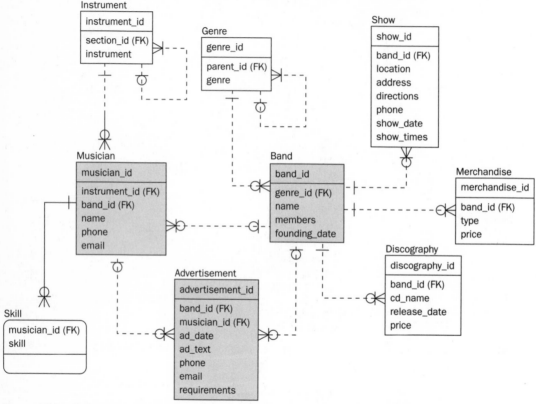

Figure 10-30: Refining relationships as identifying, non-identifying, and NULL valued.

Figure 10-31 refines the database model with normalization. This is about as far as this database model can be normalized. The INSTRUMENT and GENRE tables could be normalized if the number of layers in the hierarchies of the two tables is known. For the purposes of this example, it is assumed this is not the case. Some fields have been removed from various tables for being inappropriate. For example, the PHONE, EMAIL, and REQUIREMENTS fields have been removed from the ADVERTISEMENT table, assuming they are included in the AD_TEXT field. Some fields have been renamed.

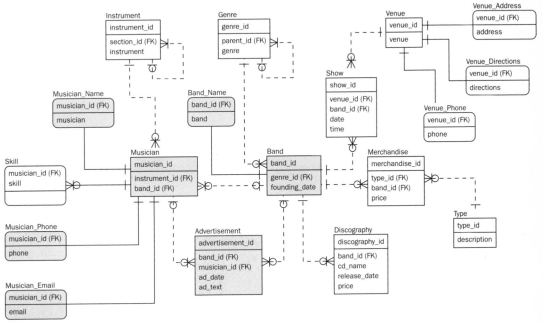

Figure 10-31: Refining the database model with normalization.

Figure 10-32 refines the database model with denormalization. All the nasty detailed Normal Forms are removed. The VENUE is retained since venues are static (dimensional) and shows are dynamic (fact data).

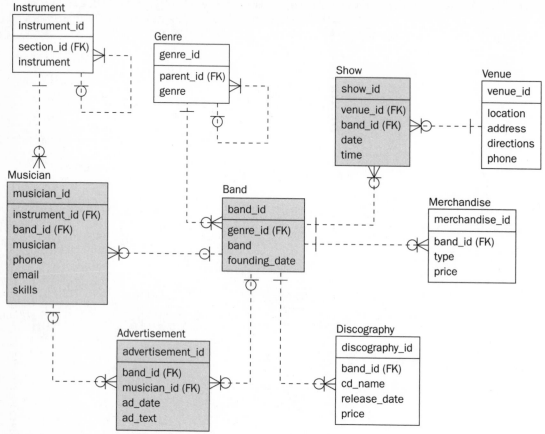

Figure 10-32: Refining the database model with denormalization.

Case Study: Refining a Data Warehouse Database Model

Figure 10-12 shows the most recent version of the data warehouse database model for the online auction house. From an operational perspective, you identified categories, sellers, buyers, locations, times, and a large fact table. Where do you go from here? What you need to do is probably to normalize the fact table somewhat, into separate fact tables. Separate fact tables become separate star schemas, and thus separate data marts. Figure 10-33 shows an initial split of facts into three separate fact tables (see Figure 10-12).

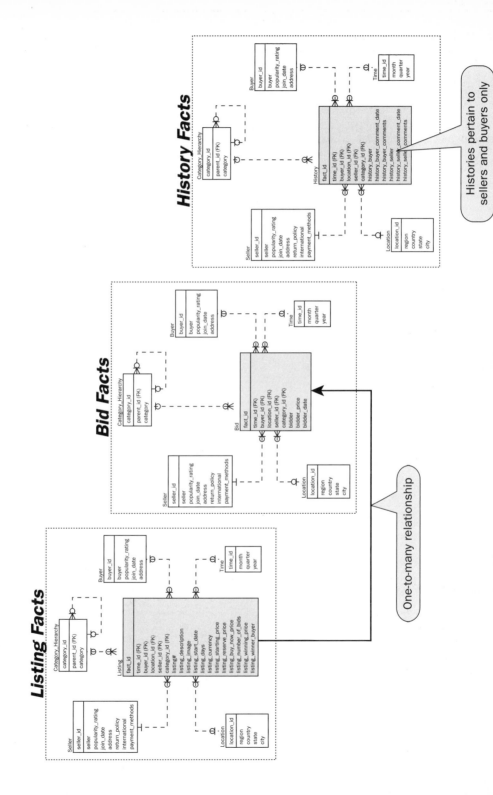

Figure 10-33: Dividing the data warehouse database model into separate facts.

The problem as shown in Figure 10-33 is that there is essentially an operational requirement for a one-to-many (master-detail) relationship between listing and bid facts. Why? Think about how this data would be used. If you wanted to track listing information alone, then there is no problem. If you wanted to analyze the pattern of bids against particular types of listings, then that LISTING to BID relationship would be required. Establishing a relationship between multiple fact tables causes serious problems. The reason why goes back to the existence of the fact-dimensional data warehouse database model itself. Data warehouse database models were devised to split very small tables, linked in a single-layer hierarchy of dimensions (a star schema), all linked to a single fact table. Fact tables are very large. The most efficient types of query joins are those between one or more small tables (the dimensions) and *only a single* large table. That great big humungous table is the fact table. And there should also be only one fact table in a star schema. Never relate or join fact tables. You might wait a week for queries to execute!

> *Linking more than one fact table together results in a join between two very large tables, which can be frighteningly inefficient — defeating the very existence of the fact-dimensional data warehouse database model. Don't do it!*

A solution is to merge and denormalize the fact tables as shown in Figure 10-34. The HISTORY fact table is not a problem because histories apply to sellers and buyers. In the real world, histories are used by sellers and buyers to assess whether they are dealing with an honest trader or a complete shyster!

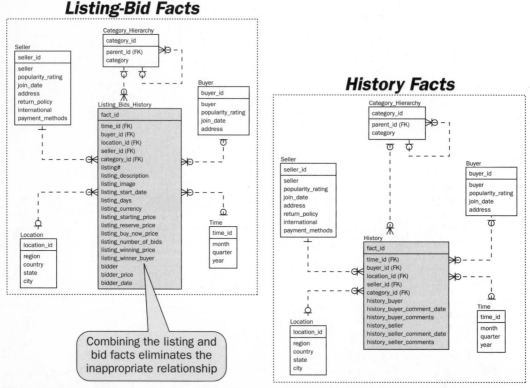

Figure 10-34: Reducing the three fact tables in Figure 10-33 to two fact tables, based on operational requirements.

A more easily readable form of the star schemas shown in Figure 10-34 is shown in Figure 10-35. If you go back briefly to Chapter 9 and examine Figure 9-23, you can see that this structure was already devised, even in the analysis stage.

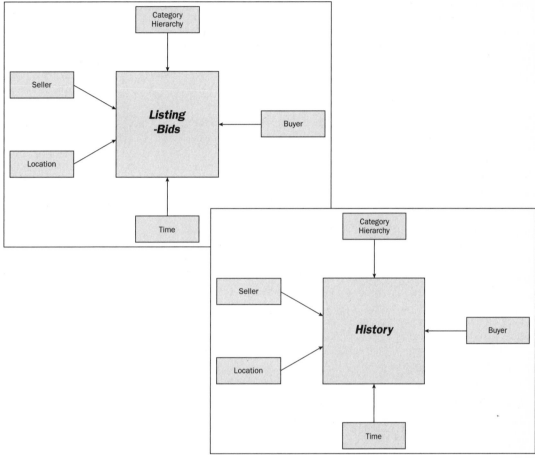

Figure 10-35: The data warehouse fact table star schemas, for the online auction house.

Essentially, Figure 10-34 and Figure 10-35 represent the best, most effective, most easily understandable, and usable database model for the online auction house data warehouse. It is possible to normalize further by normalizing the heck out of the dimensions—just don't normalize the facts. Normalizing facts (other than making operational fact table splits into multiple star schemas, as shown in Figure 10-34) defeats the purpose of the data warehouse dimensional-fact model.

> **The primary purpose of the data warehouse fact-dimensional model is to allow the fastest possible join method between two tables: one large table, and one or more very small tables.**

Figure 10-36 shows an ERD of the HISTORY fact table snowflake schema, with dimensions normalized up to gazoo! A snowflake schema is a star schema, where dimensions have been normalized.

There is no need to detail query examples for the data warehouse database model, as the same concepts apply for SQL coding of query joins for both OLTP and data warehouse databases:

❑ The fewer tables in a join, the better.

❑ It is more efficient to join between a small table and a large table, compared with equally sized tables. Obviously, joining two small tables is most efficient because there isn't much data (which should be logical by now).

Using the snowflake schema shown in Figure 10-36 is not only completely nuts, it will also drive your programmers completely nuts trying to figure it all out. And end-users simply won't know what the heck is going on in there. End-users, typically in-house type end-users, often write (or at least specify) data warehouse reporting requirements. The obsessively over-normalized data warehouse database model shown in Figure 10-36 is quite simply impractical. The end-users it will probably think it is just scary, and they will probably avoid it.

Try It Out   Designing a Data Warehouse Database Model

Create a simple design level data warehouse database model, for a Web site. This Web site allows creation of free classified ads for musicians and bands. Use the not-so-well-refined data warehouse database model presented in Figure 10-37 (copied from Figure 9-29, in Chapter 9). Here's a basic approach:

1. Refine dimensions and facts, making sure that dimensions are dimensions and facts are facts.

2. Divide facts into multiple star schemas if multiple, unrelated fact sets exist.

3. Normalize dimensions into a snowflake schema. This can help to identify and quantify dimensions more precisely.

4. Denormalize dimensions into a star schema.

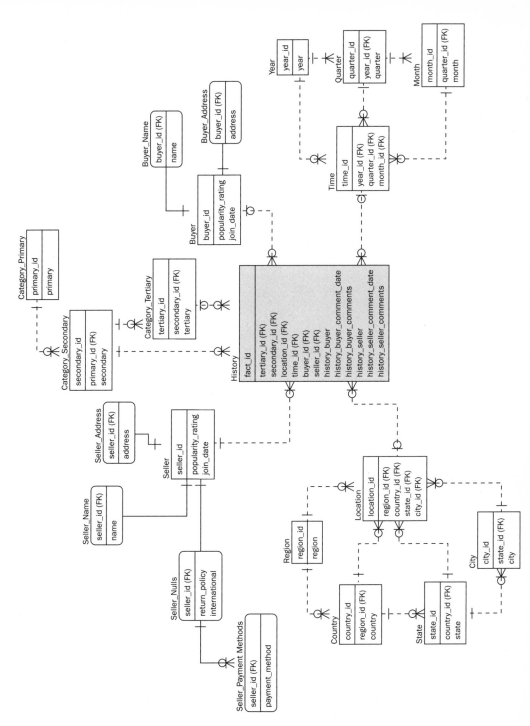

Figure 10-36: A data warehouse HISTORY fact table snowflake schema (a history data mart).

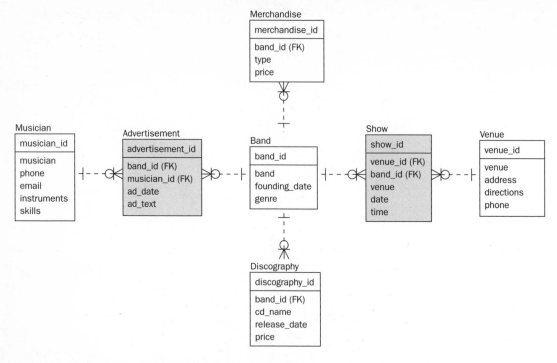

Figure 10-37: Musicians, bands, their online advertisements, and some other goodies.

How It Works

Figure 10-37 shows the analyzed data warehouse database model, for online musician and band advertisements. The most significant requirement is to ultimately produce a single star schema, if a single star schema is possible. Also add any dimensional and fact information shown as additional in Figure 10-32. Figure 10-37 shows that the SHOW table is actually fact information, not dimensional.

Examine Figure 10-37 once more. Think about the records in the tables. Yes, many advertisements are possible. However, a simple search of the Internet on Web sites such as www.themode.com and www.ticketmaster.com will reveal to you the sheer volume of advertisements, musicians, bands, shows, discography (released CDs), and venues. Figure 10-38 takes another slant on this data warehouse database model by rolling all of these tables into a single fact table.

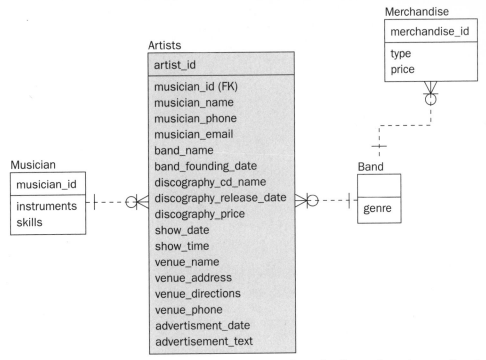

Figure 10-38: Denormalized — musicians, bands, their online advertisements, and some other goodies.

Figure 10-38 is a partially complete data warehouse database model, with all the facts rolled into a single table. Figure 10-39 shows a finalized, much more sensible star schema, based purely on relative record numbers in various tables from Figure 10-39. Larger record numbers tend to warrant tables as being factual rather than dimensional in nature.

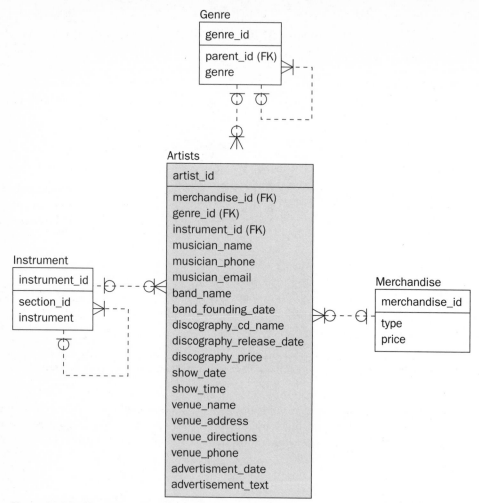

Figure 10-39: Denormalized into a single star schema — musicians, bands, their online advertisements, and some other goodies.

It is not really possible to normalize the facts in the ARTISTS table, shown in Figure 10-39, into separate star schemas because all the separate elements (such as bands, advertisements, shows, and venues) are all related to each other. Thus, a single star schema (a single fact table) is the most appropriate data warehouse database model design in this situation.

Summary

In this chapter, you learned about:

- ❏ How to expand and differentiate database model design from analysis
- ❏ The design process, as opposed to the analysis process of the previous chapter

❑   How to create and refine tables

❑   How to enforce and refine inter-table relationships and referential integrity

❑   Normalization (without going too far)

❑   Denormalization (without going too far)

❑   The folly of normalization beyond 3NFs, for both OLTP and data warehouse databases

❑   Providing for application usability, flexibility, and performance in database modeling

❑   How to ensure applications translate into happy end-users (without happy end-users, there is no profit, and, thus, no company)

This chapter has primarily expanded on Chapter 9, from analysis (what to do), into design (how to solve it). Once again, the online auction house database model has been expanded on, and detailed further by the design process, as the continuing case study. Chapter 11 digs even further into the design process by describing and specifying fields within each table, along with datatypes and indexing. The discussion on indexing is especially about alternate (secondary) indexing.

Exercises

Use the ERDs in Figure 10-32 and Figure 10-39 to help you answer these questions:

1.   Create scripts to create tables for the OLTP database model shown in Figure 10-32. Create the tables in the proper order by understanding the relationships between the tables.

2.   Create scripts to create tables for the data warehouse database model shown in Figure 10-39. Once again, create the tables in the proper order by understanding the relationships between the tables.

Filling in the Details with a Detailed Design

"Digging ever deeper gives clarity to definition, and definition of clarity." (Gavin Powell)

The further you go the more you discover.

This chapter provides the details on the internal structure of tables in terms of fields, field content, field formatting, and indexing on fields. This chapter digs a little deeper into the case study material presented in the previous two chapters. Chapter 9 introduced a database model in its infancy, by analyzing what needed to be done. Chapter 10 unearthed structural detail by describing how tables are built and how they are joined together.

This chapter delves into the details of the tables themselves, by designing the precise content and structure of individual fields. Indexing is included at this stage because indexes are created against specific table fields. An index is not quite the same thing as a key, such as a primary key. A primary key is required to be unique across all records in a table; therefore, many database engines usually create an automatic unique index for that primary key (which helps performance by checking for uniqueness). Foreign keys, on the other hand, do not have to be unique, and even the most sophisticated of relational databases does not automatically create indexes on foreign keys. This is intentional of course. If an index is required on a foreign key field (which it more often than not is), an index must be manually created for that foreign key.

By the end of this chapter, you will have a good understanding of how best to structure fields, their datatype formats, how, when and where those formats apply. Also, you will have a better conceptual understanding of foreign key indexing and alternate (secondary) indexing.

In this chapter, you learn about the following:

- ❑ Refining field structure and content in tables
- ❑ Using datatypes
- ❑ The difference between simple datatypes, ANSI datatypes, Microsoft Access datatypes and some specialized datatypes

❑   Using keys and indexes

❑   Using alternate (secondary) indexing

Case Study: Refining Field Structure

In this section, you refine the field content of tables for both the OLTP and data warehouse database models. You continue with the consistent case study development of database models for the online auction house.

The OLTP Database Model

Figure 11-1 shows the most recent version of the OLTP database model for the online auction house.

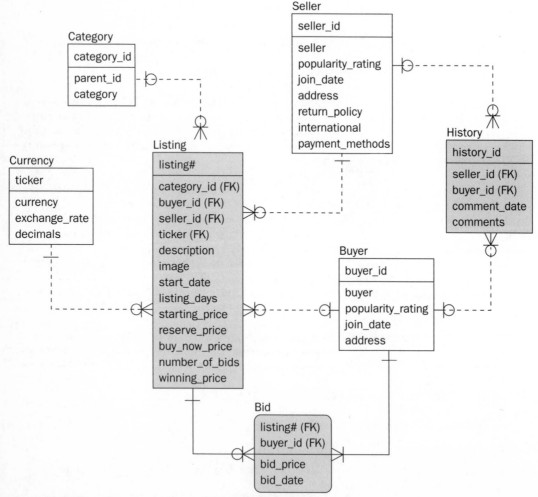

Figure 11-1: The online auction house OLTP database model.

Analysis and design are an ongoing process. Figure 11-1 shows two further examples of backtracking and refining:

❑ There is normalization of the CURRENCY table. Analytically, it is assumed that the online auction house is based in the U.S. and the U.S. dollar is the default currency. Currencies are separated because there can be a fair amount of complexity involved in currency exchange conversions.

❑ The relationships between SELLER to HISTORY, and BUYER to HISTORY tables should allow for histories with buyers or sellers. This is because the HISTORY table is a combination of buyer and seller histories. When a trader is only a buyer, that trader will have no history of activity as a seller; therefore, the relationship between BUYER and HISTORY tables is zero or one to zero, one or many. This means that for every HISTORY record, there does not necessarily have to be a SELLER record. This is because for every HISTORY record, there can be either a SELLER record, or a BUYER record.

Figure 11-2 shows a refined field structure for the online auction house OLTP database model shown in Figure 11-1.

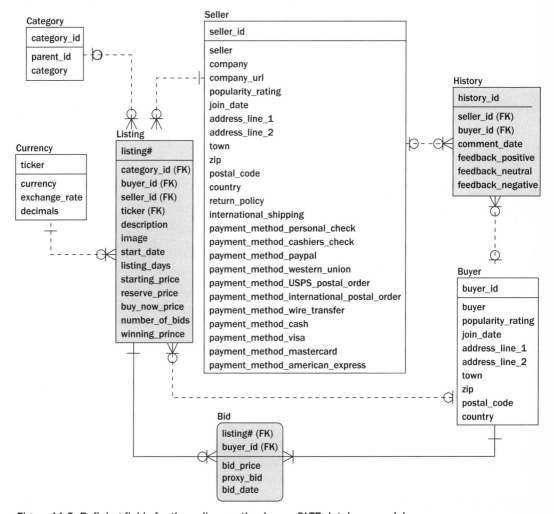

Figure 11-2: Refining fields for the online auction house OLTP database model.

Field additions and changes are refinements of both structure and application, as shown in Figure 11-2. An example of *addition refinement* is the addition of the INCREMENT field to the BID table. An example of *structural refinement* is a change to an existing field. Changing the ADDRESS field to five separate fields is a structural refinement. Field refinements are described as follows:

❑   The INCREMENT field is added to the LISTING table. Sellers can set a price increment for a listing. The application software will automatically apply bid increment values if INCREMENT is not set. The system may also override bid increments (based on all pricing factors) if an increment entered by the seller does not equate appropriately with all the pricing values set by the seller.

❑   A proxy bid (on the BID table) is where a bidder sets a maximum price a bidder is prepared to bid up to. When a bidder enters a proxy bid, it permits the online auction site to act on behalf of the bidder, increasing the bidders bid price, up to the proxy bid value (the maximum the bidder is prepared to pay).

❑   Address fields on BUYER and SELLER tables are split into ADDRESS_LINE_1, ADDRESS_LINE_2, TOWN, ZIP, POSTAL_CODE, and COUNTRY fields. The ZIP field is used in the U.S. Postal codes are used in other countries. It is necessary to divide address details up in this way for two reasons:

   ❑   It allows easy input by buyers and sellers (all sensibly broken up into separate boxes).

   ❑   Subsequent analysis of data by the system (such as in reporting by location) is much more effective with information split into separate fields.

❑   Payment methods on the SELLER table have been split into separate fields (containing simple answers of TRUE or FALSE). This allows multiple selections for sellers and is stored in one place (the SELLER table), as opposed to normalizing. The 4NF normalization, being a separate table, might make for less efficiency in joins. Additionally, this Boolean type division of multiple selectable options is best handled at the application level. It is simply too detailed for handling at the lower level of the database model.

   It might even be best to leave the PAYMENT_METHODS field in the SELLER table as a comma delimited string of options or even a comma-delimited string of TRUE and FALSE values. Applications would then dictate positions of TRUE and FALSE values (stored as T and F or Y and N, or 1 and 0, or otherwise). Remember, this is an OLTP database model. OLTP databases must be tightly controlled by applications because of the immense computing power utilized to manage huge quantities of concurrent Internet users. Allowing ad hoc access to OLTP databases and applications will kill your system and result in no users, and thus no business. If this is not the case, it is unlikely you are not building an OLTP database model.

❑   It might be possible to split up the RETURN_POLICY field in the same way that the PAYMENT_ METHODS field is split, as shown in the previous option. This one is left to your imagination.

❑   The HISTORY table COMMENTS field could be split into multiple field options, perhaps helping to direct end-user comments (for example, COMMENTS_ABOUT_SELLER, COMMENTS_ABOUT_LISTING, COMMENTS_SERVICE_LEVEL, COMMENTS_BUYER_PROMPTNESS). There are many other possibilities. Comments could even be split into a field structure based on pick list type of preset answers (or answer categories), somewhat similar to payment methods division in the SELLER table. The HISTORY table COMMENTS field has been divided into the three general feedback type fields containing options for positive, neutral, and negative feedback (perhaps even all three can be entered). When people using online Internet sites feel that they can comment, it makes them feel empowered. Empowering people encourages further business. If buyers and sellers develop poor reputations, those buyers and sellers, not the auction house, are responsible for an ill-gained reputation. This excludes the company from being involved in disputes from any respect other than the role of arbitration.

❑   The COMPANY_URL and COMPANY fields are added to the SELLER table. The inclusion of the term COMPANY in the name of the field is intentional. This implies that only bona fide company or corporate level traders should be allowed to enter company names or URLs (or both fields). Thus only sellers trading as online retailers (even competing online auctioneers) are ultimately encouraged to list themselves as full-fledged going concerns. This allows the online auction house in the case study example to become not only an auctioneer for the individual, but also a well-publicized portal to the Internet, for other auctioneers. The Internet has huge market potential. An online auction house with a well-established market presence (in the minds of potential Internet buyers) is extremely valuable for other retailers — an obvious source of profitability for the online auction house of this case study.

It is essential to note that the changes made to the OLTP database model for the online auction house, as shown in Figure 11-2, are mostly application-oriented. In other words, even though some may be analytical (back to the analysis stage) in nature, these changes are more likely design level refinements. At this stage, field refinements become less of a database modeling thing, and perhaps more to do with *how applications will handle things*. So far, the OLTP database model in this case study has been far more tightly controlled than the data warehouse model. At this point of field refinement for an OLTP database model, the OLTP database model may appear to become less mathematical.

The important thing to remember is that the database model is good at doing certain things, and that application SDKs (such as Java) are good at doing other things. You don't need to be a database expert or an experienced Java programmer to understand the basic precept of this change in approach. Essentially, the OLTP database model might become somewhat more end-user oriented at this stage, and perhaps a little less mathematically confusing to the database modeling uninitiated. So far in this book, the data warehouse modeling approach has always been more end-user oriented. The data warehouse model always looks like a company from an operational perspective. From this point in time, the OLTP database model begins to look a little friendlier and a little less *geeky*.

Overall, many of these changes may seem a little over the top. That is because many of these changes are over the top; however, you can now see what can actually be done. The SELLER table is perhaps a little too denormalized and application oriented in nature now. The SELLER table is now large and complicated because it has too many fields. You might shout, "Overkill," and you might be correct, of course! In that case, the case study is performing its demonstrative function by showing what can be done, not necessarily what should be done. You are beginning to see that a database model should not only be mathematically driven, but also application driven. The needs of front-end applications can sometimes partially dictate database model design because database model and applications are dependent on each other in many respects. The ERD shown in Figure 11-2 is a little too busy. When things are too busy, it means structure may be becoming overcomplicated.

The Data Warehouse Database Model

Figure 11-3 shows the most recent version of the data warehouse database model for the online auction house.

Listing-Bid Facts

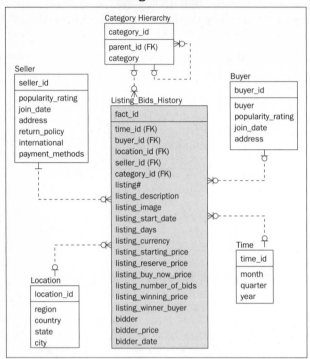

History Facts

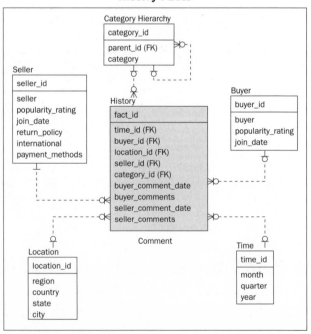

Figure 11-3: The online auction house data warehouse database model.

Analysis and design are an ongoing process. In the data warehouse database model shown in Figure 11-3, there are no structural refinement changes; however, Figure 11-4 shows a refined field structure (not structural refinements) for the online auction house data warehouse database model. These field refined field changes are all duplicated from the OLTP database model, to the database warehouse database model.

Field refinements shown in Figure 11-4 are described as follows:

❑   It is prudent to compare the OLTP database models between Figure 11-1 and Figure 11-2, and make any field additions to the data warehouse database model, already made to the OLTP database model in Figure 11-2. These changes include adding of the fields LISTING.INCREMENT, SELLER.COMPANY, SELLER.COMPANY_URL, and the three feedback comment fields in the HISTORY table. The PROXY_BID field is not added because it represents a potential maximum bid that a bidder is prepared to bid up to—not an actual bid.

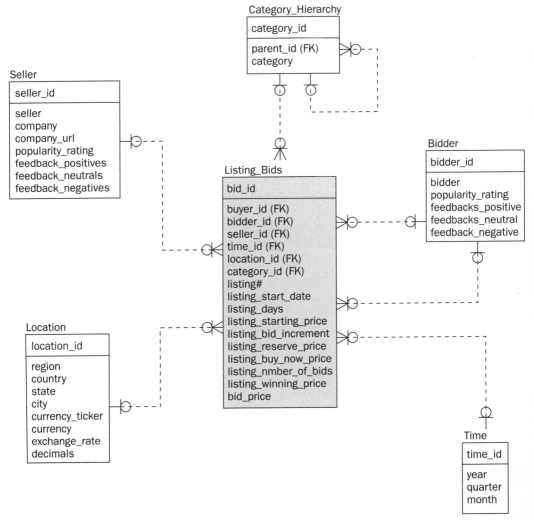

Figure 11-4: Refining fields for the online auction house data warehouse database model.

❑   ADDRESS fields are no longer required for the data warehouse database model in the SELLER and BUYER tables. Location information is actually stored in the LOCATION table in the form of REGION, COUNTRY, STATE, and CITY tables. A data warehouse is a source for reporting, be that reporting analytical or forecasting. Typical of data warehouse reporting is the need to refer to individual addresses of buyers and sellers; therefore, retaining explicit address information is pointless.

❑   The TIME table should have fields physically ordered from most significant to least significant, as for the LOCATION table. For the TIME table, field physical sequence will change from MONTH, QUARTER, YEAR to YEAR, QUARTER, MONTH.

❑   The CURRENCY dimension needs to be added to the data warehouse database model, as it was for the OLTP database model in Figure 11-2. One quite distinct difference between OLTP and data warehouse database models is that it is prudent to always use integer surrogate key fields as primary keys on dimensions. The TICKER field in the CURRENCY table for the data warehouse database model is no longer the primary key. The CURRENCY_ID field is added as the primary key for the CURRENCY table. Currency-based analysis may be required; however, there is already a LOCATION table. Currencies are location-based and, in the interests of retaining the efficiency of a star schema structure, currency fields are added to the LOCATION dimension. Also, the LISTING_CURRENCY field in the LISTING_BIDS table is removed.

Figure 11-4 shows a single step in the process of data warehouse database model field refinement changes. For a data warehouse, the changes required are often far more based on the experience of the analyst or designer. Data warehouse changes are also driven more by operational requirements. An OLTP database needs to take into account the sheer quantities of users and computing power needed to be brought to bear. What should be retained in a data warehouse database model? Some data makes no sense to be retained. Other fields may be out of the scope of possible reporting. The issue when building a data warehouse database model is that it is extremely unlikely that you can guess what will be required, and at what level (say, a few years into the future). One of the easiest rules to follow is that data warehouse facts are usually quantifiable, such as being numbers. If not quantifiable, those fields are probably more dimensional in nature.

The following structural changes apply in this respect (from Figure 11-4, as shown in Figure 11-5):

❑   All the feedback fields in the HISTORY fact table are great big strings. Remember that fields in data warehouse fact tables should be quantifiable numbers. Numbers can be aggregated by methods, such as summing up or averaging. Strings cannot be added together. All feedback fields are moved to SELLER and BIDDER dimensions, now as integer totals of positive, neutral, and negative feedback responses. This also makes the HISTORY table empty, redundant, and thus removed completely from the model. Feedback fields could be moved from dimension to fact structures, stored perhaps as a single value for each fact record, avoiding unnecessary updating of the SELLER and BUYER dimensions. It was decided this was unnecessary.

❑   In SELLER and BUYER tables, the RETURN_POLICY and PAYMENT_METHODS are likely irrelevant to a data warehouse database model. Why? RETURN_POLICY contains a variable string value. PAYMENT_METHODS data warehouse analytical reporting is probably completely unnecessary, as this information pertains to buyers and sellers specifically, and not to bid and listing facts.

❑   Joining dates of sellers and buyers does not really apply to listings and bids, and is thus not factual. Additionally dates are temporal in nature, and included in the TIME dimension. Listing and bid facts have their own dates and times. SELLER and BUYER JOIN_DATE fields are very likely superfluous.

❑ The INTERNATIONAL field on the SELLER table implies a seller is willing to ship internationally (all over the world), instead of just their home country. This information should be stored with listings and bids, and is catered for by the LOCATION dimension. This field can be removed from the SELLER table. Data warehouses are about analysis of facts across dimensions, and particularly into the past. Completed auctions are stored in the fact table as listings with all bids. All those facts are historical. They are in the past. The INTERNATIONAL field looks into the future, denoting that a SELLER is willing to ship internationally, not that the seller has shipped internationally in the past.

❑ Now attack the LISTING_BIDS fact table:

    ❑ In reality, the LISTING_BIDS table contains one listing, and many bids. Think about what is actually in the fact table. The unique identifying field (primary key) of the LISTING_BIDS fact table is actually a field unique to each and every bid, regardless of which listing a bid applies to (as an auto counter surrogate key unique to each bid). The FACT_ID field is renamed to BID_ID. Each fact can be uniquely identified as a unique bid.

    ❑ Retaining the LISTING_IMAGE field (a picture of the listed item) in a data warehouse is just completely dumb.

    ❑ LISTING_DESCRIPTION is a string that cannot be quantified or added up. It is removed.

    ❑ The BID_PRICE field remains in the fact table, because it is the only fact. The BID_DATE field is irrelevant because dates are represented by the TIME table. Also, the BUYER table becomes the BIDDER table since facts are stored as bids, and not exclusive to winning bids. Only buyers have winning bids; not all bidders win auctions. A buyer is a bid winner. A bidder may not have ever won any auctions and is not necessarily a buyer.

    ❑ There are a number of factual dates. The TIME table takes factual temporal information into account; therefore, fields containing dates should not be stored in the fact table. Bear in mind that data warehouse analysis reporting is aggregation over dimensions, such as "give me all listings in June, over the last five years." Storing dates implies that perhaps someone might ask for a report of all listings occurring at 10h22:33:02 (22 minutes past 10 in the morning, at 33.02 seconds past that 20 second minute), on every day of each year, for the past 20 years. That's obsessive precision to the point of complete uselessness in a practical situation. It's ridiculous. Retaining dates would be a case of far too much granularity. Dates need to be removed. The only thing that needs to be decided is what exactly the TIME dimension should represent. You can choose only one date. The TIME dimension will be constructed from that single date field. It makes sense that the date should be either the listing start date, the listing end date, or the bidding date.

    Look at it this way. A listing exists as a biddable auction for a specific number of days (LISTING_DAYS), from a specified date of LISTING_START_DATE, until the auction closes at the sum of the field values LISTING_START_DATE and LISTING_DAYS. An easy way to make this decision is to remember that each fact record represents a bid, not a listing; therefore, the TIME table will contain the BID_DATE (as YEAR, QUARTER and MONTH), and the BID_DATE field is removed from the fact table. The difficult decision is whether to retain the start date for a listing. It could cause a lot of confusion and some poor ad-hoc reporting choices—perhaps with attempts to aggregate and analyze facts based on the LISTING_START_DATE field. This could cause serious performance problems. The LISTING_START_DATE could be removed. If this were the case, the LISTING_DAYS field could be removed as well. On the contrary, these fields could become relevant to materialized view aggregations of listings (not bids). They are retained for now.

The biggest and most blatantly obvious issue when examining the star schema in Figure 11-4 shows something really unusual. "Unusual" in a database model usually means "nonstandard" ("nonconforming" to acceptable practices), and probably completely incorrect! The BIDDER dimensional table is joined to the LISTING_BIDS fact table twice, as both a bidder who lost the auction (BIDDER_ID), and a bidder who won the auction (BUYER_ID). It might even make sense to create two fact tables — one table containing listings, and the other bids. It could also be argued that listing fields are dimensional with respect to bids, but are factual with respect to the number of records. The result is the horribly ugly structure of the two links between the BIDDER and LISTING_BIDS tables, of BIDDER_ID and BUYER_ID foreign keys.

The LISTING_BIDS table could be split into two fact tables, and, thus, two star schemas. The problem with this approach would be a table of listings, and then a bids table, containing massive duplication of all listing information. For a data warehouse, this is unacceptable overuse of storage space. The better solution is the retain the data warehouse database model as it stands in Figure 11-4, and create a materialized view, which summarizes LISTING_BIDS fact records to the listing level. The result would be two layers. Remember from Chapter 3 that a materialized view creates a physical copy of data. That copy is generated using a query against one or more underlying tables. The copy can be an exact duplicate of all records in a fact table. It can also be an accumulation. An accumulation summarizes some of the facts in a fact table — for example, summing fact values across groups of records, such as each country, producing a single summed-up record, in the materialized view, for each country. If the fact table contains five million records and there are only 250 countries, your materialized view will contain only 250 records. The difference between a query reading five million records, and a query reading 250 records, can produce an enormous performance improvement.

Materialized views are generally available only in high-end (expensive) relational database engines.

Using a materialized view to break up facts into listings and bids would give a structure somewhat similar to that shown in Figure 11-5.

Creation of a materialized view creates a physical copy. You still end up with a copy of listings, and then a copy of listings containing all bids as well. Effectively, you still have two table-like structures, with a one-to-many relationship between. The only difference is that updates to add more data to the data warehouse are only performed on the LISTING_BIDS table. The database engine itself can automate updating of materialized views.

Now let's refine field datatypes.

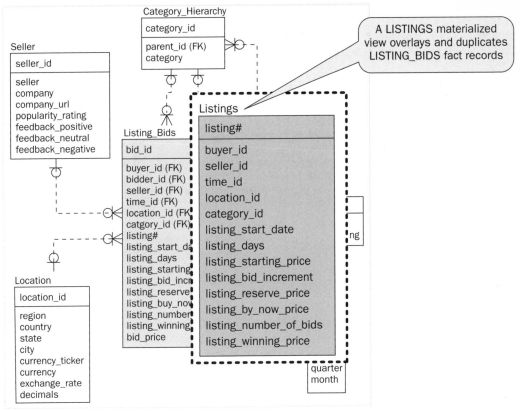

Figure 11-5: Refining facts and dimensions using materialized views to replace fact hierarchical structures.

Understanding Datatypes

A *datatype* is a format applied to a field. That format sets the field to be restricted as something. Numbers, dates, and strings are the most commonly used datatypes. In general, values in fields are made up a sequence of one or more characters. When you type your name on the keyboard of your computer, you get a sequence of characters appearing on your screen.

Simple Datatypes

Simple datatypes are numbers, dates, and strings. A *string* is an alphanumeric sequence of characters. An alphanumeric string can contain any character, including both numbers and alpha characters. An alpha character is any letter character on your keyboard. An alphanumeric character is any character on your keyboard, including numbers, letters and even all the funky characters like those things you get when you press a number key across the top of the keyboard, with the shift key pressed down. For example, Shift+2 gives you the "@" character (the "at" character).

Keyboards might be different in different countries.

A *number* datatype allows only digits between 0 and 9. In other words, 33425009 is a valid number. However, 44498.,kSDF09 is not a valid number, because some characters are not between 0 and 9 (it is alphanumeric). Attempting to add an alphanumeric value into a number datatype field will cause an error to be returned from a database (usually).

Date fields allow only date values such as 04/31/2004, or Apr 4, 2004. A specific date format is generally predetermined in the database engine and can be overridden for individual dates.

ANSI (American National Standards Institute) Datatypes

There are many different database engines, each having its distinct set of datatypes. Datatypes across all different database engines generally fulfill the same functions. Each database usually has its own specific naming conventions (for different datatypes), but not always. Many of the datatypes across different database are often the same.

ANSI datatypes attempt to establish a standard. Standards are formulated and documented in an attempt to maintain some form of consistency across different software tools, databases, and applications. Consider the following:

Items enclosed between [ ] *square brackets are optional.*

❑ CHAR[ACTER]([n]), CHAR([n]) — This represents a *fixed-length* string. CHAR(4) set to "A" will contain "A   " (that's A and 3 spaces). Setting CHAR(2) to "ABCDE" will either truncate to "AB" or a return an error, depending on the database engine. CHAR with no length specifier, defaults to a CHAR(1), allowing one character at most.

❑ CHAR[ACTER] VARYING(n) — *Variable-length strings* (sometimes called *dynamic strings*) contain any number of characters up to a maximum. As for the CHAR datatype, CHAR VARYING without a length, will default to CHAR VARYING(1). Unlike CHAR(4), with "A" producing "A   ", CHAR VARYING(4) set to "A" will contain just the character "A" and no padding space characters.

❑ NUMERIC([p],[s]), DECIMAL([p], [s]) — This represents a *fixed-length number* with precision [p] or scale [s] (or both). *Precision* is a number of digits. *Scale* is a number of decimal places. If precision or scale (or both) are omitted, then precision is set to a value greater than 1 (database engine-specific) and scale is set to zero (no decimal places). NUMERIC will allow integers only (no decimal point). NUMERIC(10, 2) will only allow numbers of less than 10 digits in length (excluding the decimal point). Numbers with more than two decimal points will be truncated or rounded, depending on the database engine. For example, 10.125 truncated to two decimal places is 10.12, while 10.125 rounded to two decimal places is 10.13 (the 5 is rounded up).

❑ SMALLINT, INT[EGER] — This represents *whole numbers* only. An integer is a whole number. A whole number has no decimal places (no decimal point). Whole numbers can be of varying sizes and thus SMALLINT (small numbers) and INTEGER (large numbers). SMALLINT occupies fewer bytes than INTEGER and takes less space. Some database engines also have LONG or LONG INTEGER datatypes, representing very large integer values.

❑ FLOAT[(n)], DOUBLE PRECISION, REAL — These are all *real numbers* of one variation or another, floating-point and otherwise. A floating point is literally that — the decimal point can exist anywhere in a number (1.223344, 11223, and 2342342334.23 are all valid real numbers). A real number is the opposite of a whole number. A real number has a decimal point, and a whole number has no decimal point.

Microsoft Access Datatypes

Take a look at Microsoft Access datatypes. There are numerous specifics, exclusive to Microsoft Access database. Figure 11-6 shows a screen in Microsoft Access for selecting a datatype for a field. General datatypes are: Text (shorter strings), Memo (big strings), Number, Date/Time (dates and timestamps), Currency, AutoNumber, Yes/No (equivalent of a Boolean datatype storing TRUE or FALSE), OLE (Object Linked Embedding) Object (a specialized object datatype), and finally Hyperlink (a Web site URL). The Lookup Wizard allows the building of specific datatype settings for any datatype. At the bottom left of Figure 11-6, various specific attributes of each datatype can be selected.

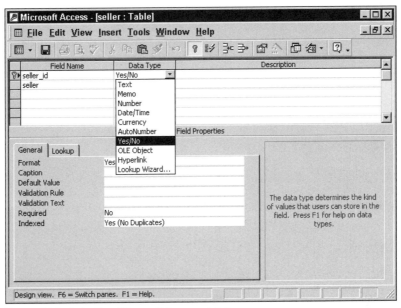

Figure 11-6: Selecting Microsoft Access datatypes.

Specialized Datatypes

Other database engines (such as Oracle, SQL-Server, Ingres, Sybase, the list is long) all have their own specific datatypes. Many databases have some very advanced and specialized datatypes. The following list describes these specialized datatypes briefly, so that you have an inkling of relational databases, their fields, and what their datatypes are capable of:

❑ *Binary objects* — Binary objects are generally a few megabytes and are used to store large text objects and binary-encoded files (such as images). Binary objects store binary data inline within a relational database table.

❑ *Pointers* — These are special datatypes used to store simple address pointers to binary data stored outside the table structure of a relational database. The actual file (such as an image) is stored on disk, externally to the database. File pointers are usually the most efficient method of storing static binary data (such as JPG, BMP, and GIF images).

❑ *XML Documents*—Some databases allow structured storage of XML documents where the XML Document Object Model (DOM) is actively available through the XML datatype field. What this means is that when accessing an XML document, you can access and manipulate the definitions and attributes of the XML document (its structure), and not just the XML data. Some relational databases can effectively mimic an XML native database using XML Document datatypes.

❑ *Any (generic)*—Some relational databases will allow use of a datatype that is completely generic. The term "generic" implies that this datatype can be used to store any datatype structure. Obviously, some definition is lost, depending on the database engine and the complexity of the datatype to be stored.

❑ *User-defined*—A user-defined datatype is just that. You can define and build your own datatypes. Typically, user-defined datatypes are used to create array or object structures. For arrays, each element contains a multiple field structure within it (such as creating a table within a table). User-defined datatypes are commonly used to build object structures within the confines of a relational database. The following example creates an address structure within a table containing customers—begin by creating a structured type:

```
CREATE TYPE TYPE_ADDRESS
(
    ADDRESS_LINE_1 CHAR VARYING(64),
    ADDRESS_LINE_2 CHAR VARYING(64),
    TOWN CHAR VARYING(32),
    STATE CHAR(2),
    ZIP NUMBER(5)
);
```

Declare a variable against the user-defined type:

```
VAR_ADDRESS TYPE_ADDRESS;
```

Now, create a table, including the address of the customer as an iteration of the type substructure:

```
CREATE TABLE CUSTOMER
(
    NAME CHAR VARYING(32),
    ADDRESS VAR_ADDRESS,
    GOOD_CREDIT_OR_NOT BOOLEAN
);
```

Case Study: Defining Datatypes

Now you can use the details learned about different datatypes to refine the OLTP and data warehouse database models for the online auction house.

The OLTP Database Model

Figure 11-2 contains the most recent version of the OLTP database model for the online auction house. Figure 11-7 defines datatypes for the OLTP database model shown in Figure 11-2.

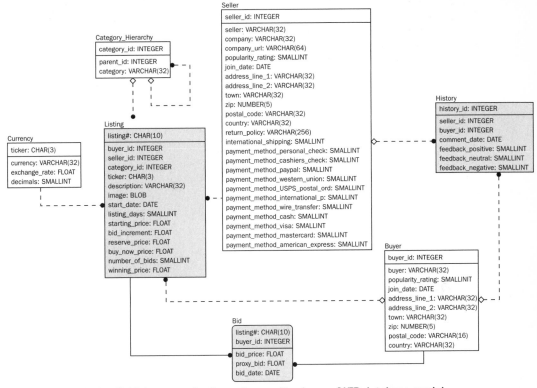

Figure 11-7: Defining field datatypes for the online auction house OLTP database model.

All that has been done in Figure 11-7 is that the field datatypes have been specified. Because of limitations of the version of the database modeling tool in use (and other software), note the following in Figure 11-7:

❑ All variable length strings (ANSI CHAR VARYING datatypes) are represented as VARCHAR.

❑ All monetary amounts (MONEY or CURRENCY datatypes) are represented as FLOAT. Not all FLOAT datatype fields are used as monetary amounts.

❑ All BOOLEAN datatypes (containing TRUE or FALSE, YES or NO) are represented as SMALLINT. For example, SELLER.PAYMENT_METHOD_PERSONAL_CHECK should be a BOOLEAN datatype. BOOLEAN datatypes are not to be confused with other fields that do not contain BOOLEAN values, such as BUYER.POPULARITY_RATING (contains a rating number).

Datatypes are specifically catered for in the following script, adapting OLTP database model structure, according to the points made previously:

```
CREATE TABLE CURRENCY
(
        TICKER              CHAR(3) PRIMARY KEY NOT NULL,
        CURRENCY            CHAR VARYING(32) UNIQUE NOT NULL,
```

```
        EXCHANGE_RATE          FLOAT NOT NULL,
        DECIMALS               SMALLINT NULL
);

CREATE TABLE BUYER
(
        BUYER_ID               INTEGER PRIMARY KEY NOT NULL,
        BUYER                  CHAR VARYING(32) UNIQUE NOT NULL,
        POPULARITY_RATING      SMALLINT NULL,
        JOIN_DATE              DATE NOT NULL,
        ADDRESS_LINE_1         CHAR VARYING(32) NULL,
        ADDRESS_LINE_2         CHAR VARYINGR(32) NULL,
        TOWN                   CHAR VARYING(32) NULL,
        ZIP                    NUMERIC(5) NULL,
        POSTAL_CODE            CHAR VARYING(16) NULL,
        COUNTRY                CHAR VARYING(32) NULL
);

CREATE TABLE CATEGORY
(
        CATEGORY_ID            INTEGER PRIMARY KEY NOT NULL,
        PARENT_ID              INTEGER FOREIGN KEY REFERENCES CATEGORY WITH NULL,
        CATEGORY               CHAR VARYING(32) NOT NULL
);

CREATE TABLE SELLER
(
        SELLER_ID              INTEGER PRIMARY KEY NOT NULL,
        SELLER                 CHAR VARYING(32) UNIQUE NOT NULL,
        COMPANY                CHAR VARYING(32) UNIQUE NOT NULL,
        COMPANY_URL            CHAR VARYING(64) UNIQUE NOT NULL,
        POPULARITY_RATING      SMALLINT NULL,
        JOIN_DATE              DATE NOT NULL,
        ADDRESS_LINE_1         CHAR VARYING(32) NULL,
        ADDRESS_LINE_2         CHAR VARYING(32) NULL,
        TOWN                   CHAR VARYING (32) NULL,
        ZIP                    NUMERIC(5) NULL,
        POSTAL_CODE            CHAR VARYING (32) NULL,
        COUNTRY                CHAR VARYING(32) NULL,
        RETURN_POLICY          CHAR VARYING(256) NULL,
        INTERNATIONAL_SHIPPING BOOLEAN NULL,
        PAYMENT_METHOD_PERSONAL_CHECK BOOLEAN NULL,
        PAYMENT_METHOD_CASHIERS_CHECK BOOLEAN NULL,
        PAYMENT_METHOD_PAYPAL BOOLEAN NULL,
        PAYMENT_METHOD_WESTERN_UNION BOOLEAN NULL,
        PAYMENT_METHOD_USPS_POSTAL_ORDER BOOLEAN NULL,
        PAYMENT_METHOD_INTERNATIONAL_POSTAL_ORDER BOOLEAN NULL,
        PAYMENT_METHOD_WIRE_TRANSFER BOOLEAN NULL,
        PAYMENT_METHOD_CASH BOOLEAN NULL,
        PAYMENT_METHOD_VISA BOOLEAN NULL,
        PAYMENT_METHOD_MASTERCARD BOOLEAN NULL,
        PAYMENT_METHOD_AMERICAN_EXPRESS BOOLEAN NULL
);

CREATE TABLE LISTING
```

```
(
        LISTING#                 CHAR(10) PRIMARY KEY NOT NULL,
        CATEGORY_ID              INTEGER FOREIGN KEY REFERENCES CATEGORY NOT NULL,
        BUYER_ID                 INTEGER FOREIGN KEY REFERENCES BUYER WITH NULL,
        SELLER_ID                INTEGER FOREIGN KEY REFERENCES SELLER WITH NULL,
        TICKER                   CHAR(3) NULL,
        DESCRIPTION              CHAR VARYING(32) NULL,
        IMAGE                    BINARY NULL,
        START_DATE               DATE NOT NULL,
        LISTING_DAYS             SMALLINT NOT NULL,
        STARTING_PRICE           MONEY NOT NULL,
        BID_INCREMENT            MONEY NULL,
        RESERVE_PRICE            MONEY NULL,
        BUY_NOW_PRICE            MONEY NULL,
        NUMBER_OF_BIDS           SMALLINT NULL,
        WINNING_PRICE            MONEY NULL
);

CREATE TABLE BID
(
        LISTING#                 CHAR(10) PRIMARY KEY NOT NULL,
        BUYER_ID                 INTEGER FOREIGN KEY REFERENCES BUYER NOT NULL,
        BID_PRICE                MONEY NOT NULL,
        PROXY_BID                MONEY NULL,
        BID_DATE                 DATE NOT NULL,
        CONSTRAINT PRIMARY KEY (LISTING#, BUYER_ID)
);
```

The primary key for the BID *table is declared out of line with field definitions because it is a composite of two fields.*

```
CREATE TABLE HISTORY
(
        HISTORY_ID               INTEGER PRIMARY KEY NOT NULL,
        SELLER_ID                INTEGER FOREIGN KEY REFERENCES SELLER WITH NULL,
        BUYER_ID                 INTEGER FOREIGN KEY REFERENCES BUYER WITH NULL,
        COMMENT_DATE             DATE NOT NULL,
        FEEDBACK_POSITIVE        SMALLINT NULL,
        FEEDBACK_NEUTRAL         SMALLINT NULL,
        FEEDBACK_NEGATIVE        SMALLINT NULL
);
```

Some field names in Figure 11-7 are truncated by the ERD tool. The previous script has full field names.

A number of points are worth noting in the previous script:

❑ Some fields are declared as being unique (UNIQUE). For example, the BUYER table has a surrogate key as its primary key; however, the name of the buyer must still be unique within the buyer table. You can't allow two buyers to have the same name. Therefore, the BUYER.BUYER field (the name of the buyer) is declared as being unique.

❑ Some fields (other than primary keys and unique fields) are specified as being NOT NULL. This means that there is no point in having a record in that particular table, unless there is an entry for that particular field. NOT NULL is the restriction that forces an entry.

❏ Foreign keys declared as WITH NULL imply the foreign key side of an inter-table relationship does not require a record (an entry in the foreign key field).

❏ CHAR VARYING is used to represent variable-length strings.

❏ DATE contains date values.

❏ MONEY represents monetary amounts.

❏ BINARY represents binary-stored objects (such as images).

The Data Warehouse Database Model

Figure 11-4 contains the most recent version of the data warehouse database model for the online auction house. Figure 11-8 defines datatypes for the data warehouse database model shown in Figure 11-4.

Once again, as in Figure 11-7, Figure 11-8 explicitly defines datatypes for all fields, this time for the data warehouse model of the online auction house. Once again, note the following in Figure 11-8:

❏ All variable length strings (ANSI CHAR VARYING datatypes) are represented as VARCHAR.

❏ All monetary amounts (MONEY or CURRENCY datatype) are represented as FLOAT.

❏ All BOOLEAN datatypes (containing TRUE or FALSE, YES or NO) are represented as SMALLINT.

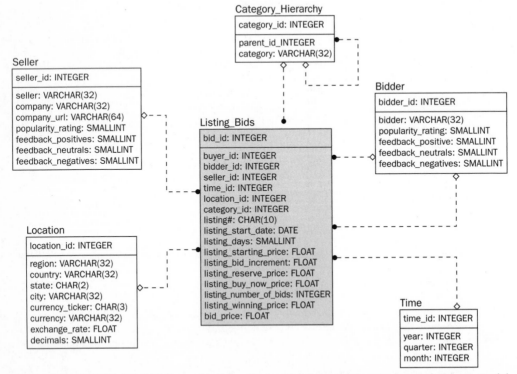

Figure 11-8: Refining field datatypes for the online auction house data warehouse database model.

Once again, datatypes are changed in the following script to adapt to the points previously made:

```
CREATE TABLE CATEGORY
(
        CATEGORY_ID          INTEGER PRIMARY KEY NOT NULL,
        PARENT_ID            INTEGER FOREIGN KEY REFERENCES CATEGORY WITH NULL,
        CATEGORY             CHAR VARYING(32) NOT NULL
);

CREATE TABLE SELLER
(
        SELLER_ID            INTEGER PRIMARY KEY NOT NULL,
        SELLER               CHAR VARYING(32) UNIQUE NOT NULL,
        COMPANY              CHAR VARYING(32) UNIQUE NOT NULL,
        COMPANY_URL          CHAR VARYING(64) UNIQUE NOT NULL,
        POPULARITY_RATING    SMALLINT NULL,
        FEEDBACK_POSITIVES   SMALLINT NULL,
        FEEDBACK_NEUTRALS    SMALLINT NULL,
        FEEDBACK_NEGATIVES   SMALLINT NULL
);

CREATE TABLE BIDDER
(
        BIDDER_ID            INTEGER PRIMARY KEY NOT NULL,
        BIDDER               CHAR VARYING(32) UNIQUE NOT NULL,
        POPULARITY_RATING    SMALLINT NULL
);

CREATE TABLE LOCATION
(
        LOCATION_ID          INTEGER PRIMARY KEY NOT NULL,
        REGION               CHAR VARYING(32) NOT NULL,
        COUNTRY              CHAR VARYING(32) NOT NULL,
        STATE                CHAR(2) NULL,
        CITY                 CHAR VARYING(32) NOT NULL,
        CURRENCY_TICKER      CHAR(3) UNIQUE NOT NULL,
        CURRENCY             CHAR VARYING(32) UNIQUE NOT NULL,
        EXCHANGE_RATE        FLOAT NOT NULL,
        DECIMALS             SMALLINT NULL
);

CREATE TABLE TIME
(
        TIME_ID              INTEGER PRIMARY KEY NOT NULL,
        YEAR                 INTEGER NOT NULL,
        QUARTER              INTEGER NOT NULL,
        MONTH                INTEGER NOT NULL
);

CREATE TABLE LISTING_BIDS
(
        LISTING#             CHAR(10) PRIMARY KEY NOT NULL,
        BID_ID               INTEGER FOREIGN KEY REFERENCES BID NOT NULL,
        BUYER_ID             INTEGER FOREIGN KEY REFERENCES BUYER WITH NULL,
```

```
        BIDDER_ID                INTEGER FOREIGN KEY REFERENCES BUYER WITH NULL,
        SELLER_ID                INTEGER FOREIGN KEY REFERENCES SELLER WITH NULL,
        TIME_ID                  INTEGER FOREIGN KEY REFERENCES TIME WITH NULL,
        LOCATION_ID              INTEGER FOREIGN KEY REFERENCES LOCATION WITH NULL,
        CATEGORY_ID              INTEGER FOREIG KEY REFERENCES CATEGORY WITH NULL,
        LISTING_STARTING_PRICE   MONEY NOT NULL,
        LISTING_RESERVE_PRICE    MONEY NULL,
        LISTING_BUY_NOW_PRICE    MONEY NULL,
        LISTING_START_DATE       DATE NOT NULL,
        LISTING_DAYS             SMALLINT NOT NULL,
        LISTING_NUMBER_OF_BIDS   INTEGER NULL,
        LISTING_WINNING_PRICE    MONEY NULL,
        LISTING_BID_INCREMENT    MONEY NULL,
        BID_PRICE                MONEY NULL
);
```

Once again, similar points apply in the previous script for the data warehouse database model, as for the previously described OLTP database model:

❑ Some fields are declared as being unique (UNIQUE) where the table uses a surrogate primary key integer, and there would be no point having a record in the table without a value entered.

❑ Some fields (other than primary keys and unique fields) are specified as being NOT NULL. This means that there is effectively no point in having a record in that particular table, unless there is an entry for that particular field.

❑ Foreign keys declared as WITH NULL imply that the subset side of an inter-table relationship does not require a record. Thus, the foreign key can be NULL valued.

❑ CHAR VARYING is used to represent variable-length strings.

❑ MONEY represents monetary amounts.

The next step is to look at keys and indexes created on fields.

Understanding Keys and Indexes

Keys and indexes are essentially one and the same thing. A *key* is a term applied to primary and foreign keys (sometimes unique keys as well) to describe referential integrity primary and foreign key indexes. A *primary key*, as you already know, defines a unique identifier for a record in a table. A *foreign key* is a copy of a primary key value, placed into a subset related table, identifying records in the foreign key table back to the primary key table. That is the essence of referential integrity. A unique key enforces uniqueness onto one or more fields in a table, other than the primary key field. Unique keys are not part of referential integrity but tend to be required at the database model level to avoid data integrity uniqueness errors.

A key is a specialized type of *index* that might be used for referential integrity (unique keys are excluded from referential integrity). An index is just like a key in all respects, other than referential integrity and that an index can't be constructed at the same time as a table is created. Indexes can be created on any field or combination of fields. The exception to this rule (applied in most database engines) is that an index can't be created on a field (or combination of fields), for which an index already exists. Most database engines do not allow creation of indexes on primary key and unique fields, because they already exist internally (created automatically by the database engine). These indexes are created automatically because primary and unique keys are both required to be unique. The most efficient method of verifying uniqueness of primary and unique keys (on insertion of a new record into a table) is an automatically created index, by the database, on those primary and unique key fields.

Indexes created on tables (not on primary keys or foreign keys) are generally known as *alternate* or *secondary keys*. They are named as such because they are additional or secondary to referential integrity keys.

As far as database modeling is concerned, alternate indexing is significant because it is largely dependent on application requirements, how applications use a database model, and most often apply to reporting. Reports are used to get information from a database in bulk. If existing database model indexing (primary and foreign keys) does not cater to the sorting needs of reports, extra indexes (in addition to that covered by primary and foreign keys) are created. In fact, alternate indexing is quite common in OLTP database environments because OLTP database model structure is often normalized too much for even the smallest on-screen listings (short reports). Reporting tends to denormalize tables and spit out sets of data from joins of information gathered from multiple tables at once.

Let's begin by briefly examining different types of indexing from an analytical and design perspective.

Types of Indexes

From an analytical and design perspective, there are a number of approaches to indexing:

❑   *No Indexes* — Tables with no indexing are heap-structured. All data is dumped on the disk as it is added, regardless of any sorting. It is much like overturning a bucket full of sand and simply tipping the sand onto the floor in a nice neat pile. Assume something absurd, and say the bucket was really big, and you were Jack in Jack and the Beanstalk. Say the pile of sand was 50 feet high when the giant overturned the bucket of sand. Finding a coin in that monstrous heap of sand, without a metal detector, means sifting through all of the sand by hand, until you find the coin. Assuming that you are doing the searching, you are not the giant, and the coin is small, you might be at it for a while. Using a metal detector would make your search much easier. The pile of sand is a little like a table containing gazillions of records. The metal detector is a little like an index on that great big unorganized table. The coin is a single record you are searching for. You get my drift.

❑   *Static Table Indexes* — A static table is a table containing data that doesn't change very often — if at all. Additionally, static tables are quite often very small, containing small numbers of fields and records. It is often more efficient for queries to simply read the entire table, rather than read parts of the index, and a small section of the table. Figure 11-9 shows the latest versions of both of the OLTP database model and the data warehouse database model for the online auction house. Dynamic (facts in the data warehouse database model) are highlighted in gray. The static tables are not highlighted. For example, the BIDDER table in the data warehouse database model, at the bottom of Figure 11-9, has a primary key field and two other fields. Creating any further indexing on this table would be over-designing this table, and ultimately a complete waste of resources. Try not to create alternate indexing on static data tables. It is usually pointless!

❑   *Dynamic Table Indexes* — The term "dynamic" implies consistent and continual change. Dynamic tables change all the time (fact tables are dynamic; dimension tables are static). Indexing on dynamic tables should expect changes to data. The indexes are subject to overflow. As a result, indexes may require frequent rebuilding. Indexing should be used for dynamic data because of the nature of potential for change in data.

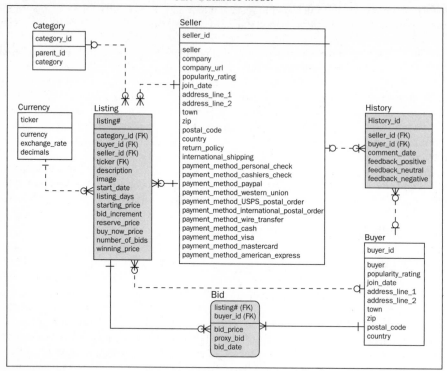

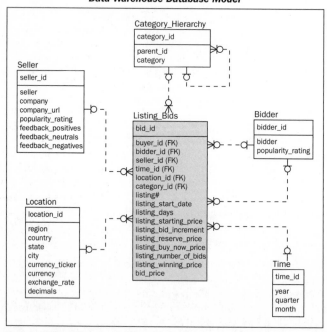

Figure 11-9: Refining fields for the online auction house data warehouse database model.

For example, the LISTING_BIDS fact table shown in Figure 11-9 changes drastically when large amounts of data are added, perhaps even as much as on a daily basis. Additionally, the LISTING_BIDS table contains data from multiple dynamic sources, namely listings and past bids on those listings. Reporting will not only need to retrieve listings with bids but also listings without bids. Even more complexity is needed because reporting will sort records retrieved based on factors such as dates, locations, amounts, and the list goes on. In the OLTP database model shown at the top of the diagram in Figure 11-9, the LISTING, BID, and HISTORY tables are also highly dynamic structures. If OLTP database reporting is required (extremely likely), alternate indexing will probably to be needed in the OLTP database model dynamic tables, as well as for the data warehouse model.

Two issues are important:

❑ *OLTP database model* — Inserting a new record into a table with, for example, five indexes, submits six physical record insertions to the database (one new table record and five new index records). This is inefficient. Indexing is generally far more real-time dynamic in OLTP databases than for data warehouses, and is better kept under tight control by production administrators.

❑ *Data warehouse database model* — Complex and composite indexing is far more commonly used in data warehouse database models, partially because of denormalization and partially because of the sheer diversity and volume of fact data. Data warehouses contain dynamic fact tables, much like OLTP databases; however, there is a distinct difference. OLTP dynamic tables are updated in real-time. Data warehouse dynamic fact tables are usually updated from one or more OLTP databases (or other sources) in batch mode. Batch mode updates imply periodical mass changes. Those periodical updates could be once a day, once per month, or otherwise. It all depends on the needs of people using data warehouse reporting.

Data warehouses tend to utilize specialized types of indexing. Specialized indexes are often read-only in nature (making data warehouse reporting very much more efficient). Read-only data has little or no conflict with other requests to a database, other than concurrently running reports reading disk storage.

Where data warehouses are massive in terms of data quantities, OLTP databases are heavy on concurrency (simultaneous use). The result is that OLTP databases focus on provision of real-time accurate service, and data warehouses focus on processing of large chunks of data, for small numbers of users, on occasion. Some of the large and more complex database engines allow many variations on read-only indexing, and pre-constructed queries for reporting, such as clustering of tables, compacted indexing based on highly repetitive values (bitmaps), plus other special gadgets like materialized views.

There is one last thing to remember about alternate indexing — the critical factor. If tables in a database model (static and dynamic) have many indexes, there could be one of two potential problems: the native referential structure of the database model is not catering to applications (poor database modeling could be the issue); and indexing has either been loosely controlled by administrators, such as developers being allowed to create indexing on a production database server, whenever they please. Clean up redundant indexing! The more growth in your database, the more often you might have to clean out unused indexing.

What, When, and How to Index

There are a number of points to consider when trying to understand what to index, when to index it, and how to build those indexes:

❑ Tables with few fields and few records do not necessarily benefit from having indexes. This is because an index is actually a pointer, plus whatever field values are indexed (field values are actually copied into the index). An index is a copy of all records in a table and must usually be relatively smaller than the table, both in terms of record length (number of fields), and the number of records in the table.

❑ In partial contradiction to the previous point, tables with few fields and large numbers of records can benefit astronomically from indexing. Indexes are usually specially constructed in a way that allows fast access to a few records in a table, after reading on a small physical portion of the index. For example, most database engines use BTree (binary tree) indexes. A BTree index is an upside-down tree structure. Special traversal algorithms (an *algorithm* is another name for a small, but often complex, computer program that solves a problem) through that tree structure can access records by reading extremely small portions of the index. Small portions of a massive index can be read because of the internal structure of a BTree index, and specialized algorithms accessing the index.

❑ The two previous points beg the following additional comments. Large composite indexes containing more than one field in a table may be relatively large compared with the table. Not only is physical size of composite indexing an issue but also the complexity of the index itself. As those rapid traversals mentioned in the previous point become more complex algorithmically, the more complex an index becomes. The more fields a composite index contains, the less useful it becomes. Also, field datatypes are an issue for indexing. Integer values are usually the most efficient datatypes for indexing, simply because there are only ten different digits (0 to 9, as opposed to A to Z, and all the other funky characters when indexing strings).

Relative physical size difference between index and table is likely the most significant factor when considering building multiple field (composite) indexes. The smaller the ratio between index and table physical size, the more effective an index will be. After all, the main objective of creating indexes is better efficiency of access to data in a database.

❑ Try to avoid indexing NULL field values. In general, NULL values are difficult to index if they are included in an index at all (some index types do not include NULL values in indexes, when an index is created). The most efficient types of indexes are unique indexes containing integers.

❑ Tables with few records, regardless of the number of fields, can suffer from serious performance degradation — the table is over-indexed if an index is created. This is not always the case, though. It is usually advisable to manually create indexes on foreign keys fields of small, static data tables. This helps avoid hot block issues with referential integrity checks where a foreign key table, containing no index on the foreign key field, are full table scanned by primary key table referential integrity verification. In highly concurrent OLTP databases, this can become a serious performance issue.

When Not to Create Indexes

Some alternate indexing is usually created during the analysis and design stages. One of the biggest issues with alternate indexing is that it is often created after the fact (after analysis and design) — quite often in applications development and implementation, and even when a system is in production. Alternate indexing is often reactive rather than preemptive in nature, usually in response to reporting requirements, or OLTP GUI application programs that do not fit the existing underlying database model structure (indicating possible database model inadequacies).

There are a number of points to consider as far as not creating indexes:

❑ When considering the creation of a new index, don't be afraid of not creating that index at all. Do not always assume that an existing index should exist, simply because it does exist. Don't be afraid of destroying existing indexes.

❑ When considering use of unusual indexes (such as read-only type indexing), be aware of their applications. The only index type amenable to data changes is a standard index (usually a BTree type index).

Some database engines only allow a single type of indexing and will not even allow you to entertain the use of more sophisticated indexing strategies such as read-only indexing like bitmaps.

❑ When executing data warehouse reporting, tables often contain records already sorted in the correct physical order. This is common because data warehouse tables are often added by appending (added to the end of), where records are copied from sources (for example, an OLTP database), on, for example, a daily basis, and probably in the order of dates. Don't re-create indexes where sorting has already been performed by the nature of structure and table record appending processing, into a data warehouse.

❑ Production administrators should monitor existing indexing. Quite often, individual indexes are redundant, and even completely forgotten about. Redundant indexes place additional strain on computing power and resources. Destroy them if possible! Be especially vigilant of unusual and weird and unusual index types (such as bitmaps, clusters, indexes created on expressions, and clustering).

It is just as important to understand when and what not to index, as it is to understand what should be indexed.

Case Study: Alternate Indexing

As stated previously in this chapter, alternate indexes are created in addition to referential integrity indexes. Use the case study in this book to examine the OLTP and data warehouse database models once again.

The OLTP Database Model

Many database engines do not automatically create indexes on foreign keys, like they do for primary and unique keys. This is because foreign keys are not required to be unique. Manual creation of indexes for all foreign keys within a database model is sometimes avoided, if not completely forgotten. They are often forgotten because developers and administrators are unaware that database engines do not create them automatically, as is done for primary and unique keys.

You may need to create indexes on foreign keys, manually because constant referential integrity checks will use indexes for both primary and foreign keys, when referential integrity checks are performed. Referential integrity checks are made whenever a change is made that might affect the status of primary-to-foreign key relationships, between two tables. If a foreign key does have an index created, a full table scan of the foreign key subset table results. This situation is far more likely to cause a performance problem in an OLTP database, rather than in a data warehouse database.

This is because an OLTP database has high concurrency. High concurrency is large numbers of users changing tables, constantly, and all at the same time. In the case of a highly active, globally accessed, OLTP Internet database, the number of users changing data at once, could be six figures, and sometimes even higher. Not only will full table scans result on foreign key (unindexed) tables, but those foreign key tables are likely be locked because of too many changes made to them at once. This situation may not cause just a performance problem, but even possibly a potential database halt, apparent to the users as a Web page taking more than seven seconds to refresh in their browsers (the time it takes people to lose interest in your Web site is seven seconds). Sometimes waits can be so long that end-user browser software actually times-out. This is not a cool situation, especially if you want to keep your customers.

Another issue for foreign key use is the zero factor in a relation between tables. Take a quick look back to Figure 11-4. Notice how all of the relationships are all optionally zero. For example, A SELLER record does not have to have any entries in the LISTING_BIDS table. In other words, a seller can be a seller, but does not have to have any existing listings of bids (even in the data warehouse database). Perhaps a seller still exists in the SELLER table, but has been inactive for an extended period. The point to make is that the SELLER_ID foreign key field on the LISTING_BIDS table can contain a NULL value. In reality, NULL-valued foreign key fields are common in data warehouses. They are less common in OLTP databases, but that does not mean that NULL-valued foreign key fields are a *big bad ugly thing* that should be avoided at all costs. For example, in Figure 11-2, a LISTING can exist with no bids because if no one makes any bids, then the item doesn't sell. NULL-valued foreign key fields are inevitable.

Refer to Figure 11-2 and the OLTP database model for the online auction house. The first order of the day with respect to alternate indexing is manual creation of indexes on all foreign key fields, as shown by the following script for the OLTP database model for the online auction house:

```
CREATE INDEX FKX_CATEGORY_1 ON CATEGORY (PARENT_ID);
CREATE INDEX FKX_LISTING_1 ON LISTING (CATEGORY_ID);
CREATE INDEX FKX_LISTING_2 ON LISTING (BUYER_ID);
CREATE INDEX FKX_LISTING_3 ON LISTING (SELLER_ID);
CREATE INDEX FKX_LISTING_4 ON LISTING (TICKER);
CREATE INDEX FKX_HISTORY_1 ON HISTORY (SELLER_ID);
CREATE INDEX FKX_HISTORY_1 ON HISTORY (BUYER_ID);
CREATE INDEX FKX_BID_1 ON BID (LISTING#);
CREATE INDEX FKX_BID_2 ON BID (BUYER_ID);
```

Now, what about alternate indexing, other than foreign key indexes? Without applications under development or a database in production, it is unwise to make a guess at what alternate indexing will be needed. And it might even be important to stress that it is necessary to resist guessing at further alternate indexing, to avoid overindexing. Over indexing and creating unnecessary alternate indexes can cause more problems than it solves, particularly in a highly normalized and concurrent OLTP database model, and its fully dependent applications.

Some of the best OLTP database model designs often match most (if not all) indexing requirements, using only existing primary and foreign key structures. In other words, applications are built around the normalized table structure, when an OLTP database model is properly designed. Problems occur when reporting (or even short on-screen listings joining more than one table) are required in applications. This is actually quite common.

A buyer might want to examine history records for a specific seller, to see if the seller is honest. This would at the bare minimum require a join between SELLER and HISTORY tables. Similarly, a seller examining past bids made by a buyer, would want to join tables, such as BUYER, BID and LISTING. Even so, with joins between SELLER and LISTING tables (or BUYER, BID and LISTING tables), all joins will be executed using primary and foreign key relationships. As it appears, no alternate indexing is required for these joins just mentioned. For these types of onscreen reports, the database model itself is providing the necessary key structures. Problems do not arise with joins when the database model maps adequately to application requirements.

Problems do, however, appear when a user wants to sort results. For example, a buyer might want to sort a report of the SELLER and HISTORY tables join, by a date value, such as the date of each comment made about the seller. That would be the COMMENT_DATE on the HISTORY table, as in the following query:

```
SELECT S.SELLER, H.COMMENT_DATE,
    H.FEEDBACK_POSITIVE, H.FEEDBACK_NEUTRAL, H.FEEDBACK_NEGATIVE
FROM SELLER S JOIN HISTORY H USING (SELLER_ID)
ORDER BY H.COMMENT_DATE ASCENDING;
```

It is conceivable that an alternate index could be created on the HSITORY.COMMENT_DATE field. As already stated, this can be very difficult to assess in analysis and design and is best left for later implementation phases. The reason why is because perhaps the GUI will offer a user different sorting methods (such as by COMMENT_DATE, by combinations of SELLER table fields and the HISTORY.COMMENT_DATE field, in unknown orders). You can never accurately predict what users will want. Creating alternate indexing for possible reporting, or even brief OLTP database on-screen listing is extremely difficult without developer, programmer, administrator, and, most important, customer feedback.

The Data Warehouse Database Model

Refer to Figure 11-4 and the data warehouse database model for the online auction house. Once again, as for the OLTP database model, create indexes on all foreign key fields in the data warehouse database model:

```
CREATE INDEX FKX_CATEGORY_HIERARCHY_1 ON CATEGORY_HIERARCHY (PARENT_ID);
CREATE INDEX FKX_LISTING_BIDS_1 ON LISTING (BUYER_ID);
CREATE INDEX FKX_LISTING_BIDS_2 ON LISTING (BIDDER_ID);
CREATE INDEX FKX_LISTING_BIDS_3 ON LISTING (SELLER_ID);
CREATE INDEX FKX_LISTING_BIDS_4 ON LISTING (TIME_ID);
CREATE INDEX FKX_LISTING_BIDS_5 ON LISTING (LOCATION_ID);
CREATE INDEX FKX_LISTING_BIDS_6 ON LISTING (CATEGORY_ID);
```

Foreign key indexes are only needed to be created on the LISTING_BIDS fact table, and the CATEGORY_ HIERARCHY tables. Categories are stored in a hierarchy and, thus, a pointer to each parent category is stored in the PARENT_ID field (if a parent exists). The fact table is the center of the data warehouse database model star schema, and, thus, is the only table (other than categories) containing foreign keys.

Creating alternate indexing for a data warehouse database model might be a little easier to guess at, as compared to an OLTP database model; however, data warehouse reporting is often ad-hoc (created on the fly) when the data warehouse is in production.

Once again, as for the OLTP database model, making an educated guess at requirements for alternate indexing, in the analysis and design stages of a data warehouse database model, is like flying blind on no instruments. Unless you have immense forehand knowledge of applications, it is more likely that you will create indexing that is either incorrect or even redundant (before it's even used).

Try It Out   Fields, Datatypes, and Indexing for an OLTP Database Model

Figure 11-10 shows an ERD for the now familiar musicians OLTP database model. The following is a basic approach to field refinement, datatype setting, and indexing:

1. Refine fields in tables by changing names, restructuring, and removing anything unnecessary.

2. Specify datatypes for all fields.

3. Create alternate indexing that might be required, especially foreign key indexes.

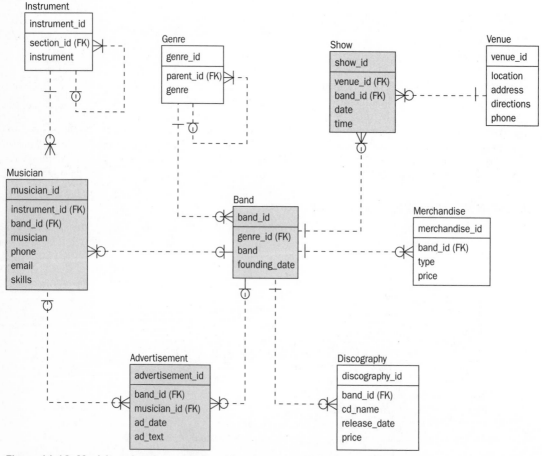

Figure 11-10: Musicians, bands, and online advertisements OLTP database model.

How It Works

Figure 11-11 shows the field-refined version of the OLTP database model shown in Figure 11-10. Changes are minimal:

❏ The fields AD_DATE and AD_TEXT in the ADVERTISEMENT table are changed to DATE and TEXT respectively.

❏ The ADDRESS field in the VENUE table is divided up into 6 separate fields: ADDRESS_LINE_1, ADDRESS_LINE_2, TOWN, ZIP, POSTAL_CODE, COUNTRY.

Figure 11-12 shows the datatype definitions for all fields in the database model.

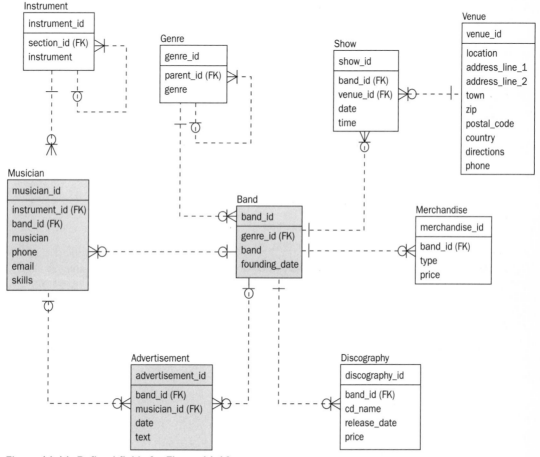

Figure 11-11: Refined fields for Figure 11-10.

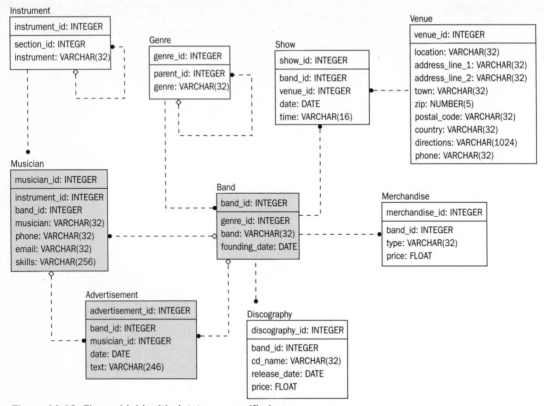

Instrument

instrument_id: INTEGER
section_id: INTEGR
instrument: VARCHAR(32)

Genre

genre_id: INTEGER
parent_id: INTEGER
genre: VARCHAR(32)

Show

show_id: INTEGER
band_id: INTEGER
venue_id: INTEGER
date: DATE
time: VARCHAR(16)

Venue

venue_id: INTEGER
location: VARCHAR(32)
address_line_1: VARCHAR(32)
address_line_2: VARCHAR(32)
town: VARCHAR(32)
zip: NUMBER(5)
postal_code: VARCHAR(32)
country: VARCHAR(32)
directions: VARCHAR(1024)
phone: VARCHAR(32)

Musician

musician_id: INTEGER
instrument_id: INTEGER
band_id: INTEGER
musician: VARCHAR(32)
phone: VARCHAR(32)
email: VARCHAR(32)
skills: VARCHAR(256)

Band

band_id: INTEGER
genre_id: INTEGER
band: VARCHAR(32)
founding_date: DATE

Merchandise

merchandise_id: INTEGER
band_id: INTEGER
type: VARCHAR(32)
price: FLOAT

Advertisement

advertisement_id: INTEGER
band_id: INTEGER
musician_id: INTEGER
date: DATE
text: VARCHAR(246)

Discography

discography_id: INTEGER
band_id: INTEGER
cd_name: VARCHAR(32)
release_date: DATE
price: FLOAT

Figure 11-12: Figure 11-11 with datatypes specified.

As discussed previously in this chapter, alternate indexing is best avoided in database analysis and design stages because there are too many unknown factors; however, foreign keys can be indexed for the musicians OLTP database model as follows:

```
CREATE INDEX FKX_INSTRUMENT_1 ON INSTRUMENT (SECTION_ID);
CREATE INDEX FKX_GENRE_1 ON GENRE (PARENT_ID);
CREATE INDEX FKX_SHOW_1 ON SHOW (BAND_ID);
CREATE INDEX FKX_SHOW_2 ON SHOW (VENUE_ID);
CREATE INDEX FKX_MERCHANDISE_1 ON MERCHANDISE (BAND_ID);
CREATE INDEX FKX_DISCOGRAPHY_1 ON DISCOGRAPHY (BAND_ID);
CREATE INDEX FKX_BAND_1 ON BAND (GENRE_ID);
CREATE INDEX FKX_MUSICIAN_1 ON MUSICIAN (INSTRUMENT_ID);
CREATE INDEX FKX_MUSICIAN_2 ON   (BAND_ID);
CREATE INDEX FKX_ADVERTISEMENT_1 ON ADVERTISEMENT (BAND_ID);
CREATE INDEX FKX_ ADVERTISEMENT _1 ON ADVERTISEMENT (MUSICIAN_ID);
```

Fields, Datatypes, and Indexing for a Data Warehouse Database Model

Figure 11-13 shows an ERD for the now familiar musicians data warehouse database model. Here's a basic approach to field refinement, datatype setting and indexing:

1.   Refine fields in tables by changing names, restructuring, and removing anything unnecessary.

2.   Specify datatypes for all fields.

3.   Create alternate indexing that might be required, especially foreign key indexes.

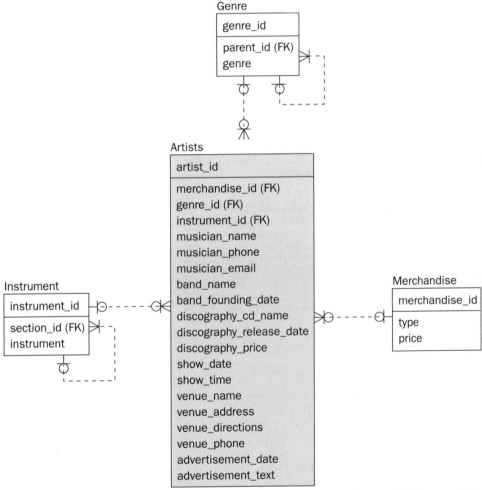

Figure 11-13: Musicians, bands, their online advertisements data warehouse database model.

Chapter 11

How It Works

In the previous chapter, it was argued that musicians, bands, discography, and venues are effectively dimensional in nature. The problem is that these dimensions have potentially such large quantities of records as to force them to be factual. This was, of course, incorrect. Look once again at the fields in the ARTIST table shown in Figure 11-13. Based on the guise that facts are supposed to be potentially cumulative, there is nothing cumulative about addresses and names. So I have reintroduced dimensions from the fact table, regardless of record numbers, and added some new fields (not seen so far in this book), to demonstrate the difference between facts and dimensions for this data warehouse database model. Figure 11-14 shows the field-refined version of the data warehouse database model shown in Figure 11-13, with new dimensions, and newly introduced fact fields.

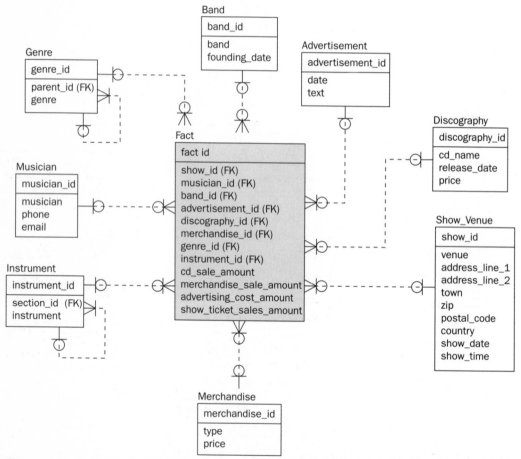

Figure 11-14: Refined fields for Figure 11-13.

Keep in mind the following:

❑ All dimensions are normalized to a single hierarchical dimensional layer.

❑ The SHOW_VENUE table is a denormalized dimension containing shows and the venues where the shows took place. This retains the efficiency of the star schema table structure because shows and venues are not broken into two tables: SHOW and VENUE.

❑ The ADDRESS field in the SHOW_VENUE table is divided up into 6 separate fields: ADDRESS_LINE_1, ADDRESS_LINE_2, TOWN, ZIP, POSTAL_CODE, COUNTRY.

Figure 11-15 shows the datatypes for all fields in the data warehouse database model, as shown in Figure 11-14.

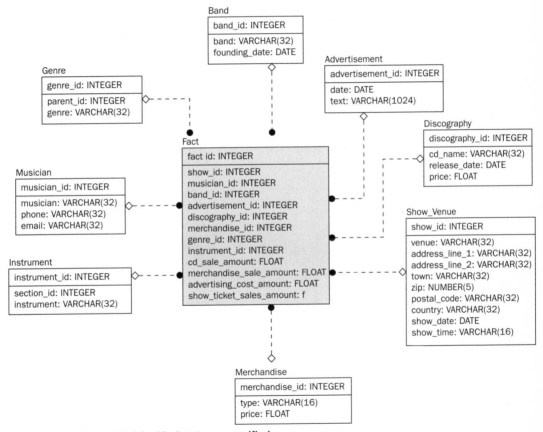

Figure 11-15: Figure 11-14 with datatypes specified.

Once again, as discussed previously in this chapter, alternate indexing is best avoided in database analysis and design stages. There are too many unknown factors; however, foreign keys can be indexed for the musicians data warehouse database model as follows:

```
CREATE INDEX FKX_FACT_1 ON FACT (SHOW_ID);
CREATE INDEX FKX_FACT_2 ON FACT (MUSICIAN_ID);
CREATE INDEX FKX_FACT_3 ON FACT (BAND_ID);
CREATE INDEX FKX_FACT_4 ON FACT (ADVERTISEMENT_ID);
CREATE INDEX FKX_FACT_5 ON FACT (DISCOGRAPHY_ID);
CREATE INDEX FKX_FACT_6 ON FACT (MERCHANDISE_ID);
CREATE INDEX FKX_FACT_7 ON FACT (GENRE_ID);
CREATE INDEX FKX_FACT_8 ON FACT (INSTRUMENT_ID);
CREATE INDEX FKX_INSTRUMENT ON INSTRUMENT (SECTION_ID);
CREATE INDEX FKX_GENRE_1 ON GENRE (PARENT_ID)
```

Summary

In this chapter, you learned about:

❑ Refining field structure and content in tables as a case study

❑ The difference between simple datatypes, ANSI datatypes, Microsoft Access datatypes and some specialized datatypes

❑ Using keys and indexes

❑ The difference between a key and an index

❑ Using alternate (secondary) indexing

❑ Using different types of indexes

❑ Deciding what to index

❑ Knowing when not to create an index

This chapter has refined and built on the previous chapters for the case study example using the online auction house OLTP and data warehouse database models. The next chapter goes a stage further into the case study, examining advanced application of business rules to a database model, such as field check constraints, database procedural coding, and advanced database structures.

Exercise

Use the ERDs in Figure 11-11 and Figure 11-14 to help you perform these exercises:

1. Create scripts to create tables for the OLTP database model shown in Figure 11-11. Create the tables in the proper order by understanding the relationships between the tables. Also include all NULL settings for all fields, all primary and foreign keys, and unique keys.

2. Create scripts to create tables for the data warehouse database model shown in Figure 11-14. Create the tables in the proper order by understanding the relationships between the tables. Also include all NULL settings for all fields, all primary and foreign keys, and unique keys.

Business Rules and Field Settings

"In business or in life, don't follow the wagon tracks too closely." (H. Jackson Brown)

Database modeling analysis and design are an art form. Use your imagination and you might find that, sometimes rules are made to be bent — if not broken altogether

This chapter covers the deepest layer of implementation into a database model — business rules. Business rules are implemented into a database model by creating tables, establishing relationships between tables, identifying fields, their datatypes, and various other factors including things such as validation. Field settings including display formats, input maskings, default values, and check constraints are included. There is also a brief section on applying business rules by way of storing code in the database model.

This chapter is the last of four chapters using the case study example of the online auction house. By reading through the last few chapters and this one, you should have a good idea of the analysis and design process for both OLTP and data warehouse database models, all the way through from start to finish.

By the end of this chapter, you should know how to apply field setting business rules in the extreme, and also that this extreme might be best left to application Software Development Kits (SDKs). Application SDKs are much more powerful than database modeling methods when it comes to number crunching, and some of the more detailed aspects of database modeling.

In this chapter, you learn about the following:

❑   Database model business rules classification

❑   Implementation of business rules can be implemented as table and relations (links between tables) design

❑   Using individual field settings as applications of deeper level business rules

❑   Using stored database code to implement highly complex business rules

What Are Business Rules Again?

When applied as a database model, the business rules of a company become the structure of that database model. The most basic implementation of business rules in a database model, are the tables, relationships between those tables, and even constraint rules, such as validation checks. Validation checks apply to individual fields. For example, a field called SEX can be restricted to having values of M for Male and F for Female. Insisting that a field only be set to M or F is a business rule, applied to the field SEX. Now I should have your full attention!

The application of normalization and Normal Forms to a set of not yet normalized data tables, applies a progressively more complex implementation of business rules, as you apply the successive Normal Form layers to the data set — 1NF, 2NF, 3NF, and so on.

As already seen previously in this book, a definition of the term *business rules* appears to be somewhat open to debate. Technically speaking, business rules require that intra-table and inter-table validation be placed into a database model. Database implementation of business rules includes validation for some or all fields in tables. Even any type of coding stored and executed within the bounds of a database engine is, technically speaking, business rules implementation. So business rules are not just about normalization, Normal Forms, and field validation checks. Business rules are also about stored procedures.

> A *stored procedure* is a chunk of code stored in a database — ostensibly to execute against data stored in one or more tables. In other words, the function of a stored procedure should be directly associated with some data in a database. On the contrary, the function of a stored procedure is not always directly associated with data in a database. This would not be an implementation of business rules. Business rules in a database model imply company operations as applied to data. In other words, not all stored procedures are an implementation of business rules. Stored procedures can implement number crunching as well.

Number crunching *is computer jargon for large quantities of extremely complex calculations.*

An object database model can encapsulate processing into class methods. A relational database can use stored (database) procedures and event or rule triggers to perform a similar function to that of object class methods. For the purposes of efficiency, it is usually best to avoid business rules in the database, unless they are included within the relationship structure of the database itself. You don't want to go too far in forcing business rules implementation into a database model. The most efficient implementation of business rules in a database model is anything non-coded and non-field-specific validation (validation checks or CHECK constraints). The only business rules that should absolutely be implemented in a database model is referential integrity (primary keys, foreign keys, and their representative inter-table relationships). Other layers can be, but are not strictly necessary.

So, it should be clear that implementing all types and layers of business rules into a database model may not the most prudent approach. As already stated, the most effective and efficient implementation of business rules in a database model is that of referential integrity. Other, deeper and more complex layers of business rules implementation are more often than not far more effectively managed in application coding. Why? Database models need to avoid number crunching processing. Application SDKs such as the Java SDK (incorporating the Java programming language) simply excel at managing large numbers of hugely complex calculations.

Excluding number-crunching processing from a database model applies to relational databases only. Quite to the contrary, object databases (object database modeling) are as adept at number crunching as an SDK such as Java is. In fact, an object database may even be more adept at complexity than a front-end application SDK such as Java. An object database is a data-processing tool, not weighed down with all the GUI bits and pieces that Java is.

Classifying Business Rules in a Database Model

Previously in this book, business rules have been classified from an operational perspective. Now classify business rules, and their implementation in a relational database model, according to the sequence in which they are implemented in a database model.

Normalization, Normal Forms, and Relations

Applying the normal form layers of normalization to a set of data applies business rules to that data. For example, a trucking company, owning many trucks, has trucks on the road with loads, and other trucks in a depot undergoing maintenance for two weeks. Over a period of a week, the trucks on the road could be hauling one or more loads. Trucks undergoing maintenance have not necessarily hauled any loads in the last two weeks. These points are important:

❏ There is potentially more than one load hauled, per truck, over the two-week period.

❏ Trucks always exist as either being on the road and working, or in a depot undergoing maintenance.

❏ Trucks in the maintenance depot haul nothing.

The following implement the previous operational facts as business rules:

❏ The relationship between trucks and loads is one-to-many. The one-to-many relationship implements the business rule between trucks and hauled loads.

❏ Trucks must always be defined as one and only one.

❏ Trucks being maintained are hauling nothing, and thus have no loads; therefore, loads are defined as zero, one, or many. This implies that each truck could have one load, many loads, or no loads at all; therefore, the one-to-many relationship between trucks and loads is more specific, as being, one and only one, to zero, one or many.

That's a simple form of implementing business rules for a trucking company and its hauled loads over a two-week period. Figure 12-1 shows an equivalent database model ERD representation.

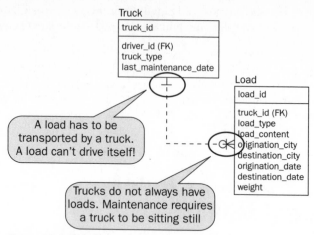

Figure 12-1: Trucks are related to hauled loads as one to zero, one or many.

Classifying Relationship Types

The ERD shown in Figure 12-1 demonstrates a one to zero, one, or many relationship between trucks and the loads they haul. You can see that relationships are not only classified as one containing many, but also, more specifically, where a related item is not necessarily required (represented by zero). In general, relationships are classified as follows:

❑   *One-to-many* — This is the most common and usually represents a 1NF master detail relationship, or a 2NF static-to-transactional referential relationship (dimensional to fact table, in a data warehouse database model).

❑   *One-to-one* — These are common of the higher Normal Forms beyond 3NF, where perhaps less commonly used fields are separated out to new tables.

❑   *Many-to-many* — This relationship represents an unresolved relationship between two tables. For example, students in a college can take many courses at once. So, a student can be enrolled in many courses at once, and a course can contain many enrolled students. The solution is to resolve the many-to-many relationship into three, rather than two tables. Each of the original tables is related to the new table as a one-to-many relationship, allowing access to unique records (in this example, unique course and student combinations).

   Zero can apply to a many-to-many relationship, such as a course with no enrolled students. This is unusual, quite probably pointless and, therefore, usually ignored.

One-to-many and one-to-one relationships can have either side of their specifications set as zero. So, all the following combinations are valid:

❑   *One or zero, to one or many* — For example, publishers publish many books. Some books are self-published (no publisher). A publisher has to publish at least one book to be called a publisher; therefore, a publisher can't exist without at least one book published, and a book can exist without a publisher.

❑   *One to zero, one, or many* — In this case, a publisher does not have to publish any books to be called a publisher. Also, self-publishing is not allowed — perhaps the author becomes the publisher.

❑   *One or zero to one, many, or zero* — In this case, a publisher is called a publisher, even if no books are published. Also, self-publishing with no publisher is allowed.

All these combinations apply to one-to-one relationships, as for one-to-many relationships, except that many is prohibited.

You can see that business rules are implemented in a relational database model using normalization (Normal Forms), the relationships established between tables, and even down to the specific value allowances, by the ends of each relationship (the crow's foot).

Explicitly Declared Field Settings

This topic area includes NULL values, uniqueness, and individual field settings (validation checks are included). You begin with NULL values and uniqueness, as these are simple:

❑   NULL *and default values* — NULL value requirements can be set for each field and are usually coded in data definition language (DDL) commands as NULL, NOT NULL, or WITH NULL. The default setting is usually NULL for any field with nothing specified. WITH NULL is often not necessary. This is not the case for all database engines. Ingres 6.04 defaulted to NOT NULL, requiring explicit declaration of WITH NULL to allow NULL values into fields. NULL simply means that a field does not have to have a value entered when a record is inserted into (or updated in) a table. NOT NULL is completely the opposite and always requires a value. If inserting or updating, a field specified as NOT NULL is not specified (insertion), or is set to NULL (updating), an error should be returned by the database.

❑   *Default values* — This is an interesting one because when a record is added to a table, if nothing is specified for a NOT NULL set field, then the default value is added to the NOT NULL field. This can somewhat restrict the purpose of specifying a field as NOT NULL. For example, a primary key field is always NOT NULL by default. Setting a default insertion value for an auto counter surrogate primary key field not specified in an insertion could ignore the auto counter, and produce an out of sequence, or worse, a duplicated surrogate key value. Default value settings are more often utilized in power-user type database engines such as Microsoft Access, rather than SQL Server or Oracle Database.

A power user is a user who is between an end-user and an expert computer programmer, in terms of knowing how to use a computer. An end-user uses a computer as a tool to solve business problems. A computer programmer writes the software that end-users make use of. A power user is someone in between, typically an end-user who writes his or her own software.

❑   *Uniqueness* — This is simply a declaration of a field as being a unique key. You have seen these specifications before in this book where a non-surrogate unique field is declared as being UNIQUE. For example, a table of customers, using a surrogate primary key auto counter integer CUSTOMER_ID, with a customer name, would not want to store customers having the same name. That could make things confusing, to say the least. The customer's name field would be declared as being unique.

❑   *Validation Check* — These settings are sometimes called *check constraints*. All they do is to check the value in a field when a new record is added, or an existing record is changed. The validation check itself can be a simple list check (such as a person being Male or Female). Validation checks can also be fairly complex executing functions or even stored procedures. Some database engines will even allow check constraints on a record as a whole, as opposed to being an individual field validation restriction. A check constraint made against an entire record would apply to multiple fields in a record, as opposed to just a single field. An example validation check would be declared for a field something like the following:

```
SEX CHAR(1) CHECK(SEX IN (M,F))
SEX CHAR(1) CHECK(SEX = "M" OR SEX = "F")
```

The following is for more than a single column check constraint:

```
CREATE TABLE INVOICES
(
        INVOICE# INTEGER PRIMARY KEY NOT NULL,
        CUSTOMER CHAR VARYING(32) NOT NULL,
        INVOICE_AMOUNT MONEY NOT NULL,
        SALES_TAX MONEY,
        SALES_COMMISSION MONEY,
        CONSTRAINT TOTAL_CHECK
            CHECK((INVOICE_AMOUNT + SALES_TAX + SALES_COMMISSION) > 0)
);
```

❑ *Other field settings* — The term "other field settings" is a little vague. That is the intention. These include field settings such as formatted input masks, default value settings, field lengths, and a host of other possibilities. The easiest way to demonstrate this is by showing graphical snapshots from with Microsoft Access. Figure 12-2 shows the different settings that can be applied to a simple short string datatype (Microsoft Access Text datatype).

Figure 12-3 shows some detail for various field-setting options for a Microsoft Access Number datatype. A Number datatype can be of a specific field size, in the form of Byte, Integer, Long Integer, Single, Double, Replication ID, Decimal. These format options are all different types of numbers. The format setting is essentially the way in which the number is displayed when queried in the database. As you can see from the central picture in Figure 12-3, there are various currency display formatting options. The last screen on the right of Figure 12-3 shows optional decimal place selection for each number value.

Date datatypes, as shown in Figure 12-4, often require some specialized formatting. Figure 12-4 shows various options.

Storing Code in the Database

Code can be stored in a database in the form of modular scripted sections. These scripts can be completely independent of anything in the database, or can operate on data in the database. These coded procedures can be called *stored procedures, database procedures, triggers, rules, events, macros, modules,* or other names, depending on the database engine in use. They all mean the same thing — code stored with data. A distinction needs to be made in that stored procedural code can operate on data in the database but not necessarily. For the purposes of database modeling, it should be stated that any stored procedure code, embedded in the database, is likely an application of business rules to a database model, if that stored procedure code operates on data stored in the database.

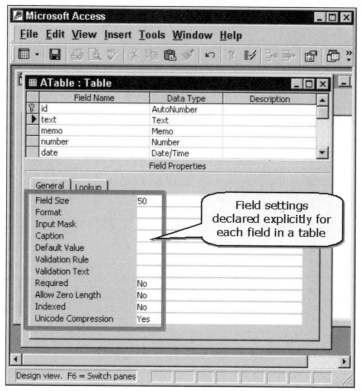

Figure 12-2: Text datatype field property (settings) in Microsoft Access.

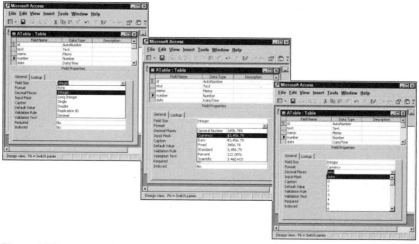

Figure 12-3: Number datatype field size, format and decimal places settings in Microsoft Access.

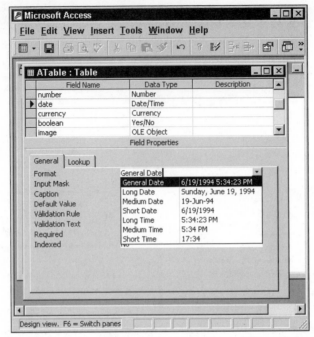

Figure 12-4: `Date` datatype field properties in Microsoft Access.

Some database engines allow extremely versatile stored procedural coding, whereas other databases only allow extremely simplistic stored procedural coding. Oracle Database allows a more or less full-fledged programming language in the form of Programming Language for SQL (PL/SQL). Ingres 6.04 database, on the other hand, allows only the simplest of commands, such as `INSERT`, `UPDATE`, `DELETE`, `COMMIT`, `ROLLBACK`—and a few others. In other words, some database engines go to town with stored procedure coding and others severely restrict it. It's not a matter of preference or lack of development. It's more of how the original writers of these various database engines, pictured how stored procedures should be used. Some database engines essentially allow anything, and some database engines deliberately restrict what can be coded in a database model. Essentially, the more coding options allowed in database engine, the more likely that coding will be over-utilized, become overcomplicated, and the less likely that coding database embedded coding (stored procedures) will cover only business rules. That's the theory, anyway. On the contrary, some benefits to using stored procedures to contain database activity can help to protect a database from misuse and abuse. Then again, proper training for developers in writing efficient SQL code might be a better option.

Take a very brief look at the different types of database embedded coding allowed, and what the various general types of embedded coding blocks are.

Stored Procedure

A stored procedure is just that—a modular chunk of code stored in the database. It does not have to operate on data, but if custom-written, that is usually the most prudent option. Any procedural code not directly written about database data, or not operating on data in a database, might be best migrated to application code. To demonstrate briefly, return to the trucking company example, as shown in Figure 12-1.

Add to the trucking company model a little, as shown in Figure 12-5. Long field names have been used in Figure 12-5 for descriptive purposes. It is inadvisable to name fields with great big, nasty, long names — programmers can get confused, and so can end users for that matter.

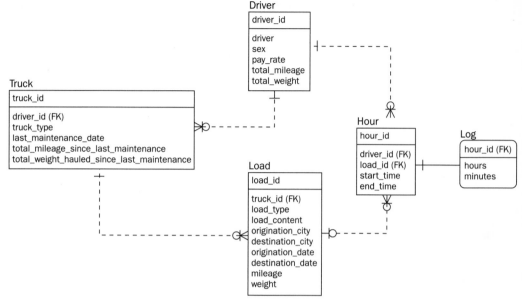

Figure 12-5: Expanding the trucking company database model ERD from Figure 12-1.

Figure 12-5 shows the LOAD table containing a WEIGHT field (the weight of each load hauled), and a MILEGAGE field (the distance in miles that each load was hauled over). The following procedure can be used to periodically update the totals, up through the table hierarchy, on both the TRUCK and DRIVER tables, from the LOAD.WEIGHT and LOAD MILEAGE fields.

```
CREATE PROCEDURE AGGREGATE_TOTALS AS
BEGIN

      UPDATE TRUCK SET TOTAL_MILEAGE_SINCE_LAST_MAINTENANCE,
            TOTAL_WEIGHT_HAULED_SINCE_LAST_MAINTENANCE
      = (
      SELECT S.MILEAGE, S.WEIGHT FROM
      (
            SELECT TRUCK_ID,
                    SUM(MILEAGE) "MILEAGE",
                    SUM(WEIGHT) "WEIGHT"
            FROM LOAD
      ) S
      WHERE S.TRUCK_ID = LOAD.TRUCK_ID
      );

      UPDATE DRIVER SET TOTAL_MILEAGE, TOTAL_HAULED
      = (
```

```
              SELECT MILEAGE, WEIGHT FROM
              (
                  SELECT DRIVER_ID,
                      SUM(TOTAL_MILEAGE_SINCE_LAST_MAINTENANCE) "MILEAGE",
                      SUM(TOTAL_WEIGHT_HAULED_SINCE_LAST_MAINTENANCE) "WEIGHT"
                  FROM TRUCK
              ) S
              WHERE S.DRIVER_ID = TRUCK.DRIVER_ID
              );

              COMMIT;

      EXCEPTION TRAP WHEN ERROR THEN
              PRINT("ERROR IN PROCEDURE AGGREGATE_TOTALS");
              ROLLBACK;
      END;
```

The preceding procedure would be executed with a comment like this:

```
EXECUTE AGGREGATE_TOTALS;
```

The preceding procedure is nice and neat and tidy; however, this type of coding can cause serious performance problems because it can lock of all three tables.

Stored Function

A stored function is precisely the same as a stored procedure, except that it returns a single value. In programming parlance, a procedure accepts parameter values, but does not return anything (unless resetting dynamic parameters). By definition, in programming terms, a function (much like a mathematical function) always returns a value, even if the return value is NULL. Additionally, because a function always returns a value, a function is always executed as an expression, or embedded within another expression. A function is actually an expression itself. The following function directly accesses data in the LOAD table, producing a calculation based on the MILEAGE and WEIGHT fields. All fields are input with zero-valued defaults, and a COST_FACTOR is defaulted to 1.304 (arbitrary) for the purposes of making a calculation. The function accepts and returns simple values.

```
CREATE FUNCTION LOAD_COST
(
        MILEAGE INTEGER DEFAULT 0,
        WEIGHT INTEGER DEFAULT 0,
        COST_FACTOR FLOAT DEFAILT 1.304
)
   RETURN INTEGER
BEGIN
   RETURN (MILEAGE * WEIGHT) * COST_FACTOR;
END;
```

The preceding function would be executed similar to this:

```
SELECT
  LOAD_TYPE, LOAD_CONTENT, MILEAGE, WEIGHT,
     LOAD_COST(MILEAGE, WEIGHT)
FROM LOAD;
```

Event Trigger

Event triggers are used to automatically trigger events, generally in response to something that happens inside a database. Triggers typically are executed automatically based on specific database change commands (such as INSERT, UPDATE, and DELETE commands). The easiest way to demonstrate use of triggers is that of log file generation, as in the trigger shown here:

```
CREATE TRIGGER LOG_ENTRIES
      AFTER INSERT ON HOUR
BEGIN
     INSERT INTO LOG (DRIVER_ID, LOAD_ID, HOURS, MINUTES)
     VALUES (:NEW.DRIVER_ID, :NEW.LOAD_ID,
          TO_CHAR(END_TIME - START_TIME, "HH"),
          TO_CHAR(END_TIME - START_TIME, "MI")
     );
     COMMIT;
EXCEPTION TRAP WHEN ERROR THEN
      PRINT("ERROR IN TRIGGER LOG_ENTRIES");
      ROLLBACK;
END;
```

Formatting of dates into "HH" and "MI" is a pseudo-like interpretation of what a database engine may allow. TO_CHAR converts a time stamp date value (the subtraction) to a string, where the HH and MM format specify extraction of hours and minutes from the timestamp, respectively.

> **The most significant factor to note about triggers is that they are not allowed to contain COMMIT or ROLLBACK commands. Triggers are automatically executed either before or after the execution of a database change command. Database change commands are INSERT, UPDATE, and DELETE commands. Transactional control is essentially the control of where and when a transaction is terminated. Transactions are terminated either by direct or indirect execution of a COMMIT or ROLLBACK command. A trigger is contained within a parent transaction. If the trigger doesn't change any database data, then you don't want the calling procedure or change command to execute a COMMIT command (storing all as-of-yet uncommitted changes).**
>
> **Transactional control must be retained outside of a trigger. Even if a trigger does change database data, transactional control must still remain within the purview of the calling command or procedure. Triggers can't directly call each other, but if a trigger includes a database change command, it can also execute other triggers, or even itself.**
>
> **One of the biggest dangers with profligate use of triggers is recursive activity. Quite often, a trigger-generated recursive execution (of the same trigger) is inadvertent and can result in a database slowing down, tying itself up in great big granny knots, and even appearing to halt.**

Some database engines call event triggers just triggers, some call them rules (used for expert system construction), and some call them database events (implying something happens in a database, to trigger the database event to occur).

External Procedure

External procedures are very similar to stored procedures, except they are written a non-database-specific programming language. External procedures are a chunk of code written in a language not native to the database engine (such as Java or C++). However, external procedures are still executed from within the database engine itself, perhaps on data within the database.

Macro

A macro is a little like a pseudo-type series of commands, typically not really a programming language, and sometimes a sequence of commands built from GUI-based actions (such as those seen on the File menu in Microsoft Access). In other words, a highly computer-literate person, who is not a programmer, stores a sequence of mouse clicks and software tool executed steps, stores them in a file, to be executed at some other time.

Now get back to the case study, and continue with more in depth business model development, for the OLTP and data warehouse database models — using the online auction house.

Case Study: Implementing Field Level Business Rules in a Database Model

The whole objective of this chapter is to show very detailed application of business rules into a database model. This can be placing too much detail into a database model. It might be too much detail because this type of business rules implementation is nearly always much more effectively and efficiently handled by application SDK programming languages. Typically, this level of business rules implementation into a database model can overcomplicate a database model, and quite often lead to serious performance problems, and serious difficulty in the day-to-day maintenance of production level databases.

Table and Relation Level Business Rules

In the case study so far in previous chapters, all factors for both OLTP and data warehouse database models, for all table and relational level business rules have already been covered in detail. This means that for both OLTP and data warehouse database models, for the online auction house, all the tables and relationships between them have been analyzed and designed. There is nothing more to do in this respect, as it's already been done. In other words, everything to do with normalization, Normal Forms, relations, relation types classification, referential integrity, primary and foreign keys, is already completed. No more need be said at this point.

Individual Field Business Rules

Individual field business rules for case study data modeling in the previous chapter has been partially covered. NULL settings and UNIQUE keys are catered for already. Default values, validation checks, and other settings (such as formatting and input maskings) are not yet covered.

Field Level Business Rules for the OLTP Database Model

Figure 12-6 shows the most recent version of the ERD for the OLTP database model, for the online auction house. Figure 12-6 shows that a CURRENT_PRICE field has been added to the LISTING table to contain the highest current bid price. If a listing has ended, CURRENT_PRICE will be equal to WINNING_PRICE. If a listing has no bids, CURRENT_PRICE will be NULL.

As mentioned, NULL and UNIQUE key settings have already been covered in previous chapters. Previous chapters have also covered the lengths of fields, be they differences between SMALLINT and INTEGERS, or varying lengths of string fields, such as CHAR(5) and CHAR(10). Go through each table and examine default values, check constraints, plus any formatting and input masking requirements. Field setting options will be added using scripting only, interspersed with appropriate notes to elucidate.

First, examine the CURRENCY table:

```
CREATE TABLE CURRENCY
(
        TICKER          CHAR(3) PRIMARY KEY FORMAT "AAA" MASK "AAA" NOT NULL,
        CURRENCY        CHAR VARYING(32) UNIQUE NOT NULL,
        EXCHANGE_RATE   FLOAT DEFAULT 1.0 NOT NULL,
        DECIMALS        SMALLINT DEFAULT 2 FORMAT "9" MASK "9"
                        CHECK(DECIMALS IN(0,2,3))
                        NULL
);
```

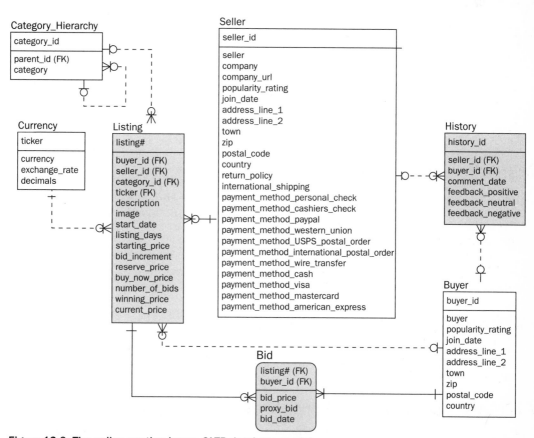

Figure 12-6: The online auction house OLTP database model.

The TICKER field has a FORMAT display setting which forces all output to be returned as three alphabetic characters. The "A" character is used to represent a single alphabetic a character. An alphabetic character is any character from A to Z.

A ticker is a currency code for a country's currency, such as GBP for British Pounds or USD for US Dollars. MASK "AAA" forces the entry of at least three alphabetic characters so no currency ticker can be less than three characters in length.

The exchange rate is set to a default value of 1.0 because most transactions will be national. The rate of exchange between USD and USD is quite obviously 1 because there is no currency conversion to be made.

The number of decimals in the currency code makes the decimal point for any amounts in the currency flexible at 0, 2 or 3. Some weaker currencies have no decimal place such as Italian Lire. USD has 2 decimals, which is the default, some very strong currencies, such as some Middle Eastern currencies have three decimals.

Now take a look at the BUYER table:

```
CREATE TABLE BUYER
(
        BUYER_ID                INTEGER PRIMARY KEY NOT NULL,
        BUYER                   CHAR VARYING(32) UNIQUE NOT NULL,
        POPULARITY_RATING       SMALLINT NULL,
        JOIN_DATE               DATE FORMAT "DD MON, YEAR" MASK "MM/DD/YYYY" NOT NULL,
        ADDRESS_LINE_1          CHAR VARYING(32) NULL,
        ADDRESS_LINE_2          CHAR VARYINGR(32) NULL,
        TOWN                    CHAR VARYING(32) NULL,
        ZIP                     NUMERIC(5) MASK "99999" NULL,
        POSTAL_CODE             CHAR VARYING(16) NULL,
        COUNTRY                 CHAR VARYING(32)
                                DEFAULT "United States of America"
                                NULL
);
```

The JOIN_DATE field is entry formatted for the United States of America as MM/DD/YYYY with MASK "MM/DD/YYYY". For example, 6/6/2005 for 6th June, 2005. JOIN_DATE is also display formatted, but with DD MON, YEAR, such that this date when output will appear as 06 JUN, 2005. All dates in these scripts are set this way—both for FORMAT and MASK settings.

The ZIP code field is set to force a five-character numeric entry. In other words, 1234 will be invalid and 12345 will be valid. No output format setting is required because five numeric characters will always print as five numeric characters. None of the digits are zero. If there are any ZIP codes with leading zeroes, a FORMAT "99999" can be added such that a ZIP code of 01234 will be returned as 01234 and not 1234 (the leading 0 is likely trimmed by default, for most database engines).

The default country is set as the United States of America. This is because our example online auction house is based in San Francisco, and most auction sellers and bidders live in the United States of America.

There are no changes for the CATEGORY table:

```
CREATE TABLE CATEGORY
(
        CATEGORY_ID          INTEGER PRIMARY KEY NOT NULL,
        PARENT_ID            INTEGER FOREIGN KEY REFERENCES CATEGORY WITH NULL,
        CATEGORY             CHAR VARYING(32) UNIQUE NOT NULL
);
```

Next up is the SELLER table:

```
CREATE TABLE SELLER
(
        SELLER_ID            INTEGER PRIMARY KEY NOT NULL,
        SELLER               CHAR VARYING(32) UNIQUE NOT NULL,
        COMPANY              CHAR VARYING(32) UNIQUE NOT NULL,
        COMPANY_URL          CHAR VARYING(64) UNIQUE FORMAT "WWW.[X...].XXX"
                                             MASK "HTTP://WWW.[X...].XXX"
                                             NOT NULL,
        POPULARITY_RATING    SMALLINT NULL,
        JOIN_DATE            DATE FORMAT "DD MON, YEAR" MASK "MM/DD/YYYY" NOT NULL,
        ADDRESS_LINE_1       CHAR VARYING(32) NULL,
        ADDRESS_LINE_2       CHAR VARYING(32) NULL,
        TOWN                 CHAR VARYING (32) NULL,
        ZIP                  NUMERIC(5) MASK "99999" NULL,
        POSTAL_CODE          CHAR VARYING (32) NULL,
        COUNTRY              CHAR VARYING(32)
                                     DEFAULT "United States of America"
                                     NULL,
        RETURN_POLICY        CHAR VARYING(256) DEFAULT "No Returns" NULL,
        INTERNATIONAL_SHIPPING BOOLEAN
            CHECK(<FIELD> IN ("Y","N"))
            DEFAULT "N"
            NULL,
        PAYMENT_METHOD_PERSONAL_CHECK BOOLEAN
            CHECK(<FIELD> IN ("Y","N"))
            DEFAULT "N"
            NULL,
        PAYMENT_METHOD_CASHIERS_CHECK BOOLEAN
            CHECK(<FIELD> IN ("Y","N"))
            DEFAULT "Y"
            NULL,
        PAYMENT_METHOD_PAYPAL BOOLEAN
            CHECK(<FIELD> IN ("Y","N"))
            DEFAULT "Y"
            NULL,
        PAYMENT_METHOD_WESTERN_UNION BOOLEAN
            CHECK(<FIELD> IN ("Y","N"))
            DEFAULT "N"
            NULL,
        PAYMENT_METHOD_USPS_POSTAL_ORDER BOOLEAN
            CHECK(<FIELD> IN ("Y","N"))
            DEFAULT "Y"
            NULL,
        PAYMENT_METHOD_INTERNATIONAL_POSTAL_ORDER BOOLEAN
            CHECK(<FIELD> IN ("Y","N"))
            DEFAULT "N"
            NULL,
```

```
          PAYMENT_METHOD_WIRE_TRANSFER BOOLEAN
              CHECK(<FIELD> IN ("Y","N"))
              DEFAULT "N"
              NULL,
          PAYMENT_METHOD_CASH BOOLEAN
              CHECK(<FIELD> IN ("Y","N"))
              DEFAULT "N"
              NULL,
          PAYMENT_METHOD_VISA BOOLEAN
              CHECK(<FIELD> IN ("Y","N"))
              DEFAULT "N"
              NULL,
          PAYMENT_METHOD_MASTERCARD BOOLEAN
              CHECK(<FIELD> IN ("Y","N"))
              DEFAULT "N"
              NULL,
          PAYMENT_METHOD_AMERICAN_EXPRESS BOOLEAN
              CHECK(<FIELD> IN ("Y","N"))
              DEFAULT "N"
              NULL
);
```

In the COMPANY_URL field, the FORMAT and MASK settings are slightly different in that the MASK setting requires the prefix HTTP://. Both format and mask settings will force a URL to be "WWW.[X...].XXX" where the "X" character represents an alphanumeric string (not alphabetic as for "A"), and the "[X...]" implies that a string of one or more alphanumeric characters is allowed. XXX at the end of the string restricts to three characters, such as "COM" or "BIZ." There is also "TV," which is two characters but, for the purposes of simplicity, this format sticks to three characters.

Dates, ZIP code and COUNTRY default values are set as before.

RETURN_POLICY is defaulted as "No Returns", implying that most sellers do not want things returned. In reality this is unlikely, of course.

All BOOLEAN datatype fields are set as CHECK(<FIELD> IN ("Y","N")) and DEFAULT"N". This is pseudo code and the field names are monstrously long. Thus, <FIELD> should be replaced with the actual field name. The CHECK constraint forces a "Y" or "N" entry, as opposed to "T" or "F", "1" or "0". Technically, this is only relevant to entry, and display as BOOLEAN datatypes are generally stored internally as 1 or 0 anyway. Also the default is set to "N," implying that if a field is not entered, it is set to "N," rather than left as NULL valued.

Now tackle the LISTING table:

```
CREATE TABLE LISTING
(
        LISTING#                CHAR(10) PRIMARY KEY NOT NULL,
        CATEGORY_ID             INTEGER FOREIGN KEY REFERENCES CATEGORY NOT NULL,
        BUYER_ID                INTEGER FOREIGN KEY REFERENCES BUYER WITH NULL,
        SELLER_ID               INTEGER FOREIGN KEY REFERENCES SELLER WITH NULL,
        TICKER                  CHAR(3) FOREIGN KEY REFERENCES CURRENCY WITH NULL,
        DESCRIPTION             CHAR VARYING(32) NULL,
```

```
            IMAGE                   BINARY NULL,
            START_DATE              DATE FORMAT "DD MON, YEAR" MASK "MM/DD/YYYY" NOT NULL,
            LISTING_DAYS            SMALLINT FORMAT "9" MASK "9" DEFAULT 7 NOT NULL,
            STARTING_PRICE          MONEY NOT NULL,
            BID_INCREMENT           MONEY NULL,
            RESERVE_PRICE           MONEY NULL,
            BUY_NOW_PRICE           MONEY NULL,
            NUMBER_OF_BIDS          SMALLINT FORMAT "999" NULL,
            WINNING_PRICE           MONEY NULL,
            CURRENT_PRICE           MONEY NULL,
            CONSTRAINT CHECK_RESERVE CHECK(RESERVE_PRICE IS NULL
                            OR (RESERVE_PRICE > STARTING_PRICE
                            AND RESERVE_PRICE <= BUY_NOW_PRICE)),
            CONSTRAINT CHECK_BUY_NOW CHECK(BUY_NOW_PRICE IS NULL
                            OR (BUY_NOW_PRICE > STARTING_PRICE
                            AND BUY_NOW_PRICE >= RESERVE_PRICE))
    );
```

The LISTING_DAYS field is output formatted and input masked as a single numerical character. It is also defaulted to seven days because most listings last seven days. Sellers can pay extra to have shorter three- and five-day listings, or even longer nine-day listings.

The NUMBER_OF_BIDS field is output formatted as three numeric digits. Personally, I have never seen an online auction with more than 99 bids, even the longer nine-day auctions.

The CURRENT_PRICE field is added, as already stated.

The two CHECK_RESERVE and CHECK_BUY_NOW constraints verify prices against the STARTING_PRICE field, and each other.

Monetary amounts can't be output formatted because in these database models, they are based on currency decimal places. Currency decimal places can be 0, 2, or 3 decimal places. There is no point placing an output display format of FORMAT "9999990.99" *on one of the monetary amount fields because this particular format specifies two decimal places only — which would be incorrect for these database models.*

Take a look at the BID table:

```
CREATE TABLE BID
(
        LISTING#                CHAR(10) NOT NULL,
        BUYER_ID                INTEGER FOREIGN KEY REFERENCES BUYER NOT NULL,
        BID_PRICE               MONEY NOT NULL,
        PROXY_BID               MONEY NULL,
        BID_DATE                DATE FORMAT "DD MON, YEAR" NOT NULL,
        CONSTRAINT PRIMARY KEY (LISTING#, BUYER_ID)
);
```

There is nothing new for the BID table except that the BID_DATE has only a FORMAT setting and no MASK setting. This is because the BID_DATE is inserted into a new bid record automatically, when a bidder clicks a mouse button. In other words, the bidders do not enter the data on which they make a bid — the computer system does that for them.

Finally, consider the HISTORY table:

```
CREATE TABLE HISTORY
(
        HISTORY_ID              INTEGER PRIMARY KEY NOT NULL,
        SELLER_ID               INTEGER FOREIGN KEY REFERENCES SELLER WITH NULL,
        BUYER_ID                INTEGER FOREIGN KEY REFERENCES BUYER WITH NULL,
        COMMENT_DATE            DATE FORMAT "DD MON, YEAR"  NOT NULL,
        FEEDBACK_POSITIVE       SMALLINT NULL,
        FEEDBACK_NEUTRAL        SMALLINT NULL,
        FEEDBACK_NEGATIVE       SMALLINT NULL
) ;
```

There is nothing new for the HISTORY table other than the COMMENT_DATE field, with the same function and restriction as the BID table BID_DATE field.

Field Level Business Rules for the Data warehouse Database Model

Figure 12-7 shows the most recent version of the ERD for the data warehouse database model for the online auction house.

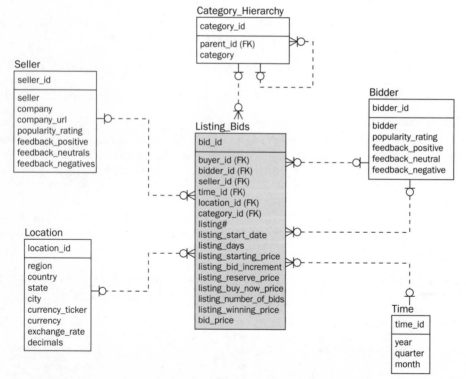

Figure 12-7: The online auction house data warehouse database model.

Bear in mind that field settings for the OLTP database model discussed in the previous section, are input mask restrictions (MASK), CHECK constraints, and output display formats (FORMAT). Data warehouse tables are rarely, if ever, manually entered into. Data warehouse tables are fully generated. using coding and scripting, all generated from source databases, such as an OLTP database. Therefore, no MASK settings are required. This approach applies to CHECK constraints as well because CHECK constraints are intended to check specific values on field input. FORMAT settings are useful for output only and thus do apply for a data warehouse, where those fields may someday be output in reports. In short, there are very few changes for the data warehouse model shown in the following scripts. Additionally, for any CHECK constraints across multiple fields, you should assume them to be correct, because the code generating data warehouse entries should be correct.

First up are the CATEGORY and SELLER tables:

```
CREATE TABLE CATEGORY
(
        CATEGORY_ID            INTEGER PRIMARY KEY NOT NULL,
        PARENT_ID              INTEGER FOREIGN KEY REFERENCES CATEGORY WITH NULL,
        CATEGORY               CHAR VARYING(32) UNIQUE NOT NULL
);

CREATE TABLE SELLER
(
        SELLER_ID              INTEGER PRIMARY KEY NOT NULL,
        SELLER                 CHAR VARYING(32) UNIQUE NOT NULL,
        COMPANY                CHAR VARYING(32) UNIQUE NOT NULL,
        COMPANY_URL            CHAR VARYING(64) FORMAT "WWW.[X...].XXX" UNIQUE NOT
NULL,
        POPULARITY_RATING      SMALLINT NULL,
        FEEDBACK_POSITIVE      SMALLINT FORMAT "99990" NULL,
        FEEDBACK_NEUTRAL       SMALLINT FORMAT "99990" NULL,
        FEEDBACK_NEGATIVE      SMALLINT FORMAT "99990" NULL
);
```

The FORMAT setting for the COMPANY_URL field is the same as for the SELLER table in the OLTP database model, shown in the previous section.

All UNIQUE settings could be deleted. There is no reason why UNIQUE key restrictions should be retained within data warehouse tables because data warehouse table data is supposed to be automatically generated. The generation code could take uniqueness into account.

The FORMAT "99990" settings for the feedback aggregations means that the number 0 is returned as "0", 456 is returned as "456" — not "00456". Obviously, "12345" is returned as "12345".

Now look at the BIDDER and LOCATION tables:

```
CREATE TABLE BIDDER
(
        BIDDER_ID              INTEGER PRIMARY KEY NOT NULL,
        BIDDER                 CHAR VARYING(32) UNIQUE NOT NULL,
```

```
        POPULARITY_RATING    SMALLINT NULL
);

CREATE TABLE LOCATION
(
        LOCATION_ID          INTEGER PRIMARY KEY NOT NULL,
        REGION               CHAR VARYING(32) NOT NULL,
        COUNTRY              CHAR VARYING(32) NOT NULL,
        STATE                CHAR(2) NULL,
        CITY                 CHAR VARYING(32) NOT NULL,
        CURRENCY_TICKER      CHAR(3) NOT NULL,
        CURRENCY             CHAR VARYING(32) UNIQUE NOT NULL,
        EXCHANGE_RATE        FLOAT NOT NULL,
        DECIMALS             SMALLINT FORMAT "9" NULL
);
```

The CURRENCY_TICKER *field is not* UNIQUE *in the* LOCATION *table because locations are duplicated within countries by both states and cities.*

Next, consider the TIME table:

```
CREATE TABLE TIME
(
     TIME_ID         INTEGER PRIMARY KEY NOT NULL,
     YEAR            INTEGER FORMAT "9999" NOT NULL,
     QUARTER         INTEGER FORMAT "9" NOT NULL,
     MONTH           INTEGER FORMAT "99" NOT NULL
);
```

Years are output formatted to ensure all four digits are always returned. Quarters are formatted to show only 1, 2, 3, or 4. Months are formatted to show "01" for January and "12" for December.

Finally, look at the LISTING_BIDS table:

```
CREATE TABLE LISTING_BIDS
(
        LISTING#               CHAR(10) PRIMARY KEY NOT NULL,
        BID_ID                 INTEGER FOREIGN KEY REFERENCES BID NOT NULL,
        BUYER_ID               INTEGER FOREIGN KEY REFERENCES BUYER WITH NULL,
        BIDDER_ID              INTEGER FOREIGN KEY REFERENCES BUYER WITH NULL,
        SELLER_ID              INTEGER FOREIGN KEY REFERENCES SELLER WITH NULL,
        TIME_ID                INTEGER FOREIGN KEY REFERENCES TIME WITH NULL,
        LOCATION_ID            INTEGER FOREIGN KEY REFERENCES LOCATION WITH NULL,
        CATEGORY_ID            INTEGER FOREIG KEY REFERENCES CATEGORY WITH NULL,
        LISTING_STARTING_PRICE MONEY NOT NULL,
        LISTING_RESERVE_PRICE  MONEY NULL,
        LISTING_BUY_NOW_PRICE  MONEY NULL,
        LISTING_START_DATE     DATE FORMAT "DD MON, YEAR" NOT NULL,
        LISTING_DAYS           SMALLINT NOT NULL,
```

```
          LISTING_NUMBER_OF_BIDS      INTEGER FORMAT "999" NULL,
          LISTING_WINNING_PRICE       MONEY NULL,
          LISTING_BID_INCREMENT       MONEY NULL,
          BID_PRICE                   MONEY NULL
    );
```

The `LISTING_NUMBER_OF_BIDS` is output formatted as for number of bids in the OLTP database model `LISTING` table.

Encoding Business Rules

As with the previous section covering individual field business rules, this section covers the case study online auction house database models, but this time attempting to encode a few things into a pseudo database programming language. The intention here is to demonstrate what can be done. It is a matter for some debate among computer professionals as to whether business rules should be written into stored procedures. Some think implementing business rules in stored procedures is good for some reasons. Others consider that applications handle this type of complexity more effectively and efficiently.

Encoding Business Rules for the OLTP Database Model

You already know the difference between a stored procedure, a stored function, and an event-based trigger. What can be done to the OLTP database model for this case study, to utilize some type of database stored coding? The `BID` table is a good candidate for some basic stored functions:

```
CREATE TABLE BID
(
        LISTING#            CHAR(10) NOT NULL,
        BUYER_ID            INTEGER FOREIGN KEY REFERENCES BUYER NOT NULL,
        BID_PRICE           MONEY
                            CHECK(VERIFY_BID(LISTING#, BID_PRICE))
                            NOT NULL,
        PROXY_BID           MONEY
                            CHECK(PROXY_BID > BID_PRICE
                               AND VERIFY_BID(LISTING#, PROXY_BID))
                            NULL,
        BID_DATE            DATE FORMAT "DD MON, YEAR" NOT NULL,
        CONSTRAINT PRIMARY KEY (LISTING#, BUYER_ID)
);
```

The preceding script has a `CHECK` constraint on the `BID_PRICE` and `PROXY_BID` fields. Both of these `CHECK` constraints execute a function. A bid price is entered by a bidder. That bid price must exceed the starting and current prices, both of which are stored in the listing table. This can be encoded using a stored function as follows:

```
CREATE FUNCTION VERIFY_BID(LISTNUM CHAR(10), BID MONEY DEFAULT NULL)
        RETURN BOOLEAN
DECLARE
        START_PRICE MONEY;
```

```
        CURR_PRICE MONEY;
BEGIN


    REMARK --- Throw out bids that are incorrectly passed in
    IF LISTING# IS NULL OR BID IS NULL OR BID <= 0 THEN RETURN FALSE;

    REMARK --- bidding price (including proxy bids) must exceed starting price
    REMARK --- if current price is NULL, otherwise must exceed current price

    SELECT STARTING_PRICE, CURRENT_PRICE
    INTO START_PRICE, CURR_PRICE
    FROM LISTING WHERE LISTING# = LISTNUM;

    IF CURR_PRICE IS NULL THEN
        IF BID <= START_PRICE THEN RETURN FALSE;
    ELSE
        IF BID <= CURR_PRICE THEN RETURN FALSE;
    END IF;

    RETURN TRUE;

END;
```

The preceding script applies to both normal (regular) bids and to proxy bids as well. A proxy bid must always be greater than the current bid price; otherwise, the proxy bid is just a normal bid. A proxy bid is where a buyer sets a maximum price that they will bid to. Whenever other bidders place bids, the system automatically increments the highest bid price with the current increment, until the proxy bid is reached. If the competing bidder exceeds the proxy bid, the other buyer becomes the current highest bidder.

Encoding Business Rules for the Data Warehouse Database Model

In short, there is nothing that you would want to attach to a data warehouse database model in the form of database model embedded coding, acting on the database model structures. It would simply be contrary to the existence of a data warehouse.

Try It Out   Field Level Business Rules for an OLTP Database Model

Figure 12-8 shows an ERD for the musicians OLTP database model. Here's a basic approach to business rules field settings:

1. Individual field business rules (including defaults, CHECK constraints, display formats, and input masks)

2. Encoding business rules using some kind of stored database coding, if and where appropriate (usually CHECK constraint functions)

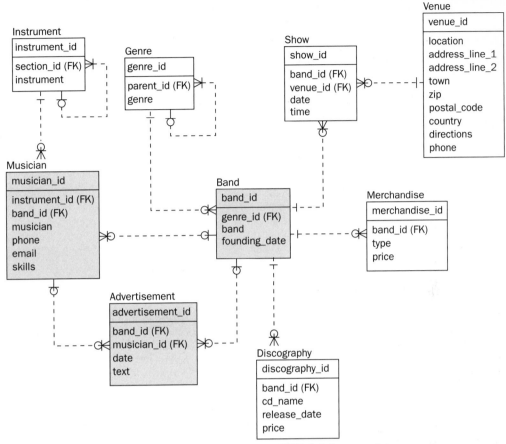

Figure 12-8: Musicians, bands, online advertisements OLTP database model.

How It Works

There are no appropriate CHECK constraints and no appropriate stored encoding. This script contains appropriate changes:

```
CREATE TABLE INSTRUMENT
(
        INSTRUMENT_ID          INTEGER PRIMARY KEY NOT NULL,
        SECTION_ID             INTEGER FOREIGN KEY REFERENCES INSTRUMENT WITH NULL,
        INSTRUMENT             CHAR VARYING(32) UNIQUE NOT NULL
);

CREATE TABLE GENRE
(
        GENRE_ID               INTEGER PRIMARY KEY NOT NULL,
        PARENT_ID              INTEGER FOREIGN KEY REFERENCES GENRE WITH NULL,
        GENRE                  CHAR VARYING(32) UNIQUE NOT NULL
);

CREATE TABLE VENUE
```

```
(
        VENUE_ID                INTEGER PRIMARY KEY NOT NULL,
        LOCATION                CHAR VARYING(32) UNIQUE NOT NULL,
        ADDRESS_LINE_1          CHAR VARYING(32) NOT NULL,
        ADDRESS_LINE_2          CHAR VARYING(32) NULL,
        TOWN                    CHAR VARYING(32) NOT NULL,
        ZIP                     NUMBER(5) FORMAT "99999" MASK "99999" NULL,
        POSTAL_CODE             CHAR VARYING(32) NULL,
        COUNTRY                 CHAR VARYING(32) NULL,
        DIRECTIONS              MEMO NULL,
        PHONE                   CHAR VARYING(32) NULL
);

CREATE TABLE MERCHANDISE
(
        MERCHANDISE_ID          INTEGER PRIMARY KEY NOT NULL,
        BAND_ID                 INTEGER FOREIGN KEY REFERENCES BAND NOT NULL,
        TYPE                    CHAR VARYING(32) UNIQUE NOT NULL,
        PRICE                   MONEY FORMAT "$9,999,990.99" MASK "9999990.00" NOT NULL
);

CREATE TABLE DISCOGRAPHY
(
        DISCOGRAPHY_ID          INTEGER PRIMARY KEY NOT NULL,
        BAND_ID                 INTEGER FOREIGN REFERENCES BAND NOT NULL,
        CD_NAME                 CHAR VARYING(32) NOT NULL,
        RELEASE_DATE            DATE FORMAT "DD MON, YEAR" MASK "MM/DD/YYYY" NOT NULL,
        PRICE                   MONEY FORMAT "$9,999,990.99" MASK "9999990.00" NOT NULL
);

CREATE TABLE SHOW
(
        SHOW_ID                 INTEGER PRIMARY KEY NOT NULL,
        BAND_ID                 INTEGER FOREIGN KEY REFERENCES BAND NOT NULL,
        VENUE_ID                INTEGER FOREIGN KEY REFERENES VENUE NOT NULL,
        DATE                    DATE FORMAT "DD MON, YEAR" MASK "MM/DD/YYYY" NOT NULL,
        TIME                    CHAR VARYING(16)
                                    FORMAT "90:90:90" MASK "90:90:90"
                                    NOT NULL
);

CREATE TABLE BAND
(
        BAND_ID                 INTEGER PRIMARY KEY NOT NULL,
        GENRE_ID                INTEGER FOREIGN KEY REFERENCES GENRE NOT NULL,
        BAND                    CHAR VARYING(32) UNIQUE NOT NULL,
        FOUNDING_DATE           DATE FORMAT "DD MON, YEAR" MASK "MM/DD/YYYY" NOT NULL
);

CREATE TABLE MUSICIAN
(
        MUSICIAN_ID             INTEGER PRIMARY KEY NOT NULL,
        INSTRUMENT_ID           INTEGER FOREIGN KEY REFERENCES INSTRUMENT NOT NULL,
        BAND_ID                 INTEGER FOREIGN KEY REFERENCES BAND WITH NULL,
        MUSICIAN                CHAR VARYING(32) UNIQUE NOT NULL,
        PHONE                   CHAR VARYING(32) NULL,
```

```
          EMAIL              CHAR VARYING(32) NULL,
          SKILLS             CHAR VARYING(256) NULL
);

CREATE TABLE ADVERTISEMENT
(
          ADVERTISEMENT_ID   INTEGER PRIMARY KEY NOT NULL,
          BAND_ID            INTEGER FOREIGN KEY REFERENCES BAND WITH NULL,
          MUSICIAN_ID        INTEGER FOREIGN KEY REFERENCES MUSICIAN WITH NULL,
          DATE               DATE FORMAT "DD MON, YEAR" MASK "MM/DD/YYYY" NOT NULL,
          TEXT               MEMO NOT NULL
);
```

Try It Out — Field Level Business Rules for a Data Warehouse Database Model

Figure 12-9 shows an ERD for the musician's data warehouse database model. Here's a basic approach to business rules field settings:

1. Individual field business rules (including defaults, CHECK constraints, display formats, and input masks)

2. Encoding business rules using some kind of stored database coding, if and where appropriate (usually CHECK constraint functions).

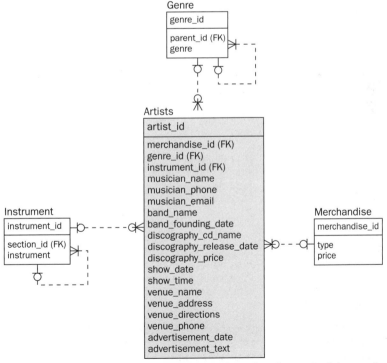

Figure 12-9: Musicians, bands, and their online advertisements data warehouse database model.

How It Works

There are no appropriate CHECK constraints and no appropriate stored encoding. Remember that input to a data warehouse is unlikely to be manual input, so input MASK settings and CHECK constraints generally do not apply. Additionally, UNIQUE constraints are not needed either (they are overhead) when data is application generated anyway. This script contains appropriate changes:

```
CREATE TABLE INSTRUMENT
(
        INSTRUMENT_ID           INTEGER PRIMARY KEY NOT NULL,
        SECTION_ID              INTEGER FOREIGN KEY REFERENCES INSTRUMENT WITH NULL,
        INSTRUMENT              CHAR VARYING(32) NOT NULL
);

CREATE TABLE MUSICIAN
(
        MUSICIAN_ID             INTEGER PRIMARY KEY NOT NULL,
        MUSICIAN                CHAR VARYING(32) NOT NULL,
        PHONE                   CHAR VARYING(32) NULL,
        EMAIL                   CHAR VARYING(32) NULL
);

CREATE TABLE GENRE
(
        GENRE_ID                INTEGER PRIMARY KEY NOT NULL,
        PARENT_ID               INTEGER FOREIGN KEY REFERENCES GENRE WITH NULL,
        GENRE                   CHAR VARYING(32) NOT NULL
);

CREATE TABLE BAND
(
        BAND_ID                 INTEGER PRIMARY KEY NOT NULL,
        BAND                    CHAR VARYING(32) NOT NULL,
        FOUNDING_DATE           DATE FORMAT "DD MON, YEAR" NOT NULL
);

CREATE TABLE ADVERTISEMENT
(
        ADVERTISEMENT_ID        INTEGER PRIMARY KEY NOT NULL,
        DATE                    DATE FORMAT "DD MON, YEAR" NOT NULL,
        TEXT                    MEMO NOT NULL
);

CREATE TABLE DISCOGRAPHY
(
        DISCOGRAPHY_ID          INTEGER PRIMARY KEY NOT NULL,
        CD_NAME                 CHAR VARYING(32) NOT NULL,
        RELEASE_DATE            DATE FORMAT "DD MON, YEAR" NULL,
        PRICE                   MONEY FORMAT "$9,999,990.99" NULL
);

CREATE TABLE MERCHANDISE
(
        MERCHANDISE_ID          INTEGER PRIMARY KEY NOT NULL,
        TYPE                    CHAR VARYING(32) NOT NULL,
```

```
        PRICE                   MONEY FORMAT "$9,999,990.99" NOT NULL
);

CREATE TABLE SHOW_VENUE
(
        SHOW_ID                 INTEGER PRIMARY KEY NOT NULL,
        LOCATION                CHAR VARYING(32) NOT NULL,
        ADDRESS_LINE_1          CHAR VARYING(32) NOT NULL,
        ADDRESS_LINE_2          CHAR VARYING(32) NULL,
        TOWN                    CHAR VARYING(32) NOT NULL,
        ZIP                     NUMBER(5) FORMAT "99999" NULL,
        POSTAL_CODE             CHAR VARYING(32) NULL,
        COUNTRY                 CHAR VARYING(32) NULL,
        DIRECTIONS              MEMO NULL,
        PHONE                   CHAR VARYING(32) NULL
        SHOW_DATE               DATE FORMAT "$9,999,990.99" NOT NULL,
        SHOW_TIME               CHAR VARYING(16) FORMAT "90:90:90" NOT NULL
);

CREATE TABLE FACT
(
        FACT_ID                 INTEGER NOT NULL,
        SHOW_ID                 INTEGER FOREIGN KEY REFERENCES SHOW WITH NULL,
        MUSICIAN_ID             INTEGER FOREIGN KEY REFERENCES MUSICIAN WITH NULL,
        BAND_ID                 INTEGER FOREIGN KEY REFERENCES BAND WITH NULL,
        ADVERTISEMENT_ID        INTEGER FOREIGN KEY REFERENCES ADVERTISEMENT
                                        WITH NULL,
        DISCOGRAPHY_ID          INTEGER FOREIGN KEY REFERENCES DISCOGRAPHY
                                        WITH NULL,
        MERCHANDISE_ID          INTEGER FOREIGN KEY REFERENCES MERCHANDISE
                                        WITH NULL,
        GENRE_ID                INTEGER FOREIGN KEY REFERENCES GENRE WITH NULL,
        INSTRUMENT_ID           INTEGER FOREIGN KEY REFERENCES INSTRUMENT WITH NULL,
        CD_SALE_AMOUNT          MONEY FORMAT "$9,999,990.99" NULL,
        MERCHANDISE_SALE_AMOUNT MONEY FORMAT "$9,999,990.99" NULL,
        ADVERTISING_COST_AMOUNT MONEY FORMAT "$9,999,990.99" NULL,
        SHOW_TICKET_SALES_AMOUNT MONEY FORMAT "$9,999,990.99" NULL
);
```

Summary

In this chapter, you learned about:

❑ How basic database model business rules classifications are normalization, Normal Forms, tables, and relations

❑ How more complex business rules can be implemented in a database model using field settings, such as display FORMATs, input MASKings, CHECK constraints, UNIQUE key constraints, and DEFAULT settings

❑ How stored database code can be used to implement highly complex business rules, using stored procedures, stored functions and event triggers

This chapter ends the case study of the OLTP and data warehouse database models using the online auction house. This chapter has refined the implementation of business rules to the hilt by applying field-level attributes and settings as being part of table field structure. Additionally, very advanced business rules can be applied using stored database coding (encoding). The next chapter discusses hardware resources, as applied to database modeling.

Part IV

Advanced Topics

In this Part:

Advanced Database Structures and Hardware Resources

This final chapter of this book wraps up the database modeling design process, delving a bit into some advanced aspects of the implementation process. Implementation is essentially the actual database building process. When you build a database, as opposed to just the database model, you create the database itself. During the database-creation process, implementing the database model, you might want to consider various other factors. These other factors include specialized database model structures (other than tables and indexes). Additionally, there are certain hardware issues such as how big of a computer do you need? Other than hardware, there are certain database installation issues to consider, with respect to configuration. Configuration can affect various factors, such as how fast your database ultimately performs. Or how much recoverability do you need? How often should backups be executed?

> Configuration is computer jargon used to describe the way in which a computer system, or part thereof (such as a database) is installed and set up. For example, when you start up a Windows computer, all your desktop icons are part of the configuration of you starting up your computer. What the desktop icons are, and where on your desktop they are placed, are stored in a configuration file on your computer somewhere. When you start up your computer, the Windows software retrieves that configuration file, interprets its contents, and displays all your icons on the screen for you.

This chapter essentially appears at the culmination of database model analysis and design; however, its contents should in the very least be considered as a part of the design process, before going ahead and purchasing hardware, and creating the physical database itself.

By the end of this chapter, you will realize that database modeling is not just about creating tables, getting the correct relationships between them, and doing lots of hairy stuff with fields. Between the database modeling phase and the creation of a database, you might want to consider materialized views for a data warehouse, for example. Or, perhaps you might consider a specialized type of hardware configuration using something called a RAID array.

In this chapter, you learn about the following:

- ❏ Views
- ❏ Materialized views
- ❏ Different types of indexes
- ❏ Auto counters
- ❏ Partitioning and parallel processing
- ❏ Hardware factors (including memory usage, as applied to OLTP or data warehouse databases)
- ❏ RAID arrays
- ❏ Standby databases
- ❏ Replication
- ❏ Grid computing and clustering

Advanced Database Structures

This section covers those logical objects in a relational database, either overlaying one or more tables or making duplicates of records in one or more tables. Objects of interest are views, materialized views, index types and clustering, auto counters, and, finally, partitioning and parallel processing.

What and Where?

"What and where" implies what objects can be used, and in which scenarios. These specialized objects do fall under the guise of database modeling design because they are generally used to enhance a database model, and its attendant applications, in one way or another. Enhancements imply easier usability, easier access, controlled access, better performance, and the list goes on. Examine the practical applications of each of these additional specialized database objects in turn, in terms of where they can and should be used.

Views

A *view* overlays underlying records in tables. It does not copy records from tables. A view contains a query that reads underlying tables when the view is accessed, and is accessed in a query in exactly the same way that a table is.

Views can cause performance problems because they are often inappropriately used. The most appropriate use of views is to implement table and field level security. You can restrict users to examining only specific fields in a table, for example. One of the most problematic uses of views is to ease and speed the development process. What typically happens is that developers will use a view, and filter over the top of the view with WHERE clauses. If the view executes a full table scan, even a single record retrieved from a view accessing 1 million records from an underlying table will still effectively read all 1 million records. That's a serious waste of resources!

Materialized Views

A *materialized view* copies records from one or more underlying tables. Unlike a view, when a query is executed against a materialized view, the materialized view is physically accessed, rather than the underlying tables.

Materialized views aggregate large data sets down to smaller sized hierarchical layers. Materialized views are nearly always utilized in data warehouses and data marts. They can also be used to make simple duplicates for backup and performance separation of data sets.

Views are not the same as materialized views. Views are logical overlays of tables, without actually physically copying data. Materialized views are duplications of data. Views will always interfere with underlying source tables; materialized views will not, unless being refreshed. Views often cause far more in the way of performance problems than the application design issues that they might seek to ease.

Indexes

The standard use *index* in relational databases is a *BTree (binary tree) index*. A BTree index allows for rapid tree traversal searching through an upside-down tree structure. Reading a single record from a very large table using a BTree index, can often result in a few block reads — even when index and table are millions of blocks in size. *Bitmap indexes* allow rapid searches into heavily duplicated field values, such as M for Male and F for Female. Another type of index is called either a *clustered index*, or an *index-organized table (IOT)*, depending on the database engine. An IOT or a clustered index is a table sorted and stored in the structure of a BTree index.

BTree indexes should be used in most cases, especially for unique key values. Bitmap indexes and clustered indexes are best suited for read-only databases such as data warehouses. In general, any index structure other than a BTree index is subject to overflow. *Overflow* is where any changes made to tables (such as adding new records) will not have records added into the original index structure, but rather tacked onto the end. Subsequent searches will likely bounce all over the disk — unpleasant for performance to say the least.

Clusters

A *cluster* allows a single table or multiple table partial copy of records, from underlying tables. Clusters are usually used for read-only applications in data warehouses.

Clusters have been somewhat superseded by materialized views. Also, a cluster is not the same as a clustered index or IOT. A cluster creates physical clustered copies of tables. A clustered index does the same thing, except with an index and a table.

Auto Counters

An *auto counter* allows automated generation of sequences of numbers, usually one after the other, such as 101, 102, 103, and so on. Some database engines call auto counters *sequences*. Auto counters are usually used to generate surrogate primary key field values.

Partitioning and Parallel Processing

Partitioning allows splitting of physical table spaces into separate physical chunks. Typically, *parallel processing* functions best when executing against multiple physical table partitions concurrently (simultaneously).

Partitioning and parallel processing can be advantageous for both OLTP and data warehouse databases; however, it is most commonly used in large data warehouses. Partitioning and parallel processing are suited to fairly large amounts of data to realize performance improvements.

Non-BTree indexes, materialized views, clusters, and partitioning are specialized database object structures. They are generally only available in high-end relational database engines, such as SQL Server, Ingres, Oracle, and DB2.

Understanding Views

Figure 13-1 shows a copy of the OLTP database model for one of the Try It Out sections in Chapter 12.

This is a simple view of all advertisements, placed by all musicians, for the month of June, 2005:

```
CREATE VIEW MUSICIAN_ADVERTS AS
    SELECT M.MUSICIAN, M.PHONE, M.EMAIL, A.TEXT "Advertisement"
    FROM MUSICIAN M JOIN ADVERTISEMENT A USING (MUSICIAN_ID)
    WHERE A.DATE BETWEEN "01-JUN-2005" AND "30-JUN-2005";
```

Records can be read from the preceding view with a query like this:

```
SELECT * FROM MUSICIAN_ADVERTS;
```

Here's another example view, but this time retrieving from four tables (a join). Also there is no filter (WHERE clause) as in the preceding query:

```
CREATE VIEW ADVERTS AS
    SELECT M.MUSICIAN, M.PHONE, M.EMAIL, A.TEXT "Advertisement"
    FROM INSTRUMENT I JOIN MUSICIAN M USING (INSTRUMENT_ID)
        JOIN BAND USING (BAND_ID)
            JOIN ADVERTISEMENT A USING (MUSICIAN_ID, BAND_ID);
```

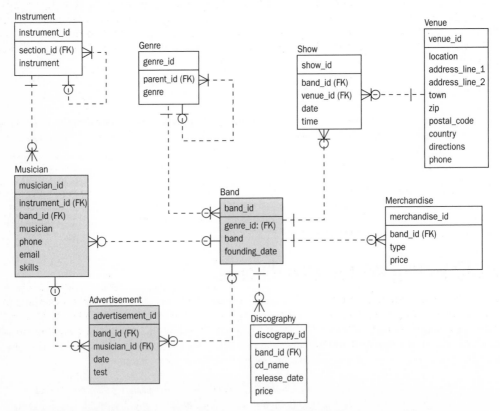

Figure 13-1: Musicians, bands, and online advertisements OLTP database model.

This query reads all the records from the previous view:

```
SELECT * FROM ADVERTS;
```

The following query reads one or only a few records from the view, but because it is reading a view, the underlying view will read all records from the table. This is extremely inefficient and a complete waste of processing time.

```
SELECT * FROM ADVERTS WHERE MUSICIAN = "Jim Bean";
```

The preceding query, reading records from the ADVERTS query, is a perfect example of misuse of views. These next example views are a more applicable application of use of views, where fields are restricted:

```
CREATE VIEW MUSICIANS_PRIVATE AS
     SELECT M.MUSICIAN, M.PHONE, M.EMAIL, B.BAND
     FROM MUSICIAN M JOIN BAND USING (BAND_ID);

CREATE VIEW MUSICIANS_PUBLIC AS
     SELECT M.MUSICIAN, B.BAND
     FROM MUSICIAN M JOIN BAND USING (BAND_ID);
```

The first view above is for the private use of musicians, allowing access to phone numbers and email addresses of all musicians. The second query is restricted, where only bands and their associated musicians can be examined. In other words, you don't want the general public to have complete access to the private phone numbers and email addresses of all musicians. This is a much more sensible use of views. What you would then want to do is to grant and revoke specific access rights to different types of users, as shown in the following command, which removes all access privileges from all users, for all tables and views:

```
REVOKE ALL FROM MUSICIAN, BAND;
```

A command such as the following allows only musicians and bands to examine their own personal data (MUSICIANS and BANDS are database users):

```
GRANT SELECT ON MUSICIANS_PRIVATE TO MUSICIANS, BANDS;
```

The following command allows all of the general public to look at only the publicly available fields and records (personal information is excluded):

```
GRANT SELECT ON MUSICIANS_PUBLIC TO EVERYONE;
```

Understanding Materialized Views

Materialized views are most often used to create hierarchical structures of aggregation in data warehouse databases. Figure 13-2 shows an enhanced copy of the data warehouse database model for one of the Try It Out sections in Chapter 11. Figure 13-2 is enhanced by the addition of the data warehouse standard TIME and LOCATION dimensions.

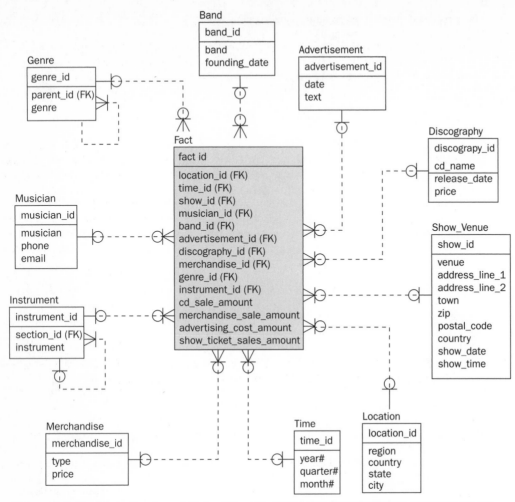

Figure 13-2: Musicians, bands, and their online advertisements data warehouse database model.

It is common practice to create a nested materialized view structure for a data warehouse database. Why? Because, typically, reporting on a data warehouse requires aggregations, such as summaries, on different levels. Where one user might want a summary by country, another may want one by state, and another by city; therefore, a nested materialized view structure could be created to summarize table records into cities, summarize the aggregated city materialized view into states, and the aggregated state materialized view into countries. In other words, materialized views in a nested structure can use data from less aggregated materialized views more efficiently than reading all the table records all over again. One method of creating a nested hierarchy of materialized views is to join all dimensions to the single fact table in a star schema, as a single, huge join query. This is shown in the following script for the data warehouse model of Figure 13-2:

```
CREATE MATERIALIZED VIEW MV_MUSIC
    ENABLE REFRESH ENABLE QUERY REWRITE
SELECT F.*, I.*, MU.*, F.*, B.*, A.*, D.*, SV.*, ME.*, T.*, L.*
FROM FACT F JOIN INSTRUMENT I ON (I.INSTRUMENT_ID = A.INSTRUMENT_ID)
  JOIN MUSICIAN MU ON (MU.MUSICIAN_ID = F.MUSICIAN_ID)
```

```
       JOIN GENRE G ON (G.GENRE_ID = F.GENRE_ID)
        JOIN BAND B ON (B.BAND_ID = F.BAND_ID)
         JOIN ADVERTISEMENT A ON (A.ADVERTISEMENT_ID = F.ADVERTISEMENT_ID)
          JOIN DISCOGRAPHY D ON (D.DISCOGRAPHY_ID = F.DISCOGRAPHY_ID)
           JOIN SHOW_VENUE SV ON (SV.SHOW_ID = F.SHOW_ID)
            JOIN MERCHANDISE ON (M.MERCHANDISE_ID = F.MERCHANDISE_ID)
             JOIN TIME ON (T.TIME_ID = F.TIME_ID)
              JOIN LOCATION ON (L.LOCATION_ID = F.LOCATION_ID);
```

Why would you want to create a single huge join query, of all facts and dimensions, into a single materialized view of all data, without any aggregation? The answer to that question really comes down to how much data is read from a data warehouse whenever a query is executed. Most data warehouse reports are large. Consequently, they read large amounts of data. The result is that, even though reports will use WHERE clauses, they read so much of the data in the database, that it is extremely likely that tables will be full scanned anyway. In other words, data warehouse reports read large amounts of data and usually do not benefit from reading indexes. When over a small percentage of a table's records are read (usually something between 5 percent and 15 percent of all records), most database engine SQL query optimizers ignore indexes, and read the entire contents of all underlying tables.

The ENABLE REFRESH *and* ENABLE QUERY REWRITE *options allow the materialized view to be automatically refreshed and allow it to be used to rewrite queries.* REFRESH *allows changes to underlying tables to be copied to the dependent materialized view.* QUERY REWRITE *automatically selects a query to read smaller materialized views, rather than larger underlying tables.*

Now you can create multiple hierarchical layers of nested materialized views. This first materialized view creates a summary of CD sales for each month (one sum for each month):

```
CREATE MATERIALIZED VIEW MV_CD_SALES_BY_MONTH
    ENABLE REFRESH ENABLE QUERY REWRITE
SELECT CD_NAME, YEAR#, QUARTER#, MONTH#, SUM(CD_SALE_AMOUNT) "CD_SALE_AMOUNT"
FROM MV_MUSIC
GROUP BY CD_NAME, YEAR#, QUARTER#, MONTH#;
```

Next, create a summary for each quarter — reading the materialized view created previously, the MV_CD_SALES_BY_MONTH materialized view, not the original MV_MUSIC join materialized view:

```
CREATE MATERIALIZED VIEW MV_CD_SALES_BY_QUARTER
    ENABLE REFRESH ENABLE QUERY REWRITE
SELECT CD_NAME, YEAR#, QUARTER#, SUM(CD_SALE_AMOUNT) "CD_SALE_AMOUNT"
FROM MV_CD_SALES_BY_MONTH
GROUP BY CD_NAME, YEAR#, QUARTER#;
```

The SUM(CD_SALE_AMOUNT) *field summary is renamed to* CD_SALE_AMOUNT *in each successive nested materialized view layer. This allows access with the name* CD_SALE_AMOUNT *from the parent materialized view.*

Once again, the next layer is a summary by year:

```
CREATE MATERIALIZED VIEW MV_CD_SALES_BY_YEAR
    ENABLE REFRESH ENABLE QUERY REWRITE
SELECT CD_NAME, YEAR#, SUM(CD_SALE_AMOUNT) "CD_SALE_AMOUNT"
FROM MV_CD_SALES_BY_QUARTER
GROUP BY CD_NAME, YEAR#;
```

And, finally, comes a summary of all CD sales, for each CD, regardless of year, month, or quarter:

```
CREATE MATERIALIZED VIEW MV_CD_SALES_BY_CD
    ENABLE REFRESH ENABLE QUERY REWRITE
SELECT CD_NAME, SUM(CD_SALE_AMOUNT) "CD_SALE_AMOUNT"
FROM MV_CD_SALES_BY_YEAR
GROUP BY CD_NAME;
```

When a query is executed reading records from the FACT table, joining with dimensions, the materialized views will be read because query rewrite changes the query, reading a materialized view, not underlying tables. Consider this query:

```
SELECT CD_NAME, YEAR#, SUM(CD_SALE_AMOUNT)
FROM FACT F JOIN DISCOGRAPHY ON (D.DISCOGRAPHY_ID = F. DISCOGRAPHY_ID)
    JOIN TIME T ON (T.TIME_ID = F.TIME_ID)
GROUP BY CD_NAME, YEAR#;
```

The preceding query may actually be executed as the following query, if the database engine allows QUERY REWRITE:

```
SELECT CD_NAME, YEAR#, CD_SALE_AMOUNT
FROM MV_SALES_BY_YEAR;
```

The previous query reads summary records from the materialized view in the nested materialized view structure, reading the MV_SALES_BY_YEAR materialized view. If there are 1 million fact records, spread over a period of 5 years, with 20 different CDs, the preceding query only reads 100 records instead of 1 million records. That is a seriously reduced quantity of I/O activity, don't you think? That is the primary benefit of using materialized views.

> Let's repeat the concepts of materialized views and query rewrite, just to make sure that the benefits of using materialized views are fully understood. Materialized views create copies of data, even of each other. When reading a materialized view, the materialized view copy is read, not underlying tables, or any other underlying materialized views. Query rewrite allows a query against an underlying table, to be satisfied by reading a materialized view. It rewrites the query internally in the database engine (it automatically rewrites the query for you). Remember, a materialized view copies data from underlying structures; a view does not. A view contains a query to be executed whenever the view is accessed, reading underlying structures (tables). A materialized view creates copies of data; a view does not!

Understanding Types of Indexes

The easiest way to understanding different indexes, how they work and where they apply, is perhaps to show you how some of the different index types work.

BTree Index

Figure 13-3 shows a picture of the internal structure of a BTree index, created in a surrogate primary key integer field of a table. Block 1 is the *root block*. Integers placed in the root block point to subsidiary *branch blocks*. The branch blocks contain links to *leaf blocks*. The root and branch blocks contain only pointers to subsidiary branch and leaf blocks, respectively. The leaf blocks contain primary key values and pointers to the primary key records in the table for which the index is built. Only four example leaf blocks are shown in Figure 13-3. The rest are not shown and left to your imagination. Block 1 has three records: 1, 100, and 105. Record 1 in Block 1 has two subsidiary branch blocks: Block 2 and Block 3. Block 2 has three branch values: 1, 10, and 25 record. Record 1 points to Block 8, containing all the records between 1 and 9 (10 is in Block 9).

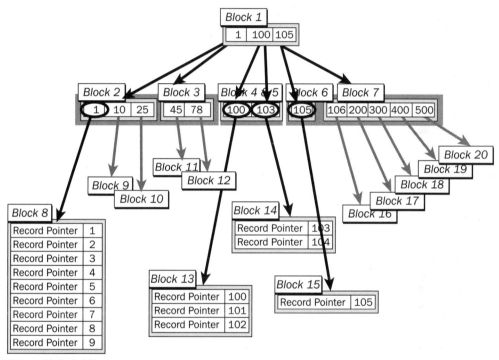

Figure 13-3: A BTree index for an integer surrogate primary key field.

That is how a BTree index is structured. Tree traversals can be used to find records in the BTree index shown in Figure 13-3. When searching for record primary key value 101, Block 1 is read, pointing to branches of Block 4 and Block 5, based on the second value in Block 1 (100). It should be plain to see that Block 4 contains values from 100 to 102. (Block 5 contains 103.) So, Block 4 is read. Block 4 contains the value 100, pointing to Block 13. Block 13 is a leaf block and contains the actual records for Block 4: 100, 101, and 102. Out of all the 20 blocks in the index, only three blocks are read to find record key number 101. In very large tables, BTree index single record searches (or very small range searches) can cut down drastically on I/O activity.

Bitmap Index

Figure 13-4 shows a picture of a bitmap index. Essentially, a bitmap is created on a field, based on the unique values in that field, across all records. In the bitmap index shown in Figure 13-4, when the COUNTRY is Canada, only the COUNTRY="Canada" field is set to 1 (meaning ON); all others COUNTRY="..." fields are set to 0 (meaning OFF).

It is sensible to use bitmap indexes when there are few distinct values, in relation to the total number of records in a table. In other words, creating a bitmap index on the STATE or CITY fields makes much less sense than creating bitmap indexes on either the REGION or COUNTRY fields.

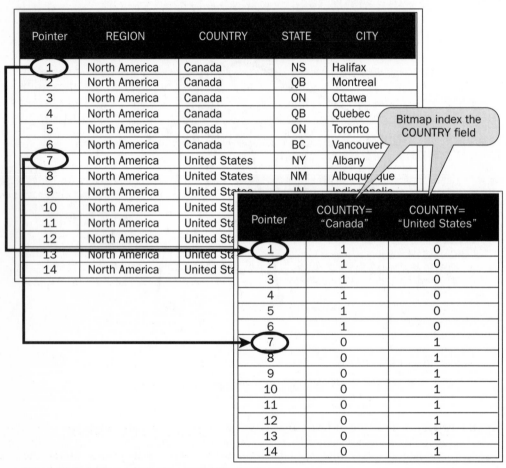

Figure 13-4: A bitmap index for a repetitive field value.

Hash Keys and ISAM Keys

There are other, less commonly used indexes, such as hash keys and Indexed Sequential Access Method (ISAM) keys. Both are somewhat out of date in the larger-scale relational database engines; however, Microsoft Access does make use of a mixture of ISAM/BTree indexing techniques, in its JET database. Both ISAM and hash indexes are not good for heavily changing data because their structures will overflow with newly introduced records. Similar to bitmap indexes, hash and ISAM keys must be rebuilt regularly to maintain their advantage in processing speed advantage. Frequent rebuilds minimize on performance killing overflow.

Clusters, Index Organized Tables, and Clustered Indexes

Clusters are used to contain fields from tables, usually a join, where the cluster contains a physical copy of a small portion of the fields in a table — perhaps the most commonly accessed fields. Essentially, clusters have been somewhat superseded by materialized views. A clustered index (index organized table, or IOT) is a more complex type of a cluster where all the fields in a single table are reconstructed, not in a usual heap structure, but in the form of a BTree index. In other words, for an IOT, the leaf blocks in the diagram shown in Figure 13-3 would contain not only the indexed field value, but also all the rest of the fields in the table (not just the primary key values).

Understanding Auto Counters

Sequences are commonly used to create internally generated (transparent) counters for surrogate primary keys. Auto counters are called sequences in some database engines. This command would create a sequence object:

```
CREATE SEQUENCE BAND_ID_SEQUENCE START=1 INCREMENT=1 MAX=INFINITY;
```

Then you could use the previous sequence to generate primary keys for the BAND table (see Figure 13-1), as in the following INSERT command, creating a new band called "The Big Noisy Rocking Band."

```
INSERT INTO BAND (BAND_ID, GENRE_ID, BAND, FOUNDING_DATE)
VALUES
(
    BAND_ID_SEQUENCE.NEXT,
    (SELECT GENRE_ID FROM GENRE WHERE GENRE="Rock"),
    "The Big Noisy Rocking Band", 25-JUN-2005
);
```

Understanding Partitioning and Parallel Processing

Partitioning is just that — it partitions. It separates tables into separate physical partitions. The idea is that processing can be executed against individual partitions and even in parallel against multiple partitions at the same time. Imagine a table with 1 million records. Reading those 1 million records can take an inordinately horrible amount of time; however, dividing that 1 million record table into 100 separate physical partitions can allow queries to read much fewer records. This, of course, assumes that records are read within the structure of partition separation. As in previous sections of this chapter, the easiest way to explain partitioning, what it is, and how it works, is to just demonstrate it. The diagram in Figure 13-5 shows the splitting of a data warehouse fact table in separate partitions.

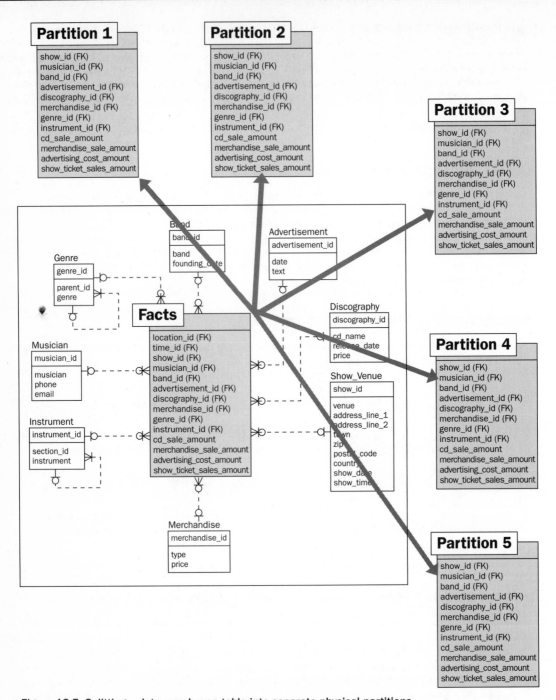

Figure 13-5: Splitting a data warehouse table into separate physical partitions.

In some database engines, you can even split materialized views into partitions, in the same way as tables can be partitioned. The fact table shown in Figure 13-5 is (as fact tables should be) all referencing surrogate primary keys, as foreign keys to dimensions. It is easier to explain some of the basics of partitioning using the materialized view created earlier in this chapter. The reason is because the materialized view contains the descriptive dimensions, as well as the surrogate key integer values. In other words, even though not technically correct, it is easier to demonstrate partitioning on dimensional descriptions, such as a region of the world (North America, South America, and so on), as opposed to partitioning based on an inscrutable LOCATION_ID foreign key value. This is the materialized view created earlier:

```
CREATE MATERIALIZED VIEW MV_MUSIC
    ENABLE REFRESH ENABLE QUERY REWRITE
SELECT F.*, I.*, MU.*, F.*, B.*, A.*, D.*, SV.*, ME.*, T.*, L.*
FROM FACT A JOIN INSTRUMENT I ON (I.INSTRUMENT_ID = A.INSTRUMENT_ID)
 JOIN MUSICIAN MU ON (MU.MUSICIAN_ID = F.MUSICIAN_ID)
  JOIN GENRE G ON (G.GENRE_ID = F.GENRE_ID)
   JOIN BAND B ON (B.BAND_ID = F.BAND_ID)
    JOIN ADVERTISEMENT A ON (A.ADVERTISEMENT_ID = F.ADVERTISEMENT_ID)
     JOIN DISCOGRAPHY D ON (D.DISCOGRAPHY_ID = F.DISCOGRAPHY_ID)
      JOIN SHOW_VENUE SV ON (SV.SHOW_ID = F.SHOW_ID)
       JOIN MERCHANDISE ON (M.MERCHANDISE_ID = F.MERCHANDISE_ID)
        JOIN TIME ON (T.TIME_ID = F.TIME_ID)
         JOIN LCOATION ON (L.LOCATION_ID = F.LOCATION_ID);
```

Now, partition the materialized view based on regions of the world — this one is called a *list partition*:

```
CREATE TABLE PART_MV_REGIONAL PARTITION BY LIST (REGION)
(
    PARTITION PART_AMERICAS VALUES ("North America","South America"),
    PARTITION PART_ASIA VALUES ("Middle East","Far East","Near East"),
    PARTITION PART_EUROPE VALUES ("Europe","Russian Federation"),
    PARTITION PART_OTHER VALUES (DEFAULT)
) AS SELECT * FROM MV_MUSIC;
```

The DEFAULT *option implies all regions not in the ones listed so far.*

Another type of partition is a *range partition* where each separate partition is limited by a range of values, for each partition. This partition uses the release date of CDs stored in the field called DISCOGRAPHY.RELEASE_DATE:

```
CREATE TABLE PART_CD_RELEASE PARTITION BY RANGE (RELEASE_DATE)
(
    PARTITION PART_2002 VALUES LESS THAN (1-JAN-2003),
    PARTITION PART_2003 VALUES LESS THAN (1-JAN-2004),
    PARTITION PART_2004 VALUES LESS THAN (1-JAN-2005),
    PARTITION PART_2005 VALUES LESS THAN (MAXIMUM),
) AS SELECT * FROM MV_MUSIC;
```

The MAXIMUM *option implies all dates into the future, from January 1, 2005, and beyond the year 2005.*

You can also create indexes on partitions. Those indexes can be created as locally identifiable to each partition, or globally to all partitions created for a table, or materialized view. That is partitioning. There are other more complex methods of partitioning, but these other methods are too detailed for this book.

That's all you need to know about advanced database structures. Take a quick peek at the physical side of things in the guise of hardware resources.

Understanding Hardware Resources

This section briefly examines some facts about hardware, including some specialized database server architectural structures, such as RAID arrays and Grid computing.

How Much Hardware Can You Afford?

Windows computers are cheap, but they have a habit of breaking. UNIX boxes (computers are often called "boxes") are expensive and have excellent reliability. I have heard of cases of UNIX servers running for years, with no problems whatsoever. Typically, a computer system is likely to remain stable as long as it is not tampered with. The simple fact is that Windows boxes are much more easily tampered with than UNIX boxes, so perhaps Windows machines have an undeserved poor reputation, as far as reliability is concerned.

How Much Memory Do You Need?

OLTP databases are memory- and processor-intensive. Data warehouse databases are I/O-intensive, and other than heavy processing power, couldn't care less how much RAM is allocated. The heavy type of memory usage for a relational database usually has a lot to do with concurrency and managing the load of large number of users, accessing your database all at the same time. That's all about concurrency and much more applicable to OLTP databases, rather than data warehouse databases. For an OLTP database, quite often the more RAM you have, the better. Note, however, that sizing up buffer cache values to the maximum amount of RAM available is pointless, even for an OLTP database. The more RAM allocated for use by a database, the more complex those buffers become for a database to manage.

In short, data warehouses do not need a lot of memory to temporarily store the most heavily used tables in the database into RAM. There is no point, as data warehouses tend to read lots of data from lots of tables, occasionally. RAM is not as important in a data warehouse as it is in an OLTP database.

Now, briefly examine some specialized aspects of hardware usage, more from an architectural perspective.

Understanding Specialized Hardware Architectures

This section examines the following:

- RAID arrays
- Standby databases
- Replication
- Grids and computer clustering

RAID Arrays

The acronym RAID stands for Redundant Array of Inexpensive Disks. That means a bunch of small, cheap disks. Some RAID array hardware setups are cheap. Some are astronomically expensive. You get what you pay for, and you can purchase what suits your requirements. RAID arrays can give huge performance benefits for both OLTP and data warehouse databases.

Some of the beneficial factors of using RAID arrays are recoverability (mirroring), fast random access (striping and multiple disks with multiple bus connections — higher throughput capacity), and parallel I/O activity where more than one disk can be accessed at the same time (concurrently). There are numerous types of RAID array architectures, with the following being the most common:

- *RAID 0* — RAID 0 is striping. *Striping* splits files into pieces, spreading them over multiple disks. RAID 0 gives fast random read and write access, and is thus appropriate for OLTP databases. Rapid recoverability and redundancy is not catered for. RAID 0 is a little risky because of lack of recoverability. Data warehouses that need to be highly contiguous (data on disk is all in one place) are not catered for by random access; however, RAID 0 can sometimes be appropriate for data warehouses, where large I/O executions utilize parallel processing, accessing many disks simultaneously.

- *RAID 1* — RAID 1 is mirroring. *Mirroring* makes multiple copies of files, duplicating database changes at the I/O level on disk. Mirroring allows for excellent recoverability capabilities. RAID 1 can sometimes cause I/O bottleneck problems because of all the constant I/O activity associated with mirroring, especially with respect to frequently written tables — creating mirrored hot blocks. A *hot block* is a block in a file that is accessed more heavily than the hardware can cope with. Everything is trying to read and write that hot block at the same time. RAID 1 can provide recoverability for OLTP databases, but can hurt performance. RAID 1 is best used in data warehouses where mirroring allows parallel read execution, of more than one mirror, at the same time.

- *RAID 0+1* — RAID 0+1 combines the best of both worlds from RAID 0 and RAID 1 — using both striping and mirroring. Both OLTP and data warehouse I/O performance will be slowed somewhat, but RAID 0+1 can provide good all-around recoverability and performance, perhaps offering the best of both worlds, for both OLTP and data warehouse databases.

- *RAID 5* — RAID 5 is essentially a minimized form of mirroring, duplicating only parity and not the real data. RAID 5 is effective with expensive RAID architectures, containing large chunks of purpose-built, RAID-array contained, onboard buffering RAM memory.

Those are some of the more commonly implemented RAID array architectures. It is not necessary for you to understand the details but more important that you know this stuff actually exists.

Standby Databases

A *standby database* is a failover database. A standby database has minimal activity, usually only adding new records, changing existing records, and deleting existing records. Some database engines do allow for more sophisticated standby database architectures, but once again, the intention in this chapter is to inform you of the existence of standby databases.

Figure 13-6 shows a picture of how standby databases work. A primary database in Silicon Valley (San Jose) is used to service applications, catering to all changes to a database. In Figure 13-6, two standby databases are used, one in New York and one in Orlando. The simplest form of change tracking is used to transfer changes from primary to standby databases. The simplest form of transfer is log entries. Most larger database engines have log files, containing a complete history of all transactions.

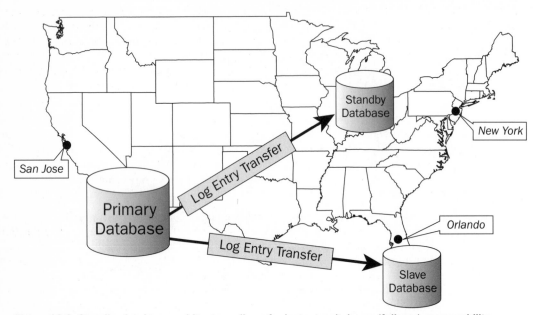

Figure 13-6: Standby database architecture allows for instant switchover (failover) recoverability.

Log files allow for recoverability of a database. Log files store all changes to a database. If you had to recover a database from backup files that are a week old, the database could be recovered by applying all changes stored in log files (for the last week). The result of one week-old cold backups, plus log entries for the last week, would be an up-to-date database.

The most important use of standby database architecture is for that of failover. In other words, if the primary database fails (such as when someone pulls the plug, or San Jose is struck by a monstrous earthquake), the standby database automatically takes over. In the case of Figure 13-6, if the big one struck near San Jose, the standby database in New York or Orlando would automatically failover, assuming all responsibilities, and become the new primary database. What is implied by failover is that a standby database takes over the responsibilities of servicing applications, immediately—perhaps even within a few seconds. The purest form of standby database architecture is as a more or less instant response backup, generally intended to maintain full service to end-users.

Some relational database engines allow standby databases to be utilized in addition to that of being just a failover option. Standby databases can sometimes be used as read-only, *slightly behind*, reporting databases. Some database engines even allow standby databases to be changeable, as long as structure and content from the primary database is not disturbed. In other words, a standby database could contain extra and additional tables and data, on top of what is being sent from the primary database.

Typically, this scenario is used for more sophisticated reporting techniques, and possibly standby databases can even be utilized as a basis for a data warehouse database.

Replication

Database replication is a method used to duplicate (replicate) data from a primary or master database, out to a number of other copies of the master database. As you can see in Figure 13-7, the master database replicates (duplicate) changes made on the master, out to two slave databases in New York and Orlando. This is similar in nature to standby database architecture, except that replication is much more powerful, and, unfortunately, more complicated to manage than standby database architecture. Typically, replication is used to distribute data across a wide area network (WAN) for a large organization.

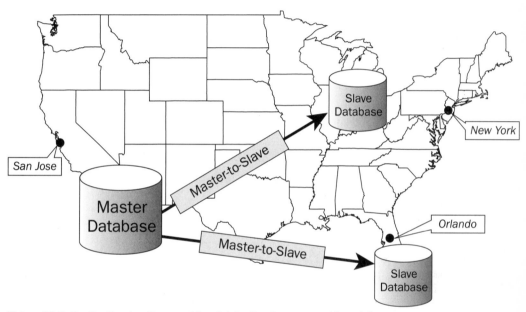

Figure 13-7: Replication is often used for distributing large quantities of data.

Tables and data can't be altered at slave databases — only by changes passed from the master database. In the case of Figure 13-8, a *master-to-master*, rather than *master-to-slave*, configuration is adopted.

A master-to-slave relationship implies that changes can only be passed in one direction, obviously from the master to the slave database; therefore, database changes are distributed from master to slave databases. Of course, being replication, slave databases might need to have changes made to them. However, changes made at slave databases can't be replicated back to the master database.

Figure 13-8 shows just the opposite, where all relationships between all replicated (distributed databases) are master-to-master. A master-to-master replication environment implies that changes made to any database are distributed to all other databases in the replicated environment across the WAN. Master-to-master replication is much more complicated than master-to-slave replication.

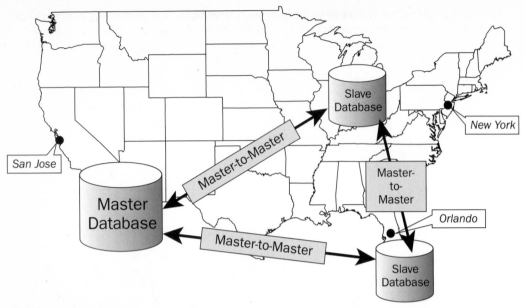

Figure 13-8: Replication can be both master-to-slave and master-to-master.

> Replication is all about distribution of data to multiple sites, typically across a WAN. Standby is intentionally created as failover; however, in some database engines, standby database technology is now so sophisticated, that it is very close in capability to that of even master-to-master replicated databases.

Grids and Computer Clustering

Computer grids are clusters of cheap computers, perhaps distributed on a global basis, connected using even something as loosely connected as the Internet. The Search for Extra Terrestrial Intelligence (SETI) program, where processing is distributed to people's personal home computers (processing when a screensaver is on the screen), is a perfect example of grid computing. Where RAID arrays cluster inexpensive disks, grids can be made of clusters of relatively inexpensive computers. Each computer acts as a portion of the processing and storage power of a large, grid-connected computer, appearing to end users as a single computational processing unit.

Clustering is a term used to describe a similar architecture to that of computer grids, but the computers are generally very expensive, and located within a single data center, for a single organization. The difference between grid computing and clustered computing is purely one of scale — one being massive and the other localized.

Common to both grids and clusters is that computing resources (CPU and storage) are shared transparently. In other words, a developer writing programs to access a database does not even need to know that the computer for which code is being written is in reality a group of computers, built as either a grid or a cluster. Grid Internet-connected computers could be as much as five years old, which is geriatric for a computer — especially a personal computer. They might have all been purchased in a yard sale. If there are enough *senior* computers, and they are connected properly, the grid itself could contain enormous computing power.

Clustered architectures are used by companies to enhance the power of their databases. Grids, on the other hand, are often used to help processing for extremely large and complex problems that perhaps even a super computer might take too long to solve.

Summary

In this chapter, you learned about:

- ❑ Views and how to create them
- ❑ Sensible and completely inappropriate uses of views
- ❑ Materialized views and how to create them
- ❑ Nested materialized views and QUERY REWRITE
- ❑ Different types of indexes (including BTree indexes, bitmap indexes, and clustering)
- ❑ Auto counters and sequences
- ❑ Partitioning and parallel processing
- ❑ Creating list and range partitions
- ❑ Partitioning materialized views
- ❑ Hardware factors (including memory usage as applied to OLTP or data warehouse databases)
- ❑ RAID arrays for mirroring (recoverability) and striping (performance)
- ❑ Standby databases for recoverability and failover
- ❑ Replication of databases to cater to distribution of data
- ❑ Grid computing and clustering to harness as much computing power as possible

This chapter has moved somewhat beyond the realm of database modeling, examining specialized database objects, some brief facts about hardware resources, and finally some specialized database architectures.

Glossary

1st Normal Form (1NF) — Eliminate repeating groups, such that all records in all tables can be identified uniquely, by a primary key in each table. In other words, all fields other than the primary key must depend on the primary key. All Normal Forms are cumulative. (*See* **Normal Forms.**)

1st Normal Form made easy — Remove repeating fields by creating a new table, where the original and new tables are linked together with a master-detail, one-to-many relationship. Create primary keys on both tables, where the detail table will have a composite primary key, containing the master table primary key field as the prefix field of its primary key. That prefix field is also a foreign key back to the master table.

2nd Normal Form (2NF) — All non-key values must be fully functionally dependent on the primary key. No partial dependencies are allowed. A partial dependency exists when a field is fully dependant on a part of a composite primary key. All Normal Forms are cumulative. (*See* **Normal Forms.**)

2nd Normal Form made easy — Performs a seemingly similar function to that of 1st Normal Form, but creates a table, where repeating values (rather than repeating fields) are removed to a new table. The result is a many-to-one relationship rather than a one-to-many relationship (*see* 1st Normal Form), created between the original (master table) and the new tables. The new table gets a primary key consisting of a single field. The master table contains a foreign key pointing back to the primary key of the new table. That foreign key is not part of the primary key in the original table.

3rd Normal Form (3NF) — Eliminate transitive dependencies. What this means is that a field is indirectly determined by the primary key because the field is functionally dependent on another field, where the other field is dependent on the primary key. All Normal Forms are cumulative. (*See* **Normal Forms.**)

3rd Normal Form made easy — Elimination of a transitive dependency, which implies creation of a new table, for something indirectly dependent on the primary key in an existing table.

4th Normal Form (4NF) — Eliminate multiple sets of multi-valued dependencies. All Normal Forms are cumulative. (*See* **Normal Forms.**)

5th Normal Form (5NF) — Eliminate cyclic dependencies. This is also known as *Projection Normal Form* (*PJNF*). All Normal Forms are cumulative. (*See* **Normal Forms.**)

Abstraction — In computer jargon, this implies something created to generalize a number of other things. It is typically used in object models, where an abstract class caters to the shared attributes and methods of inherited classes.

Active data — Information in a database constantly accessed by applications, such as today's transactions, in an OLTP database.

Ad-hoc query — A query sent to a database by an end-user or power user, just trying to get some information quickly. Ad-hoc queries are subjected to a database where the content, structure, and performance of said query, are not necessarily catered for by the database model. The result could be a performance problem, and in extreme cases, even an apparent database halt.

Aggregated query — A query using a GROUP BY clause to create a summary set of records (smaller number of records).

Algorithm — A computer program (or procedure) that is a step-by-step procedure, solving a problem, in a finite number of steps.

Alternate index — An alternate to the primary relational structure of a table, determined by primary and foreign key indexes. Alternate indexes are "alternate" because they are in addition to primary and foreign key indexes, existing as alternate sorting methods to those provided by primary and foreign keys.

Analysis — The initial fact-finding process discovering what is to be done by a computer system.

Anomaly — With respect to relational database design, essentially an erroneous change to data, more specifically to a single record.

ANSI — American National Standards Institute.

Application — A front-end tool used by developers, in-house staff, and end-users to access a database.

Ascending index — An index built sorted in a normally ascending order, such as A, B, C.

Attribute — The equivalent of a relational database field, used more often to describe a similar low-level structure in object structures.

Auto counter — Allows automated generation of sequences of numbers, usually one after the other, such as 101, 102, 103, and so on. Some database engines call these *sequences*.

Backus-Naur form — A syntax notation convention.

BETWEEN — Verifies expressions between a range of two values.

Binary object — Stores data in binary format, typically used for multimedia (images, sound, and so on).

Bitmap index — An index containing binary representations for each record using 0's and 1's. For example, a bitmap index creates two bitmaps for two values of M for Male and F for Female. When M is encountered, the M bitmap is set to 1 and the F bitmap is set to 0.

Black box — Objects or chunks of code that can function independently, where changes made to one part of a piece of software will not affect others.

Boyce-Codd Normal Form (BCNF) — Every determinant in a table is a candidate key. If there is only one candidate key, then 3rd Normal Form and Boyce-Codd Normal Form are one and the same. All Normal Forms are cumulative. (*See* **Normal Forms.**)

BTree index — A binary tree. If drawn out on a piece of paper, a BTree index looks like an upside-down tree. The tree is called "binary" because binary implies two options under each branch node: branch left and branch right. The binary counting system of numbers contains two digits, namely 0 and 1. The result is that a binary tree only ever has two options as leafs within each branch. A BTree consists of a root node, branch nodes and ultimately leaf nodes containing the indexed field values in the ending (or leaf) nodes of the tree.

Budget — A determination of how much something will cost, whether it is cost-effective, whether it is worth the cost, whether it is affordable, and whether it gives the company an edge over the competition without bankrupting the company.

Business processes — The subject areas of a business. The method by which a business is divided up. In a data warehouse, the subject areas become the fact tables.

Business rules — The processes and flow of whatever is involved in the daily workings of an organization. The operation of that business and the decisions made to execute the operational processes of that organization.

Cache — A term commonly applied to buffering data into fast access memory, for subsequent high-speed retrieval.

Candidate key — Also known as a *potential key*, or *permissible key*. A field or combination of fields, which can act as a primary key field for a table. A candidate key uniquely identifies each record in the table.

Cartesian product — A mathematical term describing a set of all the pairs that can be constructed from a given set. Statistically it is known as a *combination*, not a *permutation*. In SQL jargon, a Cartesian Product is also known as a *cross join*.

Cascade — Changes to data in parent tables are propagated to all child tables, containing foreign key field copies of a primary key from the parent table.

Cascade delete — A deletion that occurs when the deletion of a master record automatically deletes all child records in child-related tables, before deleting the record in the master table.

Central Processing Unit (CPU) — The processor (chip) in your computer.

Check constraint — A constraint attached to a field in a database table, as a metadata field setting, and used to validate a given input value.

Class — An object methodology term for the equivalent of a table in a relational database.

Client-server — An environment that was common in the pre-Internet days where a transactional database serviced users within a single company. The number of users could range from as little as one to thousands, depending on the size of the company. The critical factor was actually a mixture of both individual record change activity and modestly sized reports. Client-server database models typically catered for low concurrency and low throughput at the same time, because the number of users was always manageable.

Cluster— Allows a single table or multiple table partial copy of records, from underlying tables. Materialized views have superseded clusters.

Clustered index— *See* **Index organized table.**

Coding— Programming code, in whatever language is appropriate. For example, C is a programming language.

Column— *See* **Field.**

COMMIT— Completes a transaction by storing all changes to a database.

Complex datatype— Typically used in object structures, consisting of a number of fields.

Composite index— Indexes that can be built on more than a single field. Also known as *composite field indexes* or *multiple field indexes*.

Composite key— A primary key, unique key, or foreign key consisting of more than one field.

Concurrent— More than one process executed at the same time means two processes are executing simultaneously, or more than one process accessing the same piece of data at the same time.

Configuration— A computer term used to describe the way in which a computer system (or part thereof, such as a database) is installed and set up. For example, when you start up a Windows computer, all of your desktop icons are part of the configuration (of you starting up your computer). What the desktop icons are, and where on your desktop they are placed, are stored in a configuration file on your computer somewhere. When you start up your computer, the Windows software retrieves that configuration file, interprets it contents, and displays all your icons on the screen for you.

Constraint— A means to constrain, restrict, or apply rules both within and between tables.

Construction— A stage at which you build and test code. For a database model, you build scripts to create tables, referential integrity keys, indexes, and anything else such as stored procedures.

Cross join— *See* **Cartesian product.**

Crow's foot— Used to describe the many sides of a one-to-many or many-to-many relationship. A crows foot looks quite literally like the imprint of a crow's foot in some mud, with three splayed toes.

Cyclic dependency— In the context of the relational database model, X is dependent on Y, which in turn is also dependent on X, directly or indirectly. Cyclic dependence, therefore, indicates a logically circular pattern of interdependence. Cyclic dependence typically occurs with tables containing a composite primary key with three or more fields, where, for example, three fields are related in pairs to each other. In other words, X relates to Y, Y relates to Z, and X relates to Z.

Data — A term applied to organized information.

Data Definition Language (DDL) — Commands used to change metadata. In some databases, these commands require a COMMIT command; in other database engines, this is not the case. When a COMMIT command is not required, these commands automatically commit any pending changes to the database, and cannot be rolled back.

Data Manipulation Language (DML) — Commands that change data in a database. These commands are INSERT, UPDATE, and DELETE. Changes can be committed permanently using the COMMIT command, and undone using the ROLLBACK command. These commands do not commit automatically.

Data mart — A subset part of a data warehouse. Typically, a data mart is made up of a single start schema (a single fact table).

Data warehouse — A large transactional history database used for predictive and planning reporting.

Database — A collection of information, preferably related information, and preferably organized.

Database block — A physical substructure within a database and the smallest physical unit in which data is stored on disk.

Database event — *See* **Trigger.**

Database model — A model used to organize and apply structure to other disorganized information.

Database procedure — *See* **Stored procedure.**

Datatype — Restricts values in fields, such as allowing only a date or a number.

Datestamp — *See* **Timestamp.**

DDL — *See* **Data Definition Language.**

Decimal — Datatypes that contain decimal or non-floating-point real numbers.

Decision Support System (DSS) — Commonly known as *DSS databases*, these support decisions, generally more management-level and even executive-level decision-type of objectives.

DEFAULT — A setting used as an optional value for a field in a record, when a value is not specified.

DELETE — A command that can be used to remove one, some, or all rows from a table.

Delete anomaly — A record cannot be deleted from a master table unless all sibling records are deleted first.

Denormalization — Most often the opposite of normalization, more commonly used in data warehouse or reporting environments. Denormalization decreases granularity by reversing normalization, and otherwise.

Dependency — Something relies on something else.

Descending index — An index sorted in a normally descending order (such as in C, B, A).

Design — Analysis discovers what needs to be done. Design figures out how what has been analyzed, can and should be done.

Determinant — Determines the value of another value. If X determines the value Y (at least partially), then X determines the value of Y, and is thus the determinant of Y.

Dimension table — A descriptive or static data table in a data warehouse.

DISTINCT **clause** — A query SELECT command modifier for retrieving unique rows from a set of records.

DML — *See* **Data Manipulation Language.**

Domain Key Normal Form (DKNF) — The ultimate application of normalization. This is more a measurement of conceptual state, as opposed to a transformation process in itself. All Normal Forms are cumulative. (*See* **Normal Forms.**)

DSS — *See* **Decision Support System.**

Dynamic data — Data that changes significantly, over a short period of time.

Dynamic string — *See* **Variable length string.**

End-user — Ultimate users of a computer system. The clients and staff of a company who actually use software to perform business functions (such as sales people, accountants, and busy executives).

Entity — A relational database modeling term for a table.

Entity Relationship Diagram (ERD) — A diagram that represents the structural contents (the fields) in tables for an entire schema, in a database. Additionally included are schematic representations of relationships between entities, represented by various types of relationships, plus primary and foreign keys.

Event Trigger — *See* **Trigger.**

Expression — In mathematical terms, a single or multi-functional (or valued) value, ultimately equating to a single value, or even another expression.

External procedure — Similar to stored procedures, except they are written in non-database-specific programming language. External procedures are chunks of code written in a language not native to the database engine, such as Java or C++; however, external procedures are still executed from within the database engine itself, perhaps on data within the database.

Fact table — The biggest table in a data warehouse, central to a Star schema, storing the transactional history of a company.

Fact-dimensional structure — *See* **Star schema.**

Field — Part of a table division that imposes structure and datatype specifics onto each of the field values in a record.

Field list — This is the part of a SELECT command listing fields to be retrieved by a query. When more than one field is retrieved, then the fields become a list of fields, or field list.

Fifth Normal Form — *See* **5th Normal Form.**

File system — A term used to describe the files in a database at the operating system level.

Filtered query — *See* **Filtering.**

Filtering — Retrieve a subset of records, or remove a subset of records from the source. Filtering is done in SQL using the WHERE clause for basic query records retrieved, and using the HAVING clause to remove groups from an aggregated query.

First Normal Form — *See* **1st Normal Form.**

Fixed-length records — Every record in a table must have the same byte-length. This generally prohibits use of variable-length datatypes such as variable-length strings.

Fixed length string — The CHAR datatype is a fixed-length string. For example, setting a CHAR(5) datatype to "ABC" will force padding of spaces on to the end of the string up to five characters ("ABC ").

Flat file — A term generally applying to an unstructured file, such as a text file.

Floating point — A real number where the decimal point can be anywhere in the number.

Foreign key — A type of constraint where columns contain copies of primary key values, uniquely identified in parent entities, representing the child or sibling side of what is most commonly a one-to-many relationship.

Formal method — The application of a theory, a set of rules, or a methodology. Used to quantify and apply structure to an otherwise completely disorganized system. Normalization is a formal method used to create a relational database model.

Format display setting — A field setting used to determine the display format of the contents of a field. For example, the datatype definition of INTEGER $9,999,990.99, when set to the value 500, will be displayed as $500.00 (format models can be database specific).

FROM clause — The part of a query SELECT command that determines tables retrieved from, and how tables are joined (when using the JOIN, ON, and USING clauses).

Front-end — Customer facing software. Usually, applications either purchased, online over the Internet, or in-house as custom-written applications.

Full Functional dependence — X determines Y, but X combined with Z does not determine Y. In other words, Y depends on X and X alone. If Y depends on X with anything else then there is not full functional dependence. (*See* **Functional dependency.**)

Full outer join — A query finding the combination of intersection, plus records in the left-sided table, but not in the right-sided table, and records in the right-sided table, not in the left (a combination of both left and right outer joins).

Function — A programming unit or expression returning a single value, also allowing determinant values to be passed in as parameters. Thus, parameter values can change the outcome or return result of a function. The beauty of a function is that it is self-contained and can thus be embedded into an expression.

Functional dependence — Y is functionally dependent on X if the value of Y is determined by X. In other words if Y = X +1, the value of X will determine the resultant value of Y. Thus, Y is dependent on X as a function of the value of X. Functional dependence is the opposite of determinance. (*See* **Full Functional dependence.**)

Generic database model — A database model usually consisting of a partial set of metadata, about metadata; in other words, tables that contain tables which contain data. In modern-day, large, and very busy databases, this can be extremely inefficient.

Granularity — The depth of detail stored, typically applied to a data warehouse. The more granularity the data warehouse contains, the bigger fact tables become because the more records they contain. The safest option is include all historical data down to the lowest level of granularity. This ensures that any possible future requirements for detailed analysis can always be met, without needed data perhaps missing in the future (assuming hardware storage capacity allows it).

Grid computing — Clusters of cheap computers, perhaps distributed on a global basis, connected using even something as loosely connected as the Internet.

GROUP BY **clause** — A clause in the query SELECT command used to aggregate and summarize records into aggregated groups of fewer records.

Hash index — A hashing algorithm is used to organize an index into a sequence, where each indexed value is retrievable based on the result of the hash key value. Hash indexes are efficient with integer values, but are usually subject to overflow as a result of changes.

Heterogeneous system — A computer system consisting of dissimilar elements or parts. In database parlance, this implies a set of applications and databases, where database engines are different. In other words, a company could have a database architecture consisting of multiple database engines, such as Microsoft Access, Sybase, Oracle, Ingres, and so on. All databases, regardless of type, are melded together into a single (apparently one and the same) transparent database-application architecture.

Hierarchical database model — An inverted tree-like structure. The tables of this model take on a child-parent relationship. Each child table has a single parent table, and each parent table can have multiple child tables. Child tables are completely dependent on parent tables; therefore, a child table can only exist if its parent table does. It follows that any entries in child tables can only exist where corresponding parent entries exist in parent tables. The result of this structure is that the hierarchical database model can support one-to-many relationships, but not many-to-many relationships.

Homogeneous system — Everything is the same, such as database engines, application SDKs, and so on.

Hot block — A small section of disk that, when accessed too frequently, can cause too much competition for that specific area. It can result in a serious slow-down in general database and application performance.

Hybrid database — A database installation mixing multiple types of database architectures. Typically, the mix is including both OLTP (high concurrency) and data warehouse (heavy reporting) into the same database. (*See* **Online Transaction Processing.**)

Identifying relationship — The child table is partially identified by the parent table, and partially dependent on the parent table. The parent table primary key is included in the primary key of the child table. In other words, if the child record exists, then the foreign key value, in the child table, must be set to something other than NULL. So, you can't create the child record unless the related parent record exists. In other words, the child record can't exist without a related parent record.

Implementation — The process of creating software from a design of that software. A physical database is an implementation of a database model.

Inactive data — Inactive data is information passed from an OLTP database to a data warehouse, where the inactive data is not used in the customer facing OLTP database on a regular basis. Inactive data is used in data warehouses to make projections and forecasts, based on historical company activities. (*See* **Online Transaction Processing.**)

Index — Usually (and preferably) a copy of a very small section of table, such as a single field, and preferably a short-length field.

Index Organized Table (IOT) — Build a table in the sorted order of an index, typically using a BTree index. It is also called a *clustered index* in some database engines because data is clustered into the form and structure of a BTree index.

Indexed Sequential Access Method (ISAM) index — A method that uses a simple structure with a list of record numbers. When reading the records from the table, in the order of the index, the indexed record numbers are read, accessing the records in the table using pointers between index and table records.

In-house — A term applied to something occurring or existing within a company. An in-house application is an application serving company employees only. An intranet application is generally in-house within a company, or within the scope of its operational capacity.

Inline constraint — A constraint created when a field is created and applies to a single field.

Inner join — An SQL term for an intersection, where records from two tables are selected, but only related rows are retrieved, and joined to each other.

Input mask setting — A field setting used to control the input format of the contents of a field. For example, the datatype definition of INTEGER $990.99, will not accept an input of 5000, but will accept an input of 500.

INSERT — The command that allows addition of new records to tables.

Insert anomaly — A record cannot be added to a detail table unless the record exists in the master table.

Integer — A whole number. For example, 555 is an integer, but 55.43 is not.

Internet Explorer — A Microsoft Windows tool used to gain access to the Internet.

Intersection — A term from mathematical set theory describing items common to two sets (existing in both sets).

IOT — *See* **Index Organized Table.**

Iterative — In computer jargon, a process can be repeated over and over again. When there is more than one step, all steps can be repeated, sometimes in any order.

Java — A powerful and versatile programming language, often used to build front-end applications, but not restricted as such.

Join — A joined query implies that the records from more than a single record source (table) are merged together. Joins can be built in various ways including set intersections, various types of outer joins, and otherwise.

Key — A specialized field determining uniqueness, or application of referential integrity through use of primary and foreign keys.

KISS rule — "Keep it simple stupid."

Kluge — A term often used by computer programmers to describe a clumsy or inelegant solution to a problem. The result is often a computer system consisting of a number of poorly matched elements.

Left outer join — A query finding the combination of intersection, plus records in the left-sided table but not in the right-sided table.

Legacy system — A database or application using an out-of-date database engine or application tools. Some legacy systems can be as much as 30, or even 40 years old.

Linux — An Open Source operating system with similarities to both UNIX and Microsoft Windows.

Location dimension — A standard table used within a data warehouse, constructed from fact table address information, created to facilitate queries dividing up facts based on regional values (such as countries, cities, states, and so on).

Macro — A pseudo-type series of commands, typically not really a programming language, and sometimes a sequence of commands built from GUI-based commands (such as those seen on the File menu in Microsoft Access). Macros are not really programming language-built but more power-user, GUI driven-built sequences of steps.

Many-to-many — This relationship represents an unresolved relationship between two tables. For example, students in a college can take many courses at once. So, a student can be enrolled in many courses at once, and a course can contain many enrolled students. The solution is resolve the many-to-many relationship into three, rather than two, tables. Each of the original tables is related to the new table as a one-to-many relationship, allowing access to unique records (in this example, unique course and student combinations).

Materialized view — A physically preconstructed view of data containing data copied into the materialized view. Materialized views can be highly efficient in read-only environments and are often used for replication, distribution and in data warehouses.

Metadata — The tables and the fields defining the structure of the data; the data about the data.

Method — The equivalent to a relational database stored procedure, except that it executes on the data contents of an object, within the bounds of that object.

Microsoft Windows — The Microsoft Windows operating system.

Multi-valued dependency — A field containing a comma-delimited list or collection of some kind. A collection could be an array of values of the same type. Those multiple values are dependent as a whole on the primary key, the whole meaning the entire collection in the comma-delimited list. Each individual value is not dependent on the primary key.

Nested query — A query executed from within another query. In theory, queries can be nested up to any number of hierarchical layers. The only limitation is on complexity and the abilities of the programmer.

Network — A system of connected computers. A local area network (LAN) is contained within a single company, in a single office. A wide area network (WAN) is generally distributed across a geographical area — even globally. The Internet is a very loosely connected network, meaning that it is usable by anyone and everyone.

Network database model — Essentially a refinement of the hierarchical database model. The network model allows child tables to have more than one parent, thus creating a networked-like table structure. Multiple parent tables for each child allow for many-to-many relationships, in addition to one-to-many relationships.

Non trivial multi-valued dependency — A multi-valued dependency with more than two fields in the table. (*See* **Multi valued dependency.**)

Non-identifying relationship — The child table is not dependent on the parent table, such that the child table includes the parent table primary key as a foreign key, but not as part of the child table's primary key. In other words, the parent record does not require, that a related record, exists in the child table. A foreign key field can contain a NULL value, and it can't be a part of the primary key because a primary key requires uniqueness.

Normal Forms — The steps contained within the process of Normalization. Normal Forms are cumulative, such that a database model in 3rd Normal Form is in both 2nd and 1st Normal Forms, but not Boyce-Codd (can be the same as 3rd Normal Form), 4th, 5th Normal Form, or Domain Key Normal Form.

Normalization — The process of simplifying the structure of data. Normalization increases granularity and Granularity is the scope of a definition for any particular thing. The more granular a data model is, the easier it becomes to manage, up to a point, depending, of course, on the application of the database model.

NOT NULL **constraint** — A constraint that implies a field must have a value placed into it; otherwise, an error is returned.

413

NULL — A field that has never been initialized with any value. A NULL field setting allows a field to contain nothing when a record is created or changed in a table.

Number — A numeric datatype allowing only numbers of various formats.

Number crunching — Computer jargon for large quantities of extremely complex calculations.

Object — In object methodology, the creation (instantiation) of a class at run-time, such that multiple object instances can be created from a class. An object is also a generic term applied to anything tangible, such as a table in a relational database.

Object database model — A model that provides a three-dimensional structure to data where any item in a database can be retrieved from any point very rapidly. Whereas the relational database model lends itself to retrieval of groups of records in two dimensions, the object database model is very efficient for finding unique items. Consequently, the object database model performs very poorly when retrieving more than a single item, at which the relational database model is very good.

Object-relational database model — The object-relational database model includes minimal aspects of the object database model into the relational database model. In some respects, the object-relational database model was created in answer to conflicting capabilities of relational and object database models — and also as a commercial competitor to the object database model. The object database model is somewhat spherical in nature, allowing access to unique elements anywhere within a database structure, with extremely high performance. The object database model performs extremely poorly when retrieving more than a single data item. The relational database model, on the other hand, contains records of data in tables across two dimensions. The relational database model is best suited for retrieval of groups of data but can also be used to access unique data items fairly efficiently.

OLAP — *See* **Online Analytical Processing.**

OLTP — *See* **Online Transaction Processing.**

ON **clause** — The ON clause is an ANSI standard join format that allows exact field join specifications when you want to include one or more fields in a join, which have different names in different tables.

One-to-many relationship — The relationship between two tables dictated by having one record in one table, and many related records in another table.

One-to-one relationship — The relationship between two tables dictated by having one record in each table, and not more than one record in either table, related back to the other table.

Online Analytical Processing (OLAP) — A functionality that provides rapid interactive analysis of data into multiple dimensions, usually involving extremely large databases. The objective of analysis is to highlight trends, patterns and exceptions.

Online Transaction Processing OLTP — Databases that were devised to cater for the enormous concurrency requirements of Internet (online) applications. OLTP databases cause problems with concurrency. The number of users that can be reached over the Internet is an unimaginable order of magnitude larger than that of an in-house company client-server database. Thus, the concurrency requirements for OLTP database models explodes — well beyond the scope of previous experience with client-server databases.

Operating system — The lowest level of software on a computer, generally managing the interface and the hardware. Windows, UNIX, and Linux are all operating systems.

Operations — A term describing what a company does to make a profit.

Optimizer — A term applied to a process, within a database engine, that attempts to find the fastest method of executing a SQL command against a database.

ORDER BY **clause** — Query SELECT command adjustment allowing resorting (reordering) of records as they are returned from a query to a database.

Outer join — An intersection plus rows outside the intersection, in one table and not in the other table of a join.

Overflow — A situation where new data is added to a table or index, but outside of the most effective structure, making subsequent reads potentially very inefficient. Certain types of indexes are subject to overflow.

Paper trail — The pieces of paper a company produces, and those passing through it, while it conducts its day-to-day affairs. A company in the process of performing its day-to-day business is likely to have a paper trail of orders, invoices, bills, checks, and so on. Analysis can gain copious amounts of information from a company paper trail. Following the paper trail is a very useful method of gathering analytical details of the business operational processes of a company.

Parallel processing — Execution of more than one thing at the same time, typically using multiple CPUs (but not always). Additionally, parallel processing used in hand with partitioning can result in some very effective performance improvements.

Partitioning — Physical splitting of tables into separate sections (partitions), including parallel processing on multiple partitions and individual operations on individual partitions. One particularly efficient aspect is the capability when querying a table to read fewer than all the partitions making up a table, perhaps even a single partition. This is also known as *partition pruning*.

Performance — Performance is a measure of how fast a database services applications, and ultimately end-users.

Planning — A process whereby a project plan and timeline are used for larger projects. Project plans typically include, who does what and when. More sophisticated plans integrate multiple tasks, sharing them out among many people, ensuring dependencies are catered for. For example, if task B requires completion of task A, the same person can do both tasks A and B. If there is no dependency, two people can do both tasks A an B at the same time.

Power-user — A user who is between an end-user and an expert computer programmer, in terms of knowing how to use a computer. An end-user uses a computer as a tool to solve business problems. A computer programmer writes the software that end-users make use of. A power user is someone in between, typically an end-user who writes his or her own software.

Precedence — The order of resolution of an expression, and generally acts from left to right, across an expression.

Primary key — A key uniquely identifying each row in a table. The entity on the many side of the relationship has a foreign key. The foreign key column contains primary key values of the entity on the one side of the relationship.

Projection Normal Form (PJNF) — *See* **5th Normal Form.**

Query — A statement interrogating the database and returning information. Most often tables are interrogated and records from those tables are returned. Queries can be both simple and complex. A query is executed using the SQL SELECT command.

Random access memory (RAM) — The memory chips inside your computer. RAM provides an ultrafast buffering storage area between CPU (the processor) and your I/O devices (disks).

RDBMS — *See* **Relational Database Management System.**

Record — A repetition of a field structure across a table. Records repeat field structure in a table, where each repeated field can (and sometimes should) have a different value. Tables are divided into fields and records. Fields impose structure and datatype specifics onto each of the field values, in each record.

Redundant Array of Inexpensive Disks (RAID) — A bunch of small, cheap disks. A RAID array is a group of disks used together as a single unit logical disk. RAID arrays can help with storage capacity, recoverability and performance, using what are called mirroring and striping. Mirroring creates duplicate copies of all physical data. Striping breaks data into many small pieces, where those small pieces can be accessed in parallel.

Referential integrity — A process (usually contained within a relational database model) of validation between related primary and foreign key field values. For example, a foreign key value cannot be added to a table unless the related primary key value exists in the parent table. Similarly, deleting a primary key value necessitates removing all records in subsidiary tables, containing that primary key value in foreign key fields. Additionally, it follows that preventing the deletion of a primary key record is not allowed if a foreign key exists elsewhere.

Relational Database Management System (RDBMS) — A system that uses a database that contains tables with data. The management system part is the part allowing you access to that database, and the power to manipulate both the database and the data contained within it.

Relational database model — A model that provides a two-dimensional structure to data. The relational database model more or less throws out the window the concept and restriction of a hierarchical structure, but does not completely abandon data hierarchies. Any table can be accessed directly with having to access all parent objects. Precise data values (such as primary keys) are required to facilitate skirting the hierarchy (to find individual records) in specific tables.

Replication — A method used to duplicate (replicate) and distribute data from a primary or master database, out to a number of other copies of the master database. Those copies can be fully dependent slave databases, or even other master databases, capable of passing their own changes back.

Right outer join — A query finding the combination of intersection, plus records in the right-sided table, but not in the left-sided table.

ROLLBACK — This command undoes any database changes not yet committed to the database using the COMMIT command.

SDK — Software development kit is a tool containing a programming language (Java, for example). SDKs are often used to build applications software.

Secondary Index — *See* **Alternate index.**

SELECT **command** — A command used to execute a query on a database. A SELECT command contains all the fields to be retrieved from tables. Additionally, a SELECT command can have optional additions used to perform special alterations to queries, such as filtering using a WHERE clause, and sorting using an ORDER BY clause.

Self join — Joins records in a table to the same table. Typically used for a table containing hierarchically structured records, such as a family tree.

Semi-join — Join two tables using a subquery, but not necessarily returning any field values to the calling query. Semi-joins occur when using IN and EXISTS operators.

Sequence — Allows automated generation of sequences of numbers, usually one after the other, such as 101, 102, 103, and so on. Some database engines call these *auto counters.*

Simple datatype — A term used to describe the most basic of datatypes, containing a simple value, such as an integer or a string.

Snowflake schema — A data warehouse, single fact table structure, with dimension tables in multiple layered hierarchies of dimensional tables.

Sorted query — *See* ORDER BY **clause.**

SQL — *See* **Structured Query Language.**

Standby database — A failover database. A standby database has minimal activity, usually only adding new records, changing existing records, and deleting existing records. Some database engines, however, allow standby databases to be utilized as secondary, active database platforms.

Star schema — A single fact table surrounded by a single hierarchical layer of dimensional tables, in a data warehouse database.

Static data — Data that does not change significantly.

Stored function — The same as a stored procedure, except that it returns a single value.

Stored procedure — Also called a *database procedure,* a chunk of code stored within and executed from within a database, typically on data stored in a database (but not always).

String — A simple datatype containing a sequence of alphanumeric characters.

Structured Query Language (SQL) — A non-procedural language that does not allow dependencies between successive commands. SQL is the language used to access data in a relational database. Generally, for any relational database other than Microsoft SQL-Server, SQL is pronounced "ess-queue-ell" and not "sequel."

Surrogate key — Used as a replacement or substitute for a descriptive primary key, allowing for better control, better structure, less storage space, more efficient indexing, and absolute surety of uniqueness. Surrogate keys are usually integers, and usually automatically generated using auto counters or sequences.

Table — An entity that is divided into fields and records. Fields impose structure and datatype specifics onto each of the field values in a record.

Tertiary index — *See* **Alternate index.**

Time dimension — Used for temporal analysis in data warehouses.

Timeline — For a project plan, a plotting of who does what and when. A project plan and timeline are useful for larger projects. Project plans typically include who does what and when. More sophisticated plans integrate multiple tasks, sharing them out among many people, ensuring dependencies are catered for. For example, if task B requires completion of task A, the same person can do both tasks A and B. If there is no dependency, two people can do both tasks A an B at the same time.

Timestamp — A datatype used to store date values, with a time of day attached as well.

Transaction — In SQL, a sequence of one or more commands where changes are not as yet committed permanently to a database. A transaction is completed once changes are committed or undone (rolled back).

Transactional control — A transaction is comprised of one or more database change commands, which make database changes. A transaction is completed on the execution of a COMMIT or ROLLBACK command, manually or automatically. The concept of transactional control is that SQL allows sets of commands to be permanently stored all at once, or undone all at once.

Transactional data — Data about the day-to-day dynamic activities of a company, such as invoices.

Transitive dependence — Z is transitively dependent on X when X determines Y and Y determines Z. Transitive dependence thus describes that Z is indirectly dependent on X through its relationship with Y.

Trigger — A chunk of code that executes when a specified event occurs, usually before or after an INSERT, UPDATE, or DELETE command.

Trivial multi-valued dependency — A multi-valued dependency with only two fields in the table. (*See* **Multi valued dependency.**)

Truncate — A term implying the removal of characters from a value, typically a number, where no rounding occurs.

Tuple — *See* **Record.**

Unique key — A key created on a field containing only unique values throughout an entire table.

UNIX — An operating system that is far more complex and far more difficult to manage than an operating system like Microsoft Windows. UNIX is, however, far more versatile and far more powerful but also much more expensive.

UPDATE — The command used to change data in records in tables.

Update anomaly — An error caused when a database allows an error to be generated, by updating incorrectly across a primary and foreign key relationship. A record cannot be updated in a master table unless all sibling records, in all related child tables, are updated first. Note that changes can be propagated to sibling records in child tables, using cascading.

User — *See* **End-user.**

User-friendly — Describes a software application (or otherwise) that allows ease of use for the non-computer literate, or end-user population.

Validation check. — *See* **Check constraint.**

Variable-length records — Every record in a table does not have to be the same byte-length. This allows use of datatypes, such as variable-length strings (CHAR VARYING(nn)). Most modern relational database engines use variable-length records.

Variable-length string — A string with 0 or more characters, up to a maximum length of characters.

View — A logical overlay containing a query, executed whenever the view is accessed. Repeated query execution can make views very inefficient in busy environments.

WHERE **clause** — A clause that is an optional part of the SELECT statement, the UPDATE, and DELETE commands. The WHERE clause allows inclusion of wanted records, and filtering out of unwanted records.

Windows Explorer — A Microsoft Windows tool used to view and access files on disk.

Exercise Answers

This appendix contains all the answers to the exercises appearing at the ends of chapters.

Chapter 3

Exercise 1 solution

Two CREATE TABLE commands:

```
CREATE TABLE Band
(
        band_id INTEGER NOT NULL,
        band_name VARCHAR(32) NULL,
        CONSTRAINT XPK_Band PRIMARY KEY (band_id),
        CONSTRAINT XUK_B_Name UNIQUE (band_name)
);

CREATE TABLE Track
(
        track_id INTEGER NOT NULL,
        band_id INTEGER NOT NULL,
        track_name VARCHAR(32) NULL,
        description VARCHAR(256) NULL,
        CONSTRAINT XPK_Track PRIMARY KEY (track_id),
        CONSTRAINT FK_T_Band FOREIGN KEY (band_id) REFERENCES Band,
        CONSTRAINT XUK_T_Name UNIQUE (track_name)
);
```

Exercise 2 solution

One CREATE INDEX command:

```
CREATE INDEX XFK_T_Band ON Track(band_id);
```

Chapter 4

Exercise 1 solution

Five CREATE TABLE commands are shown here. Note that the order in which tables are created is important, as assignment of foreign key columns requires that primary keys in parent tables already exist:

```
CREATE TABLE Customer
(
        customer_name VARCHAR(32) PRIMARY KEY,
        customer_address VARCHAR(256),
        customer_phone VARCHAR(32)
);

CREATE TABLE Stock_Source_Department
(
        stock_source_department VARCHAR(32) PRIMARY KEY,
        stock_source_city VARCHAR(32) NOT NULL
);

CREATE TABLE Stock_Item
(
        stock# INTEGER PRIMARY KEY,
        stock_source_department VARCHAR(32) NOT NULL
                REFERENCES Stock_Source_Department,
        stock_description VARCHAR(256),
        stock_unit_price FLOAT
);

CREATE TABLE Sale_Order
(
        order# INTEGER PRIMARY KEY,
        customer_name VARCHAR(32) REFERENCES Customer,
        dte DATE,
        sales_tax_percentage FLOAT
);
CREATE TABLE Sale_Order_Item
(
        order# INTEGER PRIMARY KEY,
        stock# INTEGER NOT NULL REFERENCES Sale_Order,
        stock_quantity INTEGER
);
```

> Note how the PRIMARY KEY and FOREIGN KEY specifications are included within the specification of the column. These are called *in line constraint definitions*. This is a different method of definition from that of exercises in Chapter 3. Chapter 3 uses what are called *out of line constraint definitions*. Inline constraint definitions can only be used for constraints on single columns. For example, a multiple column primary key would have to be defined as an out of line constraint. It is also possible to define primary and foreign key constraints using an ALTER TABLE command to change a table specification, after the table has already been created.

Exercise 2 solution

Three CREATE INDEX commands to create indexes on foreign keys:

```
CREATE INDEX XFK_SI_SSD ON Stock_Item (stock_source_department);
CREATE INDEX XFK_SO_C ON Sale_Order (customer_name);
CREATE INDEX XFK_SOI_SI ON Sale_Order_Item (stock#);
```

Chapter 5

Exercise 1 solution

There are two possible answers:

```
SELECT * FROM EDITION;

SELECT ISBN,PUBLISHER_ID,PUBLICATION_ID,PRINT_DATE,PAGES,LIST_PRICE,FORMAT,RANK,
UNITS FROM EDITION;
```

Exercise 2 solution

```
SELECT ISBN FROM EDITION WHERE FORMAT='Hardcover';
```

Exercise 3 solution

```
SELECT ISBN FROM EDITION WHERE FORMAT='Hardcover' ORDER BY FORMAT, LIST_PRICE;
```

Exercise 4 solution

$3 + 4 * 5 = 23$, and $(3 + 4) * 5 = 35$. The second expression yields the greater value.

Exercise 5 solution

```
SELECT PUBLISHER_ID, SUM(LIST_PRICE) FROM EDITION GROUP BY PUBLISHER_ID;
```

Exercise 6 solution

```
SELECT * FROM SUBJECT S JOIN PUBLICATION P USING (SUBJECT_ID);
```

Exercise 7 solution

```
SELECT * FROM SUBJECT S LEFT OUTER JOIN PUBLICATION P USING (SUBJECT_ID);
```

Exercise 8 solution

```
SELECT * FROM SUBJECT WHERE SUBJECT_ID IN (SELECT SUBJECT_ID FROM PUBLICATION);

SELECT * FROM SUBJECT WHERE EXISTS
(SELECT SUBJECT_ID FROM PUBLICATION
  WHERE SUBJECT_ID = SUBJECT.SUBJECT_ID);
```

Chapter 6

Exercise 1 solution

```
CREATE TABLE BAND2 AS
SELECT B.BAND_ID, B.NAME, A.ADDRESS, P.PHONE, E.EMAIL
FROM BAND B JOIN BAND_ADDRESS A USING(BAND_ID)
    JOIN BAND_PHONE P USING(BAND_ID)
        JOIN BAND_EMAIL E USING(BAND_ID);
```

Exercise 2 solution

```
DROP TABLE BAND;
ALTER TABLE BAND2 RENAME TO BAND;
```

Chapter 7

Exercise 1 solution

```
CREATE TABLE BAND
(
        BAND_ID INTEGER PRIMARY KEY NOT NULL,
        NAME VARCHAR(32) NULL,
        ADDRESS VARCHAR(256) NULL,
        PHONE VARCHAR(32) NULL,
        EMAIL VARCHAR(32) NULL
);
CREATE TABLE CD
(
        CD_ID INTEGER PRIMARY KEY NOT NULL,
        BAND_ID INTEGER REFERENCES BAND NULL,
        TITLE VARCHAR(32) NULL,
        LENGTH INTEGER NULL,
        TRACKS INTEGER NULL
);

CREATE TABLE TRACK
(
        TRACK_ID INTEGER PRIMARY KEY NOT NULL,
        CD_ID INTEGER REFERENCES CD NULL,
        TRACK VARCHAR(32) NULL,
        LENGTH INTEGER NULL,
        GENRE INTEGER NULL,
        CHART VARCHAR(32) NULL,
        RANK INTEGER NULL
);

CREATE TABLE TIME
(
        TIME_ID INTEGER PRIMARY KEY NOT NULL,
        HOUR INTEGER NULL,
        DAY INTEGER NULL,
        MONTH INTEGER NULL,
```

```
        QUARTER INTEGER NULL,
        YEAR INTEGER NULL
);

CREATE TABLE LOCATION
(
        LOCATION_ID INTEGER PRIMARY KEY NOT NULL,
        CITY VARCHAR(32) NULL,
        COUNTY VARCHAR(32) NULL,
        STATE VARCHAR(32) NULL,
        COUNTRY VARCHAR(32) NULL
);

CREATE TABLE RADIO
(
        STATION_ID INTEGER PRIMARY KEY NOT NULL,
        STATION VARCHAR(32) NULL
);

CREATE TABLE PERFORMER
(
        PERFORMER_ID INTEGER PRIMARY KEY NOT NULL,
        PERFORMER VARCHAR(32) NULL
);

CREATE TABLE RECORDINGARTIST
(
        RECORDING_ARTIST_ID INTEGER PRIMARY KEY NOT NULL,
        RECORDING_ARTIST VARCHAR(32) NULL
);

CREATE TABLE ROYALTY
(
        ROYALTY_ID INTEGER PRIMARY KEY NOT NULL,
        TRACK_ID INTEGER REFERENCES TRACK NULL,
        RECORDING_ARTIST_ID INTEGER REFERENCES RECORDINGARTIST NULL,
        PERFORMER_ID INTEGER REFERENCES PERFORMER NULL,
        STATION_ID INTEGER REFERENCES RADIO NULL,
        LOCATION_ID INTEGER REFERENCES LOCATION NULL,
        TIME_ID INTEGER REFERENCES TIME NULL,
        AMOUNT FLOAT NOT NULL
);
```

Exercise 2 solution

```
CREATE TABLE TEMP AS
    SELECT B.NAME AS BAND_NAME, B.ADDRESS AS BAND.ADDRESS, B.PHONE AS BAND_PHONE,
        B.EMAIL AS BAND_EMAIL, CD.TITLE AS CD_TITLE, CD.LENGTH AS CD_LENGTH,
        CD.TRACKS AS CD_TRACKS,T.TRACK, T.LENGTH AS TRACK_LENGTH, T.GENRE AS
        TRACK_GENRE, T.CHART AS TRACK_CHART, T.RANK AS TRACK_RANK
    FROM BAND B JOIN CD CD JOIN TRACK T;

--
```

```
--DISABLE THE ROYALTY.TRACK_ID FOREIGN KEY COLUMN
--

DROP TABLE TRACK;
DROP TABLE CD;
DROP TABLE BAND;
CREATE TABLE TRACK AS SELECT * FROM TEMP;
DROP TABLE TEMP;
--
--RENABLE THE ROYALTY.TRACK_ID FOREIGN KEY COLUMN, TO POINT AT THE NEW TRACK TABLE
--
```

Chapter 8

Exercise 1 solution

High concurrency and real-time response to end-users are both correct answers:

❑ *Very High Concurrency* — Concurrency implies a very high degree of sharing of the same information.

❑ *Reaction Time* — Real-time, instantaneous reaction to database changes and activities are essential. If you withdraw cash from an ATM at your bank and then check your statement online in an hour or so, you would expect to see the transaction. Similarly, if you purchase something online, you would hope to see the transaction on your credit card account within minutes, if not seconds.

Exercise 2 solution

Very large database is the only correct answer:

❑ *Frightening Database Size* — Data warehouses can become incredibly large. Administrators and developers have to decide how much detail to retain, when to remove data, when to summarize, what to summarize. A lot of these decisions are done during production when the data warehouse is in use. Also, ad-hoc queries can cause serious problems because if the database is very large. User education in relation to how to code proper joins may be essential; otherwise, provision of efficiency providing structures such as pre-built joins and aggregations in materialized views can also help.

Exercise 3 solution

The number of tables in a join query is the best answer.

Exercise 4 solution

The second query is the best performing option because it finds a single record on a primary key, using the primary key index. The first option is a negative search and scans all records in the table, ignoring any indexing, searching for what is not in the table.

Chapter 9

Exercise 1 solution

```
CREATE TABLE INSTRUMENT(INSTRUMENT VARCHAR(32) NULL);

CREATE TABLE SKILL(SKILL VARCHAR(32) NULL);

CREATE TABLE GENRE(GENRE VARCHAR(32) NULL);

CREATE TABLE MUSICIAN
(
      NAME VARCHAR(32) NULL,
      PHONE VARCHAR(32) NULL,
      EMAIL VARCHAR(32) NULL
);

CREATE TABLE SHOWS
(
      LOCATION VARCHAR(32) NULL,
      ADDRESS VARCHAR(32) NULL,
      DIRECTIONS VARCHAR(32) NULL,
      PHONE VARCHAR(32) NULL,
      SHOW_DATE DATE NULL,
      SHOW_TIMES VARCHAR(32) NULL
);

CREATE TABLE MERCHANDISE
(
      TYPE VARCHAR(32) NULL,
      PRICE FLOAT NULL
);

CREATE TABLE DISCOGRAPHY
(
      CD_NAME VARCHAR(32) NULL,
      RELEASE_DATE DATE NULL,
      PRICE FLOAT NULL
);

CREATE TABLE BAND
(
      NAME VARCHAR(32) NULL,
      MEMBERS VARCHAR(32) NULL,
      FOUNDING_DATE DATE NULL
);

CREATE TABLE ADVERTISEMENT
(
      AD_DATE DATE NULL,
      AD_TEXT VARCHAR(1000) NULL,
      PHONE VARCHAR(32) NULL,
      EMAIL VARCHAR(32) NULL,
      REQUIREMENTS VARCHAR(1000) NULL
);
```

Exercise 2 solution

```
CREATE TABLE MUSICIAN
(
        NAME VARCHAR(32) NULL,
        PHONE VARCHAR(32) NULL,
        EMAIL VARCHAR(32) NULL,
        INSTRUMENTS VARCHAR(32) NULL,
        SKILLS VARCHAR(32) NULL
);

CREATE TABLE SHOWS
(
        LOCATION VARCHAR(32) NULL,
        ADDRESS VARCHAR(32) NULL,
        DIRECTIONS VARCHAR(32) NULL,
        PHONE VARCHAR(32) NULL,
        SHOW_DATE DATE NULL,
        SHOW_TIMES VARCHAR(32) NULL
);

CREATE TABLE MERCHANDISE
(
        TYPE VARCHAR(32) NULL,
        PRICE FLOAT NULL
);

CREATE TABLE DISCOGRAPHY
(
        CD_NAME VARCHAR(32) NULL,
        RELEASE_DATE DATE NULL,
        PRICE FLOAT NULL
);

CREATE TABLE BAND
(
        NAME VARCHAR(32) NULL,
        FOUNDING_DATE DATE NULL,
        GENRES VARACHAR(32) NULL
);
CREATE TABLE ADVERTISEMENT
(
        AD_DATE DATE NULL,
        AD_TEXT VARCHAR(1000) NULL,
        AD_PHONE VARCHAR(32) NULL,
        AD_EMAIL VARCHAR(32) NULL,
        AD_REQUIREMENTS VARCHAR(1000) NULL
);
```

Chapter 10

Exercise 1 solution

```
CREATE TABLE INSTRUMENT
(
        INSTRUMENT_ID INTEGER PRIMARY KEY,
        SECTION_ID INTEGER FOREIGN KEY REFERENCES INSTRUMENT WITH NULL,
        INSTRUMENT STRING NOT NULL
);
```

INSTRUMENT *is* NOT NULL, *because there is no point in storing an instrument without a name.*

```
CREATE TABLE GENRE
(
        GENRE_ID INTEGER PRIMARY KEY,
        PARENT_ID INTEGER FOREIGN KEY REFERENCES GENRE WITH NULL,
        GENRE STRING NOT NULL
);

CREATE TABLE VENUE
(
        VENUE_ID INTEGER PRIMARY KEY,
        VENUE STRING NOT NULL,
        ADDRESS STRING NULL,
        DIRECTIONS STRING NULL,
        PHONE STRING NULL
);
```

The field for the name of the VENUE *should be* VENUE, *not* LOCATION. *It is thus changed in the preceding script.*

```
CREATE TABLE BAND
(
        BAND_ID INTEGER PRIMARY KEY,
        GENRE_ID INTEGER FOREIGN KEY REFERENCES GENRE,
        BAND STRING NOT NULL,
        FOUNDING_DATE DATE NULL
);

CREATE TABLE MERCHANDISE
(
        MERCHANDISE_ID INTEGER PRIMARY KEY,
        BAND_ID INTEGER FOREIGN KEY REFERENCES BAND,
        TYPE STRING NOT NULL,
        PRICE MONEY NULL
);

CREATE TABLE DISCOGRAPHY
(
        DISCOGRAPHY_ID INTEGER PRIMARY KEY,
        BAND_ID INTEGER FOREIGN KEY REFERENCES BAND,
```

```
            CD_NAME STRING NOT NULL,
            RELEASE_DATE DATE NULL,
            PRICE MONEY NULL
    );

    CREATE TABLE SHOW
    (
            SHOW_ID INTEGER PRIMARY_KEY,
            VENUE_ID INTEGER FOREIGN KEY REFERENCES VENUE,
            BAND_ID INTEGER FOREIGN KEY REFERENCES BAND,
            DATE DATE NULL,
            TIME STRING NULL
    );

    CREATE TABLE MUSICIAN
    (
            MUSICIAN_ID INTEGER PRIMARY KEY,
            INSTRUMENT_ID INTEGER FOREIGN KEY REFERENCES INSTRUMENT,
            BAND_ID INTEGER FOREIGN KEY REFERENCES BAND,
            MUSICIAN STRING NOT NULL,
            PHONE STRING NULL,
            EMAIL STRING NULL,
            SKILLS STRING NULL
    );

    CREATE TABLE ADVERTISEMENT
    (
            ADVERTISEMENT_ID INTEGER PRIMARY KEY,
            BAND_ID INTEGER FOREIGN KEY REFERENCES BAND,
            MUSICIAN_ID INTEGER FOREIGN KEY REFERENCES MUSICIAN,
            AD_DATE DATE NULL,
            AD_TEXT BIGSTRING NULL
    );
```

Exercise 2 solution

```
    CREATE TABLE INSTRUMENT
    (
            INSTRUMENT_ID INTEGER PRIMARY KEY,
            SECTION_ID INTEGER FOREIGN KEY REFERENCES INSTRUMENT WITH NULL,
            INSTRUMENT STRING NOT NULL
    );

    CREATE TABLE GENRE
    (
            GENRE_ID INTEGER PRIMARY KEY,
            PARENT_ID INTEGER FOREIGN KEY REFERENCES GENRE WITH NULL,
            GENRE STRING NOT NULL
    );

    CREATE TABLE MERCHANDISE
    (
            MERCHANDISE_ID INTEGER PRIMARY KEY,
            TYPE STRING NOT NULL,
```

```
        PRICE MONEY NULL
);

CREATE TABLE ARTISTS
(
        ARTIST_ID INTEGER PRIMARY KEY,
        MERCHANDISE_ID INTEGER FOREIGN KEY REFERENCES MERCHANDISE WITH NULL,
        GENRE_ID INTEGER FOREIGN KEY REFERENCES GENRE WITH NULL,
        INSTRUMENT_ID INTEGER FOREIGN KEY REFERENCES INSTRUMENT WITH NULL,
        MUSICIAN_NAME STRING NULL,
        MUSICIAN_PHONE STRING NULL,
        MUSICIAN_EMAIL STRING NULL,
        BAND_NAME STRING NULL,
        BAND_FOUNDING_DATE DATE NULL,
        DISCOGRAPHY_CD_NAME STRING NULL,
        DISCOGRAPHY_RELEASE_DATE DATE NULL,
        DISCOGRAPHY_PRICE MONEY NULL,
        SHOW_DATE DATE NULL,
        SHOW_TIME STRING NULL,
        VENUE_NAME STRING NULL,
        VENUE_ADDRESS STRING NULL,
        VENUE_DIRECTIONS BIGSTRING NULL,
        VENUE_PHONE STRING NULL,
        ADVERTISEMENT_DATE DATE NULL,
        ADVERTISEMENT_TEXT BIGSTRING NULL
);
```

Chapter 11

Exercise 1 solution

```
CREATE TABLE INSTRUMENT
(
        INSTRUMENT_ID          INTEGER PRIMARY KEY NOT NULL,
        SECTION_ID             INTEGER FOREIGN KEY REFERENCES INSTRUMENT WITH NULL,
        INSTRUMENT             CHAR VARYING(32) NOT NULL
);

CREATE TABLE GENRE
(
        GENRE_ID               INTEGER PRIMARY KEY NOT NULL,
        PARENT_ID              INTEGER FOREIGN KEY REFERENCES GENRE WITH NULL,
        GENRE                  CHAR VARYING(32) NOT NULL
);

CREATE TABLE VENUE
(
        VENUE_ID               INTEGER PRIMARY KEY NOT NULL,
        LOCATION               CHAR VARYING(32) NOT NULL,
        ADDRESS_LINE_1         CHAR VARYING(32) NOT NULL,
        ADDRESS_LINE_2         CHAR VARYING(32) NULL,
        TOWN                   CHAR VARYING(32) NOT NULL,
        ZIP                    NUMBER(5) NULL,
```

```
           POSTAL_CODE          CHAR VARYING(32) NULL,
           COUNTRY              CHAR VARYING(32) NULL,
           DIRECTIONS           MEMO NULL,
           PHONE                CHAR VARYING(32) NULL
);

CREATE TABLE MERCHANDISE
(
       MERCHANDISE_ID        INTEGER PRIMARY KEY NOT NULL,
       BAND_ID               INTEGER FOREIGN KEY REFERENCES BAND NOT NULL,
       TYPE                  CHAR VARYING(32) NOT NULL,
       PRICE                 MONEY NOT NULL
);

CREATE TABLE DISCOGRAPHY
(
       DISCOGRAPHY_ID        INTEGER PRIMARY KEY NOT NULL,
       BAND_ID               INTEGER FOREIGN REFERENCES BAND NOT NULL,
       CD_NAME               CHAR VARYING(32) NOT NULL,
       RELEASE_DATE          DATE NULL,
       PRICE                 MONEY NULL
);

CREATE TABLE SHOW
(
       SHOW_ID               INTEGER PRIMARY KEY NOT NULL,
       BAND_ID               INTEGER FOREIGN KEY REFERENCES BAND NOT NULL,
       VENUE_ID              INTEGER FOREIGN KEY REFERENES VENUE NOT NULL,
       DATE                  DATE NOT NULL,
       TIME                  CHAR VARYING(16) NOT NULL
);

CREATE TABLE BAND
(
       BAND_ID               INTEGER PRIMARY KEY NOT NULL,
       GENRE_ID              INTEGER FOREIGN KEY REFERENCES GENRE NOT NULL,
       BAND                  CHAR VARYING(32) NOT NULL,
       FOUNDING_DATE         DATE NOT NULL
);

CREATE TABLE MUSICIAN
(
       MUSICIAN_ID           INTEGER PRIMARY KEY NOT NULL,
       INSTRUMENT_ID         INTEGER FOREIGN KEY REFERENCES INSTRUMENT NOT NULL,
       BAND_ID               INTEGER FOREIGN KEY REFERENCES BAND WITH NULL,
       MUSICIAN              CHAR VARYING(32) NOT NULL,
       PHONE                 CHAR VARYING(32) NULL,
       EMAIL                 CHAR VARYING(32) NULL,
       SKILLS                CHAR VARYING(256) NULL
);

CREATE TABLE ADVERTISEMENT
(
       ADVERTISEMENT_ID      INTEGER PRIMARY KEY NOT NULL,
       BAND_ID               INTEGER FOREIGN KEY REFERENCES BAND WITH NULL,
```

```
                MUSICIAN_ID             INTEGER FOREIGN KEY REFERENCES MUSICIAN WITH NULL,
                DATE                    DATE NOT NULL,
                TEXT                    MEMO NOT NULL
);
```

The Microsoft Access MEMO *datatype is used to represent very large strings.*

Exercise 2 solution

```
CREATE TABLE INSTRUMENT
(
        INSTRUMENT_ID           INTEGER PRIMARY KEY NOT NULL,
        SECTION_ID              INTEGER FOREIGN KEY REFERENCES INSTRUMENT WITH NULL,
        INSTRUMENT              CHAR VARYING(32) NOT NULL
);

CREATE TABLE MUSICIAN
(
        MUSICIAN_ID             INTEGER PRIMARY KEY NOT NULL,
        MUSICIAN                CHAR VARYING(32) NOT NULL,
        PHONE                   CHAR VARYING(32) NULL,
        EMAIL                   CHAR VARYING(32) NULL
);

CREATE TABLE GENRE
(
        GENRE_ID                INTEGER PRIMARY KEY NOT NULL,
        PARENT_ID               INTEGER FOREIGN KEY REFERENCES GENRE WITH NULL,
        GENRE                   CHAR VARYING(32) NOT NULL
);

CREATE TABLE BAND
(
        BAND_ID                 INTEGER PRIMARY KEY NOT NULL,
        BAND                    CHAR VARYING(32) NOT NULL,
        FOUNDING_DATE           DATE NOT NULL
);

CREATE TABLE ADVERTISEMENT
(
        ADVERTISEMENT_ID        INTEGER PRIMARY KEY NOT NULL,
        DATE                    DATE NOT NULL,
        TEXT                    MEMO NOT NULL
);

CREATE TABLE DISCOGRAPHY
(
        DISCOGRAPHY_ID          INTEGER PRIMARY KEY NOT NULL,
        CD_NAME                 CHAR VARYING(32) NOT NULL,
        RELEASE_DATE            DATE NULL,
        PRICE                   MONEY NULL
);

CREATE TABLE MERCHANDISE
(
```

```
        MERCHANDISE_ID          INTEGER PRIMARY KEY NOT NULL,
        TYPE                    CHAR VARYING(32) NOT NULL,
        PRICE                   MONEY NOT NULL
);

CREATE TABLE SHOW_VENUE
(
        SHOW_ID                 INTEGER PRIMARY KEY NOT NULL,
        LOCATION                CHAR VARYING(32) NOT NULL,
        ADDRESS_LINE_1          CHAR VARYING(32) NOT NULL,
        ADDRESS_LINE_2          CHAR VARYING(32) NULL,
        TOWN                    CHAR VARYING(32) NOT NULL,
        ZIP                     NUMBER(5) NULL,
        POSTAL_CODE             CHAR VARYING(32) NULL,
        COUNTRY                 CHAR VARYING(32) NULL,
        DIRECTIONS              MEMO NULL,
        PHONE                   CHAR VARYING(32) NULL
        SHOW_DATE               DATE NOT NULL,
        SHOW_TIME               CHAR VARYING(16) NOT NULL
);

VENUE is changed to LOCATION
CREATE TABLE FACT
(
        FACT_ID                 INTEGER NOT NULL,
        SHOW_ID                 INTEGER FOREIGN KEY REFERENCES SHOW WITH NULL,
        MUSICIAN_ID             INTEGER FOREIGN KEY REFERENCES MUSICIAN WITH NULL,
        BAND_ID                 INTEGER FOREIGN KEY REFERENCES BAND WITH NULL,
        ADVERTISEMENT_ID        INTEGER FOREIGN KEY REFERENCES ADVERTISEMENT
                                    WITH NULL,
        DISCOGRAPHY_ID          INTEGER FOREIGN KEY REFERENCES DISCOGRAPHY
                                    WITH NULL,
        MERCHANDISE_ID          INTEGER FOREIGN KEY REFERENCES MERCHANDISE
                                    WITH NULL,
        GENRE_ID                INTEGER FOREIGN KEY REFERENCES GENRE WITH NULL,
        INSTRUMENT_ID           INTEGER FOREIGN KEY REFERENCES INSTRUMENT WITH NULL,
        CD_SALE_AMOUNT          MONEY NULL,
        MERCHANDISE_SALE_AMOUNT MONEY NULL,
        ADVERTISING_COST_AMOUNT MONEY NULL,
        SHOW_TICKET_SALES_AMOUNT_MONEY NULL
);
```

Sample Databases

This appendix contains what should the most sensible versions of some of the more complete ERD database model diagrams, as presented in this book. This appendix is intended merely as a reference of database model ERDs.

Following is a summary of the ERDs included in this appendix.

- ❑ Figure B-1 shows the book publication OLTP ERD.
- ❑ Figure B-2 shows the book publication reviews data warehouse ERD.
- ❑ Figure B-3 shows the book publication sales data warehouse ERD.
- ❑ Figure B-4 shows the musicians, bands, and advertisements OLTP ERD.
- ❑ Figure B-5 shows the musicians, bands, and advertisements data warehouse ERD.
- ❑ Figure B-6 shows the online auction house OLTP ERD.
- ❑ Figure B-7 shows the online auction house data warehouse ERD.

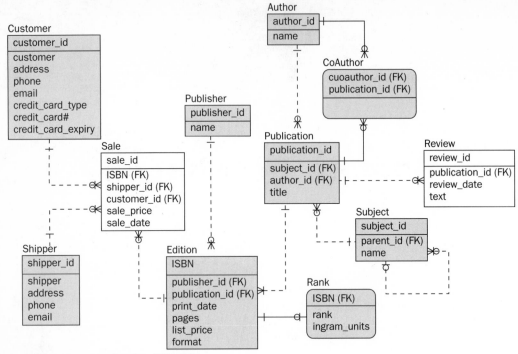

Figure B-1: Book publication OLTP ERD.

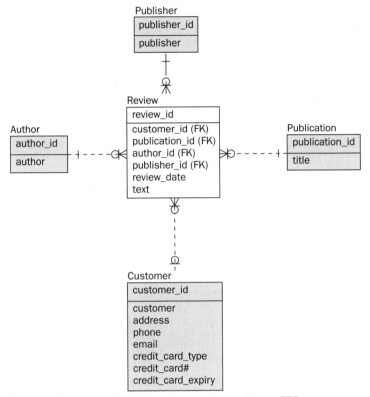

Figure B-2: Book publication reviews data warehouse ERD.

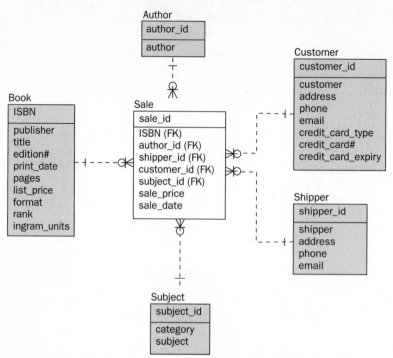

Figure B-3: Book publication sales data warehouse ERD.

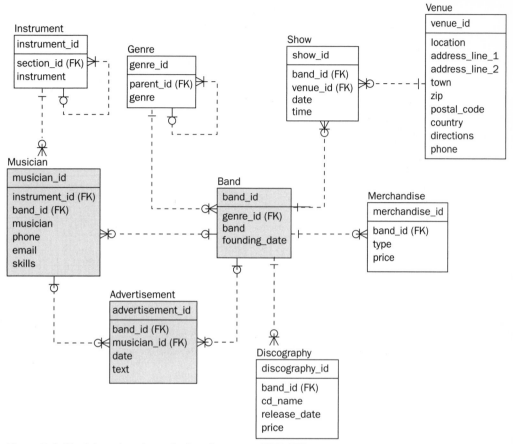

Figure B-4: Musicians, bands, and advertisements OLTP ERD.

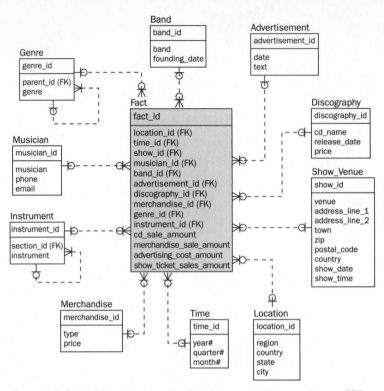

Figure B-5: Musicians, bands, and advertisements data warehouse ERD.

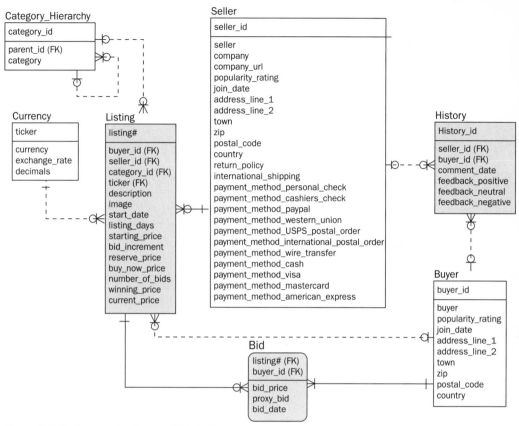

Figure B-6: Online auction house OLTP ERD.

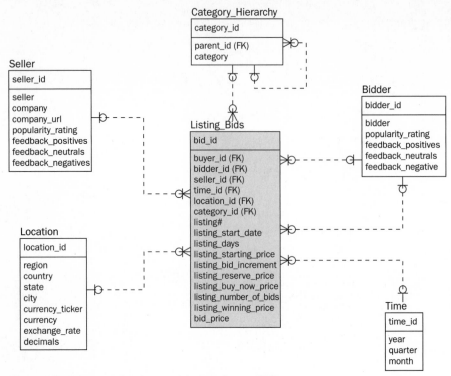

Figure B-7: Online auction house data warehouse ERD.

Index

Index

H

hardware

computer grids and clustering, 400–401

computer systems (boxes), 396

costs, 223, 256

failover database, 397–399

memory needs, 396

RAID, 397

replication, 399–400

resource usage, data warehouses reducing, 173

hash index, 68, 393, 410

HAVING **and** WHERE **clauses, mixing up, 204**

heavily and lightly access fields, separating, 164

help, hiring, 223, 256

heterogeneous databases

described, 410

homogenous integration, 33

hierarchical database model, 7, 8, 410

homogenous system, 33, 410

hot block/hot blocking

defined, 164, 411

indexes, 69

human factor, database modeling

information, getting correct, 30–31

people, talking to right, 29–30

resource, people as, 27–28

hybrid databases, 16, 411

hyperlink, 331

I

IBM, 125

identifying relationship

described, 411

non-identifying relationship versus

1NF, 92–93

OLTP database, 306

tables, 272

tables, 57, 58

image, datatype storing (BINARY**), 265**

implementation, 220–221, 411

inactive data

active, separating, 163

described, 411

including specific records

described, 130–132

performance, improving, 202–204

Index Organized Table (IOT), 68, 393, 411

Indexed Sequential Access Method. *See* **ISAM**

indexes. *See also* **metadata**

altering, 146

alternate

described, 65, 404

foreign keys, 345, 348–352

optimizing performance, 209

post-development database, tuning, 198

approaches, 339–341

bad times to create, 342–343

bitmap, 66–68, 392

BTree, 66, 385, 391

building, 68–69

caching, 211–212

clustered, 393

composite

building, 68

described, 406

WHERE clause filtering, 203

data warehouse database model,
345–346, 349–352

denormalization, 162

described, 64–65, 338–339, 411

dropping, 146

foreign key indexing, 65–66

hash keys and ISAM keys, 393

joins, 206

non-unique, 68, 208

OLTP database model, 343–348

partitions, 395

performance tuning

bad places to use, 209

fear, overcoming, 206

real-world applications, 207–209

types, 207

primary key and unique key field, 146

reading, improving performance, 200–201

what to index, when to index it,
and how to build, 342

industry standard database model, 225

L

language, general data access. *See* SQL
    (Structured Query Language)
large data sets. *See* materialized views
layers
  categories, 285–286
  snowflake schema, overabundance of, 179
left outer join, 138–139, 412
legacy system, 33, 412
`LIKE` operator, 202
Linux, 412
literal values, testing with `IN` set membership
    operator, 143
locations
  data warehouse database models, 246
  dimension, 412
  OLTP database model, 250
log files, 398
logical design, 20
logical operators (`NOT`, `AND`, and `OR`)
  described, 132
  performance, 204
lost data, preventing, 37

M

macro, 364, 412
maintenance costs, 223, 256
manageability
  client-server databases, 196
  data warehouse databases, 197
  OLTP databases, 195
managers
  finalization and approval, 260–261
  sign-off responsibility, 254
  talking to right, 29
many-to-many table relationship
  classifying, 356
  described, 53–55, 412
  4NF
    denormalizing, 155–156
    normalizing, 115–116
  OLTP database model, 263
many-to-one table relationship
  2NF creating
    described, 82
    dynamic and static tables, 90–91
  3NF, 97–103

master table, 75–76
materialized views
  data warehouse database model, 196, 387–390
  denormalization, 162
  described, 69, 413
  fact hierarchical structures, replacing, 328–329
  partitioning, 395
  performance tuning, 198
  tables, 384–385
  views versus, 36
mathematical expression
  described, 133
  order of precedence, 132–134
memory
  application caching, 211–212, 405
  hardware needs, 396
merging records, 138, 205
messed-up database, sorting out, 34
metadata
  changing, 145–146
  database structure change commands, 127
  described, 4, 413
  slots, saving in 1NF, 86
  tables fields expressing, 38
method
  database model design, 20–21
  described, 166, 413
  object model and, 165
methodology, normalization as, 221
Microsoft Access
  datatypes, 331
  field-setting options, 358, 359
Microsoft Internet Explorer, 412
Microsoft Windows
  defined, 413
  hardware reliability, 396
Microsoft Windows Explorer, 7
mirroring RAID, 397
module. *See* stored procedures
money. *See* currencies
multiple field indexes, 208
multiple tables, aggregating with join queries
  cross join, 138
  inner join, 137–138
  outer join, 138–141
  querying database using `SELECT`, 137–141
  self join, 141

Take your library wherever you go

Now you can access more than 70 complete Wrox books online, wherever you happen to be! Every diagram, description, screen capture, and code sample is available with your subscription to the **Wrox Reference Library**. For answers when and where you need them, go to wrox.books24x7.com and subscribe today!

Find books on

- ASP.NET
- C#/C++
- Database
- General
- Java
- Mac
- Microsoft Office
- .NET
- Open Source
- PHP/MySQL
- SQL Server
- Visual Basic
- Web
- XML

wrox.com